Check Point™ VPN-1®/ FireWall-1® NG

Administration

Inti Shah
Andrew Ratcliffe

McGraw-Hill/Osborne

New York   Chicago   San Francisco
Lisbon   London   Madrid   Mexico City   Milan
New Delhi   San Juan   Seoul   Singapore   Sydney   Toronto

McGraw-Hill/Osborne
2100 Powell Street, Floor 10
Emeryville, California 94608
U.S.A.

To arrange bulk purchase discounts for sales promotions, premiums, or fund-raisers, please contact **McGraw-Hill**/Osborne at the above address. For information on translations or book distributors outside the U.S.A., please see the International Contact Information page immediately following the index of this book.

Check Point™ VPN-1®/FireWall-1®NG Administration

1234567890 FGR FGR 019876543

ISBN 0-07-222342-1

Publisher	**Copy Editor**
Brandon A. Nordin	Sally Engelfried
Vice President & Associate Publisher	**Indexer**
Scott Rogers	Valerie Perry
Acquisitions Editor	**Computer Designers**
Franny Kelly	Tabitha M. Cagan, Tara A. Davis
Project Editor	**Illustrators**
Patty Mon	Melinda Lytle, Michael Mueller,
Acquisitions Coordinator	Lyssa Wald
Martin Przybyla	**Series Design**
Technical Editor	Lyssa Wald, Peter F. Hancik
Grant Markham	**Cover Series Design**
Contributor	Jeff Weeks
John Vacca	

This book was composed with Corel VENTURA™ Publisher.

ABOUT THE AUTHORS

Inti Shah has worked in the networking industry for more than 15 years in both enterprise and service provider environments. He has extensive expertise in delivering large-scale networks, complex hosting, intrusion detection, and VPN services. Inti has delivered solutions for various market sectors in diverse projects such as an interactive television service for an audience of 7 million and service-provider multi-tiered firewall architectures. He holds the Cisco CCNA, CCNP, CSS1, and Check Point CCSA NG and CCSE NG accreditations. He is currently working on various projects, including MPLS solutions and Cisco beta programs focusing on Intrusion Detection Technologies and acquiring his CCIE accreditation. Inti lives with his family in Keighley, England and his Dogue de Bordeaux, Hooch.

Andrew Ratcliffe has more than 14 years experience in delivering technical solutions to Internet Service Providers and large enterprises. He has considerable experience in delivering VPN-1/FireWall-1 solutions that focus on secure web-hosting architectures. Andrew specializes in networking, e-commerce platform design, and VPN and IDS solutions. Andrew is a Senior Product Developer for Energis, the U.K.'s largest provider of ISP connectivity, where he develops secure network services using Check Point, Nokia, and Cisco products. He currently holds the Cisco CCNA, Microsoft MCSE, and Check Point CCSE NG accreditations. Andrew lives with his wife Anne and son James in Yorkshire, England.

ABOUT THE TECHNICAL EDITOR

Grant Markham is a Check Point Certified Security Expert (CCSE) in VPN-1/FireWall-1 CP2000 and NG. He has worked in the telecommunications and data communications industry for many years. He currently works as a Senior Security Architect for Energis in Leeds, England, responsible for all aspects of security associated with the delivery of complex, hosted, fully managed e-business solutions. Although he specializes in Check Point VPN-1/FireWall-1, he also has experience of working with Nokia and Cisco Secure products.

AT A GLANCE

CONTENTS

ACKNOWLEDGMENTS

We would like to thank our friends and colleagues who have helped and supported us throughout this endeavour: Paul Simpson, Graham Smith, Nathan Allison, Adam Clarke, Jag Bains, David Thorpe, James Miller, Andrew Makin, Bill Miller, Tony Robinson, Michael Rhodes, Liz Withers-Clark, Eddie David, and Charles Aunger.

Many thanks to Marcus Goncalves for his kind assistance.

Thanks to Dino Constantinou of Check Point U.K., for always having an answer to our queries and always being happy to help. Thanks too to Rob Civil of Check Point—get that bike repaired and come trail riding with us!

Many thanks to Grant Markham for undertaking the technical reviews; your input was invaluable in producing this book.

Many Thanks to the Aladdin Knowledge Systems team for their input for Chapter 15, especially Dave Buck.

A special thank you to Niall Moynihan of Check Point for kindly authorizing and providing us access to extensive information and reference material about VPN-1/FireWall-1 NG.

We would like to give an extra big thank you to the McGraw-Hill/ Osborne team, especially Franny Kelly and Patty Mon for their tireless encouragement, support, and patience.

INTRODUCTION

C heck Point is widely accepted as a market leader in firewall and VPN technology. VPN-1/FireWall-1 NG is the latest version of their flagship product, and it incorporates a vast array of features and integration possibilities. Our work with VPN-1/FireWall-1 for an Internet Service Provider with numerous large-scale implementations on a daily basis gave rise to the idea of writing down our experience in the product's design, deployment, and administration. When we started this project, we were already working with NG in our test labs laying the groundwork for large-scale migration to the new product. We designed this book to be a practical "by example" guide to design, deployment, and administration. In keeping with this goal, we kept the Check Point theory content down to a minimum, expanding only where required to make sense of the configuration examples.

We decided to invent our own imaginary company to base our examples on, and Fiction Corporation is used throughout the book. Appendix A gives the original design proposal for all the examples we used in each of the practical hands-on sections in each chapter.

We provide the information you will need to get your firewall installed and configured on whatever platform you choose to run it using Fiction Corporation examples throughout each installation chapter. You should be able to use these in combination to serve any deployment you can think of. We have also tried to make the installation chapters stand alone because we recognize that someone installing VPN-1/FireWall-1 NG on a Windows 2000 Server will not necessarily read the Solaris installation chapter.

Where appropriate, we took a wider view, beyond VPN-1/FireWall-1 NG configuration, to include general discussions and descriptions of some of the challenges that face firewall and security administrators from both external Internet access and within. These challenges need to have a measured response appropriate to the amount of risk an organization perceives, and while we have provided some guidance for this, risk assessment is a matter that can be measured only by an organization's own technical security personnel.

Computer and communications security is one of the largest growth areas in the IT industry today. This may be associated with world events, but it is just as likely a result of cheap Internet access and ever-increasing reduction in Information Technology ownership cost. Whatever the reason for it, hackers are here to stay, and whatever motivates the hacker is largely irrelevant. We must all take the steps necessary to secure our enterprise. Firewall administrators are responsible for protecting not only the tangible assets—the networks and computers and the information that is stored on and flows over them—but also the reputation of the organization. It is only with your reputation intact that customers will have the confidence to continue to use your products and services and do business with you online.

CHAPTER 1

The Internet and the Need for Security

The requirement for organizations to connect to the Internet and ensure that that connectivity is secure has spawned a range of products called firewalls. Simply stated, a firewall is a device that provides perimeter security between internal networks and external insecure networks such as the Internet. Check Point is recognized as one of the leaders in the industry, with VPN-1/FireWall-1 their flagship product. This book is focused on all aspects of this product's rich feature set.

To set the background and lay the foundations for later chapters, this chapter will provide an introduction into what the Internet is and outline the history of this worldwide network that has become a part of our daily lives. We will start by looking at the history of the Internet and providing an overview of TCP/IP, the protocol that led to the evolution of the Internet. We will then cover the basic requirements for Internet security and look at the three most commonly used Internet services: the Web, FTP, and e-mail. Threats to these services as well as common security threats will be covered in more detail later in this chapter. It is important to recognize that successful deployment of VPN-1/FireWall-1 NG requires some knowledge of TCP/IP and some of the services that are commonly used on the Internet.

HISTORY OF THE INTERNET

The first recorded description of the social interactions that could be enabled through networking was a series of memos written by J.C.R. Licklider of MIT in 1962 discussing his "Intergalactic Network" concept. He foresaw a set of globally interconnected computers through which everyone could quickly access data and programs from any site. In spirit, the concept was very much like what the Internet of today provides. Licklider was the first head of the computer research program at the Defense Advanced Research Projects Agency (DARPA), starting in October 1962. While at DARPA he convinced his successors at DARPA, Ivan Sutherland, Bob Taylor, and MIT researcher Lawrence G. Roberts, of the importance of this networking concept.

Leonard Kleinrock at MIT published the first paper on packet-switching theory in July 1961 and the first book on the subject in 1964. Kleinrock convinced Roberts of the theoretical feasibility of communications using packets rather than circuits, which was a major step along the path to computer networking. The other key step was to make the computers talk to each other. Working with Thomas Merrill in 1965, Roberts connected the TX-2 computer in Massachusetts to the Q-32 in California with a low speed dial-up telephone line, creating the first (however small) wide-area computer network ever built. The experiment proved that the time-shared computers could work well together, running programs and retrieving data as necessary on the remote machine, but that the circuit-switched telephone system was totally inadequate for the job. Kleinrock's conviction of the need for packet switching was confirmed.

In late 1966, Roberts went to DARPA to develop the computer network concept and quickly put together his plan for the Advanced Research Project Agency Network

(ARPANET), publishing the plan in 1967. At the same conference where Roberts presented the paper, Donald Davies and Roger Scantlebury of the National Physical Library (NPL) in the United Kingdom presented their paper on a packet network concept. Scantlebury told Roberts about the NPL work, as well as that of Paul Baran and others at Research and Development (RAND). The RAND group had written a paper on packet-switching networks for secure voice in the military in 1964. It happened that the work at MIT, RAND, and NPL had all proceeded in parallel without any of the researchers knowing about the others' work. The word "packet" was adopted from the work at NPL, and the proposed line speed to be used in the ARPANET design was upgraded from 2.4Kbps to 50Kbps.

In August 1968, after Roberts and the DARPA-funded community had refined the overall structure and specifications for the ARPANET, a Request For Comments (RFC) was released by DARPA for the development of one of the key components, the packet switches called Interface Message Processors (IMPs). The RFC was won in December 1968 by a group headed by Frank Heart at Bolt, Beranek, and Newman (BBN). The BBN team worked on the IMPs, with Bob Kahn playing a major role in the overall ARPANET architectural design. At the same time, the network topology and economics were designed and optimized by Roberts working with Howard Frank and his team at Network Analysis Corporation, and the network measurement system was prepared by Kleinrock's team at UCLA.

Due to Kleinrock's early development of packet-switching theory and his focus on analysis, design, and measurement, his Network Measurement Center at UCLA was selected to be the first node on the ARPANET. All this came together in September 1969 when BBN installed the first IMP at UCLA, and the first host computer was connected. Doug Engelbart's project on "Augmentation of Human Intellect" at Stanford Research Institute (SRI) provided a second node. SRI supported the Network Information Center, led by Elizabeth Feinler, and included functions such as maintaining tables of host name-to-address mapping, as well as a directory of the RFCs.

One month later, when SRI was connected to the ARPANET, the first host-to-host message was sent from Kleinrock's laboratory to SRI. Two more nodes were added at UC Santa Barbara and the University of Utah. These last two nodes incorporated application visualization projects, with Glen Culler and Burton Fried at UCSB investigating methods for the display of mathematical functions using storage displays to deal with the problem of refresh over the Net, and Robert Taylor and Ivan Sutherland at Utah investigating methods of 3-D representations over the Net. Thus, by the end of 1969, four host computers were connected together into the initial ARPANET, and the budding Internet was off the ground. Even at this early stage, it should be noted that the networking research incorporated both work on the underlying network and how to utilize the network. This tradition continues to this day.

Computers were added quickly to the ARPANET during the following years, and work proceeded on completing a functionally complete Host-to-Host Protocol and other network software. In December 1970, the Network Working Group (NWG), working under S. Crocker, finished the initial ARPANET Host-to-Host Protocol called the Network Control Protocol (NCP). As the ARPANET sites completed implementing NCP during the period 1971–1972, network users could finally begin to develop applications.

In October 1972, Kahn organized a large, very successful demonstration of the ARPANET at the International Computer Communication Conference (ICCC). This was the first public demonstration of this new network technology to the public.

It was also in 1972 that the initial "hot" application, electronic mail, was introduced. In March, Ray Tomlinson at BBN wrote the basic e-mail message send and read software, motivated by the need of the ARPANET developers for an easy coordination mechanism. In July, Roberts expanded its capabilities by writing the first e-mail utility program to list, selectively read, file, forward, and respond to messages. From there, e-mail took off as the largest network application for over a decade. This was a harbinger of the kind of activity we see on the World Wide Web today—namely, the enormous growth of all kinds of people-to-people traffic.

ARPANET grew and grew over the following months and eventually became the modern-day Internet. In Spring 1973, Kahn realized the limitations of NCP and the existing communication protocols. This led him to ask Vint Cerf to work with him on the detailed design of the protocol. Cerf had been intimately involved in the original NCP design and development, and already knew about interfacing to existing operating systems. Armed with Kahn's architectural approach to the communications side and with Cerf's NCP experience, the two teamed up to spell out the details of what was to become TCP/IP.

TCP/IP

Initially, TCP/IP (Transmission Control Protocol/Internet Protocol) was designed to include a few basic service protocols that were essential to any communications network. These were file transfer, electronic mail, remote login, and remote printing. This enabled communication and collaboration across a very large number of client and server systems. TCP/IP could be run over a local area network (LAN) or wide area network (WAN). It also provided LAN and WAN interconnection that eventually became the basis of educational and corporate research-interconnected WANs.

These networks grew and became interconnected using the Internet Protocol (IP) to route between them. Eventually, these became the network that we call the Internet. TCP/IP is the backbone of today's Internet and is the protocol of choice for corporate LANs and WANs. Major network operating system vendors such as Novell and Microsoft have standardized on the TCP/IP for their operating systems. This eases and simplifies migration and coexistence with other systems and allows common services such as FTP and SMTP to be platform- and vendor-independent. For Novell, this was a very large and strategic step because they had used their own IPX/SPX Protocol for over a decade.

TCP and IP in the OSI Model

The OSI (Open Systems Interconnection) model is a reference model consisting of seven layers, each describing a specific function. The OSI model consists of the following seven layers:

7. Application layer

6. Presentation layer

5. Session layer

4. Transport layer

3. Network layer

2. Data-link layer

1. Physical layer

These seven layers interact and communicate with the layer directly above and the layer directly below. Above the application layer is the user, and below the physical layer is the network cable.

In contrast to the OSI model, TCP/IP was built around a four-layer model. This is referred to as the Department of Defense (DOD) or DARPA model. In this book, we will refer to it as the DOD model because TCP/IP was developed well before the advent of the OSI reference model and the DOD standards had already been set. However, the DOD model closely maps to the OSI reference model. It includes the following four layers:

- **Application/process layer** The DOD application layer defines the upper-layer functionality included in the application, presentation, and session layers of the OSI model. Support is included for application communications, code formatting, session establishment, and maintenance between applications.

- **Host-to-host layer** The DOD transport layer maps directly to the transport layer of the OSI model. The transport layer defines connectionless and connection-oriented transport functionality.

- **Internet layer** The DOD Internet layer maps directly to the network layer of the OSI model. The network layer defines internetworking functionality for routing protocols. This layer is responsible for the routing of packets between hosts and networks.

- **Network interface layer** The DOD network interface layer maps to the data-link and physical layers of the OSI model. Data-link properties, media access methods, and physical connections are defined at this layer. Figure 1-1 shows the DOD four-layer and the OSI seven-layer models.

We will refer to the TCP/IP in relation to the OSI model and not the DOD model for the rest of this chapter. Industry uses the OSI model as a reference, and it is necessary to

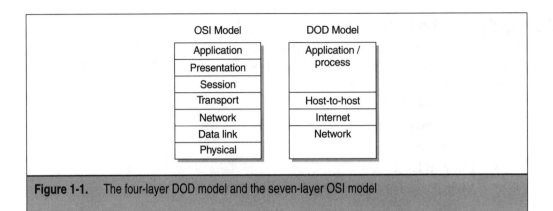

Figure 1-1.   The four-layer DOD model and the seven-layer OSI model

learn the correlation of the TCP/IP suite to the OSI model. This will also help you follow the structure of this book for troubleshooting.

Internet Protocol (IP)

The Internet Protocol (IP) is defined by RFC 791. IP is the network layer datagram service of the TCP/IP suite. IP is used by all other protocols in the TCP/IP suite, except the Address Resolution Protocol (ARP) and the Reverse Address Resolution Protocol (RARP), to route packets from host to host over an internetwork. IP operates at the network layer of the OSI model and the Internet layer of the DOD model.

NOTE   RFCs are available from the IETF website at www.ietf.org.

IP defines the set of rules for communicating across the network. Addressing and control information is included that allows the IP packets to be routed to their intended destination over the internetwork. IP has two main functions:

- The provision of a connectionless, best-effort packet delivery service routing across an internetwork.

- The provision of fragmentation and reassembly of packets to support data links with differing maximum transmission unit (MTU) sizes. This is also described as basic congestion control.

The main function of IP is the routing of packets across the internetwork. This function is unique to IP and isn't displayed by any other of the protocols contained in the TCP/IP suite. The other feature of IP, congestion control, is found on nearly every layer of the OSI model. IP performs basic congestion control because the control is very primitive in comparison with the congestion control offered by TCP.

Routing is described as the delivery of packets or datagrams from the source node to the destination node, possibly across multiple heterogeneous intermediate networks.

When the hosts are on the same physical network or subnet, they can be delivered using the routing services provided by their own IP modules. When the hosts are located on separate connected networks or different subnets, the delivery is made via a number of routers that interconnect the networks.

As just discussed, IP provides a connectionless, best-effort packet delivery system. This facilitates the delivery of packets from the source to the destination. This service has three conceptual characteristics that are important for understanding the behavior of IP routing:

- **Connectionless**   IP is classed as a *connectionless* protocol, thus each packet is delivered independently of all other packets. The packets may be sent along different routes and may arrive out of sequence at the destination. No acknowledgements are received to indicate if the IP packets were received by the intended destination.

- **Unreliable**   Due to the connectionless nature of IP, it's classed as an *unreliable* protocol. IP does not guarantee that every packet that is transmitted will be received by the host intact and in the original sequence in which it was sent.

- **Best effort**   IP uses its *best effort* to deliver the packets to their intended destination. IP will only discard packets if it is forced to do so because of hardware issues such as resource allocation problems or errors caused at the physical layer.

IP packets or datagrams consist of the IP header and the data. The data is received from the upper-layer protocols such as TCP or UDP (User Datagram Protocol) and encapsulated into the IP packet. The IP header is created by the Internet Protocol and is used by IP on intermediary systems to route the packet to its final destination. The IP header contains complete routing information to enable IP to route the packet independent of any other process. This stems from the connectionless nature of IP. Figure 1-2 shows the IP packet format.

The following details the anatomy of an IP packet:

- **Version**   Has four bits and represents the version of IP that the packet belongs to. Currently everybody uses IP version 4. In the future it is expected that everybody will use IP version 6 (IPv6) or IP Next Generation (IPng).

- **IP Header Length (IHL)**   Defines the length of the IP header. The Options field, discussed later, is optional and can affect the length of the header. The IHL field occupies 4 bits of the IP header.

- **Type of Service (TOS)**   Occupies 8 bits of the IP header. This field specifies how the packet should be handled.

- **Total Length**   Occupies 16 bits of the IP header. This field refers to the total length of the packet measured in octets.

- **Identification**   Occupies 16 bits of the IP header. This field is used in conjunction with the following two fields, Flags and Fragment Offset, to aid in the packet fragmentation and packet reassembly process.

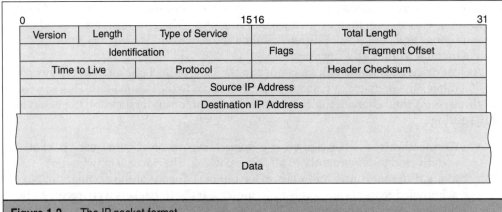

Figure 1-2.   The IP packet format

A packet is fragmented when the original packet size is larger than the MTU at the receiving node or any router along the route. IP fragments the packet into smaller packets that are within the MTU limitations. These fragmented packets are true IP packets in their own sense and contain both an IP header and IP data.

When a packet is generated at the transmitting node, a unique number is entered into the 16-bit identification field. If the packet has to be fragmented for the destination node to receive it, the original IP header is copied into the new fragmented packets. This copying process creates packets with similar identification fields in the IP header. The receiving host then uses this to identify the original packets when it reassembles the packet into its original form.

- **Flags**   Occupies 3 bits of the IP header. Its only purpose is fragmentation. Each bit is interpreted independently as follows:

  - **Bit 0**   Reserved.

  - **Bit 1**   The "don't fragment" or DF bit. When this bit is cleared, it indicates that the packet can be fragmented. When the bit is set, it indicates that the packet cannot be fragmented.

    - **Bit 2**   The "more fragments" or MF bit. When this bit is cleared, it indicates that this is the last fragment of the packet. When the bit is set, it indicates that more fragments are to follow.

- **Fragment Offset**   Occupies 13 bits of the IP header. This field identifies which part of the original packet this fragment is carrying.

- **Time to Live (TTL)**   Occupies 8 bits of the IP header. This field indicates how long the packet can exist before being dropped or copied to the bit bucket by an intermediate router. When a router receives a packet, it decrements the TTL value by one. If this value is 0, the router discards the packet by copying it to the bit bucket. Otherwise, it forwards the packet on to the next hop router or the destination network if the destination network is directly connected.

The main function of the TTL field is to avoid network congestion through routing loops. The TTL ensures that even if a misconfiguration creates a loop, the packet will be dropped when its TTL expires.

- **Protocol**   Occupies 8 bits of the IP header. This field is used to identify the protocol that should receive the data contained in the packet. Eight bits facilitates 255 different protocols, which are represented as a numeric value.

- **Header Checksum**   Occupies 16 bits of the IP header. This field is calculated as a checksum for the IP header and not for the data contained within the packet. Upper-layer protocols should have their own data integrity verification for the data contained in the IP packet.

- **Source and Destination Addresses**   Both fields occupy 32 bits of the IP header. These are the actual 32-bit IP addresses of the source and destination nodes.

- **Options and Padding**   These fields are only used for debugging and are not very useful.

Transmission Control Protocol (TCP)

The Transmission Control Protocol (TCP) is defined in RFC 761. TCP operates at the transport layer of the OSI model.

TCP sits on top of IP and provides IP with a reliable transport protocol that is used when communications have to be reliable.

Various services utilize TCP such as the Hypertext Transfer Protocol (HTTP), Simple Main Transport Protocol (SMTP), Post Office Protocol 3 (POP3), and File Transfer Protocol (FTP).

TCP is connection oriented and provides reliability with checksums and sequencing, as well as flow control through source quench and sliding windows.

The fields in the TCP header are shown in Figure 1-3.

Flow control is required to control the transmission speeds between the source and destination host and is designed to slow down the transmitting of packets if the receiving host is unable to keep up with the transmission speed.

User Datagram Protocol (UDP)

The User Datagram Protocol (UDP) is defined in RFC 768. UDP operates at the transport layer of the OSI model and is a simple packet-oriented transport layer protocol that is connectionless and therefore unreliable.

UDP packets are sent with no sequencing or flow control, so there is no guarantee that they will reach their intended destination. The receiving host compares the UDP header checksum and, if a problem is detected, the packet is dropped without reporting the error back to the sending host.

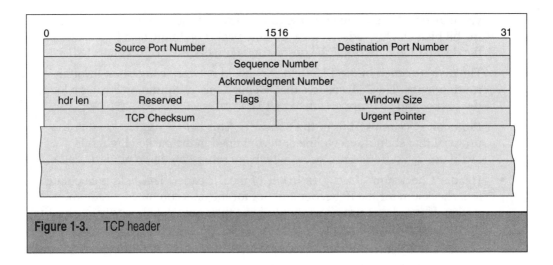

Figure 1-3.   TCP header

This is a very fast transport protocol because no acknowledgements or advanced sequencing is carried out at the transport layer. Upper-layer protocols may enforce their own error detection and recovery to use UDP's speed. UDP is typically used when the data is not essential, such as in video or voice streaming of live content over the Internet. The UDP header is shown in Figure 1-4.

Internet Control Message Protocol (ICMP)

The Internet Control Message Protocol (ICMP) is defined by RFC 792 and RFC 1700. ICMP is classed as an integral part of IP. ICMP is a separate protocol, although it does use IP transmission services. ICMP operates at the network layer of the OSI model and the Internet layer of the DOD model. Unlike IP, ICMP does not provide any services for the transport layer protocols. The ICMP message is sent encapsulated in IP datagrams as data, and these are sent at the network layer, so they are transmitted with the same best-effort, connectionless transportation used by IP.

0	1516	31
Source Port Number	Destination Port Number	
UDP Length	UDP Checksum	

Figure 1-4.   The UDP header

The main use of ICMP is to provide a reporting function that identifies error conditions on network devices. Routers usually generate ICMP messages as they receive and route the IP packet. These ICMP messages contain three fields at the beginning of the packet:

- **Type field**   An 8-bit field that identifies the message. Type fields are displayed in Table 1-1.

- **Code field**   An 8-bit field that provides further information about the ICMP message.

- **Checksum field**   A 16-bit field that is used to verify the integrity of the whole ICMP message.

Table 1-1 shows all of the ICMP message types.

Type Field	Type Description
0	Echo reply
1	Unassigned
2	Unassigned
3	Destination unreachable
4	Source quench
5	Redirect
6	Alternate host address
7	Unassigned
8	Echo
9	Router advertisement
10	Router selection
11	Time exceeded
12	Parameter problem
13	Timestamp
14	Timestamp reply
15	Information request
16	Information reply
17	Address mask request
18	Address mask reply
19	Reserved
20-29	Reserved

Table 1-1.   ICMP Message Types

Type Field	Type Description
30	Traceroute
31	Datagram conversion error
32	Mobile host redirect
33	IPv6 Where are you
34	IPv6 I am here
35	Mobile registration request
36	Mobile registration reply
37-255	Reserved

Table 1-1. ICMP Message Types *(continued)*

In network troubleshooting, one of the most frequently used tools is the Ping command. The Ping (Packet Internet Groper) command utilizes ICMP echo messages to provide a very simple way of testing that a remote node is up and running a TCP/IP protocol stack.

When you issue a Ping command, you are sending an IP packet to the destination address. The destination will translate the IP packet and use the built-in reply functionality of IP to issue an ICMP type 8 Echo message back to the source address. This command is frequently used as a first line of troubleshooting and can provide many configurations at levels 1, 2, and 3 of the OSI layer.

Address Resolution Protocols (ARP)

The Address Resolution Protocol (ARP) is defined by RFC 1122. ARP operates at the data-link layer of the OSI model. Its primary function is to resolve IP addresses to network layer addresses such as a Media Access Control (MAC) address.

Routers and hosts both operate ARP to resolve IP addresses to MAC addresses. All network communications eventually take place over the data-link layer of the OSI model, and a data-link layer address such as a MAC address is required for this to take place. The MAC address corresponding to the IP address can be either statically entered prior to communications by entering a static ARP entry, or ARP can dynamically learn the MAC address.

To dynamically learn a MAC address, ARP sends out a broadcast frame requesting the MAC address of a host with a specified IP address. All hosts on the segment will receive the broadcast, but only the host with the specified IP address will respond with its MAC address. At this point, layer 3 communication can begin.

However, if the destination address is on a remote segment or subnet, there is a slightly different process. The source host will check the destination host's IP address and subnet mask to ascertain if the host is local or remote. If the destination host is local, a broadcast frame is sent, as just described. If the destination host is remote, the source host will eventually have to pass the frame to the default gateway or router.

The MAC address will have to be learned for the router, so an ARP broadcast is sent specifying the router's IP address.

Both routers and hosts have an ARP cache. The ARP cache is always checked before an ARP packet is broadcast onto the network. The ARP cache contains previously learned MAC addresses and holds them for a predetermined duration of time before flushing them out of the cache.

Due to the normally dynamic nature of ARP, you wouldn't expect it to cause many problems in a networking environment. However, static ARP entries may cause problems if they are configured incorrectly.

Broadcasts

Broadcasts are data packets that are destined for all hosts on the network segment. There are two main classifications of broadcast:

- **Directed broadcasts** Packets that are sent to a specific network or series of networks that are determined by the destination IP address. All IP networks have a subnet or network broadcast address. This is always the last address in the subnet range. For example, a subnet with an IP address of 172.18.8.0 and a subnet mask of 255.255.248.0 would have a subnet broadcast address of 172.18.15.255.

- **Flooding** Uses the address of 255.255.255.255 as its destination address. This packet will be destined for every host on every connected network.

The abundance of broadcast packets on the network can lead to a broadcast storm. Broadcast storms can literally bring down a network because they push the network utilization up to an unacceptable amount.

By nature, routers will prevent broadcast storms from propagating out onto the network. They limit the storm to the local cable. Bridges, however, will pass broadcast. This is because a bridge is a layer 2 device and either a layer 2 or layer 3 address can define broadcasts. The layer 2 address for a broadcast is FF-FF-FF-FF-FF-FF.

The best way to identify a broadcast problem is by connecting a protocol analyser to the local segment. The analyser will identify and provide statistics as to the type of traffic on the network. There are a multitude of analysers available on the market from dedicated appliances to software that runs on laptops.

NOTE To run a protocol analyser in a switched environment a number of techniques can be used from using Port Mirroring to network taps.

Control of broadcast messages is an essential part of IP network administration, and a thorough knowledge of the broadcast process is required for the network troubleshooter.

Unicasts/Multicasts

Unicasts are IP packets that are destined for a single location on the network. This is identified by the destination's host IP address being placed into the destination field in the IP header. Unicast addresses make up the largest portion of the IP address space.

This address space is subdivided into three nonoverlapping groups. These groups define which part of the IP address is allocated for the host ID and also the Network ID. These are known as Class A, Class B, and Class C addresses.

Host-to-host communication normally occurs over multicast addresses that are direct from one host to another.

Multicasts are IP packets that are destined for a group of hosts on the network. They are identified by the destination address in the IP header. Multicast addresses use Class D addresses. Class D addresses are in the 224.0.0.0–239.255.255.255 range. Multicasts allow IP traffic to be sent from one source or multiple sources and delivered to multiple destinations. Unicasts require a single packet to be sent to each destination; multicasts send a single packet to a multicast group that is identified by a single IP address.

Hosts generally listen for multicast packets on a predetermined address and port. This can be compared to the broadcasting of radio waves. Radio waves are all around us. You can pick up a radio transmission by simply tuning in your radio receiver to the correct frequency. In a similar way, routers listen for specific packets and are tuned in to the specific multicast address. Multicasting is a very efficient way of delivering packets to multiple destinations. It reduces traffic on the network as one packet is received and processed by a group of addresses.

Domain Name Server (DNS)

Domain Name Server (DNS) is a hierarchical way to resolve host names to IP addresses. The Internet uses DNS to resolve host names.

DNS is specified in RFC 1034 and RFC 1035. Originally, the Internet used host files on all clients to facilitate name resolution. As the Internet grew, this became impossible to administer, so DNS was created to implement a hierarchical structure that allowed the namespace to be divided into subsets of names for distributing and delegating parts of the namespace to others. This eased the administrative burden of DNS and made local the namespace or domain owners responsible for this administration. A full understanding of DNS is desirable but is beyond the scope of this book. Many books have been written solely on DNS.

Most DNS problems will result from the improper configuration of the DNS servers on the client. These can be manually added or dynamically added via DHCP (Dynamic Host Configuration Protocol). If the client is using a proxy server, the client does not need specific DNS services because the proxy server will host the name resolution for the proxy client. The problems will manifest themselves into situations where you cannot reach a host by name but you can by IP address. Issuing a Ping command is a simple way to check the DNS configuration of a client.

Common TCP/UDP Ports

TCP and UDP utilize ports at the transport layer to differentiate between services. On a Windows platform, these ports are often located in the services file, which is located in the %systemdrive%\winnt\system32\drivers\etc folder on a Windows NT server.

Table 1-2 shows the common TCP/UDP ports and services.

Port	Service
20/TCP	FTP-DATA
21/TCP	FTP
23/TCP	TELNET
25/TCP	SMTP
37/UDP	TIME
49/UDP	TACACS
53/TCP/UDP	DOMAIN (DNS)
67/UDP	BOOTP/DHCP SERVER
68/UDP	BOOTP/DHCP CLIENT
69/UDP	TFTP
80/TCP	WWW
110/TCP	POP3
137/UDP	NETBIOS NAME
138/UDP	NETBIOS DATAGRAM

Table 1-2.   Common UDP/TCP Ports

The services listed in Table 1-2 are the most commonly used services. It is generally a good idea to become familiar with these when you progress on to working with VPN-1/FireWall-1 NG.

INTERNET SECURITY

The Internet is growing at a phenomenal rate. It is estimated that several thousand websites are added to the Internet on a daily basis. Never before has industry had such an aggressive medium for exploitation.

With the growth of the Internet, it has become standard for the traditional retail store to create a presence on the Internet. Initially, this presence was nothing more than a static web page that acted only as an online advertisement for the store. This progressed to being an online information source that offered information about goods and services offered by the store. Because the Internet has no geographical limits, retail stores soon realized that they had a global market with unlimited potential at their disposal, and e-commerce was born.

With this massive growth and dependence upon the technology supporting it comes, obviously, a new set of hazards. The highest risk e-commerce brings is that financial data is being transferred over the Internet. This has led to a breed of cyber-criminals, very intelligent network hackers who use tried and tested techniques to infiltrate corporate systems for their own financial gain or to cause a Denial of Service (DoS) to the corporate site, thus costing the corporation money in lost revenue.

This section will look at common web services and the attacks that are launched upon them. We will start by looking at some common security attacks that can be made over the Internet, concentrating on network intrusion and DoS attacks. Next, we will look at each individual web service, identify the common threats to the service, and look at some of the preventative steps that can be taken.

Throughout the short history of the Internet, attacks on the public servers of large corporations have been prevalent. These are usually for financial gain to the perpetrator, financial loss to the victim, a sense of personal achievement, or increased status with the perpetrator's peers.

Most Internet attacks will fall into one of two general categories (although new categories and new attacks evolve all the time): the perpetrators are either trying to gain unauthorized access into the network, or they are trying to deny service to the network. These two categories can intermingle so that a network intrusion can lead to the Denial of Service. In this section, we will look at these as separate attacks.

Network Intrusion

Network intrusion is the gaining of access to a computer system and/or computer network that you are not authorized to use. This can be achieved in many ways. We will look at two main types of network intrusion:

- Unauthorized access
- Eavesdropping

Unauthorized Access

Unauthorized access generally refers to the gaining of access to a network by using username/password pairs. These passwords can be gained by several methods, outlined next.

Social Engineering   The attacker gets someone of authority to release information such as username/password pairs. A common social engineering attack is someone telephoning a network user pretending to be from the company's network help desk and asking for the user's username and password. These attacks are very hard to overcome—the only real way is through staff training and culture.

Dictionary Attack   A brute-force attack against a password system. The attacker runs a piece of dictionary software to try numerous passwords against the system. The attack gets its name from the fact that there is usually what is called a dictionary file that contains thousands of common and not-so-common words. Each of these words in turn is attempted in the authentication attempt.

The Security Policy should stipulate the maximum number of wrong passwords that can be entered before the account is locked. This feature is implemented in most mainstream network operating systems today.

Exploitation of Service   For example, there was a bug with the UNIX Sendmail service that allowed a user to send a series of commands to the service that would gain them administrative access to the host machine.

Be sure to keep abreast of all the latest security vulnerabilities and ensure that all network services are up to the latest security patch.

Eavesdropping

An attacker uses a network analyzer or sniffer to listen and decode the frames on the network medium. This type of attack is physically hard to achieve, as it has to be done either at the same location as the network or at the office of a service provider to that network. The traffic that the attacker can capture is limited by the location of the attacker. For example, if the sniff or trace is run on the corporate LAN, the attacker will probably not see WAN routing traffic, as that traffic will not be local or contained in the LAN. A common use of sniffing is to obtain username and password pairs for either users or network services.

Sniffing can also lead to session replay attacks and session hijacking.

Session Replay Attacks   With most network analyzers available today, there is the ability to capture the data into a buffer. This buffer can then be replayed on the network. An attacker can capture a user logging in to a system and running commands. By replaying the captured session, they can re-create what the initial user did and use it to their benefit. The common way for this to be done is the attacker changes the source IP address of the capture so the session initiates with another host. Even with encryption, session replays are very hard to spot and prevent.

Session Hijacking   The attacker inserts falsified IP data packets after the initial session has been established. This can alter the flow of the session and establish communication with a different network host from which the session was originally established.

Denial of Service (DoS) Attacks

The saturation of network resources targeted against a single host or range of hosts with the intent to stop that host furnishing further network requests. This has the same effect as a server being under too much strain and unable to deal with the concentration of requests for its services.

The term Denial of Service (DoS) has been used quite a lot in the Internet community recently. This is partly due to the frequent DoS attacks that have been carried out against leading e-commerce vendors such as ebay.com and amazon.com.

The problem with DoS attacks is that most of the attacks appear to be genuine requests for service, but they come in large numbers—large enough to fill up available buffer space on the server and prevent it from responding to legitimate requests.

An attacker can run a DoS attack from anywhere. Because they are targeting a public service, they protect and hide their identity and can run the attack with a dial-up connection from anywhere in the world.

Many DoS attacks are simple to run, which has led to the increase in what are called script kiddies. A script kiddy is someone with limited knowledge who runs a prebuilt DoS script to attack an Internet host. We have even seen UNIX GUI-based applications that mimic numerous DoS attacks and make it extremely easy to use this technology against an unsuspecting host.

Numerous DoS attacks exist, and new ones are found on nearly a weekly basis. Websites run by white-hat hackers are being misused by black-hat hackers and script kiddies, and this information is being misused in the form of DoS attacks against Internet hosts. White hat hackers are ethical hackers who probe computer networks for positive outcomes. Black hat hackers are hackers who try to infiltrate computer networks to cause harm and damage. White-hat hackers, who aim to educate security administrators to the new threats and vulnerabilities that emerge almost daily, provide websites on the Internet such as www.security-focus.com and www.rootshell.com that list some of the newest types of attacks.

Another kind of DoS is a Distributed Denial of Service (DDoS) attack. This is where numerous hosts on the Internet all attack the same target. This has a distributed nature and can be catastrophic for the target.

There are hundreds of DoS attacks in existence now. Let's look at some of the common and more famous ones.

TCP SYN Flooding Attack   The TCP SYN Flood attack exploits the three-way handshake connection mechanism of TCP/IP. The attacker initiates a TCP session with the server by sending a TCP SYN packet to it. The server responds to this initial packet with a TCP SYN/ACK response. The attacker's machine should then respond to this SYN/ACK by sending its own SYN/ACK back to the server. At this point, the session would normally be established, but in a TCP SYN attack, the attacker's machine never responds to the TCP SYN/ACK sent by the server. This causes the server to wait for response and the session to start. This is called a half-open session. Each of these half-open sessions utilizes resources on the server. The attacker floods the server with thousands of these session initiation packets, causing the server to eventually run out of resources and thus denying service to any other inbound connections.

SMURF Attack   A SMURF attack is when an attacker sends an ICMP Echo request to a network address rather than a specific host. The important point is that the attacker enters the IP address of the targeted server as the ICMP Echo source address. This causes every host on the network to respond and send an ICMP Echo reply to the source address of the ICMP Echo packet. This is the address of the server that the attacker wants to attack.

In other words, the attacker uses somebody else's resources and network to attack their victim. This attack works by simply consuming the victim's bandwidth. Once this bandwidth is consumed, all access to the server from other public hosts will slowly grind to a halt.

Ping of Death   The Ping of Death is a famous denial of service attack that uses the Ping ICMP Echo request and Echo reply to crash a remote system. It is classed as an elegant one-packet kill.

This attack works by sending a large ICMP Echo request packet that gets fragmented before sending. The receiving host, which is also the victim, reconstructs the fragmented packet. Because the packet size is above the maximum allowed packet size, it can cause system crashes, reboots, kernel-dumps and buffer overflows, thus rendering the system unusable.

This attack, although still in existence, is well protected against by all recent operating systems and patches for existing operating systems. Contact your software vendor for the latest security updates.

Teardrop Attack   The Teardrop attack is a classic Denial of Service attack that normally causes memory problems on the server that is being attacked. Teardrop attacks use fragmentation and malformed packets to cause the victim host to miscalculate and perform illegal memory functions. These functions may interact with other applications running on the server and result in crashing the server.

Because this is a fragmentation attack, it can bypass some traditional intrusion detection systems.

Land Attack   To make a Land attack, the attacker sends a spoofed packet to a server that has the same source IP address and port as the destination IP address and port. For example, if the server has an IP address of 192.168.0.1, both the source and destination IP addresses of the packet would be 192.168.0.1. The port is identified as being open by a network scan that the attacker runs before sending the packet. The result is that the server, if susceptible, will crash. This attack is also known as the land.c attack. (The .c refers to the C script that it is presented in.)

As previously stated, this only represents a small percentage of the network intrusions and Denial of Service attacks that exist.

Common Internet Services

TCP/IP operates using what is called a *port* as a connection endpoint. The port is what TCP/IP uses to differentiate between the different services within the TCP/IP protocol suite. All Internet services use ports, some UDP, but mostly TCP.

We'll look at the common Internet services that most corporate businesses may employ as part of their public Internet offering. These technologies can be used on intranets, extranets, and other private networks, as well as the public Internet.

The common Internet services are as follows:

- **Web servers** The term "www" has become a part of daily life over the past five years. People would have looked at you rather strangely ten years ago if you spouted "www.yourcompanyname.com," but today, most people know what you are referring to.

  The World Wide Web is really what started the massive growth of the Internet in the early 1990s. Until that point, the Internet had mostly been used only by schools and universities across the world. The World Wide Web changed that. The Web is a collection of web pages. A web page is an informative page of information about a given subject. Figure 1-5 shows an example of a corporate website.

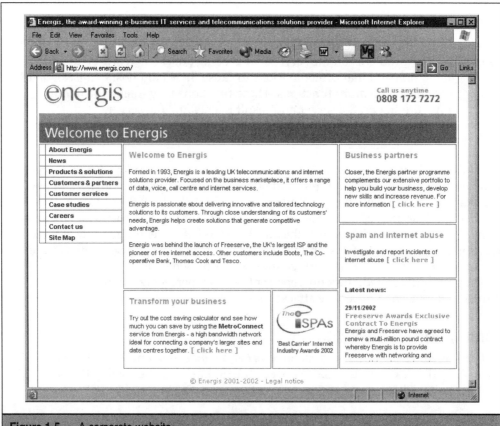

Figure 1-5. A corporate website

Web pages are traditionally created in Hypertext Markup Language (HTML). The HTML web page is viewed in what is called a web browser, which converts the HTML code into the graphical web page.

- **FTP servers**   File Transfer Protocol (FTP) is used to transfer files between hosts that are connected via a TCP/IP network. It is the easiest way to transfer files between network-attached computers. Most computer operating systems come with a built-in FTP application. The traditional applications were all command line because they stemmed from UNIX, but GUI-based FTP applications are very common now. These look and feel like the Windows Internet Explorer interface and are very easy to use for anybody already used to the Microsoft Windows environment.

- **Internet e-mail servers**   Unlike web pages, which are a newer use of the Internet, e-mail was introduced in the very early days of the Internet when new additions to existing protocols were being added all the time. With the introduction of TCP/IP came the Simple Mail Transfer Protocol (SMTP). This was later expanded with POP3 and more recently IMAP4. Everyone is familiar with the uses and advantages of electronic mail, and it has become the preferred communications method within many industries.

Web Servers

The World Wide Web is the technology that is responsible for the massive growth of the Internet today.

The Web was born in 1990 when Tim Berners-Lee developed the first browser application and launched the internal World Wide Web within the European Laboratory for Particle Physics (CERN) headquarters. At that time, the Web was only available to those who had access to the CERN system.

In 1993, the National Center for Supercomputer Applications (NCSA) released the Mosaic browser. This gave users the ability to view graphics and text at the same time over the Web. In the same year, the *New York Times* announced the appearance of the World Wide Web and the White House went online at www.whitehouse.gov.

The next seven years saw massive growth of the Web, as approximately seven thousand new websites were added daily. The largest growth sector of the Internet is the Web.

The World Wide Web is made up of numerous web servers that are located all over the world on a common network (the Internet). These servers all run the Hypertext Transport Protocol (HTTP) service. HTTP is an application-layer protocol that uses TCP as the transport protocol and maps to port 80. In addition to HTTP, there is the Secure Hypertext Transfer Protocol (HTTPS). HTTPS uses client-to-server encryption to secure the normally clear text transmission of data between the HTTP client and the HTTP server.

Threats Posed   Web servers are the most common targets for attacks within a corporate website; the majority of Denial of Service attacks are aimed at web servers. Web servers host the HTTP service and deliver the HTML pages to Internet clients browsing them. The very nature of this client/server relationship makes the web server a target for abuse. The server is addressable on a specific IP address and a specific port.

In addition to Denial of Service attacks, there are also application-related vulnerabilities. The most common web server application that is used on Windows NT is Microsoft's Internet Information Server, and the most common UNIX web server is Apache. Both of these servers are under constant scrutiny from the Internet fraternity and vulnerabilities are found quite frequently.

Solutions to the Threats   In theory, the web service that runs on TCP port 80 is intrinsically secure and does not really require protection. However, it is the web server itself and the network operating system that causes the security concerns. Any service other than the HTTP service running on the server increases the risk associated to the server. The best way to protect against this, as with most other services, is to deploy a firewall that is situated between the public Internet and the web server. The web server can then be on a private network and network address translation can provide the added security of hiding the real IP address of the web server. The firewall should be further configured to only allow access to the web server on the required ports. These are usually port 80 for general HTTP traffic and port 443 if the website is using HTTPS as well as HTTP.

To protect against application vulnerabilities, it is important to ensure that the web server applications be up to date on the latest service and security patches. These will be provided on the relevant vendor's website, and information about vulnerabilities can be obtained from white-hat hacker websites such as www.rootshell.com as well as from various e-mail lists that can be found by searching www.google.com or a similar search engine.

FTP Servers

The File Transfer Protocol (FTP) is an application-layer protocol that provides file-sharing capabilities between hosts. FTP was formally announced as part of the TCP/IP protocol suite in 1971. RFC 172 covers the design and implementation of FTP.

There are two ports associated with FTP: TCP 20 and 21. FTP creates a virtual connection over TCP port 21 for control information and then creates a separate TCP connection on port 20 for data transfers.

FTP is a common application protocol that is used widely on the Internet to transfer files. Most public web servers also provide some FTP functionality for public users to download files. For example, Check Point has a corporate website that is located at www.checkpoint.com. This serves the corporate website. In addition to this, Check Point has an FTP server that can be accessed at ftp.checkpoint.com. This service is provided for downloading files from the Check Point website, and registered users or users with support agreements can download required software updates.

Many companies do not run their own web servers in-house. Instead, they use an Internet Service Provider (ISP) to provide web space on a shared server, or they opt for a dedicated/co-located server. In doing this, they gain the benefit of the ISP's network and Internet connection. The ISP offers this as a service and usually provides fault-tolerant, secure access to the web services behind multitiered firewalls. In this situation, especially with shared web space, most ISPs offer FTP services to their clients in order to upload the required files to the web server. So, most websites will have an FTP service running that has direct access to the directory that contains the actual client website HTML files.

FTP, by design, is a faster method of transferring files across the Internet than HTTP. Most sites offer either HTTP or FTP file download, but normally, FTP download is the faster of the two.

Threats Posed   The major concern with FTP is that the built-in authentication system utilizes a username/password pair that is transmitted in clear-text to the FTP server. This causes obvious concerns when the remote FTP server is accessed across a public, untrusted network. If the FTP username and password get intercepted, it will allow the attacker the same access to your files and directories that you have, leading to disastrous results.

As with any other server, FTP servers are susceptible to Denial of Service attacks. These attacks will render the server unusable to the Internet public.

Solutions to the Threats   FTP access for downloading files from a web server is normally pretty safe, and anonymous access can be allowed for this purpose. The problems arise when you start to use FTP to upload files that make up the company website. Access to this information has to be protected. A good way to do this is to either run the management FTP access on a different port or utilize a different server completely for public FTP access.

A firewall should be placed in between the FTP server and the public Internet. This firewall will protect against some network-based Denial of Service attacks; it should be configured so that management FTP access is permitted from as few hosts as possible.

Internet E-mail Servers (SMTP/POP3/IMAP4)

Apart from the World Wide Web, the other major factor in the growth of the Internet has been electronic mail (e-mail). E-mail allows users to send messages to worldwide recipients instantly without cost or delay. This has had a huge impact in business: almost every business worker has an e-mail address by which they can be contacted.

As computer networks grew in the early 1990s, corporate e-mail became very common internally within companies. No longer did you have to print out memorandums and place them in the required physical mailbox or pigeonhole. You could now type a short memo and send it directly from your e-mail client to the intended recipients. The use of e-mail distribution lists allowed users to send one e-mail to multiple recipients, further improving the worth of e-mail.

With the advent and growth of the Internet, more and more corporations connected their internal e-mail systems to the Internet and provided internal users with Internet e-mail addresses. This opened up the world for internal e-mail users, as they could now e-mail anyone who had a valid Internet e-mail address direct from their usual e-mail client installed on their workstation.

Internet e-mail systems use a combination of three application layer protocols that belong to the TCP/IP suite: SMTP, POP3, and IMAP4. They operate over TCP ports 25, 110, and 143, respectively:

- **Simple Mail Transfer Protocol (SMTP)**   An application-layer protocol that operates over TCP port 25. SMTP is defined in RFC 821 and was originally modeled upon FTP. SMTP transfers e-mail messages between systems and provides notification regarding incoming e-mail.

- **Post Office Protocol ver.3 (POP3)**   An application-layer protocol that operates over TCP port 110. POP3 is defined in RFC 1939 and is a protocol that allows workstations to dynamically access a mail drop on a server host. The usual use of POP3 is on the e-mail client where the e-mail client retrieves e-mail that the e-mail server is holding for it.

- **Internet Message Access Protocol rev.4 (IMAP4)**   An application-layer protocol that operates over TCP port 143. IMAP4 is defined in RFC 2060 and is a protocol that allows an e-mail client to access and manipulate electronic mail messages that are stored on a server. IMAP adds a lot more functionality over POP3 and is the latest e-mail protocol to be devised. With IMAP, you can manipulate and control remote e-mail accounts similar to the way you can with local mailboxes in Microsoft Exchange or a similar corporate e-mail client.

E-mail will continue to help the growth of the Internet. New media-rich improvements to e-mail are occurring all the time. These improvements further enhance the benefit of e-mail both to corporate and to home users.

Threats Posed   Internet e-mail systems can be attacked by Denial of Service or they can be misused if they are incorrectly configured. One common misuse of Internet e-mail systems is spam. *Spam* is unsolicited bulk e-mail, and the people who send it are known as spammers. Spammers usually send bulk e-mails regarding get-rich-quick schemes or advertising pornography websites. Spam is enabled if the web server is running as what is called an open relay. Various Internet groups, such as the Open Relay Behavior Modification System (ORBS at www.orbs.org), have emerged to crack down on server administrators who are running open relays, either intentionally or unintentionally.

The result of spam is that the e-mail servers become heavily loaded, sending out e-mails to sometimes thousands of recipients. This increases the load on the server and uses the server's bandwidth.

Internet e-mail servers, like any other server, can be subject to the common Denial of Service attacks. These attacks render the server unusable to the general public.

There are also application vulnerabilities relating to Internet e-mail servers. The common Microsoft Windows–based e-mail system is Microsoft Exchange, and the common UNIX based e-mail system is Sendmail. Both of these applications have had vulnerabilities associated with them. Details of such vulnerabilities can be found at www.packetstorm.com.

Solutions to the Threats   The provision of a firewall between the Internet e-mail server and the public network is the easiest way to reduce the threats to the Internet e-mail server. The firewall should be configured to restrict access to the specific ports used for e-mail communication, in this case, SMTP and POP3.

Check Point VPN-1/FireWall-1 NG provides a mechanism via Content Vectoring Protocol (CVP) to integrate third-party add-ins that can verify e-mail content and attachments by checking for viruses with malicious code.

The operating system and e-mail application that is running on the mail server should both be at the latest service and security patch. This will ensure that any known vulnerabilities that exist within the operating system and application are protected.

The e-mail service should be configured to disallow spam. There are various documents on how to do this based on the e-mail server that you are running. Further information can be found at www.orbs.org.

CHECKLIST: KEY POINTS IN THE INTERNET AND THE NEED FOR SECURITY

The following is a checklist for the Internet and the need for security:

- ☐ Define Internet.
- ☐ Define the OSI model.
- ☐ List the main advances in the relatively long life span of the Internet.
- ☐ Identify TCP/IP.
- ☐ Identify the packet structures for IP, TCP, and UDP.
- ☐ Identify the basics of Internet security.
- ☐ Identify the two main types of network security attacks.
- ☐ List the common services of the modern Internet.
- ☐ Define the World Wide Web, FTP, and e-mail.
- ☐ Identify the threats posed and the solutions that are available to combat the threat to the common services of the modern Internet.

CHAPTER 2

What's New in VPN-1/FireWall-1 NG

C heck Point's FireWall-1 has long been the market leader, but with so many other firewall vendors appearing, version 4.1 was ready for a major update. With the release of VPN-1/FireWall-1 NG, Check Point's industry-leading firewall reaffirms itself as the product all the other companies will strive to emulate. Check Point VPN-1/FireWall-1 NG represents a milestone in the development of the software, providing exceptional updates to both the user interface and to the underlying code providing increased usability, better throughput, and improved support for large enterprises.

WHAT'S CHANGED SINCE 4.1

As the NG (Next Generation) tag implies, VPN-1/FireWall-1 NG is a major upgrade to FireWall-1 version 4.1. While security administrators versed in the workings of 4.1 will find much of it familiar, they will also find a great many enhancements, including the Security Dashboard, SecureUpdate, Management Server high availability, simplified module licensing, SIC (Secure Internal Communications), and other improvements.

Security Dashboard

The all-new Security Dashboard (see Figure 2-1) includes four panels that organize the display and make more relevant information available. Objects can be dragged and dropped between these panels: the Policy Editor, the Object Tree, the Objects List, and the Visual Policy Editor.

Policy Editor

The Policy Editor includes tabs for editing the Security Policy, Network Address Translation (NAT), and QoS (Quality of Service) policies for those users of FloodGate-1 NG (FloodGate-1 NG is not covered in this book); it also includes a new tab for editing the Desktop Security Policy.

The Policy Editor is the interface by which rules are created that form the rule base. The Rule Base and the policy properties together make up the Security Policy to be enforced on the firewall gateway. How to use the Policy Editor is discussed in Chapters 8 and 9.

Object Tree

The Object Tree enables administrators to quickly access network objects, services, and other configurable items, with an expanding tree view that allows access down to individual objects. This saves time for administrators who do not want to keep accessing the drop-down menus.

Objects List

The Objects List provides a summary level view of the object selected in the Object Tree. It displays the object name, IP address, and comment fields. This is useful for viewing the most pertinent information at a glance for the object selected in the tree view.

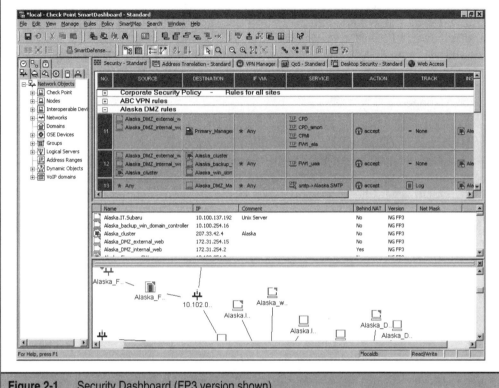

Figure 2-1.   Security Dashboard (FP3 version shown)

Visual Policy Editor

The Visual Policy Editor is a Security Policy visualization tool that provides a detailed, graphical map of an organization's security deployment.

Each object created is automatically placed in the network map at the appropriate connection point. If you create a workstation object with an IP address of 172.31.254.100 and you had previously defined a network object for 172.31.254.0/24, the workstation object will automatically show a line connector to the network object. In this way, a complete network diagram will be created showing all the relevant connections. The Visual Policy Editor provides greater control by providing a visible sanity-check so you don't lose track of the objects you've defined. It also improves security by giving an extra dimension to the Policy Editor view of the rules. This gives administrators improved visibility to validate the integrity of the Security Policy prior to deployment.

SecureUpdate

SecureUpdate provides a centralized way to guarantee that security throughout the enterprise network is automatically updated. Check Point software and OPSEC (Open

Platform for Security) certified products can be patched and maintained remotely. It also provides centralized management of product licenses. It is now easier to configure SecureUpdate in VPN-1/FireWall-1 NG.

From the SecureUpdate GUI, administrators can view and control which products, versions, and licenses are installed throughout their network. This includes some support for features that have been provided by third-party tools, such as Nokia's Horizon Manager.

Management Server High Availability

There are several solutions for high availability of enforcement modules—you can use Check Point High Availability, OPSEC partner solutions, or Nokia VRRP-based high availability. However, the Management Server has always remained a single point of failure for VPN-1/FireWall-1.

Now with the release of NG, one or more secondary management servers can act as standby management servers should the primary active Management Server become unavailable.

Simplified Module Licensing

Licenses for enforcement points are bound and managed on the Management Server rather than at the enforcement point.

Administrators in large corporations and MSSPs (Managed Security Service Providers) will be particularly pleased with this ability as they may move firewall enforcement points around more often than most. It provides more flexibility because enforcement points can have their addresses changed without having to relicense via Check Point.

Administrators can manage all their Check Point assets, licenses, product subscriptions, and support agreements online at the Check Point User Center, accessible from https:// usercenter.checkpoint.com.

Secure Internal Communications

SIC (Secure Internal Communications) is a certificate-based channel for communications between modules—Management Server, VPN/FireWall Module, FloodGate Module, OPSEC Module, and so on. This is akin to using HTTPS in a web browser, where the browser receives a certificate and can then communicate securely with the host. As is the case with HTTPS, SIC uses the underlying SSL (Secure Sockets Layer) protocol to establish a secure channel.

A Management Server includes an ICA (Internal Certificate Authority), which provides X.509-based certificate services for Check Point components. The ICA issues a certificate to each module, and the certificate authenticates all communications between the modules; for example, communications regarding policy installation. Intermodule authentication and communication is conducted using SSL, with either 3DES or RC4.

SIC, which replaces fw putkey (as used in version 4.1), has several new advantages:

- It is more reliable.
- It is easily scalable. Once the modules have certificates, they can communicate with all other modules without having to establish a secure communications channel in advance between each pair of modules (as was the case with fw putkey).
- Using SSL will accommodate future evolving standards easily, such as different symmetric algorithms.

General Improvements and Changes

Check Point has made numerous improvements with the release of NG and the subsequent release of the NG Feature Packs. The following is an overview of how these improvements will change the way you work with VPN-1/FireWall-1.

IPCOMP

IPCOMP, the Internet Engineering Task Force (IETF) data compression standard, is supported, greatly improving VPN throughput. VPN-1 supports IPCOMP for site-to-site and client-to-site connections.

Computational overhead is minimized because VPN-1 compresses only compressible data (and not, for example, binary data).

Administrator Logging

In addition to its former tracking of Policy Installs and general activity logging, the Check Point Log Viewer now tracks administrator activities, including login/logout, object creation, deletion, editing, and Rule Base changes.

Dynamic Objects

This feature greatly simplifies defining policies for large numbers of modules. You can define an object, for example, "mailserver", one time instead of having to define an object for each module, even if it is resolved differently on each module. The object's properties are defined using the dynamic objects command on the module.

Encryption Schemes

Manual IPSec and SKIP are no longer supported. These schemes were not widely used and have been removed.

Algorithms

AES (Advanced Encryption Standard) is now supported. The Rijndael (pronounced "raindoll") block cipher was chosen by the U.S. government as the successful candidate for the AES.

The VPN-1/FireWall-1 NG module supports both site-to-site and remote access clients (SecuRemote and SecureClient). AES provides these advantages:

- Variable key length (from 128 to 256 bits).

- The DES (Data Encryption Standard) key length is 56 bits, and 3DES (Triple DES) provides security equivalent to a 112-bit key.

- A threefold performance improvement over 3DES.

- Module hardware tokens.

VPN-1/FireWall-1 NG modules now support the use of PKCS#11 (Public-Key Cryptography Standards number 11, which defines hardware key storage and acceleration) and the use of cryptographic hardware tokens. These tokens provide secure key generation and storage, as well as public key hardware acceleration. Tokens are certified and available through partner vendors via the OPSEC PKI program (see www.opsec.com).

Network Address Translation (NAT)

FireWall-1 NG adds some functionality benefits with respect to Network Address Translation. These benefits are explained here:

- **A new ability to perform destination translation on the client side**   Destination translation is performed on the client-side interface in static destination (DST) mode, removing the requirement for routing changes.

- **Automatic ARP configuration**   When using address translation, the ARP table on the gateway performing the NAT will automatically be configured so that ARP requests for a translated machine, network, or address range are answered by the gateway, removing the requirement for manual ARP configuration (using the arp command on UNIX systems or the local.arp file on Windows NT systems).

These two additions remove the additional steps required when creating NAT rules of setting up a route to the destination address and having the firewall respond to ARP requests for the NATed address.

FEATURE PACKS

With the release of VPN-1/FireWall-1 NG, Check Point introduces the concept of Feature Packs. Check Point stated that a Feature Pack marks an improvement to the product in addition to fixing any bugs. A Feature Pack is therefore not just a patch; it also includes improvements to the functionality and performance of VPN-1/FireWall-1 NG. Owners of VPN-1/FireWall-1 NG can obtain the latest Feature Pack from the Check Point website (www.checkpoint.com) if they have a current software subscription for the NG product. Software subscriptions entitle the owner to all upgrades for the lifetime of the subscription. When deploying a Feature Pack, ensure that all components are upgraded in the correct order—see the accompanying information supplied with the Feature Pack for more information.

Feature Packs are cumulative in the same way that Microsoft Service Packs are. This means that you do not have to install FP1 first if you wish to go to FP2 because all the previous features and fixes are contained in the latest Feature Pack release. The following sections summarize the new features and their benefits of Feature Packs 1, 2, and 3.

VPN-1/FireWall-1 NG and Feature Pack 1

Feature Pack 1 includes all maintenance patches released since the initial version of NG up to the arrival of Feature Pack 1, along with several product enhancements.

VPN-1

The most notable changes to the VPN-1 module are a simplified setup and the addition of the concept of VPN communities.

VPN Simplified Setup   VPN-1/FireWall-1 NG's new simplified VPN setup mode greatly streamlines the VPN configuration process. This new approach requires that you understand the concepts of VPN site and VPN community.

VPN Site and VPN Community   A new management model (based on the concept of sites and communities) enables the system administrator to directly define a VPN on a group of gateways. Each gateway and all or parts of its protected domain constitute a new entity referred to as a VPN site (not to be confused with a site defined for SecuRemote/ SecureClient). By grouping an unlimited number of VPN sites, the system administrator creates a VPN community whose properties are automatically applied to each community member. The definition of the VPN community completes the VPN configuration. The structure of the community defines the encrypted connections between its members. There is no need to define encryption rules—all connections between community members (sites) are automatically encrypted.

FireWall-1 GUI

The most obvious GUI improvement is in the Policy Editor, which has been made much more visual and shows a clear view of the inter-relationships between the various objects.

Security Dashboard   There are now several places from which you can add, edit, or delete a network object:

- The Object Tree
- The menu

- The Objects List
- The toolbar
- The Rule Base
- The Visual Policy Editor

To make these changes, you can drag and drop items between panes. For example, you can drag a workstation from the Object Tree and drop it into the Source column of the Rule Base.

Strong Authentication for Administrators   You can log in to the Policy Editor using either of the following:

- Your username and password, as in previous versions
- SecureID
- RADIUS
- A PKCS#12 certificate created by the Check Point Internal Certificate Authority

In addition, the connection between the GUI client and the Management Server can be compressed. Click More Options in the Policy Editor login window to display the compression option.

Administrator Management   Check Point administrators (that is, people who are authorized to use the Check Point Policy Editor) are now defined from the Policy Editor GUI by selecting Manage | Users | Administrators. Previously administrators could only be added by using the CPConfig menu on the Management Module.

Visual Policy Editor   The new features in the Visual Policy Editor are listed here:

- **Export topology map to Microsoft Visio**   Selected portions or the entire topology map can be exported to Visio. The export format and style are fully configurable. You can use Check Point object icons or Visio shapes by choosing a user-specified mapping between Check Point objects and Visio shapes and using color, exported data from the object, and the layout of the exported drawing.

- **Export topology map to an image file**   Selected portions or the entire topology map can be saved as image files in various formats (BMP, JPEG) at various compression levels.

- **Show Rule**   Rules can be viewed in three different modes (all paths, all paths per selected pair of source-destination, or you can page through each specific path the rule applies to). Rule calculation analyzes the ability to enforce the rule, displaying the participants in the rule and highlighting modules that should participate in the rule (based on the network topology) but do not.

- **Show NAT**   The NAT status of all objects behind a specific gateway can be displayed: objects NATed by the specific gateway or other gateways, objects not NATed, and objects that may be improperly configured.

- **Show Community**   Intranet and extranet community members and the paths between them can be displayed.

- **Personalized topology view per administrator**   The administrators can configure their own preferred topology views, which are preserved between sessions.

Online Help   The online help has been improved by adding links to the public area of the SecureKnowledge database.

You can also e-mail the Technical Publications group directly from the online help.

Global Properties and Workstation Properties   The Workstation Properties window and the Global Properties window (previously known as the Properties Setup window) consist of pages with a tree-like structure displayed on the left. The result is a simpler view in which the hierarchical relationship between pages is highlighted.

SYNDefender

Both the Workstation Properties and the Global Properties windows have SYNDefender pages. The Global Properties window is relevant in upgrade situations and defines the SYNDefender properties for those workstations whose specific SYNDefender properties have not yet been set. The workstation properties apply to new installations of VPN-1/ FireWall-1 NG.

SYNDefender prevents SYN attacks and is covered in Chapter 16.

Dynamic IP Address Support

A VPN-1/FireWall-1 NG module, which is both a gateway and a host, can have a dynamic IP address rather than a fixed IP address. For example, the module IP address can be assigned by DHCP or some other mechanism. This could be useful for the increasing xDSL and cable modem connectivity market because ISPs (Internet Service Providers) often use dynamic assignment as a way of managing their address space and preventing address depletion.

Administrator Logging

The Check Point Log Viewer, in addition to its former tracking of Policy Installs and general activity logging, now tracks administrator activities, including login/logout, object creation, deletion, editing, and Rule Base changes. A new predefined Audit view is available in the Log Viewer with which to examine these activities.

Log Data Unification

Log entries are no longer static text but instead are stored in a database format that can be updated to reflect changes in the state of the connection (previously, a new entry in the log file had to be created).

Third-Party Product Status Monitoring

The Check Point Status Viewer has been redesigned and includes support for monitoring third-party OPSEC products. This gives the security administrator an improved view of all the components that enforce aspects of the Security Policy, including OPSEC-certified third-party applications.

Alerts

Two new internal VPN-1/FireWall-1 NG commands (which cannot be executed from the OS command line) are available for use with mail and SNMP trap alerts—see the Alert Commands page of the Global Properties window. These internal commands provide a significant performance improvement over the scripts used in the past.

System Status

The System Status Viewer has a new look and feel and includes support for all Check Point modules (VPN/FireWall, FloodGate, and so on) as well as for OPSEC products.

The status of two new modules, Management and Common Infrastructure, is displayed in the System Status Viewer. In addition, some 50 VPN-related statistics are collected and available for display in a separate VPN view.

TCP Service Properties

Timeouts can be configured independently for each TCP service. Previously, the only settings were global for TCP timeouts, which meant increasing the timeout setting for TCP-based connections. The only alternative to this was to edit the INSPECT code directly, which could be tricky to maintain.

NOTE   INSPECT is the language that the Rule Base is turned into and is a proprietary language developed by Check Point.

TCP timeouts can now be changed on a per-protocol basis. For example, if a an application server expects to establish a connection and have the connection remain active even if no data is sent over it for a period of time, the firewall will eventually timeout the connection. To prevent this, you may need to change the timeout property to the longest possible delay that the connection might be idle. If you don't, the next attempted data transfer will fail due to a state table check if the connection has been removed from the state table by the firewall.

High Availability

Cluster member management has been simplified, and synchronization is configurable from the GUI rather than by editing a configuration file. In version 4.1, the sync.conf file needed to be created on both synchronized gateways to maintain the state table; this is now easily achieved using the GUI interface.

ConnectControl

All IP protocols (not only TCP and UDP, as previously) can be used in Logical Server rules; SSL is supported in HTTP mode.

More timeout and persistency properties are provided. The frequency and timeout that the VPN/FireWall NG module uses to check the availability of the servers can now be configured.

ConnectControl is used to load balance requests across a group of servers creating one logical server. ConnectControl requires an additional license and is covered in Chapter 14.

VPN-1/FireWall-1 NG and Feature Pack 2

Feature Pack 2 provides a number of enhancements over the FP1 release and includes all maintenance patches released since FP1.

VPN-1

As a private network built on top of a public network, VPN hosts within the private network use encryption to talk to other hosts. The encryption excludes hosts from outside the private network even if they are on the public network. VPN-1 Net is a powerful product because it provides enhanced features such as VPN Communities for greater controls and management. VPN Communities are used to simplify the creation of intranets and extranets, although the traditional Rule Base method is still available to those who wish to use it.

VPN-1 Net   VPN-1 Net, a dedicated VPN product, provides a solution (intranet or extranet) for customers who require VPN-oriented systems and minimal access control.

VPN Communities   VPN configuration has been enhanced for Feature Pack 2 and several improvements have been made to the concept of communities. VPN Communities define the members of the community in conjunction with the network topology used for that community to simplify configuration and administration. The primary interface is the Policy Editor's VPN Manager tab, which displays the communities in either a topology or list view and enables the user to easily configure mesh or star VPNs. Access control and VPN are clearly differentiated and defined on separate tabs in the Policy Editor.

There is no longer a need for the Encrypt action. Encryption is determined by community membership and topology.

The IF VIA column in the Policy Editor's Security Policy tab is an additional match criterion that specifies access control for community connections:

- Remote access VPNs are included in the community concept.
- Multiple communities can be defined.

- A new community type (Remote Access community) is available.
- VPN gateways with dynamically assigned IP addresses (DAIP Modules) are supported for communities.

FireWall-1

FireWall-1 is a complete enterprise security suite that integrates access controls, authentication, network address translation (NAT), content security, auditing, and more. These features are discussed in detail throughout this book; the main features introduced in Feature Pack 2 are discussed next.

Network Address Translation (NAT)   NAT Hide mode supports 50,000 connections per destination IP address, rather than per-source (hiding) IP address. This gives a significant improvement in the number of connections that can be handled using a Hide NAT. See Chapter 13 for further details of a Hide NAT.

VoIP   There is improved support for both H.323 and Session Initiation Protocol (SIP)-based Voice over IP (VoIP), including gatekeepers, gateways, and SIP proxies. This will greatly enhance the firewall's ability to support VoIP applications, as this is an increasing requirement within large corporations.

Capacity Optimization   The size of the connections table and memory pool can be set in the GUI individually for each firewall module. This was something that was previously possible only by using operating system commands. These varied from platform to platform, so having this level of control moved to the GUI for the firewall greatly simplifies and speeds up administration.

Pattern-Based URL Blocking   Pattern-based signatures can be defined for blocking attacks that are characterized by the attackers' HTTP URL.

Dynamic IP Address (DAIP) Module   The current IP addresses of Dynamic IP Address (DAIP) Modules are maintained on the Management Server, enabling status monitoring of the DAIP Module and policies to be pushed from the Management Server. This means that the Management Server is aware of the module's dynamic addresses improving control and streamlines the process, pushing a new policy to the module.

OPSEC   OPSEC (Open Platform for Security) application commands (for example, starting or stopping OPSEC applications) can now be run from the Policy Editor. Once again, this shows how the command and control of OPSEC applications is being put in the hands of the administrator, providing far more integrated control of third-party applications from the GUI.

There are now more than 70 predefined OPSEC-certified products to choose from when defining an OPSEC application object. See www.opsec.com for further information on OPSEC and available third-party applications.

Security Dashboard

The Security Dashboard is a Security Policy tool that provides a detailed, graphical map, Rule Base, Object Tree and Object Lists for an organization's security deployment. The Security Dashboard provides greater control, improved security, and unparalleled ease-of-use by allowing security managers to validate the integrity of their Security Policy prior to deployment. A number of key enhancements were made in Feature Pack 2, as detailed in the next sections.

Network Objects   There are three new types of network objects, which replace the previous workstation object:

- **Check Points**   These have Check Point software installed on them and include gateways, hosts, gateway clusters, embedded devices, and externally managed gateways and hosts.

- **Nodes**   These have no Check Point software installed on them and include gateways and hosts.

- **Interoperable Device**   These are devices that participate in VPNs on which no Check Point software is installed.

A new wizard greatly simplifies the definition of gateways by taking the user through the creation of the gateway.

Policy Management   The new features in Policy Manager are listed here:

- **Revision Control**   Policy versions can be saved (either manually or automatically) and retrieved for viewing or editing.

- **Session Description**   When logging in to the Policy Editor, the administrator can enter information that will be displayed in the Audit Log entry when an object is modified or added.

- **Policy Packages**   Policies display only the tabs that have been defined for them, reducing the onscreen clutter when not all tabs are used.

These capabilities improve audit capabilities and the operation of change control as may be implemented in large organizations and MSSPs.

Visual Policy Editor (VPE)   Changes to the Visual Policy Editor in Feature Pack 2 mean it can be displayed in a dockable window. Improved export capabilities to Visio, for example, are also provided.

Installed OPSEC applications are displayed in the VPE. IP address ranges can be defined as public or private system-wide, thus enhancing the ability of the VPE to interpret interface information for networks using overlapping IP ranges.

SecuRemote/SecureClient

Feature Pack 2 introduces several enhancements for the two remote access clients for VPN, SecuRemote and SecureClient.

Simplified Management   The Remote Access page of the Global Properties window replaces the Desktop Security page and contains additional SecuRemote/SecureClient configuration options, simplifying the management of SecuRemote/SecureClient properties by locating them in a single place

SecureClient ICA Integration   Automatic ICA certificate registration is available directly from a SecureClient machine, which allows for simplified certificate retrieval.

Office Mode   Office Mode enables the organization to assign internal IP addresses to SecureClient machines. This IP address, which can now be assigned by a DHCP server, will not be exposed to the public network but will be encapsulated inside the VPN tunnel between SecureClient and the gateway.

The IP to be used externally is assigned to the SecureClient in the usual way by the ISP.

SecureClient Diagnostics Tool   The SecureClient Diagnostics Tool has been enhanced with additional information. The tool is designed to minimize the amount of time required to troubleshoot VPN client problems by providing diagnostic information, policy information, and log information.

SecureUpdate

SecureUpdate has also received an update in Feature Pack 2. All products on a Check Point node can be remotely upgraded with a single click. Product packages can be added to or deleted from the repository using the SecureUpdate GUI. Product packages can also be added to the Product Repository directly from the Web. Policy Servers can now be remotely installed. Dynamic IP Address Module Modules are supported, and GUI views are dockable and can be printed.

Log Management

Feature Pack 2 (FP2) enhances disk space management by allowing log files to be automatically switched (the current log file is time- and date-stamped and a new log is started/switched). In addition, the oldest log files are deleted when disk space is exhausted.

Remote Log Management

Log files on modules can be managed from the Log Server or Management Server.

A Log Server or Management Server can be configured to automatically forward log files from modules, and log files can be manually forwarded from a module to a Log Server or Management Server.

Status Manager

FP2 renames System Status Viewer to Status Manager. System alerting has been further enhanced to provide alert conditions when CPU usage or free disk space violates a threshold. These can be defined in the Status Manager to apply either globally or to specific modules, products, and events.

VPN-1/FireWall-1 NG and Feature Pack 3

Feature Pack 3 (FP3) provides a number of enhancements over the FP2 release and includes all maintenance patches released since Feature Pack 1. Feature Pack 3 includes some new features for VPN-1/FireWall-1 NG. The most important new features are discussed in this section.

Internal Certificate Authority

Microsoft Enterprise Certificate Authority (CA) using Active Directory on Windows 2000 server is supported in FP3. This combination was not previously supported because the CA signs the certificates using only the full name, not the full DN. This created a problem because user searches were based on the full DN. Using another identifier in the certificate enables a proper search.

- Internal CA automatic renewal for Secure Internal communication and for Remote Users is now available.

- It is possible to enlarge the key size of certificates produced by the Internal CA for VPN-1 clients or modules from the default of 1024 bits to either 2048 or 4096 bits.

- Internal CA certificates can be stored on a hardware token using CAPI interface.

L2TP Support for Microsoft Clients

VPN-1 Gateways support for MS Windows XP/2000 VPN client (which consists of L2TP/Transport IPsec).

Clientless VPN (SSL-based VPN)

VPN-1 Gateways now include GUI support for HTTPS (SSL over HTTP) termination of remote users with no SecuRemote/SecureClient or any other IPsec VPN client installed. This means that SSL enabled browsers can be used to set up VPN tunnels without a specific IPSec-based VPN Client.

SmartDefense

The SmartDefense package is now integrated into the Check Point Suite. SmartDefense provides the following:

- A unified security framework for components that identify and prevent cyber attack.

- Protection against Denial of Service attacks. To avoid exhaustion of the connection table when under a UDP (or other protocol) flood attack, it is possible to define a quota for UDP (or other non-TCP protocol) connections. When the number of non-TCP connections reaches the quota, only new TCP connections will be allowed. The non-TCP quota is disabled by default and can be set individually for each VPN-1/FireWall-1 NG Module.

Inspection of Peer-to-Peer Applications and Instant Messaging

Applications that use HTTP to tunnel their data can now be detected and blocked. This includes peer-to-peer applications like KaZaA and Gnutella, and messaging applications like ICQ, AOL Instant Messenger, and MS messenger. This is done by the HTTP Security Server, which can parse and match regular expressions over HTTP headers.

Managing File Sharing

CIFS, the Microsoft protocol for file and print sharing (also known as SMB) is supported. VPN-1/FireWall-1 NG can enforce a granular access control policy to specific disk shares and printers and log access to these shares. VPN-1/FireWall-1 NG inspects CIFS in the kernel using the Check Point high-performance TCP-streaming technology. CIFS functionality is available as a new type of a resource in the SmartDashboard.

Services   Simple Object Access Protocol (SOAP), a standard for application data sharing over the Internet using HTTP, is now supported. SOAP relies on XML to encode the information and then adds the necessary HTTP headers to send it. Using URI resources, VPN-1/FireWall-1 NG is able to parse SOAP version 1.1 traffic and validate its integrity according to a user-defined scheme. SOAP functionality is available via a new tab in the URI resource window.

There is new multicast support. The router-alert IP option used by IGMP protocol is supported. IGMP is used for multicast group membership management. In earlier versions, VPN-1/FireWall-1 NG dropped all packets with IP options (including IGMP).

X11 (X Window graphics system for UNIX) is blocked by default when it is matched with a rule that has Any service. This prevents a potential security misconfiguration where Any is used to allow outbound connections for protected servers. If such X11 connectivity is required, it should be allowed explicitly by a rule that uses this service. The old behavior can be restored by setting the reject_x11_in_any global property to false, though this is not recommended.

Discontinued Features

The following features are no longer supported:

- The Windows NT performance DLL
- The Axent Pathways Defender authentication method

NAT-Related Issues

The mechanism for resolving address ranges (applicable for connections to hosts protected by VPN-1 Gateways with multiple interfaces) is now functional even when the protecting VPN-1 Gateway is behind a NAT device, which performs static NAT for the interfaces of the protecting module.

Multiple (Dynamic) interface resolving using the RDP polling mechanism is now supported when the responding VPN-1 Gateway is hidden behind a NAT device.

NAT can be disabled inside VPN tunnels: a property to disable NAT is available on each Gateway to Gateway VPN community.

Summary for Feature Pack 3

The Management Client has been renamed Smart Client and is shown earlier in this chapter in Figure 2-1.

CHECKLIST: KEY POINTS IN WHAT'S NEW IN VPN-1/FIREWALL-1 NG

The following is a checklist for what's new in VPN-1/FireWall-1 NG:

- ☐ List the new features of VPN-1/FireWall-1 NG.
- ☐ Define Check Point VPN-1/FireWall-1 NG.
- ☐ Define Feature Pack.
- ☐ Identify all deployed Check Point components and gateways.
- ☐ Define change control.
- ☐ Define Security Dashboard.
- ☐ Define SecureUpdate.
- ☐ Define Management Server high availability.
- ☐ Define simplified module licensing.

CHAPTER 3

VPN-1/FireWall-1 NG Architecture

As e-business infrastructure proliferates and e-commerce global markets expand, corporations are being forced to enhance the level of security of client/server communications over the Internet. With that goal in mind, Check Point has developed a Secure Virtual Network (SVN) architecture. This SVN architecture unites multiple products into an integrated management framework, which allows for a sophisticated level of integration among Check Point's suite of applications. This allows it to provide an end-to-end framework for network security and enables organizations to secure business-critical Internet, intranet, and extranet traffic at the network, system, application, and end-user levels.

Check Point's SVN is an integral part of their suite of security applications, providing an integrated architecture that includes application- or protocol-specific bandwidth management (Quality of Service, or QoS), IP Address Management, private key interoperability (PKI), and a VPN/firewall solution dubbed VPN-1/FireWall-1 NG, which is a major part of Check Point's SVN architecture. Later in this chapter, Tables 3-1 through 3-3 will show a breakdown of the SVN components.

FUNDAMENTALS OF EXTRANET SECURITY

To understand the power behind SVN components, you need to understand the challenges of implementing extranet security:

- **Many-to-many interactions**   Includes news groups whose members exchange information freely.

- **One-to-many communication**   Includes information posted on the Web available to many groups and corporations on the Internet.

- **Two-way interaction**   Includes providing users with technical help and support over the Web.

There are two main guidelines when building extranets:

- **Access control is paramount**   Controlling who can access your system is one of the most important parts of a security plan. However, users who gain lawful access to a system are often forgotten. You need to know what other types of information and access are available to these users once they're inside your system.

- **Provide an easy mechanism for login**   An access system does not require a high degree of visibility. The more transparent the system is, the more efficient it will be. Consider developing an access system that can handle your entire system, as opposed to piecemeal access control that you set up as the system grows.

USING FIREWALLS FOR EXTRANET PROTECTION

The implementation of a dual-homed host VPN-1/FireWall-1 NG configuration in your LAN, as shown in Figure 3-1, is a smart solution for your extranet security. When implementing the firewall, the host can act as a router between networks sending information directly from one network to another—Internet packets can be sent from your organization's network to your supplier's network and vice-versa.

Requests for information that involve the supplier can be directly routed to bypass the supplier's network. The results of a query can then be forwarded back to the requester's browser. But don't be too optimistic! This is far from secure, yet many small to medium-sized organizations maintain such an arrangement. This architecture cannot prevent harmful information from penetrating the network.

An alternative to this scenario is screening a host setup and router combination, as shown in Figure 3-2. This approach can protect the internal network. Along with a screened host is a screening router that uses packet filtering (just discussed) to transfer information into the organization. This is a rather simple concept, yet there is quite a divide in the information technology community as to which method is preferable.

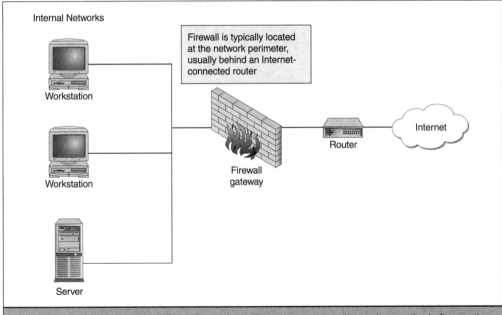

Figure 3-1.   Dual-home host VPN-1/FireWall-1 NG implementation: the easiest method of protection against unwanted packets coming from the Internet

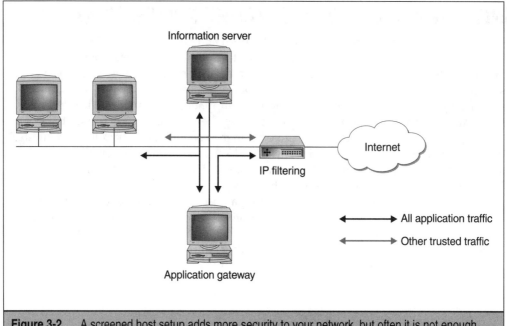

Figure 3-2.   A screened host setup adds more security to your network, but often it is not enough.

Dual-homed hosts are somewhat unreliable, and screened hosts are a small measure of defense against intruders. Moreover, once a screened host is compromised, so is the network. Thus, a better alternative is to use a screened-host setup with an advanced authentication software or firewall, as shown in Figure 3-3.

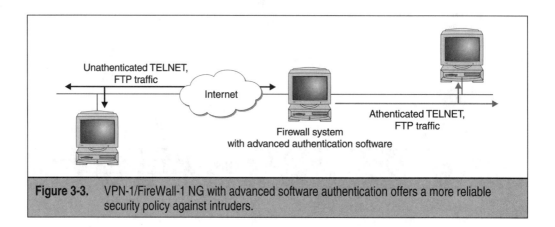

Figure 3-3.   VPN-1/FireWall-1 NG with advanced software authentication offers a more reliable security policy against intruders.

Another important area of security threats and countermeasures is of users accessing the Internet via intranets and visiting a number of websites that contain a broad array of content, including harmful ones. A user may choose to download an executable file from your website or vice-versa. Unfortunately, some of these files can carry infected code that can cause a tremendous amount of harm to the network. Check Point and others have developed methodologies to try to curb the harmful effects of such executables. Secure Virtual Networks (SVN) includes Security Servers and Content Vectoring Protocol which allow third-party plug-ins to Check Point VPN-1/FireWall-1 NG solutions to protect networks against malicious code. An example of this would be Anti-Virus Content Checking software. Content Checking software is discussed in detail in Chapter 15.

Firewalls alone will not take care of the problem of downloading infected executables. End users and corporations need a path back to the author or publisher of web executables to ensure accountability for the product in question. An alternative is to use *sandboxes*, which essentially guard against attacks from malicious code by preventing applets from writing to the hard drive and restricting access to memory. The sandbox confines executable code to a runtime environment, seeking to neutralize any problem by limiting the reach of the code. An example of this is a Java applet, which cannot read or write to the client computer's file system.

This approach is interesting, but it prohibits the full functionality of the applet because the applet must perform outside of the sandbox. ActiveX controls, plug-ins, and most other executables that can be downloaded over the Internet are not restricted to the sandbox. Another approach to ensure accountability with downloaded code is to have the code digitally signed, which allows a user or corporation to trace back to the author or publisher.

SECURING NETWORKS, SYSTEMS, APPLICATIONS AND USERS

Check Point has identified the components that make up any organization's network: networks, systems, applications, and users, as shown in Figure 3-4. To ensure that an enterprise security architecture could be applied to these components, Check Point's Secure Virtual Network (SVN) architecture was designed to connect these four elements. SVN addresses the security requirements for all four elements thus giving a seamless enterprise solution. This section will attempt to explain how this is achieved.

SVN Components

Tables 3-1, 3-2, and 3-3 list the products that comprise Check Point's SVN architecture. These tools are designed to meet the security requirements for networks, systems, applications, and users.

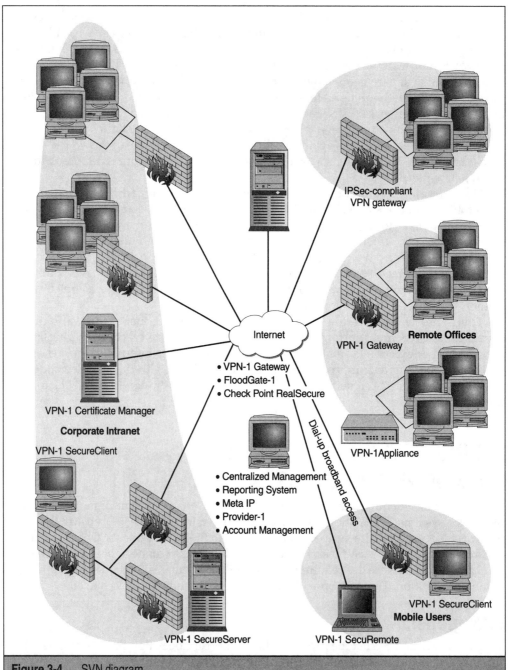

Figure 3-4. SVN diagram

Product	Description
VPN-1 Product Family	Protects communications over untrusted networks such as the Internet, and secures networks against unauthorized access
FireWall-1	Comprehensive, integrated platform for Internet security
VPN-1/FireWall-1 SmallOffice	Enterprise-class security for small businesses and branch offices
Safe@Home by Sofaware	Home network security solution providing firewall and VPN capabilities

Table 3-1.   VPN/Security

Product	Description
Meta IP	IP address management solution
Provider-1	Security management solution for managed service providers and large enterprises
SiteManager-1	Based on Provider-1, SiteManager-1 enables service providers to provide managed security services to small businesses
Reporting Module	Turns VPN-1/FireWall-1 NG log data into actionable information
Visual Policy Editor	Security policy visualization tool
UserAuthority	Provides a secure communication layer for authenticating users to applications

Table 3-2.   Management

Product	Description
FloodGate-1	Quality of Service (QoS) solution for secure networks
High Availability Module	Integrated failover solution for VPN-1/FireWall-1 NG gateways
VPN-1 Accelerator Card	Improves VPN-1 gateway performance by accelerating intensive cryptographic operations in hardware
ConnectControl	Intelligently balances incoming connections among multiple application servers

Table 3-3.   Performance/Availability

FIREWALLS: FROM PACKET FILTERS TO STATEFUL INSPECTION

The most secure method of connecting the corporate network to a public network such as the Internet is to deploy a firewall at the network perimeter. A firewall, as discussed in the previous section, is typically a gateway system that controls traffic flow between two or more networks. Figure 3-5 shows where a firewall is typically installed to control traffic between the internal network and the Internet. The firewall will typically be configured to allow data to pass bi-directionally between a protected network and an external network based on a set of defined rules. For example, the firewall may let users access external web pages but prevent all other access.

The firewall typically operates on the assumption that everything is prohibited unless expressly permitted via security rules that make up the security policy. Data that meets these specific requirements or rules is allowed to pass through the firewall gateway, while unauthorized data is dropped at the gateway.

Packet filtering and application-layer proxies were used widely within earlier firewalls and routers to secure the network. However, packet filtering and application-layer proxies alone have limitations that are discussed in further detail in the following sections. These are exactly the sort of solutions that have been superseded by Check Point Stateful Inspection Technologies and the Secure Virtual Network architecture.

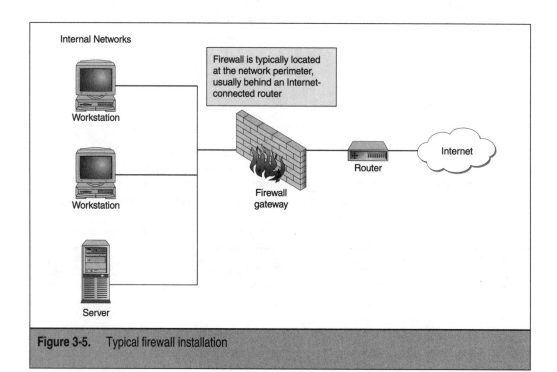

Figure 3-5.   Typical firewall installation

Packet Filtering

Packet filtering was originally deployed in routers and first-generation firewalls. The most common form of packet filtering ignores the upper four layers of the OSI (Open Systems Interconnection) model and operates at the network layer or IP layer of TCP/IP.

This type of firewall provides access control at the IP layer and either accepts, rejects, or drops packets based mainly on source and/or destination network addresses, and the type of application or service. Packet filtering firewalls provide a simple level of security at an inexpensive price. These firewalls also provide a high level of performance and are normally transparent to the users. However, packet filtering firewalls have several weaknesses:

- They allow access to only a limited part of the packet header.

- They perform only limited screening above the network layer.

- They need resource-intensive administration and configuration due to increasing complexity of ACLs.

- They provide minimal logging; alerts are usually limited to text strings sent via syslog messages that are typically logged to the /var/adm/messages file on a separate Unix system.

- They understand only network-level protocol, so they are vulnerable to attacks aimed at higher protocols.

- The network-level protocol requires certain knowledge of its technical details and not every administrator has them, so packet filtering firewalls are usually more difficult to configure and verify, increasing the risks of system misconfiguration, security holes, and failures.

- Packet-filtering firewalls cannot hide the private network topology and therefore exposes the private network to the outside world.

- These firewalls have very limited auditing capabilities, thus your company needs to audit its security policy.

- Not all Internet applications are supported by packet-filtering firewalls.

- These firewalls do not always support some of the security policies clauses such as user-level authentication and time-of-day access control.

Figure 3-6 shows the Open Systems Interconnection (OSI) 7 layer model with the packet filter operating at the network layer. Each packet entering or leaving the network is compared to a set of criteria before it is forwarded or dropped.

Packet filtering has historically been deployed on perimeter routers with the use of Access Control Lists (ACLs), which control access based on the following information:

- Source network address or host IP address

- Destination network address or host IP address

- Source protocol port number

- Destination protocol port number

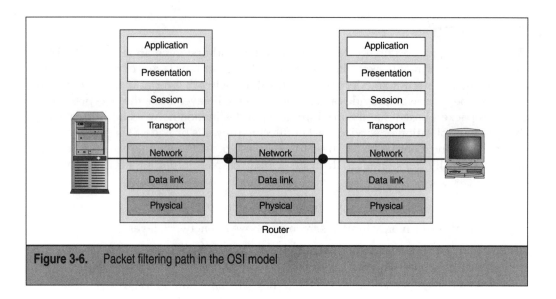

Figure 3-6.   Packet filtering path in the OSI model

Packet filters are application independent, which allows high throughput and scalability. However, large ACLs with multiple entries, known as Access Control Entries (ACE) will eventually lead to a performance impact. Access Control Lists are processed sequentially until a match is found and large lists place a load on the CPU.

Packet filters are the least secure type of firewall because they do not understand the context of a given communication.

The advantages of packet filters are as follows:

- They're inexpensive.
- They provide application transparency.
- They provide high performance and scalability.

Application-Layer Gateways (Proxies)

Because packet filters were found to be inadequate in securing corporate networks, second-generation firewalls were developed that could use application-layer information. Application-layer gateways, also called proxies, provide access control at the application-level layer; they implement firewalls above the network layer, as shown in Figure 3-7.

Because application-level firewalls function at the application layer, they have the ability to examine the traffic in detail, which makes them more secure than packet filtering firewalls. However, application-layer gateways are usually slower than packet filtering due to their scrutiny of the traffic. Application-layer gateways are to some degree intrusive and restrictive, and they usually require users to either change their behavior or use specialized software to achieve policy objectives. Application-layer gateways are thus not transparent to the users.

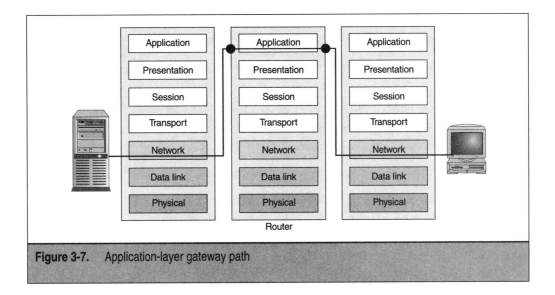

Figure 3-7.   Application-layer gateway path

As shown in Figure 3-7, proxy servers have access to the upper-layer protocols, which improves on security and provides communication context. However, this is done by interrupting the flow of communication between the client and the server, which increases the number of connections used by the firewall because one connection is required from client to the firewall and another from the firewall to the destination.

Each proxy on the application gateway requires a specific daemon or process, which makes scalability and support for new applications problematic.

In the dynamic environment of today's e-business marketplace, new applications, protocols, and services emerge frequently. For example, Napster or Microsoft Instant Messenger and the application-layer gateway struggle to keep pace because specific proxies or daemons must be developed for each application that the application gateway supports.

It is common for commercially available application proxies to also support packet filtering to compensate for the lack of application transparency inherent in application proxy firewalls. However, packet filtering should be deployed with caution as it introduces all its disadvantages to the application-layer gateway.

The advantages of application-layer gateways are as follows:

- Good security.
- Because application proxies understand application-level protocols, they can defend against higher-level protocol attacks for the supported application.
- They don't require you to know all the details about the lower-level protocols and so are usually easier to configure than packet filters.
- They can hide the private network topology.

- They have full auditing facilities including tools that monitor the traffic and manipulate the log files that contain information such as source, destination network addresses, application type, user identification and password, start and end time of access, and the number of bytes of information transferred in all directions.

- They can support more security policies, including user-level authentication and time-of-day access control.

- Full application-layer awareness providing the application is supported.

The disadvantages of application-layer gateways (proxies) are as follows:

- Poor performance, because data has to travel further up the OSI model to layers 4–7 to be processed than with a packet filtering firewall which operates at layer 3.

- Limited application support.

- Poor scalability.

Hybrid Firewalls

Because both packet filtering and application-layer gateways have their weaknesses, some IT organizations have implemented hybrid firewalls that combine both firewall techniques. While these hybrid products attempt to solve some of the weaknesses mentioned previously, they also introduce some of the weaknesses inherent in application-level firewalls as just outlined.

One of the main weaknesses of this alternative is that because hybrid firewalls still rely on packet filtering mechanisms to support certain applications, they still have the same security weaknesses.

Second-Generation Application-Layer Gateways

Second-generation application-layer gateways (or firewalls) are still application-level firewalls, but their second generation solves the transparency problem of earlier versions without compromising performance. This alternative provides a few advantages, including the following:

- These gateways can be used as an intranet firewall due to their transparency and generally higher performance.

- They can provide full network address translation (NAT) in addition to network topology hiding. NAT is the mechanism of hiding real IP addresses behind virtual IP addresses.

- They can support a more advanced user-level authentication mechanism.

SELECTING A FIREWALL FOR TODAY'S NETWORKS

Before you select a firewall, you need to develop a corporate security policy that the firewall will implement. When evaluating firewalls, make sure you understand the underlying technology used in the firewall—as we just discussed, some firewall technologies are inferior in security to others. You should evaluate a firewall based on its level of security and implementation features.

The following are some of the characteristics you should be looking for in a firewall:

- **Security assurance**   Independent assurance that the relevant firewall technology fulfills its specifications and assurance that it is properly installed.

- **Privilege control**   The degree to which the product can impose user access restrictions.

- **Authentication**   What kind of access control does the product provide? Does it support authorizations? What about authentication techniques? These techniques include security features such as source/destination computer network address authentication, password authentication, access control cards, and fingerprint verification devices.

- **Audit capabilities**   The ability of the product to monitor network traffic, including unauthorized access attempts, and the ability to generate logs and provide statistical reports and alarms.

As for implementation features, you should be looking for the ability a product has to satisfy your network management requirements and concerns. A good firewall product should have the following:

- **Flexibility**   The firewall should be open enough to accommodate the Security Policy of your company and to allow for changes in the feature. Remember, a Security Policy should very seldom change, but security procedures should always be reviewed, especially in light of Internet and new web-centric applications.

- **Performance**   A firewall should be fast enough so that users won't feel the screening of packets. The volume of data throughput and transmission speed associated with the product should be consistent with your bandwidth to the Internet.

- **Scalability**   Is the firewall scaleable? The product should be able to adapt to multiplatforms and instances within your protected network. This includes operating systems, machines, and security configurations.

As far as integrated features, look for the ability of a firewall to meet your needs as well as those of your users, such as:

- **Ease of use**   The firewall product should have a graphical user interface (GUI), which simplifies your job when creating, installing, and managing policies and configuring, monitoring, and managing the firewall.

- **Transparency**   How transparent is the firewall product to your user? If you adopt a confusing system, the users may not use it. Conversely, the more transparent the firewall is to your users, the more likely it is that they will use it appropriately.

- **Customer support**   To what extent does the vendor support customer needs, such as providing prompt access to technical expertise for installation, use and maintenance, and comprehensive training courses?

Stateful Inspection

Check Point has developed Stateful Inspection architecture that delivers full firewall capabilities, assures the highest level of network security, analyzes all packet communication layers, and extracts the relevant communication and application state information. The Inspection Module understands and can learn any protocol and application.

Check Point's Stateful Inspection technology is implemented in the Inspection Module that resides between the data link and network layers of the OSI model. An Inspection Module examines every packet. Packets are only allowed to traverse the firewall when the Rule Base has been applied and a rule allowing the communication has been found, which is how the enterprise Security Policy is enforced.

VPN-1/FireWall-1 NG never examines packets in isolation as a packet filter would. The state of each communication is recorded and matched against further connections in the state table; the application state is also recorded. Both can be used when making decisions regarding whether to accept packets.

VPN-1/FireWall-1 NG Stateful Inspection is a third-generation firewall technology that integrates the strengths of both packet filtering and application gateways (proxies) but adds full state awareness to allow the progress of any communication to be uniquely identified, monitored, and controlled. This, coupled with the SVN architecture's integrated management paradigm and strong auditing capabilities, allows administrators to manage and deploy Check Point products to secure the entire enterprise.

VPN-1/FireWall-1 NG was designed to inspect not only the information received, but also the dynamic connection and transmission state of the information being received. Control decisions are made by the following:

- **Communication information**   Information from the top five layers of the OSI model.

- **Communication-derived state**   State information derived from previous communications. For example, saving the outgoing PORT command of any FTP session so that an incoming FTP data connection can be verified against it.

- **Application-derived state**   State information derived from other applications. For example, allowing a previously authenticated user access through the firewall for authorized services only.

- **Information manipulation**   Evaluation of flexible expressions based on communication information, communication-derived state, and application-derived state.

The VPN-1/FireWall-1 NG Inspection Module

The VPN-1/FireWall-1 NG Inspection Module resides in the operating system kernel, below the network layer, at the lowest software level. By inspecting communications at this level, VPN-1/FireWall-1 NG can intercept and analyze all packets before they reach the operating systems. No packet is processed by any of the higher protocol layers unless VPN-1/FireWall-1 NG verifies that it complies with the enterprise Security Policy.

Full State Awareness

The Inspection Module has access to the "raw message" and can examine data from all packet layers. In addition, it analyzes state information from previous communications and other applications. The Inspection Module examines IP addresses, port numbers, and any other information required to determine whether packets comply with the enterprise security policy. It also stores and updates state and context information in dynamic connections tables. These tables are continually updated, providing cumulative data against which VPN-1/FireWall-1 NG checks subsequent communications. VPN-1/FireWall-1 NG follows the security principle, "All communications are denied unless expressly permitted." This means that by default, VPN-1/FireWall-1 NG drops traffic that is not explicitly allowed by the security policy and generates real-time security alerts, providing the system manager with complete network status.

Securing "Stateless" Protocols

The Inspection Module understands the internal structures of the IP protocol family and applications built on top of them. For stateless protocols such as User Datagram Protocol (UDP) and Remote Procedure Calls (RPC), the Inspection Module extracts data from a packet's application content and stores it in the state connections tables, providing context in cases where the application does not provide it. In addition, it can dynamically allow or disallow connections as necessary. These capabilities provide the highest level of security for complex protocols.

VPN-1/FireWall-1 NG Enforcement Module

The VPN-1/FireWall-1 NG Enforcement Module resides within the operating system kernel between the data link and the network layers, layers 2 and 3. The data link layer refers to the network interface card (NIC) hardware, and the network layer is the first layer of the software protocol stack. VPN-1/FireWall-1 NG is positioned at the lowest software layer, as shown in Figure 3-8.

By having access to the lowest software level in the protocol stack, the VPN-1/FireWall-1 NG Enforcement Module sees every packet and can inspect them and make decisions about whether the packet should be passed up the protocol stack to higher layer protocols. In this way, the Security Policy is enforced.

VPN-1/FireWall-1 NG has access to all OSI layers above the data link layer, allowing it to analyze data from all communication layers. State and context information is stored for each connection; this is then updated as the state of connections change. Virtual session information for connectionless protocols such as RPC and UDP-based applications is also maintained. Check Point's Stateful Inspection technology maintains state for all

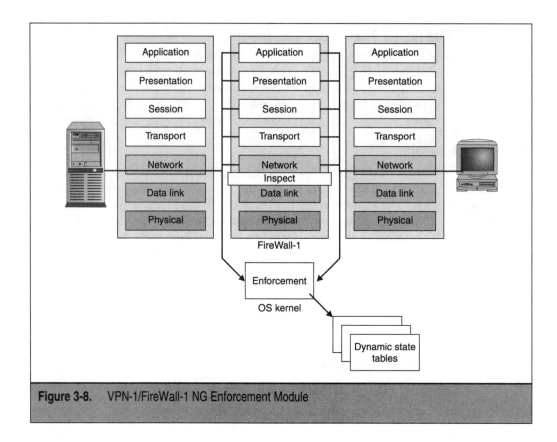

Figure 3-8. VPN-1/FireWall-1 NG Enforcement Module

protocols in the TCP/IP suite and can easily be extended to work with new protocols as they are developed.

UDP-based applications are difficult to secure with packet-filtering techniques because there is no distinction between a request and a response. Packet filters either don't allow UDP sessions or open up an entire range of ports to bidirectional communication, which has in the past been the cause of some major network breaches.

VPN-1/FireWall-1 NG secures UDP-based applications by recording each request packet and verifying packets traveling in the opposite direction against the list of pending request packet sessions built up. A packet that matches a pending session is allowed, and the rest are dropped.

As already stated, VPN-1/FireWall-1 NG has access to complete information contained in the communication request and can therefore provide application context in those cases where the application does not provide it. This application context can then be stored in the state tables and updated as required. This can then be used to check against new communication requests as they are received.

Table 3-4 displays the comparison of packet filters and application-layer gateways and how each falls short of Stateful Inspection in certain areas.

Firewall Capability	Packet Filters	Application-Layer Gateways	Stateful Inspection
Communication information	Partial	Partial	Yes
Communication-derived state	No	Partial	Yes
Application-derived state	No	Yes	Yes
Information manipulation	Partial	Yes	Yes

Table 3-4.   Comparison of Firewall Architectures

INSPECT Language

At the heart of the VPN-1/FireWall-1 NG is INSPECT, a high-level script language. The Policy Editor (or SmartDashboard) allows administrators to graphically design a Rule Base; the Rule Base is turned into INSPECT code and compiled when you install the policy. The Inspection Module installs the compiled code, and the rules are enforced as packets that are passed through the program. INSPECT is an objected-oriented language that has the ability to understand TCP/IP applications, communication data, and context information. The Inspection Module also maintains the dynamic state tables.

INSPECT provides system extensibility. The INSPECT code itself can be written by hand using a standard ASCII text editor, allowing enterprises to incorporate new applications, services, and protocols simply by modifying one of VPN-1/FireWall-1 NG's built-in script templates. INSPECT can be used to create support for unusual or new protocols. In practice, the coverage of the product is so complete, we have never had to write a single line of INSPECT code by hand.

HOW VPN-1/FIREWALL-1 NG WORKS

VPN-1/FireWall-1 NG is an extremely efficient firewall architecture. It prevents higher-layer protocols from having to do more work than necessary by operating inside the OS kernel; decisions whether to accept, reject, or drop packets occur before they are passed up the protocol stack, thus reducing load on the OS itself.

VPN-1/FireWall-1 NG minimizes the use of system resources and processing overheads by processing packets in the operating system's kernel. The operating system's applications and processes above the kernel suffer little, if any, performance degradation. The Kernel Module resides between the NICs and the TCP/IP stack. This additionally protects the TCP/IP stack because the Inspection Module examines packets against the Security Policy prior to passing them onto the TCP/IP stack.

Figure 3-9 presents a detailed flow of the packets through the Inspection Module:

1. Packets pass through the NIC to the VPN-1/FireWall-1 NG Inspection Module. The Inspection Module inspects the packet and its data.

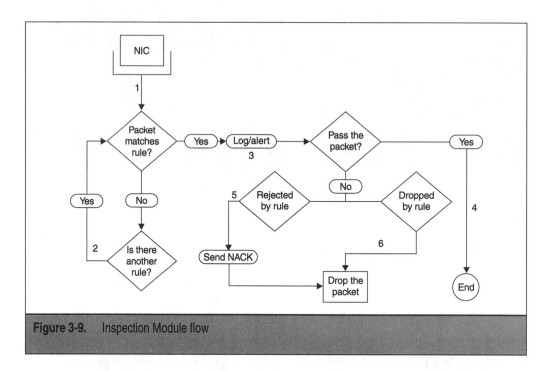

Figure 3-9.   Inspection Module flow

2. Packets are matched to the Rule Base one rule at a time.

3. Logging and/or alerts that have been defined are activated.

4. Packets that pass inspection are moved through the TCP/IP stack to their destination.

5. If a packet does not pass inspection and is rejected by rule definition, VPN-1/FireWall-1 NG sends an acknowledgement.

6. If a packet does not pass inspection and is to be dropped by rule definition, VPN-1/FireWall-1 NG drops it without sending a negative acknowledgement.

VPN-1/FireWall-1 NG Client/Server Architecture

VPN-1/FireWall-1 NG has a modular, scalable architecture. A modular architecture allows an organization to define and implement a single, centrally administered Security Policy. The policy is defined at the central management console and can then be deployed on multiple enforcement points throughout the corporate network and remote offices.

VPN-1/FireWall-1 NG consists of the following three components:

- Management Console (Policy Editor/SmartDashboard)
- Management Server
- Enforcement Module

The three components are installed along with the Check Point SVN Foundation NG (CPShared). Communication is handled via Check Point's VPN-1/FireWall-1 NG Secure Internal Communications (SIC). For more information on these features, see the sections "SVN Foundation" and "Secure Internal Communications" later in this chapter.

The Management Console

The Management Console GUI (Policy Editor/SmartDashboard) is used to create the enterprise Security Policy. The Management Console connects to the management server and configures the network objects and security rules that form the Security Policy. Organizations often have multiple Management Consoles that connect to a central management server(s). The Management Console is shown in Figure 3-10.

Management Server

The enterprise Security Policy is defined using the Management Console and saved on the Management Server. The Management Server contains the VPN-1/FireWall-1 NG databases, which include network object definitions, user definitions, network address translation, security rules for the Security Policy, and the log files for firewalled enforcement points.

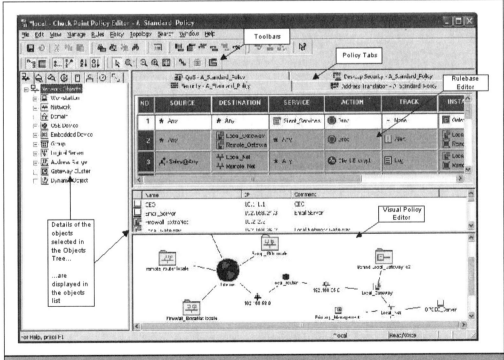

Figure 3-10.   Check Point Management Console

The enterprise Security Policy is stored on the Management Server and is defined using the Management Console (Policy Editor/SmartDashboard).

TIP   The Management Console and the Management Server can be deployed on the same machine or on separate machines in a client/server configuration.

Enforcement Module

The Enforcement Module is deployed on a gateway wherever security is required to control traffic flow between networks. The typical scenario is between an internal network and the Internet. After the Security Policy is defined using the Management Console and saved onto the Management Server, an Inspection Script, written in INSPECT, is generated from the Security Policy. Inspection Code is compiled from the script and loaded to the Enforcement Module, which protects the network in accordance with the Security Policy defined in the Rule Base.

The Enforcement Module can be installed on a broad range of platforms: Windows NT, Windows 2000, Solaris (32-bit and 64-bit), Linux (Red Hat), and a range of firewall appliances such as the Nokia IP range or Alteon Firewall Switches.

CAUTION   On some platforms, the Management Server and Enforcement Module can reside on the same system. However, due to scalability and performance issues, this is not recommended except for small installations.

The VPN-1/FireWall-1 NG Security Servers and Inspection Module are included in the Enforcement Module. The Inspection Module examines all communications according to an enterprise Security Policy. The Security Servers provide authentication and content security features at the application level. A host is considered a firewalled enforcement point if a VPN-1/FireWall-1 NG Enforcement Module is installed on that host.

SVN Foundation

SVN Foundation (Check Point SVN Foundation NG) is a key part of the Check Point infrastructure and is installed with every Check Point product. All Check Point products use the SVN Foundation services. The main components of SVN Foundation are as follows:

- **Cpstart/cpstop**   Scripts to start and stop VPN-1/FireWall-1 services
- **Check Point Registry**   Registry components
- **CPShared daemon**   The SVN foundation services for VPN-1/FireWall-1 components
- **Watch Dog for critical services**   Watch Dog for VPN-1/FireWall-1 daemons
- **Cpconfig**   Configuration Utility for VPN-1/FireWall-1
- **License utilities**   Cplic commands
- **SNMP daemon**   Service for configuring SNMP with VPN-1/FireWall-1

Secure Internal Communications (SIC)

Check Point's Secure Internal Communications (SIC) delivers network security to the product's communication between its various modules.

Secure Internal Communication (SIC) secures communication between Check Point SVN components, such as:

- Management Servers
- Management Consoles
- VPN-1/FireWall-1 NG Modules
- Customer Log Modules
- SecureConnect Modules
- Policy Servers
- OPSEC Applications

SIC simplifies the administration of large installations by reducing the number of configuration actions. Except for backward compatibility, it is no longer necessary to perform fw putkey operations between each pair of communicating components, as required by previous versions of VPN-1/FireWall-1.

Security Benefits of SIC   Securing internal communications allows the firewall administrator to ensure that a Management Console connecting to the Management Server is authorized and not a machine pretending to be the Management Console. SIC ensures that data integrity is maintained.

SIC Certificates   SIC for Check Point SVN components use certificates for authentication and standards-based SSL for encryption. SIC certificates uniquely identify Check Point–enabled machines, or OPSEC applications, across the VPN-1/ FireWall-1 NG system. Certificates are created by the Internal Certificate Authority (ICA) on the Management Server.

VPN certificates, such as those used for Internet Key Exchange (IKE), are used for VPNs and should not be confused with SIC certificates, which are shown in Figure 3-11.

The ICA creates a certificate for the Management Server machine during the Management Server installation. The ICA is created automatically during the installation procedure.

Certificates for VPN-1/FireWall-1 NG modules and any other communicating component are created via a simple initialization from the Management Console. Upon initialization, the ICA creates, signs, and delivers a certificate to the communication component. Every module can verify the certificate for authenticity.

The Management Server and the modules are identified by their SIC name, also known as the Distinguished Name (DN).

Full backward compatibility allows a Management Server to communicate with a version 4.1 or earlier VPN-1/FireWall-1 NG Module, using the legacy shared secret

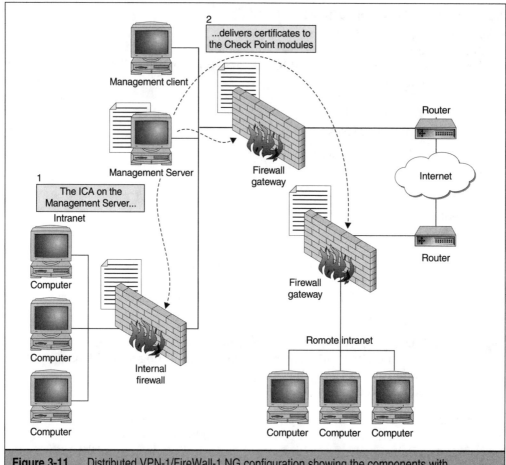

Figure 3-11. Distributed VPN-1/FireWall-1 NG configuration showing the components with SIC certificates

(fw putkey). The two communicating components use the password to create a shared key, which is used to set up an encrypted secure link between them.

SIC between Management Servers and the Management Console   For SIC communications between the Management Server and the Management Console, the Management Console must be defined as being authorized to use the Management Server. When invoking the Management Console on the client:

- The administrator is asked to identify himself/herself.
- The administrator specifies the IP address of the Management Server.
- The Management Console initiates an SSL-based connection with the Management Server.

- The Management Server verifies that the client's IP address belongs to an authorized Management Console.

- The Management Server sends back its certificate.

Once the Management Server's certificate has been authenticated, the administrator is prompted to verify the Management Server Fingerprint, a text string containing a hash value computed from the Management Server's certificate. Once the administrator approves the Fingerprint, the administrator's name and password are securely sent to the Management Server.

The Fingerprint is generated during Management Server installation. You should save it to a file for later verification.

Distributed Client/Server Deployment

VPN-1/FireWall-1 NG manages the enterprise Security Policy through a distributed client/server architecture that ensures high performance, scalability, and centralized management and control. VPN-1/FireWall-1 NG components can be deployed on the same machine or in flexible client/server configurations across a broad range of platforms. Figure 3-12 shows a distributed client/server configuration.

The Management Module can also manage routers or switches that have the VPN-1/FireWall-1 NG modules installed. The Alteon Firewall Switch is an example of this type of device.

The security administrator can configure and monitor network activity for several sites from a single desktop machine. The Security Policy is defined on the Management Console, while the firewall database is maintained on the Management Server. The Security Policy is downloaded to multiple VPN-1/FireWall-1 NG modules, each on a different platform, each protecting a network. The connections between the client, server, and the multiple enforcement points are secured, enabling safe remote management.

THE VIRTUAL PRIVATE NETWORK

A virtual private network (VPN) is a secure private network that operates over the Internet. The Internet becomes the wide area network (WAN) infrastructure, allowing the establishment of secure communication links between company offices, business partners, and mobile users. VPNs are advantageous because they are far less expensive than leased lines, frame relay circuits, or other forms of dedicated connectivity. They are especially cost effective when deployed across geographical boundaries.

In addition to being cost effective, VPNs are valuable to corporations that have a high requirement for security. Instead of trusting the integrity of data with their Telco or service providers, organizations often configure VPNs across their private network to protect against the possibility that the service provider's network may be compromised.

VPNs fall into three categories:

- Intranet for intraorganization communications

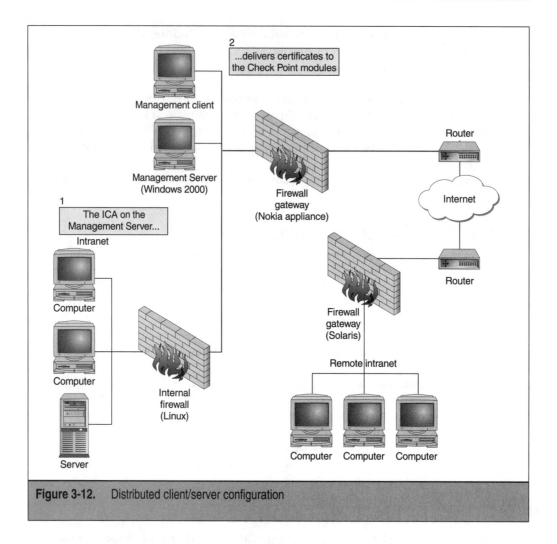

Figure 3-12.   Distributed client/server configuration

- Remote access for mobile or roaming users
- Extranet for interorganization communications

Intranet VPNs

Intranet VPNs are used to secure communications between a company's different locations; for example, between HQ and branch offices. In today's business world, responding rapidly to change in the marketplace is a key requirement for survival. Intranet VPNs can be critical to the success of organizations because they can be deployed rapidly, bringing connectivity to new locations at much lower costs than traditional WAN infrastructure. They can allow you to connect up a new store on the other side of world when entering new markets where previously the cost of connectivity would have been prohibitive, allowing businesses to extend the reach of their internal networks around the world in a secure and cost effective way. Design requirements for Intranet VPNs include the following:

- Strong data encryption to protect confidential information
- Reliability for mission-critical systems
- Scalability to accommodate growth and change

Figure 3-13 shows an intranet VPN with a central site and a remote office connected across the Internet.

Remote Access VPNs

Remote access VPNs are used to secure communications between the corporate network and remote or mobile employees. Remote access has long been established as a key requirement to allow a businesses workforce to be mobile, especially for salespeople and other company representatives. Remote Access VPNs can, for a fraction of the cost, replace traditional remote access methods with more flexible options, including

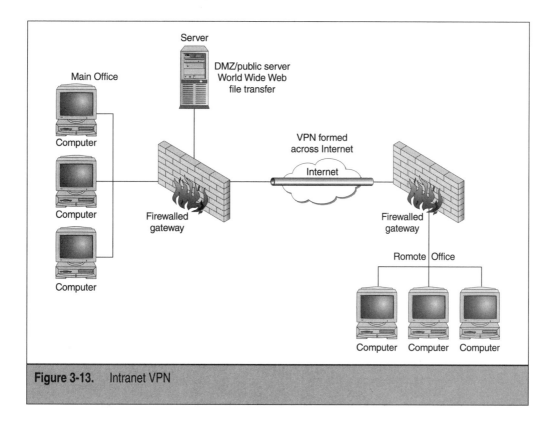

Figure 3-13. Intranet VPN

xDSL and cable Internet connections, as well as the traditional Dial-IP access. Design requirements for Remote Access VPNs include the following:

- Strong authentication to verify remote and mobile users
- Centralized policy management to control what users can access
- Scalability to accommodate growth in users
- Security to the desktop to prevent a system connected via VPN from being hijacked.

Figure 3-14 shows a basic remote access network design with Internet-connected clients.

Extranet VPNs

Extranet VPNs provide secure communications between a company and its strategic partners, customers, and suppliers. Extranet VPN design requirements include the following:

- Internet Protocol Security Standard (IPSec)
- Traffic control to prevent network access-point bottlenecks
- Fast delivery and response times for critical data
- Granular Security Policy capabilities for access control

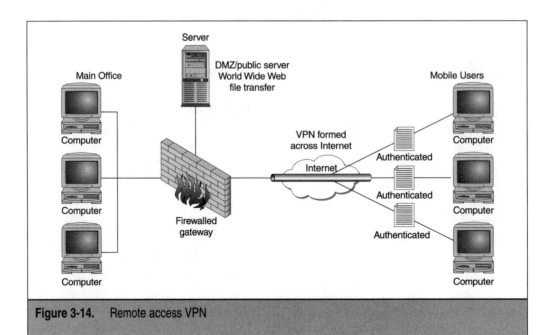

Figure 3-14.   Remote access VPN

An extranet is similar to an intranet VPN, but it connects different companies together rather than a single corporation with multiple sites.

VPN Implementation

Corporate VPN solutions frequently use all three capabilities, intranet, Remote Access, and extranet, to provide a corporation with cost savings, time-to-market advantage, and world wide access to essential data.

Without security, these advantages would be lost, so authentication, privacy, and integrity are essential for a successful implementation. Check Point provides industry-leading VPN capabilities, ensuring the most powerful encryption available keeps data private.

A large organization with highly utilized VPN links should consider deploying Quality of Service (QoS) and VPN acceleration to ensure VPN reliability and performance. Check Point has developed Floodgate NG for end-to-end QoS (Quality of Service). This is optional software that integrates with VPN-1/FireWall-1 NG as part of Check Point's SVN architecture, and it is outside the scope of this book.

VPN enterprise management should include policy-based management to guarantee the integration of VPNs within the enterprise Security Policy, local or remote centralized management of policy, and scalability of the entire deployment.

Check Point's SVN architecture meets the requirements for security, QoS, performance, and management that are essential components of a scalable and reliable enterprise VPN implementation.

CHECKLIST: KEY POINTS
IN VPN-1/FIREWALL-1 NG ARCHITECTURE

The following is a checklist for the key points in VPN-1/FireWall-1 NG Architecture:

- [ ] List the fundamentals of extranet security.
- [ ] Use firewalls for extranet protection.
- [ ] Identify the architecture components of Check Point VPN-1/FireWall-1 NG.
- [ ] Install the management and firewall modules of the VPN-1/FireWall-1 NG on the same system or in a distributed client/server architecture.
- [ ] Show how VPN-1/FireWall-1 NG utilizes Stateful Inspection technology.
- [ ] Identify the distinct advantages of Stateful Inspection technology over older packet filtering or application gateway (proxy) firewall implementations.
- [ ] Illustrate how the VPN-1/FireWall-1 NG Inspection Module resides between the NIC and the TCP/IP stack.

☐ Describe the step-by-step procedure that shows how the VPN-1/FireWall-1 NG Inspection Module examines packets immediately and how the unwanted packets are discarded prior to being passed through the TCP/IP stack.

☐ Describe in detail how the VPN-1/FireWall-1 NG offers GUI-based configuration and centralized policy management for multiple firewalled gateways, scalability, and product maturity.

☐ Show how the VPN-1/FireWall-1 NG supports the complete set of VPN deployment scenarios: intranet VPN, remote access VPN, and extranet VPN.

CHAPTER 4

Solaris
VPN-1/FireWall-1 NG
Installation and Setup

This chapter will go through the process of a first-time installation of VPN-1/ FireWall-1 NG on the Solaris operating system. By default, VPN-1/FireWall-1 NG follows this security principle:

"All communications are denied, unless expressly permitted."

Until the Security Policy is configured, VPN-1/FireWall-1 loads a default Security Policy that prevents packets from being accepted unless they are for VPN-1/FireWall-1 control connections. Until Security Policy rules are configured, VPN-1/FireWall-1 NG will prevent access to the network and drop all traffic because the Rule Bases have an implied rule that drops all traffic by default. Chapter 8 covers Rule Base creation in detail.

In this chapter, you will install Fiction Corporation's first firewall. Fiction Corporation is an imaginary company that will allow us to build an enterprise-wide VPN-1/ FireWall-1 infrastructure that we'll use to develop examples throughout the book.

INSTALLING A VPN-1/FIREWALL-1 NG ON SOLARIS

The first firewall deployment will link Fiction Corporation's head office in London to the Internet and provide a DMZ (demilitarized zone) for the company to deploy insecure services on, such as web servers and mail relay. Figure 4-1 shows a network diagram for the deployment of the firewall.

NOTE A DMZ (demilitarized zone) is a computer host or even a small network inserted as a "neutral zone" between Fiction Corporation's private network and the outside public network. It prevents outside users from accessing a server that has company data. The term originated from the geographic buffer zone that divided North Korea and South Korea following the Korean War in the early 1950s. In essence, the network is neither 'inside' nor 'outside'.

In preparation for installing VPN-1/FireWall-1 NG on Solaris, we will cover the following topics:

- **VPN-1/FireWall-1 NG Minimum System Requirements** To verify the system meets the minimum requirements.
- **Preinstallation Configuration** Outlines the required Solaris operating system configuration before installation.
- **Module Configuration** Defines the Enterprise installation options.
- **Installing VPN-1/FireWall-1 NG** Seventeen-step installation guide for installing Check Point VPN-1/FireWall-1 NG.
- **Installing Check Point management clients** Six-step installation guide for installing the management clients.

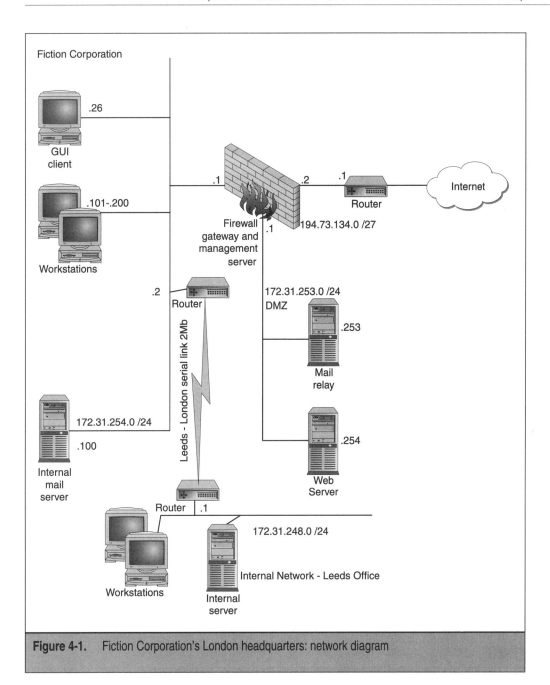

Figure 4-1.   Fiction Corporation's London headquarters: network diagram

VPN-1/FireWall-1 NG Minimum System Requirements

The minimum system requirements for VPN-1/FireWall-1 are provided as a guide so that systems can be specified to meet the software needs. Meeting the bare minimum requirements for the software will not always be sufficient for any given situation, due to variable factors such as required throughput of the system, number of VPN tunnels to be supported, number of rules and their complexity, and so on. Table 4-1 shows the minimum requirements for the installation of the management clients, the Policy Editor, Log Viewer and system Status Viewer.

The Management Module and Enforcement Point can be installed together on a single system or separately in client/server arrangement. Each component has the same basic hardware and software requirements. Table 4-2 lists the minimum hardware and software for installing the NG Management Module and Enforcement Point on Solaris.

NOTE   Check Point recommends that a management server with the VPN-1/FireWall-1 module should not be installed with minimum memory in a real-world deployment.

Preinstallation Configuration

Before you install the chosen Solaris operating system (OS), you should read the next sections on hardening and tuning the OS. You should note that the Solaris 2.7 installation, which defaults to 64-bit mode, is not supported for VPN-1/FireWall-1; you need to choose 32-bit mode when installing Solaris 2.7. Solaris versions prior to 2.7 are no longer supported and should be upgraded to at least version 2.7.

Hardening the Operating System

While VPN-1/FireWall-1 does an admirable job of securing the underlying OS, there may be times when the firewall is stopped and the policy not installed. During this

Component	Requirement
Operating Systems	Windows 98/ME, Windows NT Workstation/Server 4.0 (SP4, SP5, SP6a), Windows 2000 Server, Windows Advanced Server, Windows 2000 Professional
Disk Space	40MB
Memory	32MB minimum, 128MB recommended
Network Interface	Supported interfaces, ATM Ethernet, Fast Ethernet, Gigabit Ethernet, Token Ring. Complete list available on www.checkpoint.com.
Video	16-bit color. Large monitor recommended for Visual Policy Editor.

Table 4-1.   Minimum Requirements for the Management Clients

Component	Requirement
Operating Systems	Solaris 2.7 with patch 106327-08 (Solaris 2.7 supports 32-bit mode only) Solaris 2.8 with patches 108434-01 and 108435-01 (Solaris 2.8 supports 32- and 64-bit mode)
Disk Space	40MB
Memory	64MB minimum, 128 MB recommended
Network Interface	Supported interfaces, ATM Ethernet, Fast Ethernet, FDDI, Gigabit Ethernet, Token Ring. Complete list available on www.checkpoint.com.

Table 4-2.   VPN-1/FireWall-1/Management Module Requirements for Solaris

time, the OS is vulnerable to attack. Therefore you should remove all services from the OS that are not required and make sure that services needed from time to time are properly configured and as secure as possible. An operating system exploit could lead to a compromised gateway or firewall and then a compromised network. Secure the system by removing unnecessary software and services and applying patches for vulnerabilities.

It's recommended that the installation of the operating system be done in *isolation*, on a network that is not connected to the Internet. In this way, the server can be installed without the possibility of attack. All OS software and patches can be placed on media such as CD-ROM and transported to the build environment to ensure that no contamination of the clean-build environment occurs. A VPN-1/FireWall-1 gateway should never be installed in the gateway position on the production network.

Use the core installation option for Solaris. This option installs the minimum required software to run VPN-1/FireWall-1 NG. If the graphical environment is required, you can use the end user installation option. Other installation options will add software that is not required, which can introduce vulnerabilities into the build.

The installation of the operating system optionally creates different partitions on the hard drive for specific uses. It is best to manually create these so they can be sized appropriately for VPN-1/FireWall-1 NG. A separate /var partition is recommended of at least 400MB. The /var partition stores log files and e-mail and can fill up if left unchecked. If it were simply a directory off the root '/', then the system could become unstable and crash if the root partition were to fill up. You should create a partition for the firewall logs either on the primary disk or on a secondary drive if available. The path for the mount point is /var/opt/CPfw1-50/log. The rest of the partition space can be given over to the root '/' and the required swap space. The swap space is an area of disk used as virtual memory. The swap space should be 256MB or twice the size of the installed RAM.

By default, Solaris is a powerful multipurpose operating system that includes many useful services. However, most of these services are not required for a firewalled gateway and pose potential security risks. The /etc/inetd.conf controls the behavior of the superdaemon inetd. The inetd program starts programs dynamically when a request is received for a given service. Examine the /etc/inetd.conf file and comment out all services that are not required. A hash (#) character is used to comment out a line.

Check the active services using the grep command:

```
#grep -v "^#" /etc/inetd.conf
```

In the /etc/rc2.d and /etc/rc3.d directories, there are scripts launched at boot time by the init process. Several of these can be removed. To prevent a script from executing during a boot, change the uppercase *S* to a lowercase *s*. This allows a system administrator to easily re-enable the script if required by changing the lowercase *s* back to an uppercase *S*. Table 4-3 shows the scripts that can be safely disabled in the /etc/rc2.d and /etc/rc3.d directories.

You can check on the number of processes running before and after making these changes by using the ps command to list processes; piping the output to wc –l (Word Count –line mode) which shows the number of processes running:

```
#ps -aef | wc -l
```

If you intend to use remote access to the firewall for administration purposes, install a secure replacement for Telnet. Telnet uses clear-text user accounts and passwords that can easily be captured on the network. One such replacement is called SSH (Secure Shell). The SSH protocol uses encrypted packets to communicate with the server so the contents cannot be captured easily. SSH is available as an open software standard and a commercial product. However, vulnerabilities have been found in SSH, so make sure you update SSH with any security patches available after installing it.

Script	Directory	Description
S73nfs.client	rc2.d	Used for NFS mounting a system; a firewall should never mount another file system.
S74autofs	rc2.d	Used for automounting; a firewall should never mount another file system.
S80lp	rc2.d	Used for printing; your firewall should never need to print.
S88sendmail	rc2.d	Listens for incoming e-mail; your system can still send mail, such as alerts, with this disabled.
S71rpc	rc2.d	Portmapper daemon; a highly insecure service (required if you're running CDE).
S99dtlogin	rc2.d	CDE daemon; starts CDE by default.
S51nfs.server	rc3.d	Used to share file systems; inadvisable for firewalls.

Table 4-3.   Scripts to Disable in /etc/rc2.d and /etc/rc3.d

Tuning the OS

Performance tuning a VPN-1/FireWall-1 server is an important step both during and after installation. Before installation, capacity planning should take place and appropriate hardware should be acquired for the gateway. Keep in mind that all network traffic travels through the VPN-1/FireWall-1 Enforcement Point to reach the Internet or internal network segments.

Some good pointers for maintaining a VPN-1/FireWall-1 Enforcement Module are as follows:

1. Install a minimal amount of software. This will make the maximum amount of system resources available to VPN-1/FireWall-1.

2. Use a distributed installation of VPN-1/FireWall-1. Using the client/server capabilities of VPN-1/FireWall-1 distributes the processing load and system requirements among computers and provides more flexibility.

3. Place other services, such as CVP Servers, on separate machines. Again, this distributes load and does not place unnecessary burden on a single system.

4. Ensure the server hardware can be upgraded as the need arises. Choosing systems that have available RAM slots or even additional processor board slots can allow you to do this. Some systems even allow for live hot-swap of components without requiring the system to be taken off-line.

Remember that the hardware specifications of the gateway play an important part in the overall performance. CPU, memory, and PCI bus speed all contribute to the performance of the gateway. Symmetrical multiprocessing systems can yield a 35–54 percent increase in performance.

Expanding the VPN-1/FireWall-1 memory pool is by far the most important and frequently used tunable parameter. Many important VPN-1/FireWall-1 performance characteristics depend on the amount of memory available. These characteristics include the number of concurrent connections VPN-1/FireWall-1 is able to sustain and the number of concurrent encrypted tunnels. By default, VPN-1/FireWall-1 allocates 3MB of memory for the kernel. Every simple (not authenticated or encrypted) connection requires about 70 bytes of memory. Encrypted IKE traffic requires 3KB per encrypted tunnel. VPN-1/FireWall-1 will need to support a given number of concurrent connections or encrypted tunnels. A general guideline for the memory allocation parameter on a busy firewall is 16MB.

To change the amount of memory allocated to the kernel on Solaris, edit the /etc/system file and add the following line:

```
Set fw:fwhmem = 0x1000000
```

Some of the tasks examined in the "Hardening the Operating System" section also have a bearing on performance: by disabling as many running system processes as possible, you reduce the amount of memory required by the system and increase the CPU cycles available to other tasks.

Obtaining and Installing Solaris Patches

Before you install the Solaris patches, determine the types of patches already installed in your system by using the shell command showrev:

```
% showrev -p
```

Check to see if the patches you need are on this list and make sure which ones can be used. When checking the version of a Solaris patch, the expression "or later" that you see followed by the patch number is the patch version; it means you can use the indicated patch version or later. For example, the version of patch 123456-07 is 07. In this case, you could use version 07 of the patch 123456 or any later version, such as 08, 09, 10, and so forth.

Next, download a recommended set of patches, called a *patch cluster*, from the SunSolve website at http://sunsolve.sun.com. Use Unzip to extract the files and apply the patch cluster with the install_cluster command located in the directory created by unzipping the distribution file:

```
# cd /tmp
# unzip 7_Recommended.zip
# cd 7_Recommended
# ./install_cluster
```

See the information regarding installation as provided by Sun Microsystems (CLUSTER_README). Alternatively, you can install just the required patches detailed in Table 4-2.

TIP   Sun Microsystems runs a Sun Security Coordination Team that investigates reports of security vulnerabilities, responds to customer inquiries about security problems with Sun software, and publishes Sun Security Bulletins. You can subscribe to Sun's bulletin by sending an e-mail to security-alert@sun.com and include subscribe cws [your e-mail address] in the subject. For example: *yourname@yourdomain.com*. Should you need to contact them, send e-mail to security-alert@sun.com. Make sure to encrypt sensitive mail using the Sun Security Coordination Team's PGP key!

Adding Network Interface Cards

If you are installing additional Network Interface Cards (NICs), you should run touch /reconfigure before shutting down the system and installing the new hardware. This ensures that the system checks for new hardware when it is restarted. It is necessary to do this once just before adding new hardware.

TIP   Use the # prtconf command to display all devices found by the system.

All NICs that you intend to use with VPN-1/FireWall-1 must be configured with an IP address and subnet mask. Do this by creating a file for each NIC called hostname.<DeviceID>. This file is located in the /etc directory; the standard on-board NIC is usually hme0, which is the device identifier. If you are installing a PCI Quad Fast Ethernet Card, the device identifiers will be qfe0 through qfe3. Each hostname.<DeviceID> file has a single hostname in it that is looked up in the /etc/hosts file at boot time. The corresponding IP address found in the /etc/hosts file is then assigned to the NIC it refers to. For example:

```
# cat /etc/hostname.hme0
outside
# cat /etc/hosts | grep outside
outside          194.73.134.2
```

Similarly, to configure a subnet mask on an interface, an entry is placed in the /etc/netmasks file, which maps the network address to an interface and configures the assigned subnet mask on that interface. For example:

```
# cat /etc/netmasks | grep 194
194.73.134.0           255.255.255.224
```

As you can see, the network address is used, not the NIC address.

Once you have configured the network interfaces, you can configure routing. Note that the network addresses will not be configured until the system is rebooted after you have created the hostname.<DeviceID> and added entries to /etc/hosts and /etc/netmasks.

TIP   Use the # ifconfig –a command to verify the network interfaces after you have rebooted.

Configure Routing

Routing configuration under Solaris is straightforward, but at this point you need to decide how packets will find their way to internal networks. Firewalls are generally placed between the Internet and the internal network, though this is not the only situation in which they can be deployed (you will see this as Fiction Corporation's requirements develop). Because the firewall will be located between the ISP-supplied Internet router and your internal network, routing is simple. On one side, the firewall should use a Gateway of Last Resort, pointing to the Internet router, and on the other side, use static routes to your internal networks. A Gateway of Last Resort allows the firewall to forward *all* traffic that it does not a have a specific route for in its routing table to the Internet router. To configure a Gateway of Last Resort, you need to add a file to the /etc directory named defaultrouter. This file contains the inside interface IP address of the Internet Router (that is, the IP address of the router interface closest to the firewall external interface).

```
# cat /etc/defaultrouter
194.73.134.1
```

If you have only one internal network that the Firewall is connected to, you don't need to add any static routes as the firewall will be directly connected to your only network. If you have more than one internal network, you will need to tell the Firewall how to reach the other networks. There are two methods of doing this task. Figure 4-2 shows an example of a simple configuration that has two internal networks.

Method one uses static routes on the firewall. For example:

```
# route add 172.31.248.0 172.31.254.2 255.255.255.0 1
```

The route command is used to add a route. This is entered on the command line and is made permanent by adding it to a startup script of the system. The example shown adds a route to the 172.31.248.0 network via the gateway 172.31.254.2. To add a route to a startup script, create a file that will be executed at boot time after the system has started all the networking components by using vi or another text editor to create a file in the /etc/rc3.d directory and changing its status to executable:

```
# cd /etc/rc3.d
cat S78routes
:
route add 172.31.248.0 172.31.254.2 255.255.255.0 1
```

This file will run when the system starts. You should note that the ':' on the first line (with no spaces in front of it) of the shell script indicates that the file should be interpreted using the standard Bourne shell (sh), and the uppercase *S* in the filename is required for the file to execute at startup. The number following the uppercase *S* dictates in which order files will be run at system startup; make sure the startup script to add routes executes after the Solaris startup script that enables networking and configures IP addresses.

Set the file permissions using the chmod command:

```
# chmod 744 S78routes
```

The chmod (change mode) command is used to set the permissions on the file—in this case, read, write, and execute for root, read-only to all others.

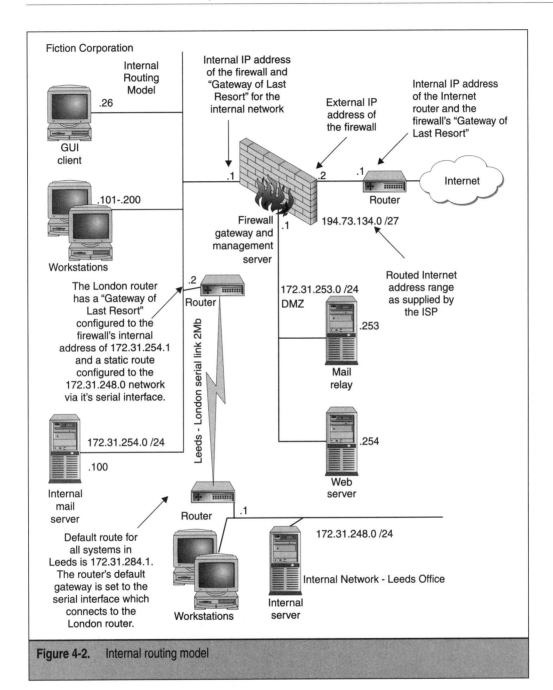

Figure 4-2. Internal routing model

CAUTION   You might be tempted to utilize the VPN-1/FireWall-1 startup scripts to add your own commands at the end, such as the route command. Don't. The startup scripts are part of the product and an upgrade or Service Pack could replace them without warning, deleting all your changes in the process.

Alternatively, Solaris can use RIP (Routing Information Protocol) to discover routes in the internal network. Routes are advertised via RIP to other devices such as internal routers. Your internal routers must also support RIP and have it configured as their routing protocol so that they advertise their own routes. The process that runs the RIP daemon (in.routed) is only started if the file /etc/defaultrouter does *not* exist. Therefore, if you want to run RIP to discover internal routed networks, you must *not* create this file and instead create an /etc/gateways file to define the Gateway of Last Resort for the Internet. The /etc/gateways file is used to add routes that will be used by the in.routed daemon.

```
# cat /etc/gateways
net 0.0.0.0 gateway 194.73.134.1 metric 1 passive
```

Here, net specifies that the destination is a network as opposed to a host. The 0.0.0.0 specifies all networks not learned about via a routing protocol (RIP), and the gateway 194.73.134.1 address is the Internet router's internal interface address where all packets should be sent if they are destined for any route that does not explicitly have an entry in the routing table (Gateway of Last Resort). The passive option tells in.routed not to expect routing updates from this gateway; it also prevents the route from being removed if no routing update verifies it after a period of time.

TIP   To verify routing on the firewall, use the # netstat –rn command to view the routing table and the # ping and # traceroute commands to verify reach ability (traceroute is only available on Solaris 2.7 and above).

To use RIP with VPN-1/FireWall-1, you must allow RIP packets to the firewall from your internal networks, and vice versa, in the Security Policy. Do this by selecting Accept Rip from the FireWall-1 Implied Rules on the Global Properties window, as shown in Figure 4-3.

The Internet router will not need to know how to route packets beyond the network it is connected to (between itself and the firewall, in the example shown in Figure 4-2). This is because it cannot route from the Internet into a private RFC1918-compliant addressed network. The firewall is normally used to hide all outbound traffic behind a registered public address using Network Address Translation (NAT), so the Internet router will never see any source addresses that are on the internal network and does not need to know how to route back to them. This scheme preserves Internet address space and hides the internal structure of a network from would-be attackers. See Chapter 13 for more details on Network Address Translation (NAT).

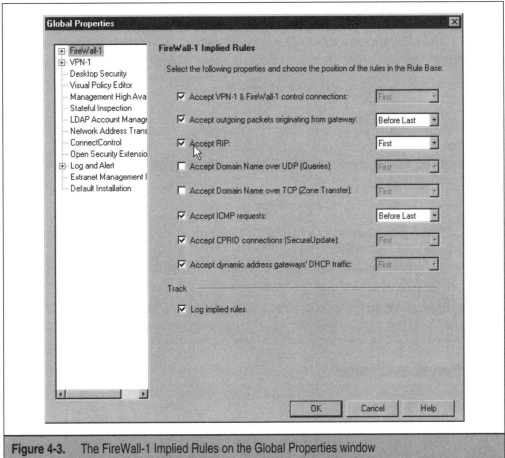

Figure 4-3.   The FireWall-1 Implied Rules on the Global Properties window

Configuring Domain Name Service (DNS)

Domain Name Service (DNS) is used to map real-world names such as www.checkpoint
.com to IP addresses. The firewall can be configured to use either an internal or external
(an ISP) DNS server. It is probably most useful to have DNS configured for use with
internal systems that can also provide Internet names to address mapping via a
forwarders or root servers configuration. This will allow VPN-1/FireWall-1 to use
domain name objects in the rules and also to resolve addresses inside the log viewer.

Solaris uses a file in the /etc directory to locate DNS servers, resolv.conf:

```
# cat /etc/resolv.conf
nameserver      172.31.254.101
```

The nameserver statement specifies a DNS server to query for domain names.

The nsswitch.conf, also located in the /etc directory, must be configured so that name resolution occurs using the DNS servers as well as the standard method of using the /etc/hosts file:

```
# cat /etc/nsswitch.conf | grep \^hosts:
hosts:        files dns
```

If the nsswitch.conf file does not have the dns entry after the files entry, add it and reboot the system.

Module Configuration

VPN-1/FireWall-1 consists of three primary modules:

- **Management clients**   Visual Policy Editor used for configuring and administering the firewall.

- **Management server**   Manages the VPN-1/FireWall-1 NG database, including the Rule Base, objects, services, and users via the Visual Policy Editor.

- **VPN-1/FireWall-1 Module**   Includes the INSPECT Module and security servers. This is the enforcement point that implements the Security Policy, logs events, and communicates with the management server.

Client Server Configuration

VPN-1/FireWall-1 components can be installed in a distributed manner as shown in the diagram in Figure 4-4.

The administrator working on the management client maintains the VPN-1/FireWall-1 NG database, which resides on the management server. The management server pushes the Security Policy to one or more enforcement points (VPN-1/FireWall-1 Module). Fiction Corporation's initial installation will be performed as a nondistributed or standalone installation where both the Enforcement Point and management server are installed on the same server.

INSTALLING VPN-1/FIREWALL-1 NG

The installation described in this chapter will consist of a standalone environment as opposed to a distributed environment. Make sure you have obtained a license for the VPN-1/FireWall-1 installation from your reseller or from www.checkpoint.com/usercenter. Distributed installation is discussed in detail in Chapter 6. The installation is described in the following 17 steps.

Insert the VPN-1/FireWall-1 NG CD in the server. Change to the /cdrom/cpsuite-ng directory. If the Solaris Removable Media Volume Manager daemon (vold) is not

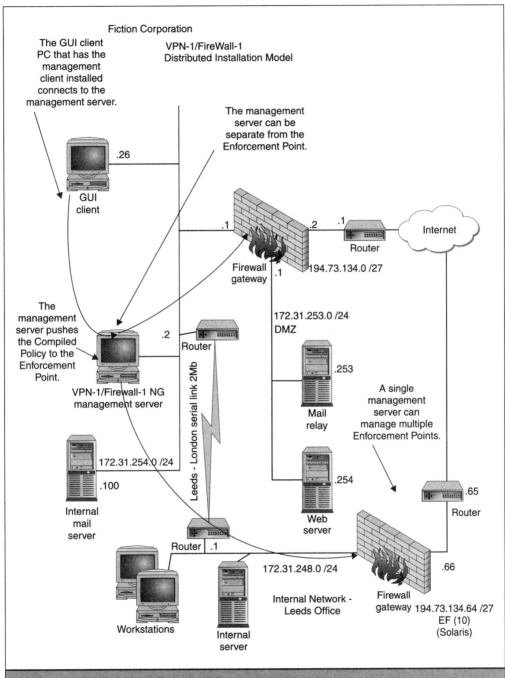

Figure 4-4. Distributed installation model

installed (SUNWvolu package) or disabled, you will need to manually mount the
CD-ROM. To do this, use the mount command:

```
# mount -o ro -F hsfs /dev/dsk/c0t0s2d0 /cdrom
```

If your Sun server does not have a CD-ROM, you will need to use FTP to transfer
the distribution source files to the server. To transfer the files, use a PC with an FTP
client on your internal network. The two required directories are as follows:

- **CPfw1**   Check Point VPN-1 and FireWall-1 Next Generation
- **CPshrd-50**   Check Point SVN Foundation Next Generation

You need to transfer the entire contents of the two directories (CPfw1-50 &
CPshrd-50), located under the Solaris2 directory, on the distribution CD-ROM to
a directory on the server.

NOTE   You can use the /tmp directory, but anything placed there will be removed after the system
is restarted.

Both these directories are then installed with the pkgadd utility:

```
# cd /usr/spool/pkg
# pkgadd -d .
```

The full stop after -d indicates the current directory; this tells pkgadd where to look
for the package you want to install. The remainder of this chapter follows the standard
install using the UnixInstallScript wrapper. Follow these steps:

1. To start the installation, change to the directory on the CD-ROM and run the
   ./UnixInstallScript.

   The UnixInstallScript is a wrapper program that allows you to choose which
   components you want to install interactively. Once the program has loaded,
   the Welcome screen is displayed, as shown in Figure 4-5.

2. Press U to install a purchased product or V for an evaluation product. The next
   screen reminds you that a valid license is required. Press N for next.

   The installation script then checks the operating system version and patch level.

3. The License screen is then displayed. Press the spacebar to scroll a page at a
   time through the license and then press Y and ENTER to confirm acceptance of
   the License Agreement.

4. The Check Point SVN Foundation is now installed. After completing this, the
   Select Product menu is displayed, as shown in Figure 4-6. Choose 1 to select
   VPN-1/FireWall-1, then press N for next.

5. The Installation Type screen is then displayed, as shown in Figure 4-7. Press 1
   for Enterprise Primary Management and Enforcement Module, then press N
   for next.

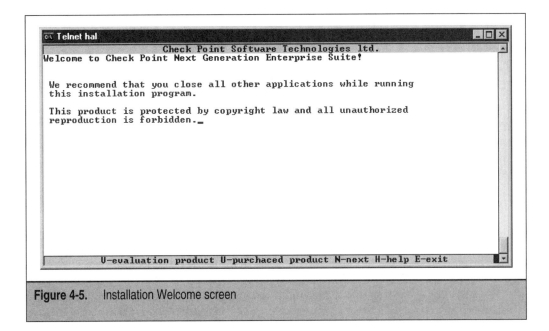

Figure 4-5. Installation Welcome screen

6. The Backward Compatibility screen is then displayed. Backward compatibility allows the management of previous versions of VPN-1/FireWall-1 product. Press 2 to continue without the backward compatibility option. Press N to continue.

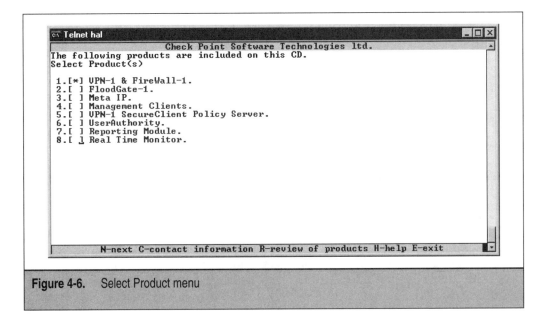

Figure 4-6. Select Product menu

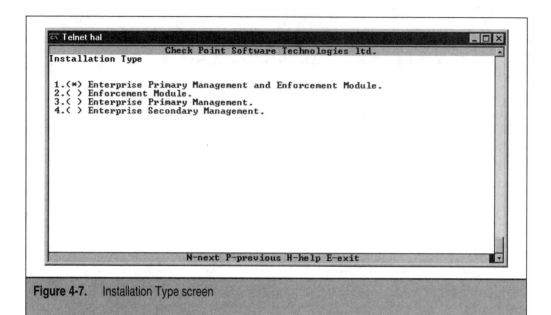

Figure 4-7.   Installation Type screen

7. A screen will now confirm that you have made valid installation choices.

8. Press N to continue the installation.

   The kernel module will be installed, IP forwarding will be disabled, and configuration of the system will start, as shown in Figure 4-8.

   The first step in configuration is to install a license. You should have already obtained a license from your Check Point reseller or directly from the Check Point website (www.checkpoint.com/usercenter). Transfer the license file to the server if you have not already done so.

9. Answer Y to the "Do you want to add licenses" question (see Figure 4-8). Press F to fetch the license from a file then enter the full path and filename when prompted. Confirmation of the license acceptance will be shown, and the configuring administrators section will start.

10. Enter the administrator name when prompted. Enter and verify the administrator's password. Press W and ENTER to configure an administrator with full rights. Confirmation of the creation of an administrator with full rights will be displayed, as shown in Figure 4-9. Press N then ENTER to decline adding another administrator at this time.

11. Now add the IP address of a PC that will be allowed to use the management client software (Security Policy Editor, Log Viewer, and System Status Viewer) and to manage the databases of objects and Rule Bases on the Management Module. Press A to add a new entry to the list, enter the IP address of the PC

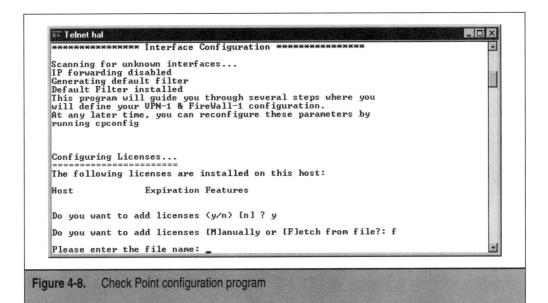

Figure 4-8.   Check Point configuration program

that will have the management client software installed on it, press ENTER, and confirm that you wish to add the entry by pressing Y, as shown in Figure 4-10. You can add more GUI clients later using the cpconfig configuration program. Press N to decline adding any more GUI Clients at this time.

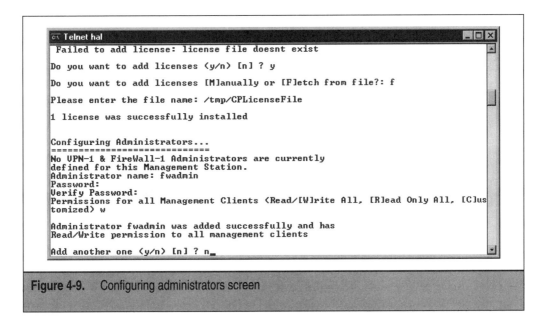

Figure 4-9.   Configuring administrators screen

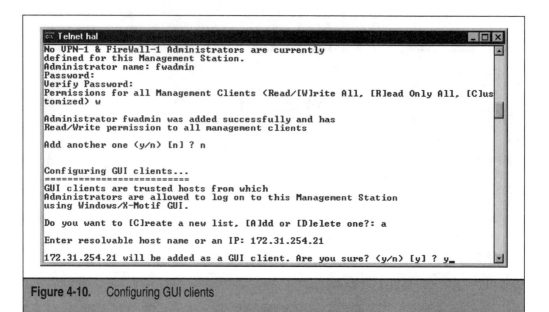

```
Telnet hal                                                          _ □ ×
No UPN-1 & FireWall-1 Administrators are currently
defined for this Management Station.
Administrator name: fwadmin
Password:
Verify Password:
Permissions for all Management Clients (Read/[W]rite All, [R]ead Only All, [C]us
tomized) w

Administrator fwadmin was added successfully and has
Read/Write permission to all management clients

Add another one (y/n) [n] ? n


Configuring GUI clients...
============================
GUI clients are trusted hosts from which
Administrators are allowed to log on to this Management Station
using Windows/X-Motif GUI.

Do you want to [C]reate a new list, [A]dd or [D]elete one?: a

Enter resolvable host name or an IP: 172.31.254.21

172.31.254.21 will be added as a GUI client. Are you sure? (y/n) [y] ? y_
```

Figure 4-10. Configuring GUI clients

12. Next, the SNMP configuration option is displayed. If you require other SNMP-based network management tools to monitor the status of VPN-1/FireWall-1, activate this option by pressing Y; otherwise, press N.

13. The Configuring Group Permissions option is now displayed.

   Group permissions are useful if you require *all* users who belong to a given group to manage the VPN-1/FireWall-1 installation. Without group permissions, only the root user will be able to start and stop services for VPN-1/FireWall-1 and modify configuration files directly. Note that group permissions do not have any effect on who can use the Policy Editor to manage the firewall—that is set up in the Administrator accounts under cpconfig or during initial configuration.

   Press ENTER for no group permissions. Confirm that no group permissions will be granted by pressing Y.

14. You will now be asked to enter some random text from the keyboard. This random data will be used in various cryptographic operations. Varying your typing speed and typing nonrepeated characters will improve the strength of the cryptographic key. Keep typing until you hear a bleep and the bar is full.

15. Next, the Certificate Authority will be configured. Press ENTER to create the Certificate Authority.

After the Certificate Authority is created, the Certificate fingerprint will be displayed, as shown in Figure 4-11.

16. Press Y to save a copy of the fingerprint to a file. Enter a filename and press ENTER then Y to confirm and save the file.

The fingerprint is used to determine the identity of the management server when connecting to it from the management clients. This confirmation is done to prevent "man in the middle" style impersonation of a system during the connection.

17. Answer Y to confirm that you want to reboot the system after installation.

Chapter 8 continues to expand upon the Fiction Corporation's London firewall installation by examining the requirements for the security policy and building an initial Rule Base.

After initial installation administration of GUI clients, administrators and licenses can be created and installed using the cpconfig program by logging on as root (or as another user that was a group member when group permissions were set during the initial install) to the firewall either on the console or via Telnet.

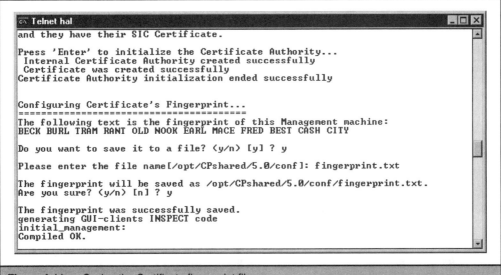

Figure 4-11.   Saving the Certificate fingerprint file

Installing Check Point Management Clients

As stated earlier, it is recommended you install the management clients on a workstation on the inside part of the network. Insert the VPN-1/FireWall-1 CD and it will Autorun. The Check Point Welcome screen appears, as shown in Figure 4-12. If Autorun is disabled, run setup from the CD and follow these steps:

1. Click Next to proceed with the installation. The License Agreement is displayed.

2. Click Yes to the License Agreement to proceed. The Product Menu screen is displayed, as shown in Figure 4-13.

3. Click Next, then click Select the Management Clients and deselect all other options. Click Next to proceed.

4. Click Next at the InstallShield Wizard Information window to confirm installation of the management client software.

5. Click Next to confirm the destination directory of the management clients.

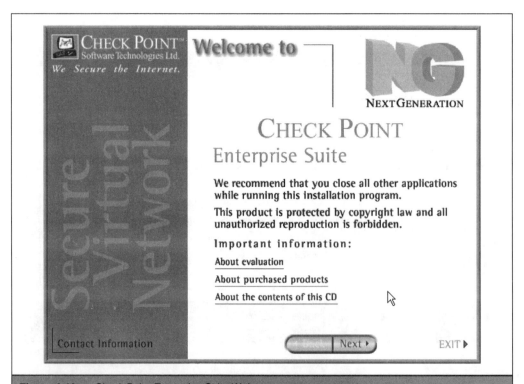

Figure 4-12. Check Point Enterprise Suite Welcome screen

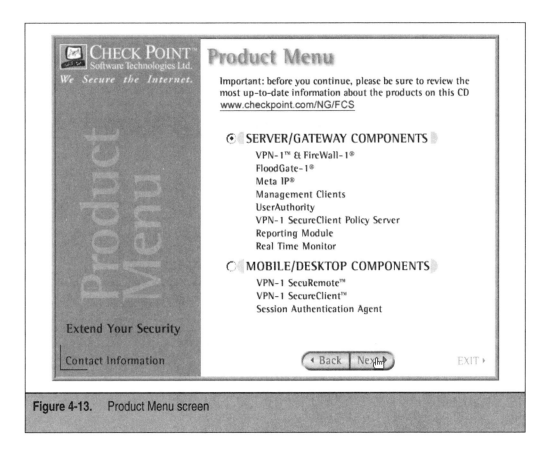

Figure 4-13.   Product Menu screen

6. You will now be presented with a list of checkbox options, as shown in
    Figure 4-14. To install the management clients, select the checkbox for the
    Policy Editor, Log Viewer, and System Status applications only and click
    Next to proceed.

The software will be installed and a dialog box will appear to report the installation
is complete.

LOCATING THE INSTALLATION DIRECTORIES

After VPN-1/FireWall-1 is installed, an environment variable is configured so that various
software components can locate the VPN-1/FireWall-1 uppermost or base directory.
The $FWDIR is used throughout this book as a shortcut for the base directory FireWall-1
was installed in. This comes from the UNIX shell environment variable that is also defined
on the Windows platform. The command processor on Windows works differently and

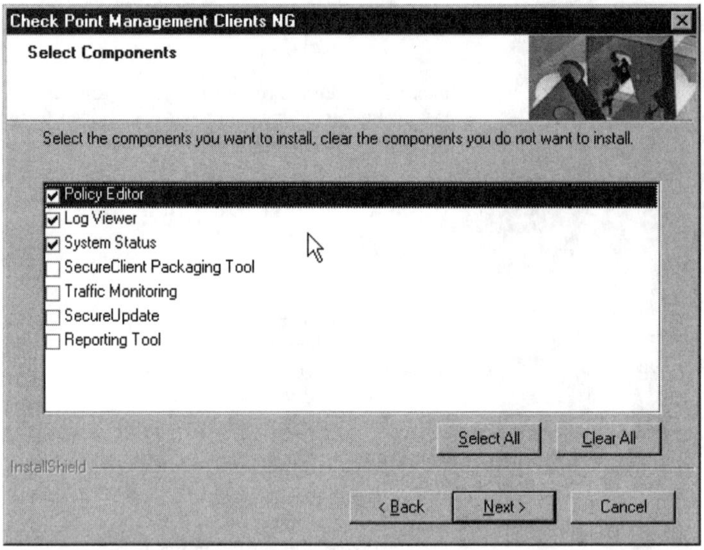

Figure 4-14. InstallShield Wizard confirms components selected

is normally referenced as %FWDIR%; however, we shall continue to refer to it as
$FWDIR throughout the book for clarity.

To check to see if the environment variable is set on the Windows platform, enter
the following in a command window:

```
echo %FWDIR%
```

If set, the path to the FireWall-1 base directory is shown.

It can be useful to get to the VPN-1/FireWall-1 without having to remember which
directory the firewall is installed in:

```
# cd $FWDIR/log
```

This is a useful shortcut to reference any directory easily either from the command
prompt or within shell scripts.

TIP   You may need to log out and then back in for the variable to be set after the system is first
installed.

CHECKLIST: KEY POINTS IN SOLARIS VPN-1/FIREWALL-1 NG INSTALLATION AND SETUP

The following is a checklist for the key points in Solaris VPN-1/FireWall-1 NG installation and setup:

- ☐ Install a VPN-1/ FireWall-1 NG on Solaris.

- ☐ Identify the prerequisites of both hardware and software for installation of VPN-1/FireWall-1.

- ☐ Implement the basic installation processes for the Solaris platform.

- ☐ List the steps that are required to support the operating system in order to prepare for and complete a successful VPN-1/FireWall-1 NG installation.

- ☐ Show how to install a VPN-1/FireWall-1 in a distributed client/server architecture.

- ☐ Identify how all of the VPN-1/FireWall-1 components can reside on a single operating system.

- ☐ Follow the single-server installation model.

- ☐ Install both the Management Module and the Enforcement Point on a single gateway server.

- ☐ Configure the basic system level components, such as adding licenses, administrator accounts, and GUI Client IP addresses.

- ☐ Install the Management Client software on a PC on the internal network.

- ☐ Locate the Installation Directories.

CHAPTER 5

Windows NT/2000
VPN-1/FireWall-1 NG
Installation and Setup

This chapter will go through the process of a first-time Windows NT/2000 installation. By default, as with the Solaris version installation, VPN-1/FireWall-1 NG follows this security principle:

"All communications are denied, unless expressly permitted."

Until the Security Policy is configured, VPN-1/FireWall-1 loads a default Security Policy that prevents packets from being accepted unless they are for VPN-1/FireWall-1 control connections. Until rules are configured, VPN-1/FireWall-1 NG will prevent access to the network and drop all traffic because the Rule Bases have an implied rule that drops all traffic by default.

In this chapter, you will install Fiction Corporation's New York firewall. (As you probably remember, Fiction Corporation is an imaginary company that will allow you to build an enterprise-wide VPN-1/FireWall-1 infrastructure that we will use to develop examples throughout the book.)

The office requires access to the Internet but would also like VPN access to resources located in the London headquarters at some point in the future. Figure 5-1 shows the network diagram for Fiction Corporation New York.

The first Windows-based VPN-1/FireWall-1 deployed will allow Fiction Corporation New York to use a VPN to the head office in London. Previously, the cost of a leased line would have been prohibitive, but virtual private networks enable this kind of long-haul connectivity for the first time for Fiction Corporation. Windows was chosen as the platform because the local support staff understands the operating system thoroughly, and Fiction Corporation can easily train the existing support staff to manage the firewall installation.

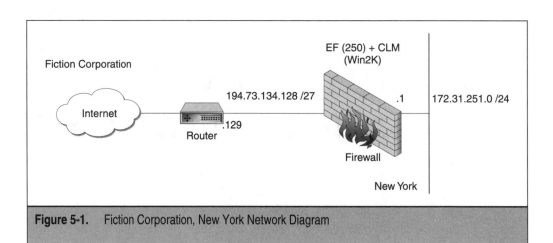

Figure 5-1. Fiction Corporation, New York Network Diagram

INSTALLING VPN-1/FIREWALL-1 NG ON WINDOWS

We will cover the following topics so that you can install FireWall-1/VPN-1 NG:

- **VPN-1/FireWall-1 NG Minimum System Requirements**   Verify systems meet the minimum requirements.

- **Preinstallation Configuration**   Check the required Windows platform configuration before installation.

- **Module Configuration**   Check the Enterprise installation options.

- **Installing VPN-1/FireWall-1 NG**   Follow the 18-step installation guide for installing Check Point FireWall-1 NG.

VPN-1/FireWall-1 NG Minimum System Requirements

Table 5-1 shows the minimum requirements for the installation of the management clients, the Policy Editor, Log Viewer and System Status Viewer.

NOTE   The Visual Policy Editor is not supported on Windows 95.

The Management Module and Enforcement Point can be installed together on a single system or separately in a client/server arrangement. Each component has the same basic hardware and software requirements. Table 5-2 lists the minimum hardware and software for installing the NG Management Module and Enforcement Point on Windows NT/2000.

Component	Requirement
Operating systems	Windows 98/Me, Windows NT Workstation/Server 4.0 (SP4,SP5,SP6a), Windows 2000 Server, Windows Advanced Server, Windows 2000 Professional
Disk space	40MB
Memory	32MB minimum, 128MB recommended
Network interface	Supported interfaces, ATM Ethernet, Fast Ethernet, Gigabit Ethernet, Token Ring Complete list available on www.checkpoint.com
Video	16-bit color; large monitor recommended for Visual Policy Editor

Table 5-1.   Minimum Requirements for the Visual Policy Editor

Component	Requirement
Operating systems	Windows NT 4.0 (SP6a), Windows 2000 Server, Windows Advanced Server (SP0 and SP1)
Disk space	40MB
Memory	64MB minimum, 128MB recommended
Network interface	Supported interfaces, ATM Ethernet, Fast Ethernet, Gigabit Ethernet, Token Ring, FDDI Complete list available on www.checkpoint.com

Table 5-2.   VPN-1/FireWall-1/Management Module Requirements for NG

NOTE   Check Point recommends that a management server with the VPN-1/FireWall-1 module should not be installed with minimum memory in a real-world deployment.

Preinstallation Configuration

While VPN-1/FireWall-1 does an admirable job of securing the underlying operating system (OS), there may be times when the firewall is stopped and the Security Policy not yet installed. During this time, the OS is vulnerable to attack. Therefore, you should remove all services from the OS that are not required and make sure that services needed from time to time are properly configured and as secure as possible.

NOTE   Before you begin installing the OS, read the following sections on hardening and tuning the OS.

Install the Windows operating system platform and apply the required patches as stated in the minimum requirements. Ensure that the routing configuration is working correctly and that all the network adapter cards are configured correctly and can pass data. Windows NT and Windows 2000 need to have IP routing/forwarding enabled because VPN-1/FireWall-1 uses the operating system. Once the INSPECT Module has examined the packets and decided to allow them, they are passed to the operating system to make a decision on how to best forward the packet, thus saving overhead and task duplication.

NOTE   Those of you familiar with MS Proxy Server will note the reverse nature of this process: withMS Proxy Server, IP forwarding is not selected because the proxy handles its own IP forwarding decisions.

TIP   Windows 2000 Server, Windows 2000 Professional, and Windows Advanced Server do not have the option to enable IP routing unless Routing and Remote Access Service (RRAS) is installed. If it's not installed, you must edit the registry and navigate to the following key: HKEY_LOCAL_MACHINE\SYSTEM\CurrentControlSet\ Services\Tcpip \Parameters. Then change the following entry to a value of 1: IPEnableRouter: REG_DWORD: 0x0.

Hardening the Operating System

Hardening the OS maximizes the security of the operating system by reducing the number of services available for remote access and making sure that all required server services are patched to remove all known vulnerabilities.

While VPN-1/FireWall-1 secures the underlying OS, there may be times when the firewall is stopped and the policy is not installed. During this time the OS is vulnerable to attack. Therefore you should remove all services from the OS that are not required and make sure that any needed services are properly configured and secured. An operating system exploit could lead to a compromised gateway or firewall and then a compromised network. Secure the system by removing unnecessary software and services and applying patches to known vulnerabilities.

The best place to start securing the operating system is during installation. Because this server is used as a firewall, previous installations cannot be validated for system integrity. Windows NT/2000 is unique in that a large portion of securing the system occurs during installation.

Install the operating system in isolation, on a network that is not connected to the Internet so the server can be installed without the possibility of attack. All OS software and patches can be placed on media such as CD-ROM and transported to the build environment to ensure that no contamination of the clean-build environment occurs. A VPN-1/FireWall-1 gateway should never be installed in the gateway position on the production network.

This installation is recommended for Windows NT/2000 Server, not Workstation or Professional systems, for several reasons. First, the Server version handles more connections than the Workstation version. Registry permissions are more restrictive on the Server platform and, finally, the Server version can support fault-tolerant disk configurations, such as RAID (Redundant Array of Inexpensive Disks).

The initial installation options let you choose which file system to install, FAT or NTFS. NTFS offers granular control over file access permissions and is recommended, whereas the FAT system offers no control over file access for a user logged in on the console itself.

After the initial installation options are chosen, the component install options allow the administrator to choose which software to install. Keep in mind that the object of this process is to install a minimal amount of services. With minimal services running, fewer exploits and security threats are available.

At the minimum, eliminate services that are not required, for example:

- Communications
- Multimedia
- Accessibility
- IIS

There are three options when determining what type of server to install for NT4: Primary Domain Controller, Backup Domain Controller, and Stand-alone. The Stand-alone selection is correct, as this is a VPN-1/FireWall-1 server and should only be performing the function of an Enforcement Module. Similarly, the Windows 2000 Server should be installed without Active Directory support. Active Directory allows permissions to be granted across the enterprise directory for access to resources located on individual servers. Because an Enforcement Point offers no services to end-users, it is not necessary to assign permissions to access it. Furthermore, it could give rise to situations where access to the firewall was granted inadvertently, which could lead to the system being compromised.

For Windows NT4, make sure that *no* other networking protocols, aside from TCP/IP, are installed. By default, IPX is installed on all network cards.

Next, select the services you want to install. By default, the system installs RPC, NetBIOS, Workstation, and Server. These services cannot be removed during installation, but they can be removed later. The only service that may need to be added is SNMP if it is required to integrate firewall monitoring into an existing network management and monitoring application such as SNMP or OpenView. The OS SNMP only needs to be on the Management Module to operate properly.

During the networking configuration phase, you should configure the IP address, default router, and DNS servers. Do not configure a WINS server or DHCP relay to eliminate unnecessary communication between the VPN-1/FireWall-1 server and other servers.

Next, configure the system to be part of a domain or workgroup. Create a workgroup that is not used anywhere in the organization for each gateway you install. To ensure uniqueness, use a naming convention similar to an obfuscated password.

Following installation, install the latest Service Packs and hot fixes. Staying current with the latest updates is critical for a secure system. Once installation of the Service Packs and hot fixes is complete, begin turning off some of the services installed earlier. In Network Properties, select Services. Remove RPC Configuration, NetBIOS Interface, Workstation, Server and Computer Browser. These services are not required to run a VPN-1/FireWall-1 Enforcement Module.

NOTE   You may lose some functionality by removing the Workstation and Server services, including the ability to modify administrator passwords and map network drives. This is a good example of making a tradeoff between functionality and security. The security administrator must decide which is more important—in this case, improved security or higher administration overhead.

You may also disable the WINS Client binding from the adapter and the TCP/IP NetBIOS helper service. No additional services should be installed on the firewall such as Telnet, FTP or PCAnywhere. Access should be limited to the console only.

Certain registry changes can further enhance security of the system. Remove the display of the last logged on user by changing the registry of DontDisplayLastUsername value to 1 in the key:

```
HKEY_LOCAL_MACHINE\SOFTWARE\Microsoft\Windows NT\CurrentVersion\Winlogon
```

This prevents the last username from being displayed while logging on to the system. You can further restrict Anonymous connections to listed account names by adding the RestrictAnonymous entry with a value of 1 to the key:

`HKEY_LOCAL_MACHINE\SYSTEM\CurrentControlSet\Control\Lsa`

Finally, you can restrict access to the Registry from the network by creating the following key:

`HKEY_LOCAL_MACHINE\SYSTEM\CurrentControlSet\Control\SecurePipeServices\winreg`

It is worth changing the administrator account name so that it does not become the target of a brute-force dictionary attack. However, you may not be able to do this if you disable the Workstation and Server services.

System auditing can also be turned on so that logins and changes to permissions can be monitored.

Tuning the Operating System

Tuning the OS helps maximize efficiency in terms of packet throughput through the firewall by making sure that VPN-1/FireWall-1 NG has as much of the system's free resources at its disposal as possible. This will help maintain a system that can cope at times of peak load, such as when you launch a new website that proves very popular with your customers.

Performance tuning a VPN-1/FireWall-1 server is an important step both during and after installation. Before installation, capacity planning should take place and appropriate hardware should be acquired for the gateway. Keep in mind that all network traffic travels through the VPN-1/FireWall-1 Enforcement Module to reach the Internet or internal network segments, so the system needs to have sufficient resources, memory, disk space, and processor speed to be able to perform acceptably for the total throughput the system will handle. Firewalls can often be under-specified because only the Internet bandwidth is taken in to account. For example, a company may have a 2Mbps Internet connection from the firewall, but they may also have used another firewall network interface to connect *all* the remote access and WAN networks, which means the system is handling 100Mbps of data and thousands of concurrent connections. Make sure to examine the overall throughput requirements and total number of concurrent connections required when setting a specification for the hardware for the firewall.

Some good pointers for maintaining a VPN-1/FireWall-1 Enforcement Module are as follows:

1. Install a minimal amount of software. This will make the maximum amount of system resources available to VPN-1/FireWall-1.

2. Use a distributed installation of VPN-1/FireWall-1. Using the client/server capabilities of VPN-1/FireWall-1 distributes the processing load and system requirements among computers and provides more flexibility.

3. Place other services, such as CVP Servers, on separate machines. Again, this distributes load and does not place unnecessary burden on a single system.

4. Ensure the server hardware can be upgraded as the need arises. Choosing systems that have available RAM slots or even additional processor board slots can allow you to do this. Some systems even allow for live hot-swap of components without requiring the system to be taken off-line.

Remember that the hardware specifications of the gateway play an important part in the overall performance. CPU, memory, and PCI bus speed all contribute to the performance of the gateway. Symmetrical multiprocessing systems can yield a 35–54 percent increase in performance.

Expanding the VPN-1/FireWall-1 memory pool is by far the most important and frequently used tunable parameter. Many important VPN-1/FireWall-1 performance characteristics depend on the amount of memory available to it. These characteristics include the number of concurrent connections VPN-1/FireWall-1 is able to sustain and the number of concurrent encrypted tunnels. By default, VPN-1/FireWall-1 allocates 3MB of memory for the kernel. Every simple (not authenticated or encrypted) connection requires about 70 bytes of memory. Encrypted IKE traffic requires 3KB per encrypted tunnel. VPN-1/FireWall-1 will need to support a given number of concurrent connections or encrypted tunnels. A general guideline for the memory allocation parameter on a busy firewall is 16MB.

To change the amount of memory allocated to the kernel on Windows, modify the key in the Windows Registry:

```
HKEY_LOCAL_MACHINE\System\CurrentControlSet
\Services\FW1\Parameters\Memory = 16000000
```

Some of the tasks already examined in the "Hardening the Operating System" section also have a bearing on performance; by disabling as many running system processes as possible you reduce the amount of memory required by the system and increase the CPU cycles available to other tasks.

Configure Routing

The firewall requires a gateway of last resort to be set for all traffic destined to the Internet. This is the address of the Internet router closest to the firewall's external interface as previously shown in Figure 5-1. In Windows 2000, this is done by selecting the interface from Network and Dial-up Connections on the Settings menu of the Start menu, clicking the Properties button, selecting Internet Protocol (TCP/IP), and clicking the Properties button. The default gateway is entered on the General Properties screen, along with IP and subnet mask details.

Static routes may need to be configured on your firewall so that all internal networks can be located by the firewall. This is done by adding static routes, but it can also be achieved by enabling RIP (Routing Information Protocol) or other routing protocols on the firewall used by your internal routers.

To add static routes on the Windows platform, use the Route Add command. If you have one network in an office in New York and another in Ohio (172.31.247.0) and both offices are connected via a WAN link and both want to use the Internet link installed in the New York office, the Firewall will need to know how to route back to systems in Ohio.

From a command prompt, enter:

```
C:\> route add 172.31.247.0 mask 255.255.255.0 172.31.251.2 -p
```

The route command creates a temporary route that is lost if the system is rebooted; the -p switch makes a static route permanent. Static routes are stored in the Windows Registry.

TIP   To view the routing table, use the Route Print command.

For more detailed information on the internal routing required for router and firewall configuration, see the "Configure Routing" section in Chapter 4.

Module Configuration

VPN-1/FireWall-1 consists of three primary modules:

- **Management clients**   Visual Policy Editor used for configuring and administering the firewall.
- **Management server**   Manages VPN-1/FireWall-1 NG database, including the Rule Base, objects, services, and users via the Visual Policy Editor.
- **VPN-1/FireWall-1 Module**   Includes the INSPECT Module and security servers. This is the enforcement point that implements the Security Policy, logs events and communicates with the management server.

Client Server Configuration

VPN-1/FireWall-1 components can be installed in a distributed manner as detailed in Chapter 4. However, because the New York Office will manage its firewall, the management server and Enforcement Point will be installed on the same system.

INSTALLING VPN-1/FIREWALL-1 NG

The installation described in this chapter will consist of a stand-alone environment as opposed to a distributed environment. Make sure you have obtained a license for the VPN-1/FireWall-1 NG installation from your reseller or from www.checkpoint.com/usercenter. Distributed installation is discussed in detail in Chapter 6.

The installation is described in the following 18 steps:

1. Insert the VPN-1/FireWall-1 NG CD in the server. If the CD does not Autorun, open the CD in Explorer and run SETUP.EXE. The Welcome screen will appear, as shown in Figure 5-2.

2. Click Next on the welcome screen and the License Agreement screen appears.

3. Click Yes to accept the License Agreement, and the Product Menu screen appears, as shown in Figure 5-3.

4. Click Next, and the Server/Gateway Components screen appears, as shown in Figure 5-4.

5. Clear all checkboxes in the Server/Gateway Components screen except for VPN-1 & FireWall-1 and Management Clients. Management client installation will commence after VPN-1/FireWall-1 NG is installed. If you elect not to install the management clients on the firewall, you can follow the installation procedure to install them on another PC in the section "Installing Check Point Management Clients" in Chapter 4.

6. Click Next, and the InstallShield Wizard appears.

7. Click Next. The SVN Foundation Software is installed. See Chapter 3 for an explanation of the SVN Foundation components. When the SVN installation is complete, you are asked to choose the Enterprise product that you wish to install, as shown in Figure 5-5.

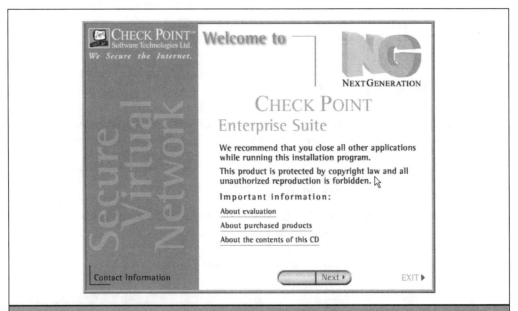

Figure 5-2. Welcome screen

Figure 5-3.   Product Menu screen

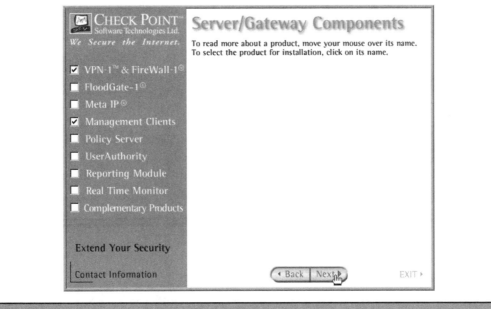

Figure 5-4.   Server/Gateway Component screen

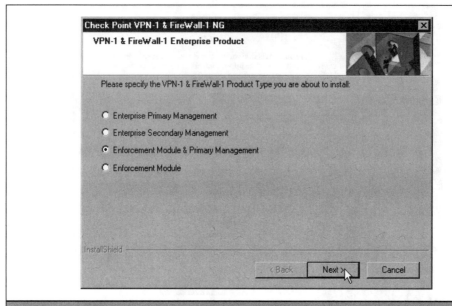

Figure 5-5.   VPN-1 & FireWall-1 Enterprise Product screen

8. You are prompted to select the option most appropriate for your environment. Because you are installing the Enforcement Module and Primary Management on the same server, click next to accept the default and continue the installation.

9. You are now presented with options to install backward compatibility. If you wish to use the Management Server on this installation to manage Check Point VPN-1/FireWall-1 4.1 Enforcement Modules, select the Install with Backward Compatibility option. Otherwise, leave the default option Install without Backward Compatibility and click Next to Continue.

10. You are now given the option to change the installation path. While there is merit in installing FireWall-1 NG to another directory path, especially for extra security, in our experience, it is better to leave the defaults. Click Next to continue the installation.

11. Once the files have been installed, you will see a variety of messages as the installation program completes various tasks, such as installing the kernel module. These are installation progress messages that require no action on the part of the installer. Once the installation tasks have been completed, the Information dialog box will be displayed, as shown in Figure 5-6.

12. The VPN-1/FireWall-1 part of the installation is completed. Click OK to continue. Proceed to step 15 if you did not elect to install the management client software on this server.

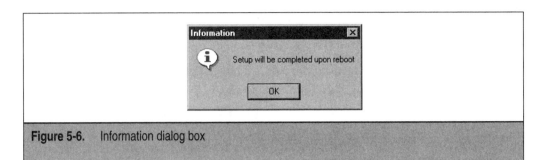

Figure 5-6. Information dialog box

13. You are now prompted for a directory location for the management client software. It is recommended that you accept the default path of C:\Program Files\CheckPoint\Management Clients\5.0\PROGRAM. Click Next to continue.

14. You are now presented with a list of options, as shown in Figure 5-7. Select Policy Editor, Log Viewer, and System Status, and click Next to continue.

    The installation will now complete.

NOTE It is not essential to deploy the management client software on the VPN-1/FireWall-1 server. Indeed, it is recommended that the management client software be deployed on a workstation on the internal network for security and convenience of management.

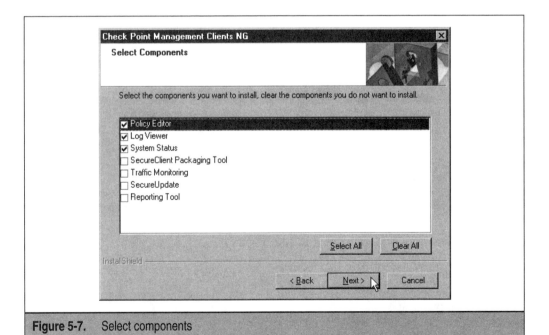

Figure 5-7. Select components

15. You will now be presented with a screen to add licenses. Select Fetch from File and open the LIC file with the license you obtained from the Check Point User Center site or your reseller. Select the file and select Open to add the license.

16. Click OK to confirm the license was successfully added. Click Next to continue. You will now be asked to add administrators to the firewall installation.

17. Select Add to define users and their permissions. You are presented with the Add Administrator dialog box, as shown Figure 5-8.

18. You can create administrators with different permissions and levels of access. In the example shown in Figure 5-8, an administrator called fwadmin is being given Read/Write All (full) access to all the default options available from the management client software of the VPN-1/FireWall-1 installation. Click OK to add the administrator.

    Now you will create a user who can use only the Log Viewer, as shown in Figure 5-9.

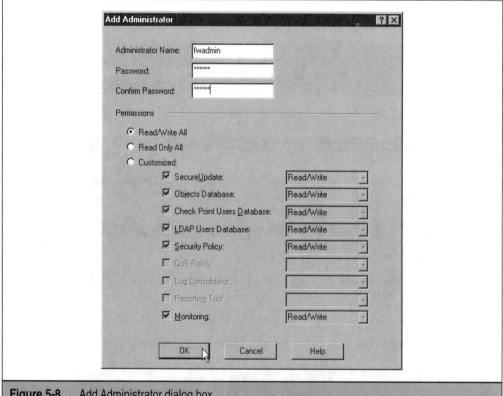

Figure 5-8. Add Administrator dialog box

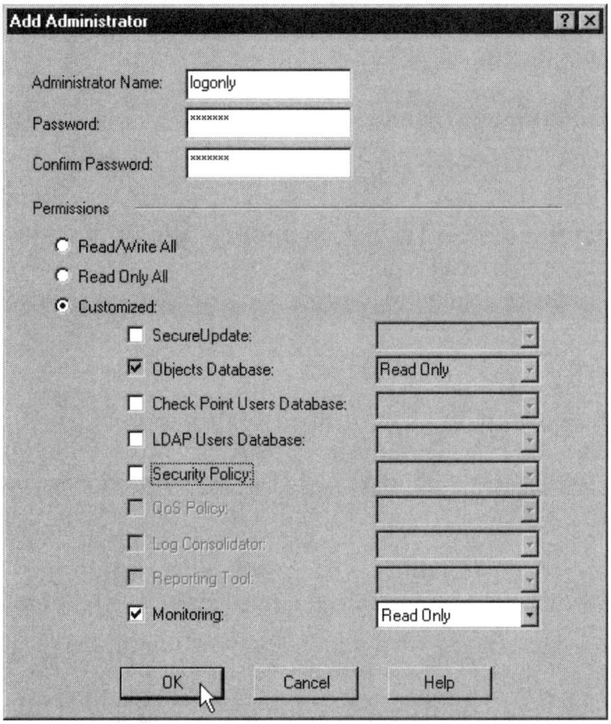

Figure 5-9.   Add Administrator dialog box

Giving an administrator read-only access to the Log Viewer is useful for first-line support personnel and for allowing customers to view the logs without giving them the ability to make changes and block intruders. See Chapter 10 for more information on the Log Viewer.

NOTE   You must select the Customized option to control the type of access that is given for each of the installed products. In this example, the user has read only permission to the Log Viewer.

Click OK to add the user, and then click Next to continue.

GUI Clients

You are now prompted to Add GUI clients, which are the IP addresses of workstations that run management client software. Adding the IP addresses allows a minimal Security Policy to be put in place that allows connections from these workstations to manage the firewall policy. Specify the IP address of any remote workstations that will have management clients installed so that they are allowed to connect to the management server. Perform the following steps:

1. Enter the IP address as required and click Add.

2. After adding GUI clients, click Next to continue the installation.

3. You will now see the Key Hit Session screen. Press keys randomly across your keyboard until you see a Thank You message appear and the Next button is activated. It is important to hit different keys and vary the speed of your typing, as this will improve the cryptographic strength of the key. Click Next to continue.

Certificate Authority

You will now be presented with a Certificate Authority Screen. The certificate authority is used for SIC (Secure Internal Communications). SIC is the method used for securing communication between Check Point VPN-1/FireWall-1 modules; see Chapter 3 for details.

1. Click Next to create a Certificate Authority. You are informed that the internal Certificate Authority was initialized successfully. Click OK to continue.

    You are now presented with a screen showing you the Management Server fingerprint, as shown in Figure 5-10.

    It is recommended that the fingerprint be exported to a file and that you make a note of its location. It is essential to compare this with the fingerprint presented to the management client when connecting to the management server for the first time.

    The fingerprint determines the identity of the management server when connecting to it from the management clients for the first time. This confirmation prevents "man in the middle" style impersonation of a system during the connection.

2. Click Finish. Click OK to the final notice displayed from the SVN integrated installation suite.

    To complete the installation, select Yes, I Want to Restart My Computer Now in the final dialog box, and then click Finish to reboot. It is strongly recommended that the server be immediately rebooted to ensure proper configuration of your Check Point VPN-1/FireWall-1 installation.

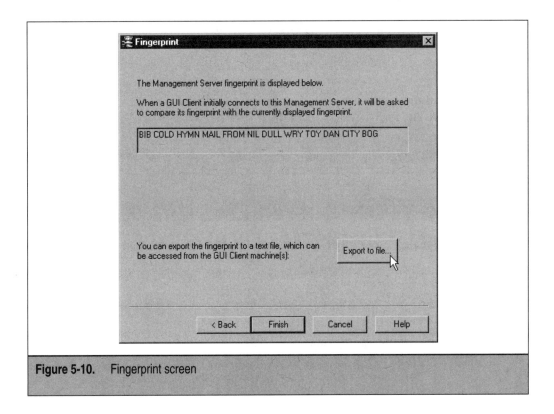

Figure 5-10. Fingerprint screen

LOCATING THE INSTALLATION DIRECTORIES

After VPN-1/FireWall-1 is installed, an environment variable is configured so that various software components can locate the VPN-1/FireWall-1 uppermost or base directory. $FWDIR is used throughout this book as a shortcut for the base directory of VPN-1/FireWall-1. This shortcut comes from the UNIX shell environment variable that is also defined on the Windows platform. Because the command processor on Windows works differently, it would normally be referenced as %FWDIR%; however, we will continue to refer to it as $FWDIR throughout the book for consistency.

To check if the environment variable is set on the Windows platform, type the following in a command window:

```
echo %FWDIR%
```

The path to the VPN-1/FireWall-1 base directory is shown.

It can be useful to get to the VPN-1/FireWall-1 without having to remember which directory the firewall is installed in. To do this, type:

```
# cd $FWDIR/log
```

This is a useful shortcut to reference any directory, either from the command prompt or within shell scripts.

TIP   You may need to log out and then back in for the variable to be set after the system is first installed.

CHECKLIST: KEY POINTS IN WINDOWS NT/2000 VPN-1/FIREWALL-1 NG INSTALLATION AND SETUP

The following is a checklist for the key points in Windows NT/2000 VPN-1/FireWall-1 NG Installation and Setup:

- ☐ List the hardware and software requirements for the installation of VPN-1/FireWall-1.
- ☐ Install the Windows platform.
- ☐ Install the VPN-1/FireWall-1 NG on Windows.
- ☐ Show how to install the VPN-1/FireWall-1 in a distributed client/server architecture.
- ☐ Show how the VPN-1/FireWall-1 components reside on a single system.
- ☐ Follow the single-server installation model for Fiction Corporation's New York office.
- ☐ Install both the Management Module and the Enforcement Point on a single gateway server.
- ☐ Install the management client software directly on to the server.
- ☐ Provide the Windows support staff in New York with a complete "firewall in a box" installation.
- ☐ Configure basic system level components, such as adding licenses and administrator accounts.

CHAPTER 6

Red Hat Linux VPN-1/FireWall-1 NG Installation and Setup

This chapter deals with a Red Hat Linux 7.0 installation. As an operating system (OS), Linux can be customized for very specific tasks. Linux can be a great platform for firewalls, in particular for VPN-1/FireWall-1 NG, as Linux has all the history of Unix behind it when it comes to stability, without the cost associated with a Unix environment.

When information technologies start to offer information services online to the whole Internet community, everyone wants to have access to it. It becomes a valuable commodity. As with any valuables, it must be protected before it is stolen. Unfortunately, there is a mob of talented hackers and crackers out there, a mix of cyberpunks and whackers, lurking around, waiting for an opportunity to break in to a secure system, whether it's a website or a corporate internal network. Worse, the Internet does not protect confidential or sensitive information. Companies and others must protect themselves! The fact that neither users nor Internet providers are regulated makes security even more difficult because the doors are open to everyone. It is like trying to protect your home without any locks on the doors. Deploying an internal firewall is akin to giving part of your building restricted access to authorized personnel only—after all, you wouldn't give every computer user physical access to the data center, would you?

BACKGROUND

Because of these security risks, Fiction Corporation has decided to segregate the Finance Department by using an internal firewall that will provide strict control over who has access to specific services in the Finance Department. This firewall installation will use the management server already installed on the Internet Gateway firewall to manage the Enforcement Point for the Finance Department. If you intend to use Linux as your platform for VPN-1/FireWall-1 and to install the management server on the same system, refer to Chapter 4 for the steps required to install both Management and Enforcement Modules in conjunction with the other instructions in this chapter.

NOTE Chapter 12 shows how you can use this firewall with authentication to secure resources on the network using VPN-1/FireWall-1 authentication services.

The Fiction Corporation's Finance Department has a payroll server and a general finance server that contains the sales and purchase ledger software and databases. By segregating and securing the access to the Finance Department and enforcing authenticated controlled access to these resources, Fiction Corporation aims to protect these servers from unauthorized access from the rest of the organization's networks.

Most organizations consider implementing security only at the perimeter of the network, but most financial fraud perpetrated against organizations using computers comes from within the organization itself. Whether this is termed "hacking" or simply fraud is not important—what's important is that one of the primary places to protect a company's resources from abuse is from within.

The diagram shown in Figure 6-1 shows the network diagram covering Fiction Corporation, including the Finance Department's firewall.

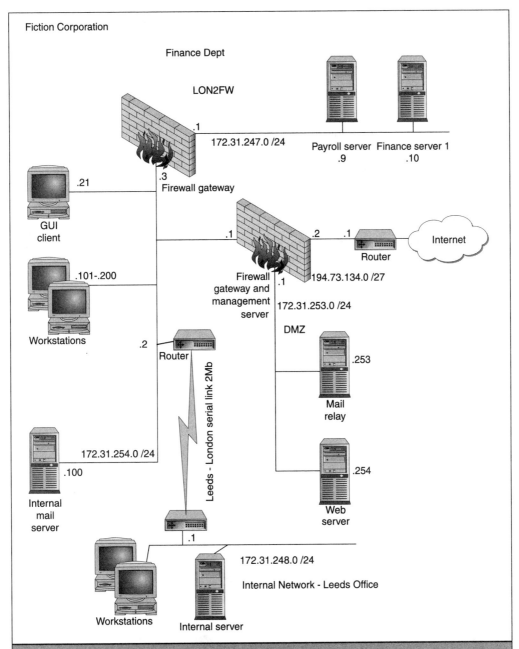

Figure 6-1.   The Fiction Corporation's network diagram with the Finance Department firewall

INSTALLING VPN-1/FIREWALL-1 ON LINUX

In preparation for installing VPN-1/FireWall-1 NG on Red Hat Linux, we will cover the following topics:

- **VPN-1/FireWall-1 NG Minimum System Requirements**   Verify systems meet the minimum requirements.

- **Preinstallation Configuration**   Check the required Red Hat Linux operating system configuration before installation.

- **Module Configuration**   Choose the appropriate Enterprise installation options.

- **Installing VPN-1/FireWall-1 NG**   Follow the 15-step installation guide for installing Check Point VPN-1/FireWall-1 Enforcement Module.

- **Post Installation Configuration**   Add the new firewall enforcement point to the existing management server and establish Secure Internal Communication (SIC).

VPN-1/FireWall-1 NG Minimum System Requirements

Table 6-1 lists the minimum hardware and software required for installing the NG Management Module and Enforcement Point on Red Hat Linux.

NOTE   Check Point recommends that a management server with the VPN-1/FireWall-1 module should not be installed with minimum memory in a real-world deployment.

Component	Requirement
Operating systems	Red Hat Linux 6.2–7.0 only Supports 32- and 64-bit mode Requires minimum Pentium II 300Mhz + or equivalent
Disk space	40MB
Memory	64MB minimum, 128MB recommended
Network interface	Supported interfaces, Ethernet, Fast Ethernet Complete list available on www.checkpoint.com

Table 6-1.   VPN-1/FireWall-1 Management Module Requirements for Red Hat Linux

Preinstallation Configuration

Red Hat Linux 7.0 was used for this installation and the installation type chosen was Server. The Server installation allows optional server components to be included, such as DNS and NFS, but these were all deselected. This installation does not install any graphical user interface on top of the operating system. DNS, NFS, and the GUI (graphical user interface) would be a drain on system resources that could be available to VPN-1/FireWall-1 NG. They may also introduce vulnerabilities that could be exploited by a hacker.

Before installing VPN-1/FireWall-1 for Red Hat Linux, confirm that the compat-libstdc++-6.2-2.9.0.9.i386.rpm package is installed. If it has not this can be obtained from ftp://ftp.redhat.com/pub/redhat/linux/7.0/en/os/i386/RedHat/RPMS.

To install the package use the rpm package management tool.

```
#rpm -i compat-libstdc++-6.2-2.9.0.9.i386.rpm
```

Before installing Linux, read the next section, "Hardening and Tuning the Operating System."

Hardening and Tuning the Operating System

Hardening the operating system (OS) maximizes its security by reducing the number of services available for remote access and making sure that all required server services are patched to remove all known vulnerabilities.

Tuning the OS helps maximize efficiency in terms of packet throughput through the firewall by making sure that VPN-1/FireWall-1 NG has as much of the system's free resources at its disposal as possible. This will help maintain a system that can cope at times of peak load, such as when you launch a new website that proves very popular with your customers.

While VPN-1/FireWall-1 secures the underlying OS, there may be times when the firewall is stopped and the policy not installed. During this time the OS is vulnerable to attack. Therefore you should remove all services from the OS that are not required and make sure that any needed services are properly configured and secured. An operating system exploit could lead to a compromised gateway or firewall and then a compromised network. Secure the system by removing all unnecessary software and services and applying patches for all known vulnerabilities.

Install the operating system in isolation, on a network that is not connected to the Internet so the server can be installed without the possibility of attack. All OS software and patches can be placed on media such as CD-ROM and transported to the build environment to ensure that no contamination of the clean-build environment occurs. A VPN-1/FireWall-1 gateway should never be installed in the gateway position on the production network.

Performance tuning a VPN-1/FireWall-1 server is an important step both during and after installation. Before installation, capacity planning should take place and appropriate hardware should be acquired for the gateway. Keep in mind that all network traffic travels through the VPN-1/FireWall-1 Enforcement Module to reach the Internet or internal network segments.

Some good pointers for maintaining a VPN-1/FireWall-1 Enforcement Module are as follows:

- Install a minimal amount of software. This will make the maximum amount of system resources available to VPN-1/FireWall-1.

- Use a distributed installation of VPN-1/FireWall-1. Using the client/server capabilities of VPN-1/FireWall-1 distributes the processing load and system requirements among computers and provides more flexibility.

- Place other services, such as CVP servers, on separate machines. Again, this distributes load and does not place unnecessary burden on a single system.

- Ensure the server hardware can be upgraded as the need arises. Choosing systems that have available RAM slots or even additional processor board slots can allow you to do this. Some systems even allow for live hot-swap of components without requiring the system to be taken off-line.

Remember that the hardware specifications of the gateway play an important part in the overall performance. CPU, memory, and PCI bus speed all contribute to the performance of the gateway. Symmetrical multiprocessing systems can yield a 35-54 percent increase in performance.

For further information on hardening and tuning the OS, see the Red Hat website at www.redhat.com.

SecurePlatform   Check Point's SecurePlatform is a tailor-made operating environment for VPN-1/FireWall-1. The product creates a ready-made VPN-1/FireWall-1 environment using the Red Hat Linux operating system which allows you to build a Linux installation without having to spend additional time hardening and tuning the system. See the Check Point website for further information at www.checkpoint.com/products/protect/secureplatform.html.

Further discussion of the SecurePlatform product is outside the scope of this book.

Performance Pack   Check Point's Performance Pack for Linux greatly improves performance on the Linux OS. The product takes advantage of specific hardware acceleration capabilities by improving device drivers for Network Interface Cards (NICs) and the operating system's processes to gain specific performance gains and offloading functions to a separate SecureXL off-load layer. The product produces one of the highest throughput systems available today. See the Check Point website for further information at www.checkpoint.com/products/accelerate/performancepack.html.

Further discussion of Performance Pack is outside the scope of this book.

Adding Network Interface Cards (NICs)

All NICs that you use with VPN-1/FireWall-1 must be configured with an IP address and subnet mask. If you do not configure all the interfaces you require during installation or you decide to add more interfaces or change the choices made during installation, you can edit the files in /etc/sysconfig/network-scripts directory to change the interface parameters.

The files in the directory are the interface configuration files used during the boot process to start the network and configure addressing details. Each ifcfg-eth*x* (where *x* is the number of interfaces) file configures that interface. If you have four Ethernet NICs, these files will be numbered 0 through 3.

```
# cd /etc/sysconfig/network-scripts
# cat ifcfg-eth0
DEVICE=eth0
BROADCAST=172.31.254.255
IPADDR=172.31.254.3
NETMASK=255.255.255.0
NETWORK=172.31.254.0
ONBOOT=yes
```

If you are installing additional NICs, you should check to see if they are supported on the hardware support page of the Red Hat website: http://hardware.redhat.com/hcl/.

TIP Use the command # dmesg | grep eth to display all Ethernet devices found by the system during startup.

Once you have configured all the network interfaces you need, you can move on to configuring routing. Note that the network addresses will not be configured until the system is rebooted after you have amended the ifcfg-eth*x* file.

TIP Use the # ifconfig –a command to verify the network Interfaces after you have rebooted.

Configuring Routing

To configure a default gateway (or gateway of last resort) under Linux, you need to edit the file /etc/sysconfig/network file. This file contains several parameters including the GATEWAY directive used to specify the default gateway for the system:

```
# cat /etc/sysconfig/network
NETWORKING=yes
FORWARD_IPV4=no
HOSTNAME=lon2fw.fictioncorp.com
```

```
DOMAINNAME=fictioncorp.com
GATEWAY=172.31.254.1
GATEWAYDEV=eth0
```

The default gateway device (GATEWAYDEV) is also specified when you have multiple NICs installed. This tells the system which device is used to reach the default gateway.

The FORWARD_IPV4 directive defines whether the system will act as a router and forward traffic between the networks it is connected to. VPN-1/FireWall-1 controls forwarding unless you change this behavior using the fw ctl ip_forwarding command:

```
fw ctl ip_forwarding (never|always|default)
```

The default operation of VPN-1/FireWall-1 controls forwarding only if forwarding is disabled in the kernel. The FORWARD_IPV4 directive should therefore be set to no. If the FORWARD_IPV4 directive is not in the network file, check the status of forwarding by examining the contents of the /proc/sys/net/ipv4/ip_forward file:

```
# cat /proc/sys/net/ipv4/ip_forward
0
```

If the output is zero, routing is disabled in the kernel; if it is one, routing is enabled. You can also change this setting directly by altering the contents of the ip_forward file:

```
# echo 1 > /proc/sys/net/ipv4/ip_forward
```

Static routes can be entered directly at the command line. For example, say Fiction Corporation needs to add two static routes so that the Leeds city office of Fiction Corporation can be routed to and from the Finance Department's firewall:

```
route add -net 172.31.248.0 netmask 255.255.255.0 gw 172.31.254.2
route add -net 172.31.201.0 netmask 255.255.255.0 gw 172.31.254.2
```

These two routes are required to get traffic to the Leeds network via the leased serial line connecting the London headquarters and the Leeds city office, as shown in Figure 6-2. Note that the route for the 172.31.201.0 network is optional and is required only for testing connectivity from and to the Leeds router. The 172.31.201.0 network is used between the two routers on the serial link.

Static routes can be made persistent across reboots by adding the routes to the /etc/sysconfig/static-routes file:

```
# cat /etc/sysconfig/static-routes
any net 172.31.248.0 netmask 255.255.255.0 eth0
any net 172.31.201.0 netmask 255.255.255.0 eth0
```

The form for these static routes uses an alternative method of directing a static route out of a particular interface, as opposed to directing it to a specific gateway. Both forms are also found on Cisco IOS Routers.

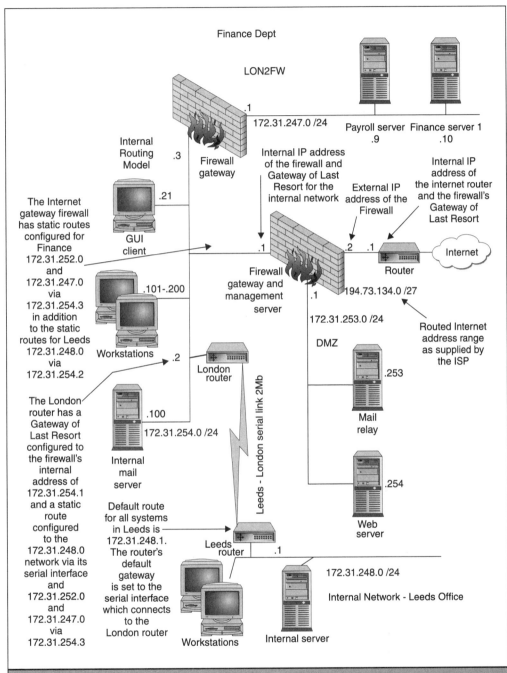

Figure 6-2.   Internal routing model

Figure 6-2 shows how the routing has evolved with the addition of an internal VPN-1/FireWall-1 Enforcement Point and further segregation of the network.

It is necessary to configure and test routing before implementing the VPN-1/FireWall-1 Enforcement Point. Figure 6-2 shows how each internetworking device must determine the path for other locations within the network. You can see from the diagram how each gateway device (firewall or router) has the information it needs to direct traffic appropriately. A Gateway of Last Resort to the Internet is maintained so that all networks can access the Internet if no local route is found to direct the traffic.

TIP   To verify routing on the firewall, use the # netstat –rn command to view the routing table. Use the # ping and # traceroute commands to verify reach ability.

Configuring DNS

DNS (Domain Name Server) is used to map real-world names such as www.checkpoint .com to IP addresses. The firewall can be configured to use either an internal or external ISP DNS. If you have DNS configured for use with internal systems that can also provide an Internet name to address mapping via a forwarder or root server configuration, this is probably the most useful. (A forwarder configuration forwards *all* requests for resolution that cannot be satisfied locally to a DNS on the Internet, normally your ISP's DNS server; a root server configuration uses the latest list of root servers available to resolve all nonlocal requests.) This will allow VPN-1/FireWall-1 to use domain name objects in the rules and will also resolve addresses inside the Log Viewer.

Linux uses a file in the /etc directory to locate DNS servers, resolv.conf:

```
# cat /etc/resolv.conf
nameserver      172.31.254.101
```

The nameserver statement specifies a DNS server to query for domain names.

The nsswitch.conf, also located in the /etc directory, must be configured so that name resolution occurs using the DNS servers as well as the standard method of using the /etc/hosts file:

```
# cat /etc/nsswitch.conf | grep \^hosts:
hosts:       files dns
```

If the nsswitch.conf file does not have the dns entry after the files entry, add it and reboot the system.

Module Configuration

VPN-1/FireWall-1 consists of three primary modules:

- **Management clients**   Visual Policy Editor used for configuring and administering the firewall.

- **Management server**   Manages VPN-1/FireWall-1 NG database, including the Rule Base, objects, services, and users via the Visual Policy Editor.
- **VPN-1/FireWall-1 Module**   Includes the INSPECT Module and security servers. This is the Enforcement Point that implements the Security Policy, logs events, and communicates with the management server.

Client Server Configuration

VPN-1/FireWall-1 components can be installed in a distributed manner as shown in the diagram in Figure 6-3.

The administrator working on the management client maintains the VPN-1/FireWall-1 NG database that resides on the management server. The management server pushes the Security Policy to one or more Enforcement Points (VPN-1/FireWall-1 Module). Fiction Corporations initial installation was performed as a nondistributed or standalone installation where both the Enforcement Point and management server were installed on the same server.

This installation will use the existing management server installation (installed with the current Enforcement Point) and add another Enforcement Point for the Finance Department. This will form a distributed installation for the Finance Enforcement Module.

INSTALLING VPN-1/FIREWALL-1 NG

The installation described in this chapter will be a distributed environment. Make sure that you have obtained a license for the VPN-1/FireWall-1 installation from your reseller or from www.checkpoint.com/usercenter.

If your Linux server does not have a CD-ROM, you will need to use FTP to transfer the distribution source files to the server. To transfer the files, use a PC with an FTP client on your internal network. The two required directories are as follows:

- **CPFirewall1-50**   Check Point VPN-1/FireWall-1 NG
- **CPshared-50**   Check Point SVN Foundation NG

You need to transfer the file contents of the two directories (CPFirewall1-50 and CPshared-50) located under the Linux directory on the distribution CD-ROM to a directory on the server. (Note that you can use the /tmp directory, but anything placed there will be removed after the system is restarted.)

The directories are then both installed with the rpm utility:

```
# rpm -i CPshrd-50-00.i386.rpm
# rpm -i CPfw1-50-00.i386.rpm
```

The -i indicates the following application is to be installed.

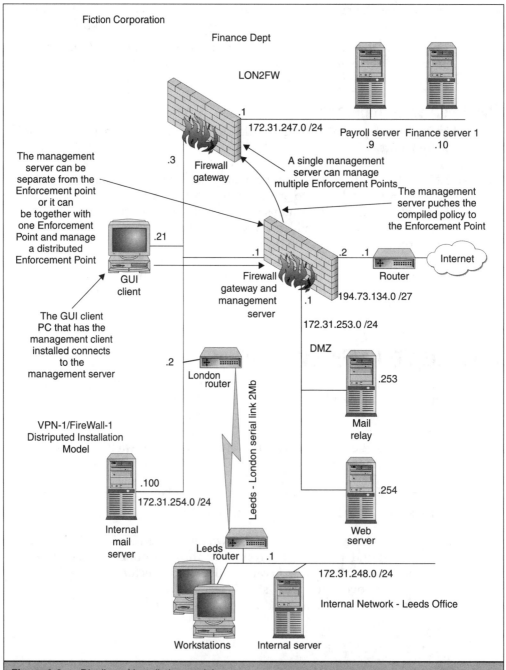

Fiction Corporation

Finance Dept

LON2FW

Payroll server .9   Finance server 1 .10

172.31.247.0 /24

.1

The management server can be separate from the Enforcement point or it can be together with one Enforcement Point and manage a distributed Enforcement Point

.3   Firewall gateway

A single management server can manage multiple Enforcement Points

The management server puches the compiled policy to the Enforcement Point

GUI client   .21

.1   Firewall gateway and management server   .2   .1   Router   Internet

194.73.134.0 /27

The GUI client PC that has the management client installed connects to the management server

.1

172.31.253.0 /24

DMZ

.2   London router

.253

Mail relay

VPN-1/FireWall-1 Distriputed Installation Model

Leeds - London serial link 2Mb

.100

172.31.254.0 /24

.254

Internal mail server

Leeds router   .1

Web server

172.31.248.0 /24

Internal Network - Leeds Office

Workstations   Internal server

Figure 6-3.   Distributed installation model

Note that the remainder of the installation instructions assume you are performing the standard install with the UnixInstallScript wrapper. The installation is described in the following 15 steps. If you are not working from the CD-ROM, begin at step 3.

1. Insert the VPN-1/FireWall-1 NG CD in the server using the mount command:

```
# mount /dev/cdrom /mnt/cdrom
```

2. To start the installation, change to the directory on the CD-ROM and run the UnixInstallScript, as shown in Figure 6-4.

   The UnixInstallScript is a wrapper program that chooses which components you want to install interactively. Once the program has loaded, the Welcome screen is displayed.

3. Press U to install a purchased product or V for an evaluation product. The next screen reminds you that a valid license is required. Press N for next.

   The installation script then checks the operating system version and patch level.

4. The License Agreement screen is then displayed. Press the spacebar to scroll a page at a time through the license and then press Y and ENTER to confirm acceptance of the License Agreement.

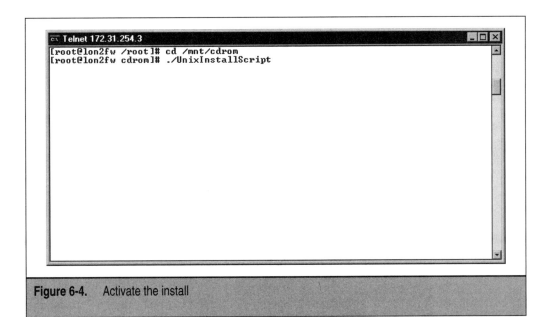

Figure 6-4.   Activate the install

5. The Check Point SVN Foundation is now installed. The Select Product menu is then displayed, as shown in Figure 6-5. Choose 1 to select VPN-1/FireWall-1, then press N for next.

6. The Installation Type screen is then displayed as shown in Figure 6-6. Press 2 for Enforcement Module, then press N for next.

7. A screen will now confirm that you have made valid installation choices.

   Press N to continue the installation. The kernel module will be installed, IP forwarding will be disabled, and configuration of the system will start.

8. Answer N to the question Would you like to install the High Availability?, then press ENTER.

   You should have already obtained a license from your Check Point reseller or directly from the Check Point website (www.checkpoint.com/usercenter); you should transfer the license file to the server if you have not already done so.

9. Answer Y to Add New License on the screen shown in Figure 6-7. Press F to fetch the license from a file, enter the full path and filename when prompted, and press ENTER. Confirmation of the license acceptance will be shown.

10. Next, the SNMP configuration option is displayed. If you require other SNMP-based network management tools to monitor the status of VPN-1/ FireWall-1, activate this option by pressing Y; otherwise, press N.

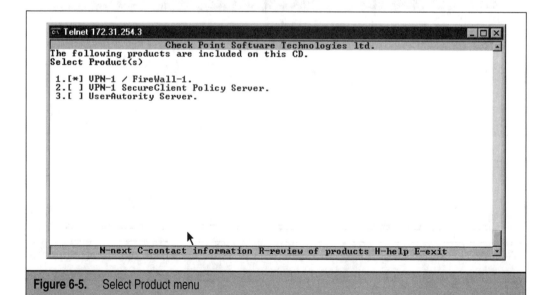

Figure 6-5. Select Product menu

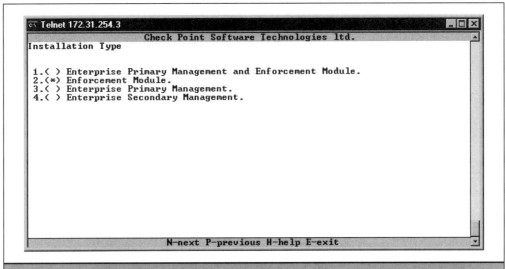

Figure 6-6.   Installation Type screen

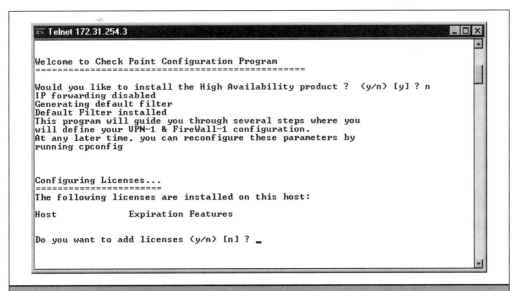

Figure 6-7.   Configuring licenses

11. The Configuring Group permissions option is now displayed.

    Group permissions are useful if you require *all* users who belong to a given group to manage the VPN-1/FireWall-1 installation. Without group permissions, only root users will be able to start and stop services for VPN-1/FireWall-1 and modify configuration files directly. Note, this option does not have any effect on who can use the Policy Editor to manage the firewall—that is set with the administrator's accounts setup under cpconfig or during initial configuration.

12. Press ENTER for no group permissions. Press Y and ENTER to confirm that no group permissions will be granted.

13. You are now asked to enter some random text from the keyboard. This random data will be used in various cryptographic operations. A varied speed of typing as well as nonrepeated characters will improve the strength of the cryptographic key produced. Keep typing until you hear a bleep and the bar is full.

14. You are now prompted to enter the one-time password used to authenticate this module to the management server, as shown in Figure 6-8. You will need this password later when you create an object on the management server for the new Enforcement Point discussed in the next section. Enter a password, press ENTER, then re-enter the password to verify the secret password and press ENTER again.

15. You are now prompted to a restart the computer.

The installation is now complete.

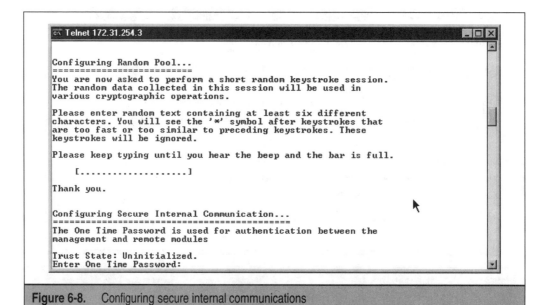

Figure 6-8.   Configuring secure internal communications

Post-installation Configuration

Once the installation of the VPN-1/FireWall-1 module is complete and the system has been restarted, the management server object for the Enforcement Point must be created with the Policy Editor.

Start the Policy Editor and log in. From the main menu, choose Manage | Network Objects, then click New and select Workstation. Enter the details for the VPN-1/FireWall-1 Enforcement Module, as shown in Figure 6-9.

Click the Communication button, and the Communication dialog box is displayed, as shown in Figure 6-10.

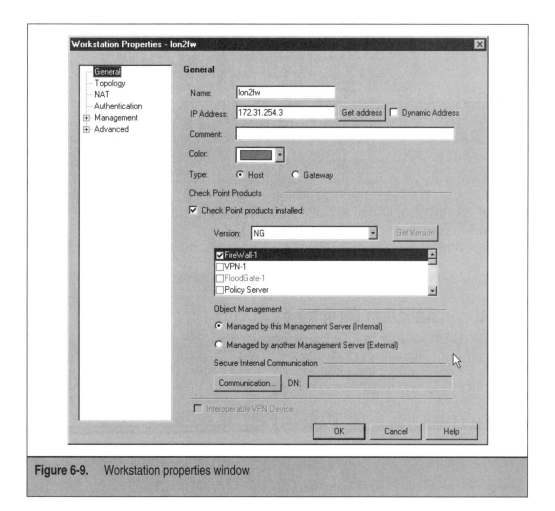

Figure 6-9.   Workstation properties window

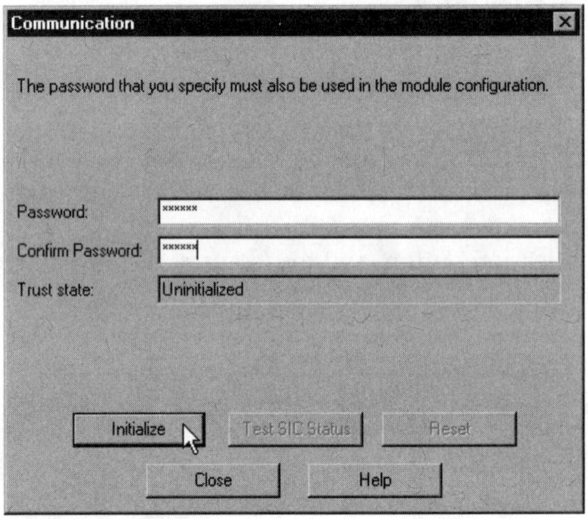

Figure 6-10. Communication dialog box

Enter the one-time password you used during the installation of the VPN-1/
FireWall-1 Enforcement Module, and then click the Initialize button. If the trust
relationship initialization is successful, "Trust Established" will be displayed in
the Trust State text box in the Communication dialog, as shown in Figure 6-11.

Once secure internal communications are configured, you can define a Rule Base
and install a policy for the Finance Department firewall. We will examine the policy
for the Finance Department when we look at authentication in Chapter 12.

Locating the Installation Directories

After VPN-1/FireWall-1 is installed, an environment variable is configured so that
various software components can locate the VPN-1/FireWall-1 uppermost, or base,
directory. $FWDIR is used throughout this book as a shortcut for the base directory
VPN-1/FireWall-1 was installed in. This comes from the Unix shell environment
variable.

It can be useful to get to the VPN-1/FireWall-1 without having to remember which
directory the firewall is installed in:

```
# cd $FWDIR/log
```

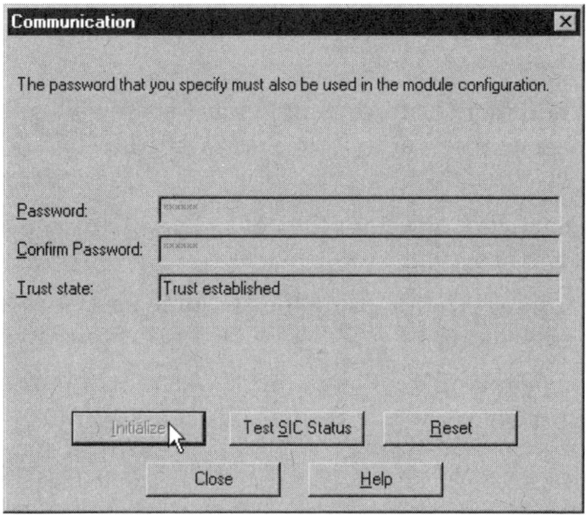

Figure 6-11. Communication trust established

As can be seen, it is a useful shortcut to reference any directory easily either from the command prompt or within shell scripts.

TIP If the $FWDIR environment variable is not defined, command-line utilities will not function.

CHECKLIST: KEY POINTS IN RED HAT LINUX VPN-1/FIREWALL-1 NG INSTALLATION AND SETUP

The following is a checklist for the key points in Red Hat Linux VPN-1/FireWall-1 NG Installation and Setup:

- ☐ Install the Linux platform.
- ☐ Install the VPN-1/FireWall-1 on Linux.
- ☐ List the installation steps required to install the VPN-1/FireWall-1 NG.
- ☐ List all of the necessary preconfiguration elements.
- ☐ List all of the preinstallation configuration steps.

☐ List the routing and path determination issues involved in the imaginary Fiction Corporation's network prior to undertaking an installation of VPN-1/FireWall-1.

☐ Show how to add more Enforcement Points (or firewall gateways) to an existing management server to form a distributed installation of VPN-1/FireWall-1.

☐ Configure the network object for the new VPN-1/FireWall-1 Finance firewall on the management server.

☐ Initialize the communication using the one-time password as entered during the module installation.

☐ List the VPN-1/FireWall-1 NG minimum system requirements.

CHAPTER 7

Nokia Appliance VPN-1/FireWall-1 NG Installation and Setup

I n the twenty-first century economy, information mobility and the Internet are converging at warp speed. However, users are not willing to take advantage of such convergence unless they can be assured that services are secure, reliable, and instantaneous. Unless access to information available via the Internet is secure and fast, convergence in the true sense, with users' support, will likely not happen. In addition, as mobile devices and network speeds evolve, more and more sensitive corporate data is being delivered via mobile networks, which again, users expect to be secure.

BACKGROUND

Nokia is well known worldwide for its mobile communications, and as a natural evolution, the company has extended its global leadership in mobility to include security applications for the Internet. Thus, Nokia security solutions enhance the end user experience by providing a trusted Internet transaction.

Nokia Appliance features exceptional remote management capabilities and is tightly integrated on a hardened, purpose-built security platform and shipped preconfigured and pretested for ease of deployment.

Protecting and extending the network has never been more important than it is today. Secure Internet communications must be simple to install and manage, be continuously available, offer significant cost savings, be flexible, and not require extensive security expertise at all remote locations. This chapter will go through the process of a first-time Nokia Appliance installation. By default, VPN-1/FireWall-1 NG follows this security principle:

"All communications are denied, unless expressly permitted."

Until the Security Policy is configured, VPN-1/FireWall-1 loads a default Security Policy that prevents packets from being accepted unless they are for VPN-1/FireWall-1 control connections. Until rules are configured, VPN-1/FireWall-1 NG will prevent access to the network and drop all traffic because the Rule Bases have an implied rule that drops all traffic by default.

In this chapter, you learn that Fiction Corporation wants to host web servers with their ISP. Rack space is at a premium, so Fiction Corporation has decided to deploy a Nokia Appliance. In addition, by integrating Check Point VPN-1/FireWall-1 software with high-performance IP routing on a network applications platform, Fiction Corporation will have one of the most powerful Internet security solutions available on the market today. Not only will the company save rack space, it will also take advantage of a single, integrated solution that provides secure Internet communications and access control for its networks at the carrier class all the way to its regional office environments.

The Nokia Appliance supports a full suite of routing protocols including RIP (Routing Information Protocol), OSPF (Open Shortest Path First), DVMRP (Distance Vector Multicast Routing Protocol), BGP (Border Gateway Protocol), VRRP (Virtual Router Redundancy Protocol), and IGRP (Interior Gateway Routing Protocol). Further, Fiction Corporation will also take advantage of Nokia's Network Voyager, a browser-based management tool, with which Fiction Corporation's administrators can securely monitor, manage, and configure the firewall from any authorized location.

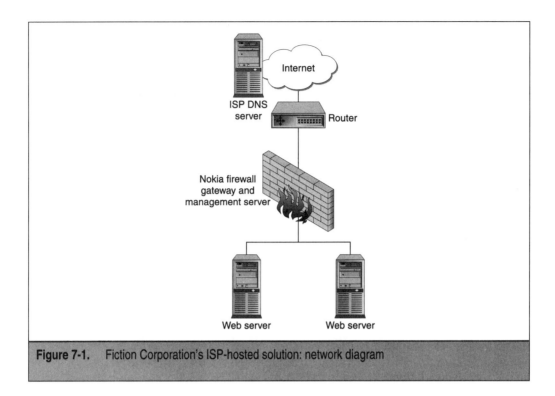

Figure 7-1.   Fiction Corporation's ISP-hosted solution: network diagram

This chapter will take you through configuring VPN-1/FireWall-1 NG on a Nokia Appliance (IP 330) from basic configuration through VPN-1/FireWall-1 NG specifics. Figure 7-1 shows a network diagram for the deployment of the firewall.

INSTALLING VPN-1/FIREWALL-1 NG ON NOKIA

In preparation for installing VPN-1/FireWall-1 NG on the Nokia IPSO platform, we will cover the following topics:

- **VPN-1/FireWall-1 NG Minimum System Requirements**   Verify systems meet the minimum requirements.

- **Preinstallation Configuration**   Detail the required Nokia Appliance configuration before installation.

- **Module Configuration**   Define the Enterprise installation options.

- **Installing VPN-1/FireWall-1 NG**   Follow the 14-step installation guide for installing Check Point VPN-1/FireWall-1 NG.

VPN-1/FireWall-1 NG Minimum System Requirements for Nokia Appliance

Mission critical applications in today's e-business environments have minimum requirements that provide continuous network availability in a fail-safe infrastructure. To address such demands, Nokia adopts the Virtual Router Redundancy Protocol (VRRP, RFC2338) standard on all of its IP network application platforms, which offers active redundancy between two or more appliances.

Nokia IP Network Security Solutions combine a very reliable security software and IP routing to provide high-performance network security solutions.

Fiction Corporation also sets as a minimum requirement the combination of the Nokia Appliance with Firewall Sync, a firewall synchronization technology provided by Check Point for high availability solutions, to ensure that access to the network is always available. By doing this, Fiction Corporation prevents substantial financial losses that could occur if a VPN gateway or firewall becomes unreachable for even a few seconds. Should a fail-over occur, Nokia Appliance and VPN-1/FireWall-1 maintain all VPN and firewall connections through VRRP. All sessions continue seamlessly without the need for users to reconnect and reauthenticate should a primary VPN gateway or firewall become unavailable.

Built for plug-and-play operation and supported top-to-bottom by Nokia support engineers, the Nokia Appliance simplifies and accelerates the deployment of Fiction Corporation's security implementations. The Nokia Appliance allows Fiction Corporation's IT group to choose the networking, performance, and redundancy options that meet the demands of their business.

Table 7-1 shows the minimum requirements for the installation of the Management and Enforcement Modules. Note that it's not possible to install the Management Console (GUI clients) on the Nokia platform.

NOTE   Check Point recommends that a management server with the VPN-1/FireWall-1 module should not be installed with minimum memory in a real-world deployment.

Component	Requirement
Nokia IP120, IP330, IP440, IP530, IP740 Appliance	IPSO 3.4.2 or later
Disk space	40MB
Memory	128MB RAM minimum
Network interface	Supported interfaces, ATM Ethernet, Fast Ethernet, Gigabit Ethernet Complete list available on www.checkpoint.com
Configuration access	Nokia-supplied console cable Web access via Voyager Interface

Table 7-1.   Minimum Requirements for the Nokia Appliance Platform

Preinstallation Configuration

The Nokia Appliance is delivered with an operating system (IPSO, which is a variant of BSDI Unix) and the Check Point packages already installed but not activated. The IPSO operating system is preconfigured to be tuned and hardened for VPN-1/FireWall-1 NG software. The IP300 series supports the addition of a 2-port 10/100 interface or a 1-port serial (X.21) interface in the expansion slot. Should you have a need to upgrade Nokia's proprietary IPSO operating system, it is recommended that you use Nokia's Horizon Manager, which provides advanced software image management, to securely install and upgrade its IPSO operating system and related applications such as Check Point VPN-1/FireWall-1 and RealSecure.

The combination of Check Point VPN-1/FireWall-1 initial configuration and backup/restore features simplify and protect appliance configuration integrity. Command-line scripting and Check Point license management offer systematic execution of actions that must otherwise be manually completed. Device configuration, action status, and action history views are immediately displayed on Nokia Horizon Manager. The product features the following:

- Full compatible installation of application and OS (operating system) versions with "Do No Harm" Constraint Tables

- Installation and upgrade for Nokia IPSO, Check Point VPN-1/FireWall-1 and RealSecure for Nokia

- Management of multiple appliances in logical groups by customer, type of service, system type, or filtered basis

- Execution of backups and restores of system configuration for Nokia IPSO, Check Point VPN-1/FireWall-1, and RealSecure for Nokia

- Execution of complete software and hardware inventories

- Execution of initial configuration and license distribution of Check Point VPN-1/FireWall-1

- Verification of connectivity to managed devices via HTTP, SSH, SCP (Secure Copy), FTP, and Telnet

In addition, the tool also features role-based administration for effective management of network security access privileges as well as SSH and SCP for secure access, enabling Fiction Corporation's IT group to keep their security appliances secure and up-to-date. After all, what good is network security without secure network management?

Upgrading IPSO

You may need to upgrade the IPSO operating system to install the latest version of VPN-1/FireWall-1 NG. You can obtain upgrades from http://support.nokia.com if you have an appropriate support contract. To install IPSO you may also need to upgrade the Boot Manager binary. Consult the release notes for the version of IPSO that you intend to install to see if this step is required.

To upgrade the Boot Manager:

1. Enable FTP via Voyager by going to the Configuration-> Network Access and Services section screen. See the section "Configuring IPSO" later in this chapter for information on getting initial access to Voyager.

2. Use an FTP client to transfer NKIPFLASH.BIN over to the Nokia.

3. Remount the root file system as read/write (read-only by default), copy the file to the /etc directory, and reboot:

```
# mount -uw /
# cp nkipflash.bin /etc
# Sync; reboot
```

4. Select Boot Manager during startup and press a character to drop into command mode when prompted to do so. Note this requires a serial terminal to be connected during the reboot so the boot process can be interrupted.

5. At the bootmgr> prompt, boot to single user mode:

```
Bootmgr> boot -s
```

6. When you see the message "Enter pathname of shell or RETURN for sh:", press ENTER to get a shell prompt. Type in the correct command for upgrading the platforms as follows:

For the IP600

```
#/etc/upgrade_bootmgr wd1 /etc/nkipflash.bin
```

For the IP300

```
#/etc/upgrade_bootmgr wd0 /etc/nkipflash.bin
```

Then use sync; reboot to restart with new flash bios.

Once the Boot Manager has been upgraded, you can install a new version of the IPSO operating system. Use FTP to transfer the following files to /var/admin and use a console connection, Telnet, or SSH to the system and run the newimage program.

```
# cd /var/admin
# newimage -i
```

The New Image program menu will be displayed. Select Local File System, option 4 and enter a "." (full stop) for the location of the current directory and press ENTER. This will cause the program to search the local directory for a new file called ipso.tgz.

Follow the prompts to install the new image and choose which image to reboot with. You can go back to a previous image at any time as long as it has not been deleted. See the Configuration-> Manage IPSO Images screen to return to previous images and delete existing unused images.

Installing Packages on IPSO

The IPSO operating system uses a package installation routine that differs from the other Check Point supported operating systems. If you add a new version of VPN-1/FireWall-1 NG to the Appliance, you can transfer the files (which usually have a .tgz extension) to the firewall and use the newpkg command:

```
# newpkg
```

This command will add a new package or upgrade an existing package.

CAUTION   Be careful if the appliance already has an installed active VPN-1/FireWall-1. Choosing New Install for a package that is already installed could overwrite the configuration information without warning.

If you are upgrading a new Feature Pack, choose the option to upgrade from the New Package menu.

TIP   For further information on the Nokia IP Series range, please refer to www.nokia.com or your reseller.

Adding Network Interface Cards

If you are installing additional Network Interface Cards (NICs), power down the system and add the interface cards. IPSO will automatically check for new hardware when the Nokia Appliance is powered on.

TIP   Unlike the addition of NICs on most PCs, it is not necessary to install drivers for the new interfaces on a Nokia Appliance—the new interfaces will be identified and configured automatically by the system.

Configuring IPSO

Use the Nokia-supplied console cable and connectors to configure a console session to your workstation. The console cable connects into the 9-pin port marked console, not the port-labeled serial. The correct settings for terminal session are 9600, 8 bits, no parity, 1 stop bit, no flow control.

TIP   It is important to ensure flow control is set to none, or the console connection can cause the Nokia to hang during power-on.

To complete initial configuration using a console connection to your workstation, follow these steps:

1. When the Nokia is powered on for the first time, you are prompted to enter a hostname, as shown in Figure 7-2.

2. Enter the hostname.

3. You are prompted for a password for the admin account. This is the equivalent of root on other Unix systems. You are prompted again for the password to confirm you have spelled it correctly.

4. You are now prompted for configuration via either the Voyager interface or the Lynx browser. It is strongly recommended that you use the Voyager interface, as this allows you to use the web browser on your workstation. You should use the vt100-based Lynx browser only when you cannot get LAN access to the Nokia Appliance. This is detailed in the Nokia manuals. Select option 1 for the Voyager interface.

5. You are now given a list of interfaces to select. For the example, use eth-s2p2, which will be the inside interface.

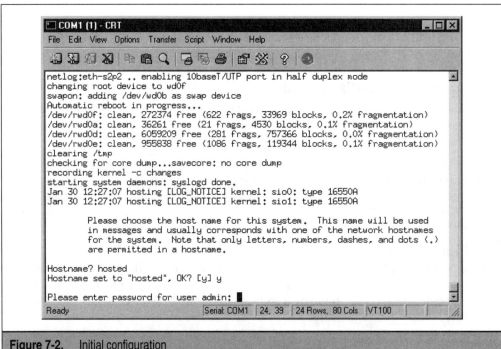

Figure 7-2. Initial configuration

TIP Use a spare interface (one which would be otherwise unused) once your final configuration is complete to avoid having to reconfigure the interface later.

6. You are prompted to supply the IP address, netmask, and default gateway. Enter the required information.

7. You are prompted to configure the port speed and duplex settings for the Interface. This should be based on the settings of the network connection you have the Appliance connected to. A summary of the IP information is shown on-screen. If this is correct, press Y to continue.

Voyager Configuration

Nokia Network Voyager is an SSL-enabled, web-based configuration and monitoring tool that allows you to easily manage each Nokia IP Security Platform. Network Voyager presents a dynamic GUI (graphical user interface) with point-and-click access to every device. IT personnel can easily look up current configuration parameters and status as well as consult event logs to track levels of network activity on each device.

You are now ready to use the Voyager interface to configure the remainder of the IPSO part of the installation.

1. Launch your workstation browser and enter **http://172.31.249.2**. You are presented with the login screen, as shown in Figure 7-3.

2. Type in **admin** as the user name and enter the password you defined earlier during the configuration process. Click OK to start using Voyager, which is

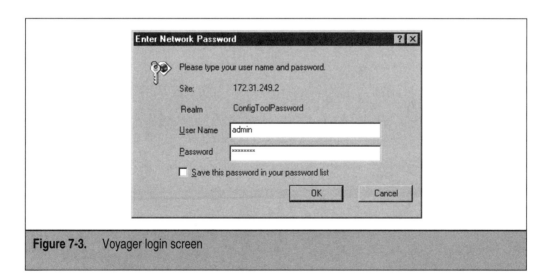

Figure 7-3.   Voyager login screen

the browser-based application that will allow you to configure the Nokia IPSO operating system.

3. You are presented with the Welcome screen and two options, Config and Monitor. Select Config to enter the Configuration screen, as shown in Figure 7-4.

4. First, select Interfaces to complete the interface configuration. The Interface Configuration screen shows a table, as shown in Figure 7-5. Physical interface attributes are configured by selecting the appropriate interface hotlink under the Physical heading. This will allow duplex and speed settings for the Ethernet Interface. Once Changes have been made, select Apply and Save. Then select Up to return to the previous menu.

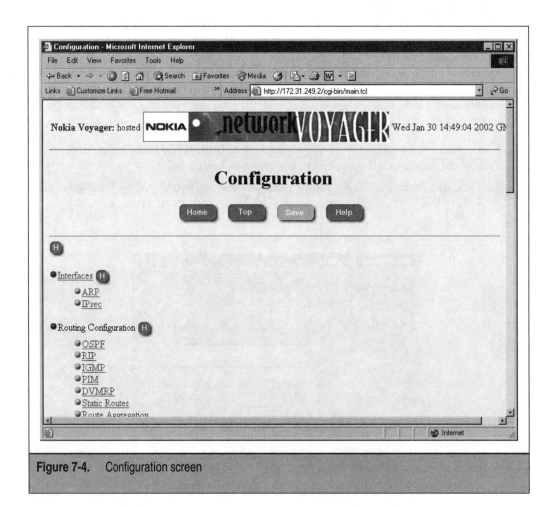

Figure 7-4.   Configuration screen

5. IP information is configured by selecting the appropriate interface hotlink under the Logical heading in the table. This allows you to enter IP address information. The browser expects subnet mask information to be entered in bits, for example, /24 designates 255.255.255.0 or a 24-bit network mask.

6. Select the interface eth-2p1 (designated to be the outside interface) under the Physical heading to define the options for port settings and to turn on the physical interface, as shown in Figure 7-6.

7. Click Apply to apply the changes and then click Save to save the changes permanently. To return to the previous menu, click the Up button.

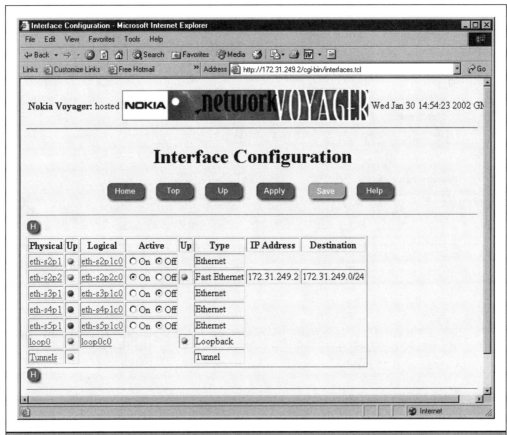

Figure 7-5. Interface Configuration screen

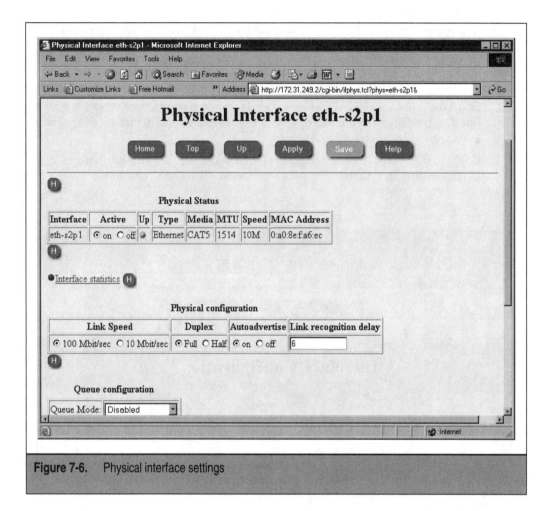

Figure 7-6.   Physical interface settings

8. Select the same interface (eth-2p1) under the Logical heading to configure the IP address information, as shown in Figure 7-7. Enter **194.73.134.98** as the IP address and **27** for the netmask and turn on the logical interface.

TIP   The Nokia Appliance requires netmasks to be entered as numbers of bits; for example, 255.255.255.0 would be 24 bits.

---

9. After you enter the information, click Apply and then Save. Click the Up button to return to the Interface Configuration window. A green light against

the interfaces indicates that the interface is connected to the network correctly. A red light indicates that the interface is not correctly connected or might not be turned on.

Static Routes

Click Top to return to the main Configuration window. Click the Static Routes hotlink. You are now in the Static Routes Configuration window. You will notice that the default route entered earlier in the configuration is configured. This is where all additional static routes that are required need to be added.

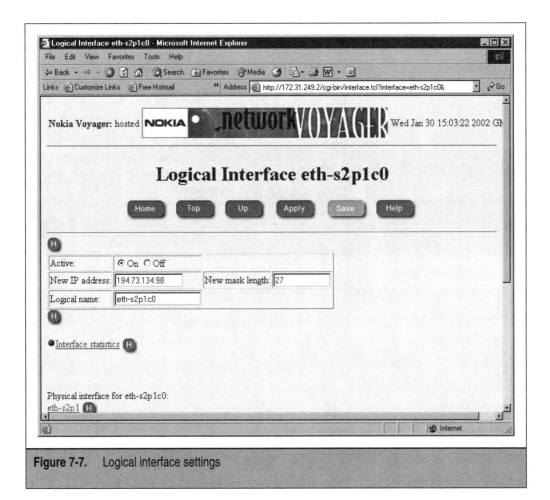

Figure 7-7.   Logical interface settings

NOTE The Top button always returns you to the configuration main window while the Up button returns you to the previous window.

DNS Configuration

To configure DNS name resolution, select DNS from the System Configuration section of the main Configuration window and enter the DNS.

Host Address Assignment

To get to the Host Address Assignment window, select Host Address Assignment from the main configuration screen. This section requires a host address and accompanying IP address to be added. This is essential. First, enter the hostname and click Apply. Next, enter the outside interface IP address, as shown in Figure 7-8, and click Apply and then Save.

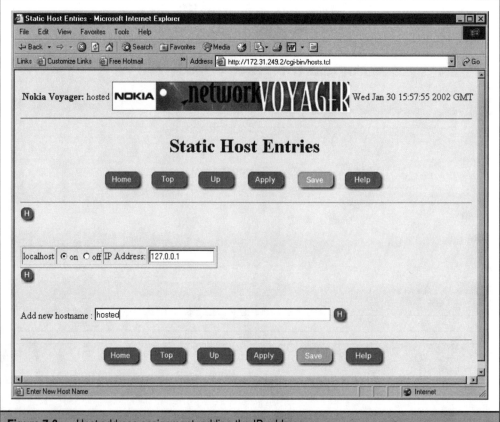

Figure 7-8. Host address assignment: adding the IP address

Activating the VPN-1/FireWall-1 NG Package

Return to the main Configuration window and scroll down until you can see and select the Manage Installed Packages link. In the Manage Installed Packages page, select the VPN-1/FireWall-1 NG version you wish to activate. Select Apply and Save.

Rebooting the Nokia Appliance

You have now completed the Nokia IPSO part of the configuration. Select Reboot from the Shutdown option on the main Configuration window.

TIP   The VPN-1/FireWall-1 NG package that you have just selected will not be available for configuration until the appliance has been rebooted.

Module Configuration

VPN-1/FireWall-1 consists of three primary modules:

- **Management clients**   Visual Policy Editor used for configuring and administering the firewall.

- **Management server**   Manages VPN-1/FireWall-1 NG database, including the Rule Base, objects, services, and users via the Visual Policy Editor.

- **VPN-1/FireWall-1 Module**   Includes the INSPECT Module and security servers. This is the Enforcement Point that implements the Security Policy, logs events, and communicates with the management server.

Client Server Configuration

VPN-1/FireWall-1 components can be installed in a distributed manner by installing a separate management server on a different server from the Enforcement Point (VPN-1/FireWall-1 Module).

The administrator working on the management client maintains the VPN-1/FireWall-1 NG database, which resides on the management server. The management server pushes the Security Policy to one or more Enforcement Points (VPN-1/FireWall-1 Module). Fiction Corporation's hosting firewall installation will be performed as a nondistributed or standalone installation where both the Enforcement Point and Management Server are installed on the same server.

Installing VPN-1/FireWall-1 NG

VPN-1/FireWall-1 comes preinstalled on the Nokia IP series devices, so it is not necessary to perform an installation. Once the package is activated, the installation is complete. Therefore, you simply need to configure a standalone or distributed environment, as outlined in the following steps. (This is usually done during the product selection phase of other platform's installations.) Figure 7-9 shows how to start the product configuration.

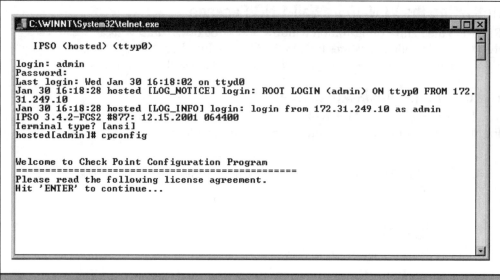

Figure 7-9. Launching cpconfig

1. Press ENTER to read the License Agreement. You can press the spacebar to scroll down through the License Agreement or press Q to exit the agreement. You are asked if you accept the terms. Press Y to continue the installation. You are now asked which components of VPN-1/FireWall-1 you wish to install. In this example, select option 1 to install the Management Station and Enforcement Module.

NOTE If you failed to correctly specify the hostname and IP address at the host address assignment phase, the installation will fail with the message "Cannot copy default filter". Use Voyager to correct the problem and rerun cpconfig.

---

2. You are prompted to add the license for this product. Select Y to add the licenses you have obtained.

3. You can either fetch the licenses from a file or add them manually. To add them manually, press M at the prompt and enter the license fields, as shown in Figure 7-10. The license should be obtained from Check Point or your reseller prior to installing VPN-1/FireWall-1 NG.

4. You are prompted to add administrators. Create an Administrator account and enter the password you wish to use. You will be asked to retype the password to ensure accuracy.

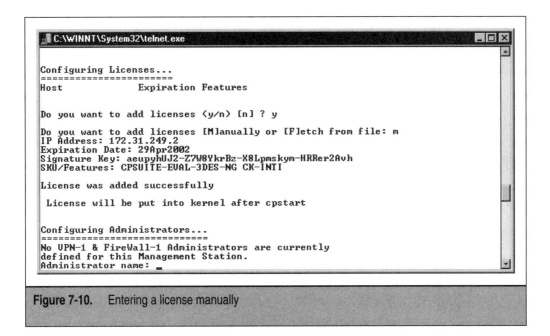

Figure 7-10. Entering a license manually

5. Assign the account you just created **W** for write permissions because this will be the account used to create the Security Policy.

6. VPN-1/FireWall-1 NG restricts the workstations that can connect using Management Console to the Management Station for security purposes. You are now prompted to define GUI clients. Select A to add a GUI client. You are prompted for an IP address. Enter the IP address of all workstations that require GUI client access to administer the firewall and press ENTER. You are prompted to confirm that this is correct. Press Y to add the entry.

Adding a Management Console

Follow these steps to add a management console:

1. You are prompted to add additional GUI client IP addresses. Press N to continue with the installation.

2. Group permissions allow you to add additional accounts that can have rights to start and stop VPN-1/FireWall-1 NG daemons. Do not assign group permissions at this time; press ENTER. Select Y to confirm this is correct.

3. You are asked to enter some random text from the keyboard to be used in various cryptographic operations. A varied speed of typing as well as nonrepeated characters will improve the strength of the cryptographic key produced. Keep typing until you hear a bleep and the bar is full.

4. To configure the Certificate Authority, press ENTER.

5. After the Certificate Authority is created, the Certificate fingerprint will be displayed.

6. Press Y to save a copy of the fingerprint to a file in /var/admin. Enter a filename and press Y to confirm and save the file. This is the admin user's home directory on the IPSO operating system and will facilitate finding the file after it is saved. The fingerprint determines the identity of the management server when connecting to it from the management clients. This confirmation prevents man-in-the-middle style impersonation of a system during the connection.

7. Answer Y to confirm that you want to reboot the system after installation. The system will now reboot with VPN-1/FireWall-1 NG configured and a default policy in place. You are now ready to use the Management Console to connect to the Management Station and start defining a Security Policy.

LOCATING THE INSTALLATION DIRECTORIES

After VPN-1/FireWall-1 is installed, an environment variable is configured so that various software components can locate the VPN-1/FireWall-1 uppermost or base directory. The $FWDIR is used throughout the book as a shortcut for the base directory VPN-1/FireWall-1 was installed into. This comes from the Unix shell environment variable.

It can be useful to get to the VPN-1/FireWall-1 without having to remember which directory the firewall is installed in. To do this, use the following command, which can be used from the command prompt or within shell scripts:

```
# cd $FWDIR/log
```

TIP   After the VPN-1/FireWall-1 is activated on IPSO, Voyager warns that it will be necessary to log out and then log in again for the environment variable to be set.

CHECKLIST: KEY POINTS IN NOKIA APPLIANCE VPN-1/FIREWALL-1 NG INSTALLATION AND SETUP

The following is a checklist for the key points in Nokia Appliance VPN-1/FireWall-1 NG installation and setup:

☐ Identify the Nokia Appliance range of firewalls.

☐ List all of the needs that the Nokia Appliance range of firewalls offers.

☐ Identify the basic IP120 firewalls supporting three interfaces to the high-end IP530 and IP740 firewalls, which also support 20-plus interfaces.

- ☐ List all interfaces.
- ☐ Deploy the Nokia Appliance range of firewalls in Internet data centers.
- ☐ Use VRRP to support the Nokia firewalls on an active standby basis.
- ☐ Show how if there is an interface failure, the second or standby firewall assumes the active role.
- ☐ Install VPN-1/FireWall-1 NG on Nokia.
- ☐ Show how to locate the Installation Directories.
- ☐ List the VPN-1/FireWall-1 NG minimum system requirements for the Nokia Appliance.

CHAPTER 8

Setting Up Security Policy Rule Base and Properties

The Security Policy is the most important part of VPN-1/FireWall-1 NG administration. The Security Policy defines the rules or criteria of your network security. This chapter will build an initial Security Policy for Fiction Corporation, the imaginary company used for examples throughout the book.

We will discuss how to create rules and modify a Security Policy's properties to give Fiction Corporation a secure connection for the installation carried out in Chapter 4. The best way to learn how to do this is by using the correct process from the beginning, so, throughout the chapter, the components that make up a Security Policy will be discussed and applied to a practical real-world scenario that is common for many companies who want to connect to the Internet.

This chapter will feature the Policy Editor tools from VPN-1/FireWall-1 NG Feature Pack 3, known as Check Point Smart Clients. For this chapter, it is our aim to use the most current version of the software to define a basic Security Policy that allows firewall administrators to be up and running quickly.

SECURITY POLICY DEFINED

The Security Policy is a set of rules that defines your network security. In VPN-1/FireWall-1 NG, a Security Policy is defined using a Rule Base, a collection of individual rules that make up your Security Policy. Each rule can be comprised of any combination of network objects, users, services, and actions. Once a Rule Base is defined, VPN-1/FireWall-1 NG distributes it to enforcement points across your entire network.

Prior to attempting to define any Security Policy, you must define a thorough set of requirements detailing services, access to the Internet, what objects are present in the network, and any user authentication required.

Process for Defining the Rule Base

We recommend that the following process be adhered to when developing Security Policies for firewall installations:

- Understand the requirements
- Produce a network diagram detailing objects and IP address information
- Produce a table of rules
- Create the Rule Base

Understanding the Requirements

Prior to defining a Security Policy for VPN-1/FireWall-1 NG, it is essential to understand what Fiction Corporation requires for its Security Policy. The following is a list of the requirements that Fiction Corporation provided:

- A firewall to allow secure access to the Internet for its internal users.
- A World Wide Web server that is accessible via the Internet yet cannot be compromised even though it's sitting on the internal network.
- The ability to send and receive e-mail to and from the Internet.

Producing a Network Design

Figure 8-1 shows a network design that details Fiction Corporation's proposed Internet firewall and documents the IP addresses. Note that the mail relay and the web server are located on a demilitarized zone (DMZ). Because these are publicly accessible servers, placing them on the internal network could compromise the security of Fiction Corporation's internal networks.

Producing a Table of Rules

It's important to define the required rules in a worksheet and check for accuracy prior to working with VPN-1/FireWall-1 NG. This gives your company or your customer a chance to check the Rule Base and sign off on its validity prior to any implementation. Table 8-1 defines the Rule Base that was built from Fiction Corporation's requirements.

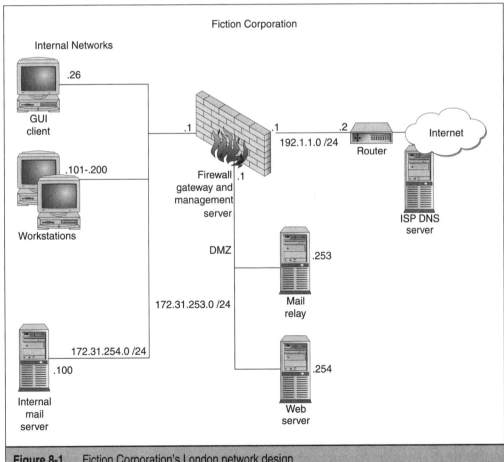

Figure 8-1. Fiction Corporation's London network design

Source	Destination	Service	Action	Description
Any	Firewall	Any	Drop and log	Stealth Rule to stop unauthorized attempts to access the firewall gateway
Any	Web server	http	Accept	Access to web server
Mail relay	Any	SMTP	Accept	Mail out to Internet from mail server (This rule allows the mail relay to also communicate with the internal mail server; no specific rule is required.)
Any	Mail relay	SMTP	Accept	Allow SMTP to mail server (This rule allows the internal mail server to communicate with the mail relay; no specific rule is required.)
Internal nets	Any	HTTP	Accept	Outbound web access
Internal nets	Any	HTTPS	Accept	Outbound HTTPS (SSL) access
Internal nets	Any	FTP	Accept	Outbound FTP access
Any	Any	Any	Drop and log	Cleanup Rule

Table 8-1.   Security Policy Worksheet

Creating the Rule Base

We have established that a VPN-1/FireWall-1 NG policy consists of network objects, users, services, properties, and a Rule Base. Each rule in a Rule Base defines the packets that match the rule, based on the source IP address, destination IP address, service, and the time the packet is inspected. The service defines the type of application or protocol used.

The first rule that matches a packet is applied, and the specified action is taken. The communication may be logged and/or an alert issued, depending on what was entered in the Track field.

TIP   Rules are matched from the top down in order. Once a match is found, the remainder of the Rule Base is not examined for any other matches for that communication even if there is a more specific rule later in the policy.

Creating VPN-1/FireWall-1 NG Objects

To create the required Rule Base, the first step is to use the Policy Editor to create the component objects. Launch the Management Console and log in as shown in Figure 8-2. The username and password you supply to log in are defined during installation. This is known as Smart Client Dashboard in VPN-1/FireWall-1 Feature Pack 3.

The first time the Policy Editor connects to the Management Server, you will see a dialog box showing the Fingerprint key. Verify this against the key generated during installation of the Management Server. This is done to prevent man-in-the-middle style

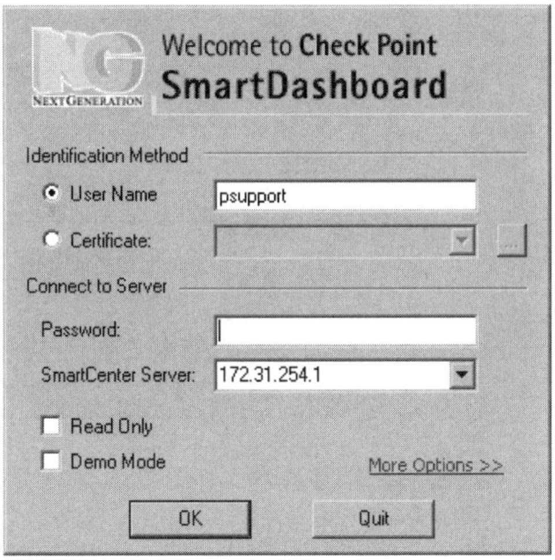

Figure 8-2. Log in to the Management Console

impersonation where a hacker could potentially pretend to be the Management Server and gain information such as sent passwords.

TIP The Management Server Fingerprint can be viewed from the Fingerprint option of the Check Point Configuration tool on the Management Server. Or, check the Fingerprint against the one saved to file when Management Server was installed.

Edit Gateway Object

You will now be presented with the Policy Editor screen shown in Figure 8-3. Verify that the Management Server object appears listed in the Visual Policy Editor. The Management Server is the first defined object in a new installation and is found under the Check Point heading of the objects tree. Follow these steps:

1. Complete the configuration of the Management Server Object labeled lonfw. Double-click the Management Server object displayed in the Objects List. The Workstation Properties screen appears for your Management Server as shown in Figure 8-4.

2. Complete the configuration of the object by entering the following information in the appropriate fields:

Comment:	Fiction Corporation Firewall
Color:	Red

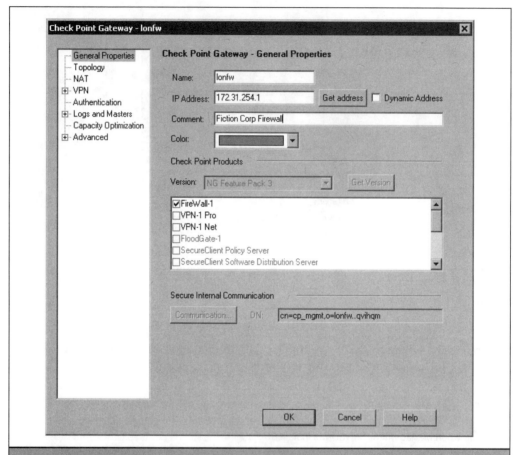

Figure 8-3.   Management Server object created during installation

---

TIP   It's standard practice for firewall administrators to color-code objects within the Rule Base for improved clarity. The usual convention is to use red for all objects that have VPN-1/FireWall-1 NG components.

---

3. Verify the object appears as detailed in Figure 8-4. Select the Topology option from the list that appears on the left-hand side of the screen. The Topology screen appears as shown in Figure 8-5.

4. Click the Get Interfaces button to ensure that all interfaces appear. It is recommended you use this option to retrieve interfaces rather than entering the interfaces manually. VPN-1/FireWall-1 NG uses SNMP to retrieve the interface information.

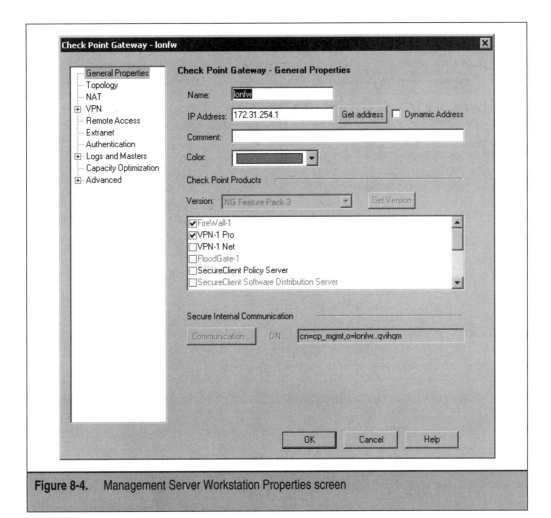

Figure 8-4.   Management Server Workstation Properties screen

5. Click OK after reviewing the information and ensuring it is correct. It is common for firewall administrators to check the interface information to ensure no mistakes have been made during initial installation. The Visual Policy Editor Topology map will now be updated with the changes you just made by showing the networks attached to the Gateway object (provided that you have enabled the Visual Policy Editor from the View menu).

6. If you are prompted to configure anti-spoofing, click OK to configure without defining anti-spoofing at this stage. We will address anti-spoofing later in this chapter.

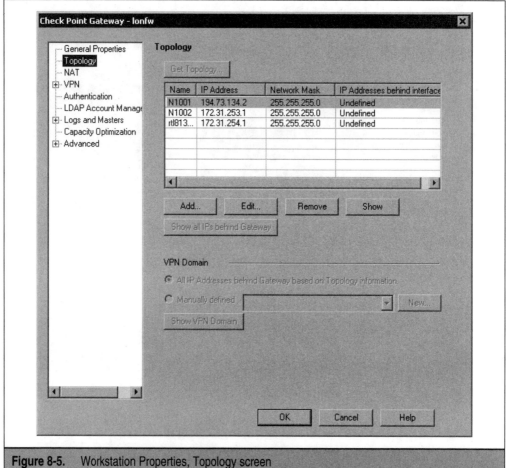

Figure 8-5.   Workstation Properties, Topology screen

Create the Web Server Object

Now you can start creating the objects that will form the basis for Fiction Corporation's Rule Base. Start by adding an object for the web server. Select Manage from the top menu and choose Network Objects. You will be presented with the Network Objects dialog. Select New and choose Workstation for the type of object to be created by the VPN-1/FireWall-1 NG Management Console.

TIP   You can also add new objects by right-clicking the Network Objects icon in the left column of the Policy Editor and selecting the type of object you want to create.

Complete the Workstation General dialog, as shown in Figure 8-6, by supplying the following information:

Name:	Web-Server
IP Address:	172.31.253.254
Comment:	Fiction Corporation Web Server
Color:	Blue

You are not required to make any amendments to the Topology screen at this stage because the Web Server object is on a DMZ, which uses RFC1918-compliant IP addressing;

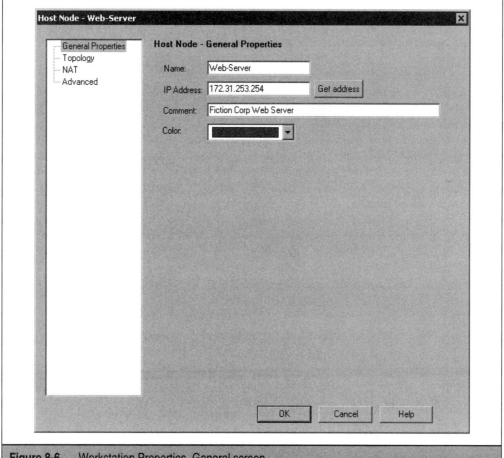

Figure 8-6.   Workstation Properties, General screen

that is, private IP addressing which is not routable via the Internet. You are, however, required to publish the Web Server object on the Internet or external interface of the firewall by allocating an IP address from Fiction Corporation's registered IP address range of 194.73.134.0 /27. To achieve this, VPN-1/FireWall-1 NG provides Network address Translation (NAT) that allows the firewall to publish a hidden internal RFC1918-compliant IP address as an Internet-visible, registered IP address (RFC1918 defines the allowed IP address ranges for use in a private network that don't conflict with registered or Internet routable IP addresses). Two types of NAT will be used to create Fiction Corporation's Rule Base: static (one-to-one) and hide (one-to-many) NAT. In this case, you will be using the automatic address translation capability of VPN-1/FireWall-1 NG to create a static NAT. Select the NAT option from the left column to display the NAT screen.

NOTE Detailed information on NAT is presented in Chapter 13. Do not be concerned if NAT appears confusing at this stage. In a nutshell, a static NAT is used to publish a server on the Internet, and a hide NAT is used to allow internal users to access the Internet.

In the Valid IP Address field, enter the required Valid IP as shown in Figure 8-7. The valid IP must be in the same network range as the external interface because VPN-1/FireWall-1 NG will process all requests from the Internet to this IP address via a technique known as Proxy ARP. This allows VPN-1/FireWall-1 NG to process to any request to the valid IP of the web server on the web server's behalf.

In earlier versions of VPN-1/FireWall-1 NG, it was necessary to map the IP addresses of published objects to the MAC (hardware) address of the firewall's external interface using startup scripts on Unix or a local.arp file and permanent static route entries on Windows Server platforms. These MAC address and static route entries are no longer required as this is all taken care of automatically by VPN-1/FireWall-1 NG. In practice we have found there are exceptions to using Automatic ARP on VPN-1/FireWall-1 with certain versions of Nokia IPSO and Windows Operating systems where Proxy ARP still has to be defined as in previous versions of the firewall software.

For this example, you need to allocate 194.73.134.3 to the web server, so create a static NAT as shown in Figure 8-7 and click OK to save the object.

CAUTION It is not recommended that the actual VPN-1/FireWall-1 NG external IP address be used in NAT because this can result in unpredictable behavior.

VPN-1/FireWall-1 NG updates the Visual Policy Editor and the left column of network objects as new objects are created.

Creating the Mail Relay

Now you will create the mail relay. This server would typically be an intermediary, which is deployed in the DMZ to intercept mail from the Internet or the internal mail

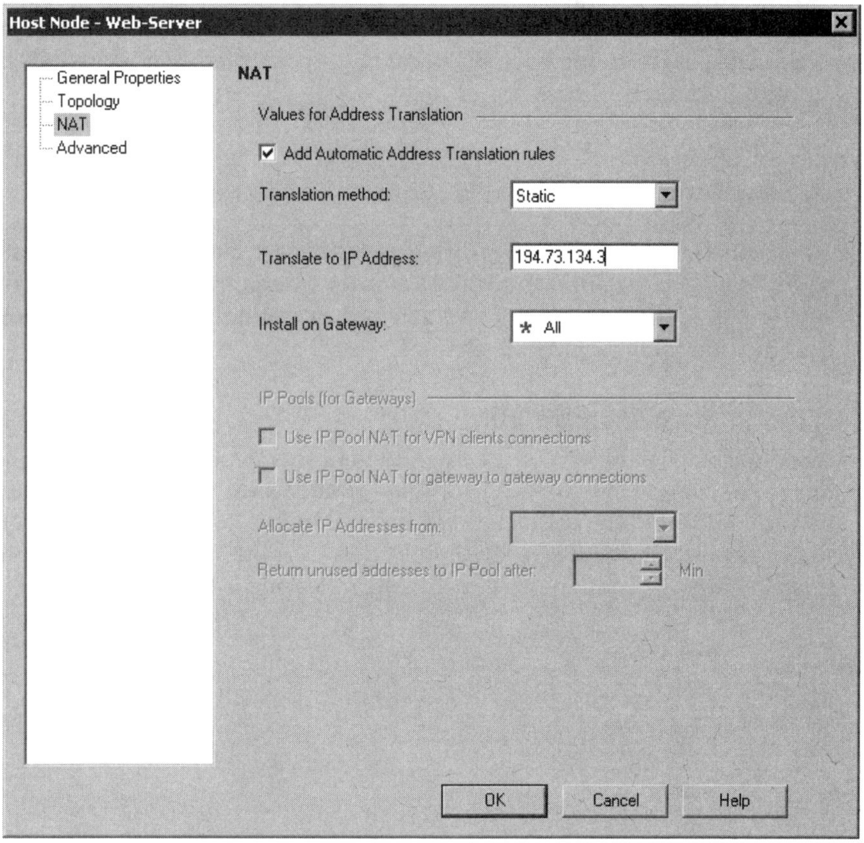

Figure 8-7. Creating a static NAT

server and route it. Commercial software that is deployed in this role typically has virus scanning and anti-spam capabilities. Supply the following information to complete the Workstation General dialog using the same procedure you used to create the web server:

Name:	Mail-Relay
IP Address:	172.31.253.253
Comment:	Fiction Corporation Mail Relay
Color:	Blue

You also need to create a static NAT for the mail relay, so select the NAT option and enter the following information. Allocate 194.73.134.4 as the valid IP for the mail relay—it is available in the range our ISP allocated for registered IP addresses. Click the NAT tab and follow these steps:

1. Check the Add Automatic Address Translation check box.

2. Select Static and enter the Valid IP address of 194.73.134.4.

Notice that the Visual Policy Editor Topology builds as objects are being created. While it is not necessary to define all the objects prior to creating rules, it is far better to focus on object definition first and then move on to creating rules. This will build a solid foundation for later parts of the chapter.

Creating the Internal Mail Server

You now need to create an object for the internal mail server that communicates with the mail relay. You won't be using NAT for this object because it will not be required to communicate with any Internet-connected system. In fact, to do so would create a security risk because the system is located on Fiction Corporation's internal network. Instead, create a new workstation object using the following information:

Name:	Internal-MailServer
IP Address:	172.31.254.100
Comment:	Fiction Corporation Mail Server
Color:	Blue

Click OK to save the Internal Mail Server Object.

Creating a Network Object

To allow internal users to connect to the Internet, a network object representing the Internal IP network is required. It is better to use network objects for internal users rather than defining each individual workstation because it makes creating rules on the firewall much easier. Where there are multiple networks internally, firewall administrators create a larger mask or group network objects together.

Fiction Corporation has several internal networks, and Internet access is required from each network. You will now create a hide NAT (many-to-one) for the internal networks 172.31.254.0 /24 and 172.31.248.0 /24. This will be expanded upon in Chapter 13.

To create a Network Object for network 172.31.254.0 /24, either right-click the Network icon in the Network Objects list or select Manage from the top menu bar and launch the Network Objects window. Choose Network as the object type. Enter the following network information for the Network object as shown in Figure 8-8.

Name:	Net_172.31.254.0
IP Address:	172.31.254.0
Net Mask:	255.255.255.0
Comments:	Fiction Corporation London Net
Color:	Blue

Notice that the Network object has a descriptive name. Naming conventions for objects are almost entirely optional, but in larger installations they are essential for rapid troubleshooting and ease of management. Typically firewall administrators who have multiple VPN-1/FireWall-1 gateways installed often use naming conventions which are structured so a given object can easily be related to an actual organizational or geographical location and function, for example, uk_lon_web01 means a Web Server in the UK at London. Some administrators also put the IP address into the name of the object, for example, Net_172.16.1.0 describes network 172.16.1.0. Naming conventions are entirely discretionary.

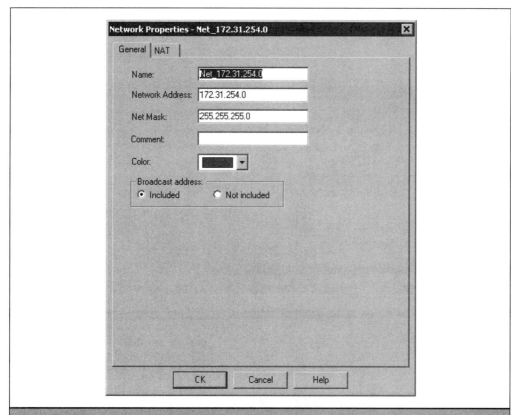

Figure 8-8.   Network Properties for Net_172.31.254.0, General tab

Now you need to create a network object for network 172.31.248.0 /24 with the following information using the same technique as used for creating the previous object:

Name:	Net_172.31.248.0
IP Address:	172.31.248.0
Net Mask:	255.255.255.0
Comments:	Fiction Corporation Leeds Net
Color:	Blue

Grouping Objects Together

The two Network objects that you have created need to be grouped together with a Group object. This will make creating rules based on these objects much easier.

To create a Group object called Internal_Nets, right-click the Network Objects icon and select the Simple Group option from the Group submenu.

You are now presented with a Group Properties dialog as shown in Figure 8-9. Select the two network objects you wish to include in the group from the Not in Group list and click Add. These can be group selected or individually added.

Click OK to save the object.

Figure 8-9.   Assigning objects to a group

The Visual Policy Editor network topology now matches your network diagram and all the objects in your initial table have been created.

Defining Rules

You can easily translate the table-based rules that you created in the preparation stage (see Table 8-1) into a VPN-1/FireWall-1 NG rule. Let's examine the anatomy of a Rule Base as detailed in Table 8-2.

Defining Basic Rules

There are two basic rules that are almost a de facto standard for VPN-1/FireWall-1 NG administrators: the Cleanup Rule and the Stealth Rule. These rules are important for basic security and help track important information in the Log Viewer (or SmartClient Tracker, as it's known in Feature Pack 3). To create a rule in the Policy Editor, select Add Rule from the Rules menu and select Top or Bottom as this is the first rule. The rule is assigned rule number 1 as it is the first rule added.

A default rule appears, as shown in Figure 8-10, that you can configure with all objects, services, and users installed in your Rule Base.

The Cleanup Rule

VPN-1/FireWall-1 NG follows the principle, "That which is not expressly permitted is prohibited." VPN-1/FireWall-1 NG does an implicit drop after any user-defined rules, but this does not log. Because of this, it is standard practice to create a Cleanup Rule that logs any packets that have passed through the preceding set of rules without being processed.

Field	Definition
No.	The Rule number defines the order in which VPN-1/FireWall-1 NG enforces each rule
Source	Packets emanating from this object—can be any defined network or workstation objects
Destination	Packets going to this object—can be any defined network or workstation objects
IF VIA	Defines the VPN community the connection passes through. Not required for just firewall functionality. This should be ignored for the purposes of this chapter or if you are only using FireWall-1 functionality and not VPN features.
Services	The protocols that are to be checked for
Action	What the firewall does with the packet—typically Accept or Drop
Track	Type of notification required for each packet action
Install On	Which firewalled object to install this rule on
Time	The time period a rule is effective—if no time is defined, the rule is constantly active
Comment	Optional description of the rule—can help with troubleshooting if used

Table 8-2.   Anatomy of a Rule

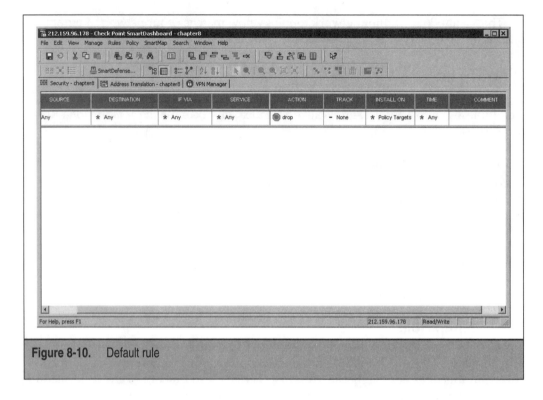

Figure 8-10.   Default rule

To change the default rule, right-click in the Track field and select Log. Double-click the Comments field and enter the text **Cleanup Rule**. Figure 8-11 shows the completed rule. Congratulations, you have just created your first rule in VPN-1/FireWall-1 NG.

Setting the Cleanup Rule's Track field to Log ensures that any packets that the VPN-1/FireWall-1 NG Rule Base does not process will be recorded so you'll be informed of potential unauthorized attempts to gain access.

Stealth Rule

The Stealth Rule prevents any attempt to directly connect to the firewall. Protecting the firewall in this manner makes the firewall transparent to the network. The firewall becomes an invisible network object that cannot be seen by users on the network. To create the Stealth Rule, right-click the No. field of the rule you just created and select Add Rule Above. Enter the following information by right-clicking in each field and selecting the appropriate object or action:

Source:	Any
Destination:	Lonfw
Service:	Any
Action:	Drop
Track:	Log

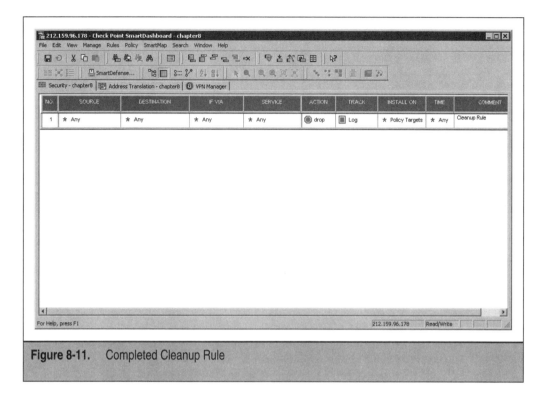

Figure 8-11.   Completed Cleanup Rule

Now right-click in the Comments Field and insert the text **Stealth Rule**, as shown in Figure 8-12.

NOTE   Figure 8-12 shows only the rules and no other parts of the Management Console. We have simply enlarged the Rule Base display, but you can reduce it again to see the other views within the Management Console. Take some time to experiment with moving and resizing the windows, or use the View option from the menu toolbar and select or deselect items to see how it affects the display.

The Stealth Rule is usually placed as the first rule in simple single gateway installations. This protects the firewall from being port scanned, a common reconnaissance technique used by hackers to identify which ports are open in a network and a prelude to more sophisticated attacks. Legitimate connections that need to be made directly to the firewall, such as client authentication, encryption, and CVP rules always go above the Stealth Rule. It is also important to allow any operating system management access before the Stealth Rule.

It is a good idea to save the Rule Base frequently if large numbers of changes are being made. To do this, select the Disk icon below the File menu or choose Save from the File menu. Remember, the Rule Base is saved on the Management Server, not on the Management Console.

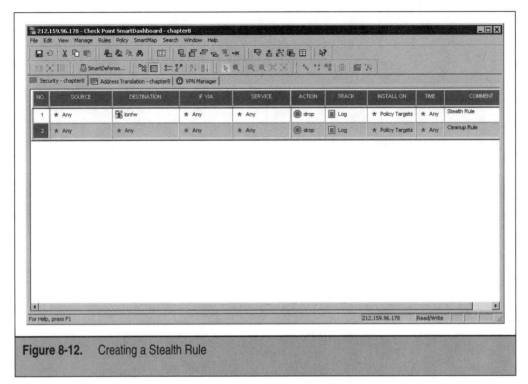

Figure 8-12. Creating a Stealth Rule

Implicit and Explicit Rules

VPN-1/FireWall-1 NG creates a Rule Base by translating the Security Policy into a collection of individual rules. VPN-1/FireWall-1 NG creates implicit rules, derived from the global policy properties and explicit rules created by the user in the Policy Editor.

NOTE   Rules do not take effect until the Rule Base is installed.

Implicit rules are defined by VPN-1/FireWall-1 NG to allow certain connections to and from the firewall with a variety of different services. VPN-1/FireWall-1 NG creates a group of implicit rules that it places first, last, or before last in the explicitly defined Rule Base. To view Implicit rules, from the View menu select Implied Rules. Examine the rules that you see. Select Implied Rules again from the View menu to hide the rules. There are three types of FW1 Control Connections:

- VPN-1/FireWall-1 NG-specific traffic that facilitates functionality, such as logging, management, and key exchange.
- Acceptance of IKE and RDP traffic for communication and encryption purposes.

- Communication with various types of servers such as RADIUS, CVP, UFP, TACACS, LDAP, and logical servers, even if these servers are not specifically defined resources, as in the Fiction Corporation Rule Base.

Policy Properties

Implied rules are generated in the Rule Base from options that you set within Global Properties. To view the properties for the Rule Base, select Global Properties from the Policy menu. Table 8-3 defines what each option within the Policy Global Properties does. These options can be placed in different positions in the Rule Base:

- **First**   Place first in the Rule Base
- **Before Last**   Place before the last rule in the Rule Base
- **Last**   Place as the last rule in the Rule Base

NOTE   The implicit drop rule is not logged. This is why it is necessary to create an explicit Cleanup Rule that generates log records.

Understanding the Rule Base Order

Before you can define Security Policy properties, you must consider the Rule Base order. Because VPN-1/FireWall-1 NG examines the Rule Base on a rule-by-rule basis, it is

Implied Rule	Description
Accept VPN-1/FireWall-1 NG control connections	Used for communications between firewall modules on different machines and for connecting to external servers, such as RADIUS and TACACS.
Accept outgoing packets originating from gateway	If checked, allows packets to pass through the firewall gateway. Can only be left unchecked if rules are enforced in both directions (eitherbound) and there is a rule that allows the packet to leave the gateway.
Accept RIP	Allows the firewall to accept RIP packets.
Accept domain name over UDP (queries)	If the firewall does not know the IP address associated with a host name, it issues a query to the name server. Enabling this option allows the firewall to receive the reply.
Accept domain name over TCP (zone transfer)	Check to allow uploading of domain name-resolving tables.
Accept ICMP Requests	IP uses ICMP to send control messages such as destination unreachable, source quench, and route change to other systems. Commonly used to allow Ping to function.
Log implied rules	If checked, the firewall generates log records for communications that match implied rules.

Table 8-3.   Policy Global Properties Definitions

important to define each rule in the appropriate order. VPN-1/FireWall-1 NG enforces the Security Policy in the following order:

- IP Spoofing/IP Options
- Security Policy "First" Rule
- Rule Base above Stealth Rule (Encryption, Client Authentication)
- Stealth Rule
- Rule Base below Stealth Rule
- Security Policy Global Properties "Before Last" rule
- Cleanup Rule
- Security Policy Global Properties "Last Rule"
- Implicit Drop

Explicit Rules

Now that you have learned about the VPN-1/FireWall-1 NG Rule Base, you are ready to start creating explicit rules for Fiction Corporation by using the objects you already created.

Because Fiction Corporation has no requirement until later in the book for Encryption or advanced services, all the rules will be defined between the Stealth Rule and the Cleanup Rule that you created earlier in this chapter. It is almost universal practice for firewall administrators to enter rules that apply to the busiest traffic early in the Rule Base. Fiction Corporation has an uncharacteristically dedicated workforce that will not spend a large number of office hours surfing the Internet, so the next rule you will deploy is for web access to the Fiction Corporation website. To do this, launch the Policy Editor, right-click the Stealth Rule, and select Add Rule Below.

A default rule is inserted between the Cleanup Rule and the Stealth Rule. Leave the source field as Any because this is a public access server and Fiction Corporation wants anyone on the Internet to access it. Right-click the Destination field and select Add to launch the Network Objects window. You will now be presented with a list of objects that you defined previously. You could add new objects, but for now, select the Web Server object that has been defined.

Click OK to add the object to the rule.

TIP   While you are in the Add Object dialog, you can add additional objects, edit existing objects, or delete objects. If you select the Show pull-down menu, you can view specific types of objects; for example, workstation objects only, which is useful if you have a large set of defined objects.

You have built a rule, which states from any source to the Web Server, but you now need to define the services you are permitting. The original table (Table 8-1) of rules stated that only HTTP was going to be accepted, so right-click in the Services field and select Add. The Add Object dialog is launched with a list of supported services. Follow these steps:

1. Select HTTP and click OK.

2. Right-click in the Action field and select Accept to allow HTTP packets to be passed if destined for the web server.

3. The rule will now accept HTTP requests to the web server from any source. To generate log records for each connection attempt, right-click in the Track field and select Log from the pop-up menu.

4. Double-click in the Comment field and enter **Access to Fiction Corporation Web Site**. This is optional, but having a good description will assist you later with administration and troubleshooting when the Rule Base grows. The Rule Base should look like Figure 8-13.

Now add the other rules as shown in Table 8-1 to complete the Rule Base. The completed Rule Base is shown in Figure 8-14.

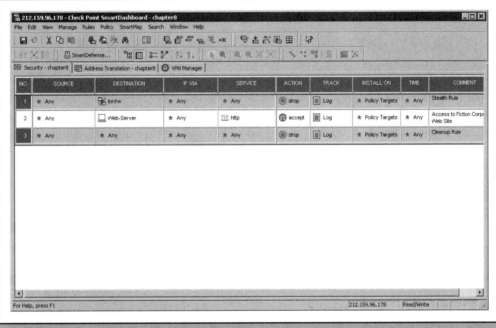

Figure 8-13.   The Rule Base with the Web Server Rule added

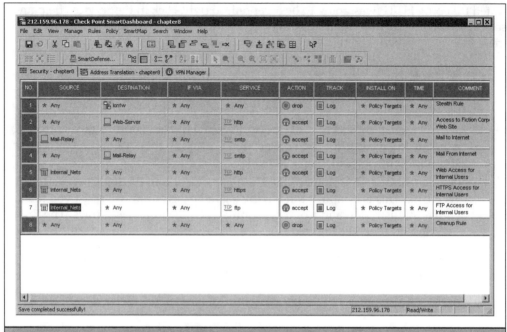

Figure 8-14. Completed Fiction Corporation Rule Base

Hide NAT

If you only had a single network object that needed outbound Internet access, you could have used an Automatic Address Translation as you did for the other servers, except you would have selected hide NAT instead of static NAT. Fiction Corporation has multiple networks, so you sensibly grouped these into the Group Internal_Nets. You now need to create a manual hide NAT and insert this in the Address Translation section of the Rule Base.

A hide NAT means that a single Valid IP will represent all the workstations on both the internal networks. VPN-1/FireWall-1 NG does this by using a technique known in the IT Industry as Port Address Translation (PAT); or a hide NAT as it is referred to in VPN-1/FireWall-1 NG terminology. The firewall IP address has been chosen to be the hide address for the Group Internal_Nets. All requests from this object via the firewall will be translated as appearing to be sent from 194.73.134.2 (the firewall gateway's registered IP address).

The Group object Internal_Nets represents the Internal Networks. To create the hide NAT rule as shown in Figure 8-15, use the firewall object as follows:

1. Select the Address Translation Tab of the Rule Base.

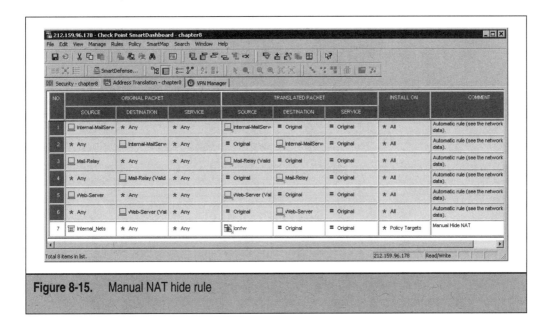

Figure 8-15. Manual NAT hide rule

2. Select Add | Bottom to insert a rule at the bottom of the Address Translations rules.

3. Add Internal_Nets under Source in the Original Packet section.

4. Add the Gateway Object lonfw under Source in the Translated Packet section.

The manual hide NAT rule will translate all requests from the internal networks to the Internet into the valid address of the firewall gateway. However, there is a problem with this. If users on the internal networks wish to communicate with the DMZ (172.31.253.0 /24), the packets will translate and the connection attempts will fail.

Firewall administrators usually create a NoNat Group object and a No Network Address Translation rule at the top of the Address Translation Rules to ensure that VPN-1/FireWall-1 NG does not translate packets that are communications from the internal networks to a DMZ. To create a NoNat rule, follow these steps:

1. Create a Network Object Net_172.31.253.0 with a /24 (255.255.255.0) netmask using the steps as shown in Creating VPN-1/FireWall-1 objects earlier in this chapter.

2. Create a Group object called NoNat and place all three Fiction Corporation Internal networks into this group.

3. Select Add Rule | Top in the Address Translation Section.

4. In both the Source and Destination fields of the Original Packet, insert the Group NoNat as shown in Figure 8-16.

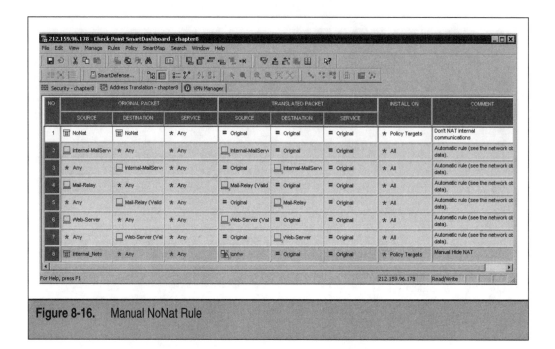

Figure 8-16.   Manual NoNat Rule

Any external object, such as the ISP DNS server defined here, is placed in the Internet space as shown in Figure 8-16. By double-clicking the Internet icon in the Visual Policy Editor, external hosts are shown. It is quite common to have a number of external objects defined for specific groups that require access into your network and that restrict access.

DNS Name Resolution

You now need to amend the Rule Base to add support for DNS queries. One way to do this is to create a rule that would allow Internal_Nets to perform DNS queries within the Rule Base, as shown in Table 8-4.

This time, however, you'll use the Global Properties option to allow DNS UDP queries and leave the default of First in the pop-up list. This will allow all systems to resolve DNS queries. This is more open because it allows DNS queries both to the DMZ servers for Fiction Corporation which is unnecessary and also those outbound for all internal systems. We recommend using the rule shown in Table 8-4 instead as it is more secure.

Anti-Spoofing

A properly configured Security Policy requires more than just some objects and rules. The Security Policy for Fiction Corporation's Internet connection is now almost complete, but you must add some additional security measures. The features that will be covered in the remainder of the chapter and throughout the book show the strength and depth

Source	Destination	Service	Action	Description
Internal_Nets	ISP-DNS	domain-udp	Accept	Allow DNS queries from specific systems in Fiction Corporation to the ISP DNS Server

Table 8-4. DNS Rule Format

of VPN-1/FireWall-1 NG capabilities. The Security Policy for Fiction Corporation will be strengthened as the company grows and as it requires additional VPN-1/FireWall-1 NG features including defining Anti-Spoofing.

Detecting Spoofing

Spoofing is a technique where an intruder attempts to gain unauthorized access by making a packet's IP address appear as if it originated in a part of the network with higher access privileges. VPN-1/FireWall-1 NG has a sophisticated anti-spoofing feature that detects such packets by requiring that the interface on which a packet enters a gateway corresponds to its IP address.

Select the workstation object for VPN-1/FireWall-1 NG and select the Topology option from the left-hand column.

NOTE Anti-spoofing rules, defined in a firewalled object's properties, are enforced before any rule in the Security Policy's Rule Base.

Configuring Anti-Spoofing

Select the firewall object. From the workstation properties dialog box, highlight the interface with 194.73.134.2 defined and select Edit. Select the Topology tab from the Interface Properties window. Select the External radio button and ensure the Perform Anti-Spoofing Based on Interface Topology check box is selected, as shown in Figure 8-17.

1. Configuring the external interface as shown in Figure 8-17 ensures that only packets that do not meet the criteria defined for other interfaces on the gateway are accepted.

2. Click OK to continue.

3. Select the Internal Interface (172.31.254.1) and select Edit. You will now be presented with an Interface Properties dialog. Select the Topology tab.

4. Under Topology, select the Internal (Leads to the Local Network) radio button.

5. Under IP Addresses Behind This Interface, select Specific. In the drop-down list box, select the group object Internal_Nets. This groups the networks that are behind this interface.

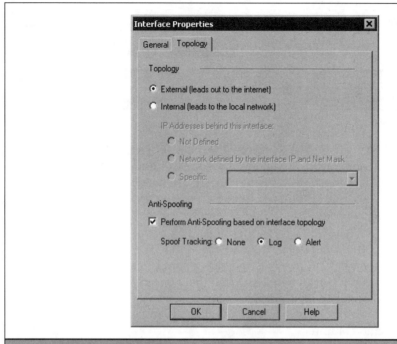

Figure 8-17. Interface Properties, Topology tab

6. Under Anti-Spoofing, check the Perform Anti-Spoofing Based on Interface Topology check box. For Spoof Tracking, select the Log radio button.

7. Click OK. The completed interface should look like Figure 8-18.

TIP If there are multiple routed networks on the Internal Network, create a group and assign the networks to that group. Under IP Addresses Behind This Interface, select the Specific option and assign the group object.

---

8. Select the DMZ Interface (172.31.253.1) and select Edit. You will be presented with an Interface Properties dialog. Select the Topology tab.

9. Under Topology, select the Internal (Leads to the Local Network) radio button.

10. Under IP Addresses Behind This Interface, select Network Defined by the Interface IP and Net Mask. You do this because the directly connected network is the only one behind this interface.

11. Under Anti-Spoofing, check the Perform Anti-Spoofing Based on Interface Topology check box. For Spoof Tracking, select the Log radio button.

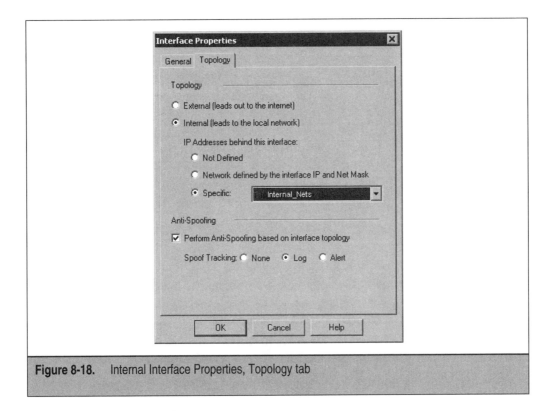

Figure 8-18.   Internal Interface Properties, Topology tab

Click OK to save changes. You have now successfully configured the Anti-Spoofing policy for the Fiction Corporation Rule Base.

Care should be taken when using Feature Pack 3 to define Anti-Spoofing. When a firewall administrator selects the Get Topology button from the Topology tab, VPN-1/FireWall-1 Feature Pack 3 will offer the option of automatically defining Anti-Spoofing and create the necessary objects. In our experience this has resulted in duplicate objects, and in some cases a misconfigured Anti-Spoofing policy. This feature is useful for a new install, but it should not be used for an established installation.

Verifying the Policy

Now you need to verify that the Rule Base is valid. Verifying a Rule Base allows you to create a policy without installing it. Verifying the Security Policy also helps you ensure your rule order is correct and keeps you from using services in rules where they are not specifically allowed.

To verify the Rule Base, select the Verify option from the Policy menu and VPN-1/ FireWall-1 NG will verify the Rule Base. If the Rule Base does not contain inconsistencies, such as multiple rules performing the same task, the Policy Verification dialog will appear as shown in Figure 8-19.

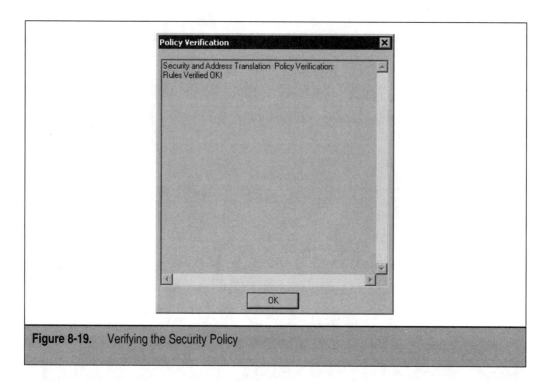

Figure 8-19.   Verifying the Security Policy

Installing the Rule Base

You are now ready to install the VPN-1/FireWall-1 NG Rule Base you have defined
for Fiction Corporation. To install the Rule Base, select Install from the Policy menu.
The Install Policy dialog will appear. Click OK to install the Security Policy. The
Security Policy is generated and installed on the enforcement point. The progress of
the Security Policy installation is detailed in the dialog, as shown in Figure 8-20.

Visual Policy Editor

As you build up Fiction Corporation's Security Policy, notice that some objects that appear
within the Visual Policy Editor cannot be edited until they are actualized (actually defined
as objects and not just assumed to be present by VPN-1/FireWall-1). This is because there
is no object defined, but VPN-1/FireWall-1 NG assumes that the object exists within the
actual network.

To demonstrate the functionality of the Visual Policy Editor, highlight the Network
object 172.31.253.0. Note that it is an implied object because you cannot edit the object,
and the object name starts with **Implied_**. To make the object real and editable, you need
to actualize it. To do this, right-click the DMZ (172.31.253.0) object and select the Actualize
option from the pop-up menu. A window appears with all the IP information already

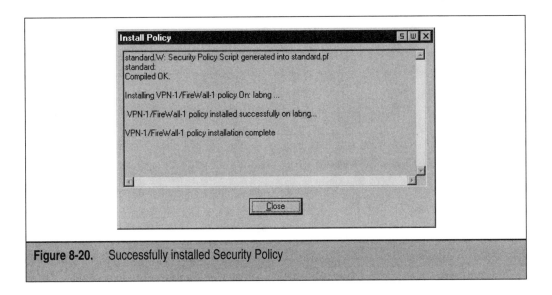

Figure 8-20. Successfully installed Security Policy

entered, as shown in Figure 8-21. Click OK to save the object. The newly created object can now be used within the Rule Base.

This is a good shortcut to creating objects within VPN-1/FireWall-1 NG. If you double-click the object in the Visual Policy Editor, you can edit it because it is an actual object that exists within VPN-1/FireWall-1 NG databases.

This is just one way to use the Visual Policy Editor.

CHECKLIST: KEY POINTS IN SETTING UP A SECURITY POLICY RULE BASE AND PROPERTIES

The following is a checklist for the key points in setting up a security policy rule base and properties:

☐ List the components that make up the Security Policy Editor functionality of VPN-1/FireWall-1 NG.

☐ Identify the basic security requirements of the Fiction Corporation.

☐ Define the Security Policy.

☐ Create the Security Policy for VPN-1/FireWall-1 NG.

☐ Implement a basic Rule Base from a real-world example.

☐ Demonstrate how easy it is to start building a Security Policy using VPN-1/FireWall-1 NG's Policy Editor.

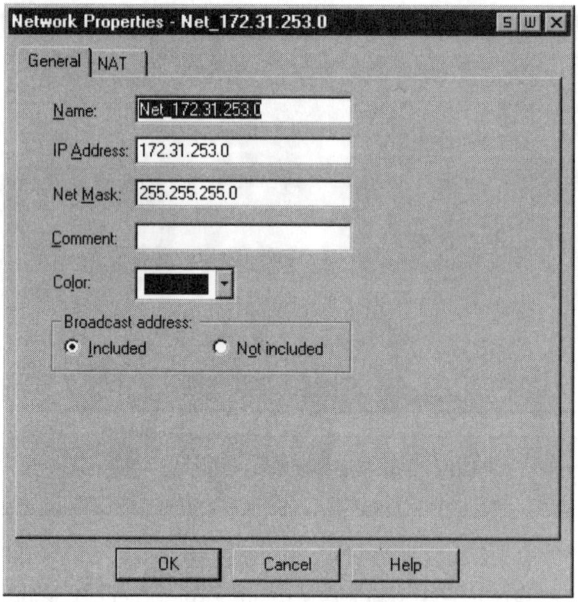

Figure 8-21. An actualized Network object

☐ Identify the required information for launching the Policy Editor with requirements capture and a network design.

☐ Amend the Security Policy as required.

☐ Define in general the initial Security Policy for Fiction Corporation's main site in London.

☐ Apply real-world deployments of a company's Security Policy.

☐ Specifically design the Rule Base so there is room for improvement.

☐ Define Network Address Translation.

☐ Deploy a complete Rule Base.

CHAPTER 9

Working with the Security Policy

Whenen discussing Security Policy, you must first consider risks, something you try to eliminate, of course. However, complete elimination is never possible: the costs of avoiding risk can sometimes be too high. Deciding how much risk you can accept and, hence, how much security you deem as sufficient for your requirements is called *risk management*.

There's an old, obscure security practice called "security through obscurity" that used to be very common, and it is still around. *Security through obscurity* defines a Security Policy that isolates information about the system it is protecting from anyone outside the implementation team. This includes, but is not limited to, hiding passwords in binary files or scripts and assuming that no one will ever find it.

Are you running an internal network and planning to run your firewall based on such a system? You'd better not! It certainly worked during the "glass walls" age of proprietary and centralized systems. But today, with the advent of open systems, internetworking, and great development of intelligent applications and applets, Security Policies need to be taken a step higher.

To run your site based on hidden information, rather than protected information, is to play with fire (without the wall!)—it's useless. Nowadays, users are more knowledgeable about the systems they are running and the technology surrounding them. If your only security is to keep information unknown, you'll find it's just a matter of time until the information becomes well known. Hackers were the first to discover that obscurity, more than security, is exciting. To keep that type of excitement to a minimum, you need a system that is genuinely secure. Although any system can be broken, developing a policy with an organized method and tools to increase security, monitor threats, catch intruders, or even pursue them, increases your odds of successfully blocking intruders. Hackers who uncover vulnerable systems via random probing will find the possibility of a system that is obscure but not very secure, quite exciting as they start to access more of the system. They will concentrate their efforts on breaking into that system. The use of stateful firewalls such as Check Point will prevent random probing from revealing information which could tempt a hacker to probe further, and then prevent attacks that are attempted.

Your site will be as secure as the people you allow or invite to access it. To make tracking easier, keeping detailed logs via VPN-1/FireWall-1 NG's comprehensive logging facilities is easily manageable when dealing with a few hundred internal users. Additional log management strategies and commercial tools are available, including the Reporting Module from Check Point, to assist with log processing for larger numbers of users. Logging is essential to keep a record of transactions that have taken place and to generate alerts on those that are deemed suspicious.

You could have a very secure site to which only corporate users have access. However, this is impractical because most businesses want to leverage the massive potential of e-commerce and the cost savings of extranet and intranet deployment.

ASSESSING FICTION CORPORATION'S SECURITY

Use formulas when assessing risk management. These are not mathematical equations based on quantitative determinations; they are algorithms that study factors such as the qualitative level of danger posed in a given situation.

In information systems security, the word "threat" describes a more limited component of risk. For the purposes of this chapter, threats are posed by organizations or individuals who intend your corporation harm and who have the capability to cause it.

As you plan your Security Policy, study the different types of threats to Fiction Corporation and the consequences that these attacks might have if successfully executed. Often threats to information systems are paired with a specific line of attack or set of vulnerabilities. A threat that can't exploit vulnerability is probably not as high on the list of possible attacks as others may be; therefore study threat-vulnerability pairings in the risk management process.

The threats that face Fiction Corporation are the same that face any company dipping its toes into the big wide world of Internet connectivity. For example, worms (malicious code that penetrates systems to do harm), such as the now famous Code Red or Nimda, damaged countless systems on the Internet and spread very rapidly.

Once Fiction Corporation has installed the correct security patches for these worms, the threat of the Code Red worm will not be high on the list of possible attacks that need serious consideration.

A line of attack or set of vulnerabilities could be defined as web-based worms and Trojans for customers who have publicly available web systems. Once systems are patched and secured correctly by utilizing SmartDefense in VPN-1/FireWall-1 NG, the web-based worm's significance recedes.

By assuming a threat to be a real possibility, valuing your potential targets highly, and conservatively estimating the uncertainties, you reduce risk management to the question, "What are our vulnerabilities and how much do countermeasures cost to eliminate them?" The management problem then becomes, "How much money can I spend and where can I spend it most wisely?"

With this kind of careful analysis, you should be able to estimate the value of each factor in your equation, balance the risk of loss or damage against the costs of countermeasures, and select a mix that provides adequate protection without excessive cost.

Ultimately, the risk management process, even when configuring VPN-1/FireWall-1 NG's Security Policy, involves making decisions. The impact of a successful attack and the level of risk that is acceptable in any given situation are fundamental policy decisions. The threat may be abated, controlled, or subdued by appropriate countermeasures, but it is beyond the direct control of the security process. The process must focus, accordingly, on *vulnerabilities* and *countermeasures*.

Vulnerabilities are design issues that must be addressed during the development, fabrication, and implementation of your facilities, equipment, systems, and networks. Although the distinction is not always clear, *countermeasures* are less characteristic of your systems than of their environments and the ways in which you use them. Typically, to make any asset less vulnerable raises its cost, not just in the design and development phase but also in its more extensive validation and testing to ensure the functionality and utility of security features, as well as the application of countermeasures during the operation and maintenance phase.

Your basic security requirement should minimize, if not eliminate, all the security holes existent in your site. Security holes are presented in four ways:

- **Physical** Unauthorized people accessing the site or the firewall server (bastion host), enabling them to trespass and peruse. For example, a browser installed in a public place, such as a reception area, gives users the chance not only to browse the Web, but also to change the browser's configuration and get the site's information such as IP addresses, DNS entries, and so on.

- **Software** "Buggy privileged" applications such as daemons executing illegal functions. As a rule of thumb, never trust scripts and applets! When using them, make sure you understand what they are supposed to do—and what they are not!

- **Incompatibility issues** A system with poor integration planning. Hardware or software may work great alone, but once you integrate it with other devices it may cause problems. These kinds of problems are very hard to spot, so test every component before integrating it into your system.

- **Lack of a Security Policy** It does not matter how secure your password authentication mechanism is if your users use their kids' names as passwords. You must have a Security Policy that addresses all the security requirements for your site as well as covering, and preventing, all the possible security holes.

Most web-based applications, as mentioned earlier, have the capability to generate traffic logs. Users are at the mercy of these servers, especially web servers, so make sure to keep them on a DMZ. Furthermore, when information about them, their connections, their address, or even specifications about their client or company are disclosed, this information can be used against those users. A web server log can threaten a user's security because it discloses a list of information, which usually includes:

- The IP address
- The server/host name
- The time of the download
- The user's name (if known by user authentication or, with Unix, obtained by the identd (identification, used in mail systems) protocol)
- The requested URL
- The data variables submitted through forms users usually fill out during their session

- The status of the request
- The size of the data transmitted

A fundamental challenge of developing a Security Policy is to link the choice of design characteristics, which reduces vulnerabilities, with the countermeasures to threat and impact to create a cost-effective balance that achieves an acceptable level of risk. Such a process might work as follows:

1. **Assess the impact of loss of or damage to the potential target.**   For example, while the emotional impact of the loss of a parental family member is beyond measure, the economic value of the member as a wage earner can be estimated to decide the amount of life insurance to purchase. The same model should be used in assessing the impact of loss or damage of a particular network resource of information.

2. **Consider that not all impacts are economic.**   For example, the loss of privacy or the integrity of a user.

3. **Specify the level of risk of damage or destruction that is acceptable.**   This may well be the most difficult part of the process. Use Table 9-1 as your boilerplate.

4. **Identify and characterize the threat.**   The damage that can be caused by criminal behavior can be described and predicted.

5. **Analyze vulnerabilities.**   Your computer systems and networks can be designed to be less vulnerable to hacker attacks. Where potential improvements that may reduce vulnerabilities are identified, the cost of their implementation must be estimated.

6. **Specify countermeasures.**   Where vulnerabilities are inherent or cost too much to eliminate during the design and development of your Security Policy, countermeasures must be selected to reduce risk to an acceptable level. Access to servers can be controlled. Computer and network use can be monitored or audited. Personnel can be vetted to various degrees by performing background checks. Not all available countermeasures need be used if the business requirements of an organization are addressed by a subset of countermeasures that will reduce risk to an acceptable level. Costs of each type of countermeasure must be estimated in order to determine the most cost-effective mix.

7. **Expect and allow for uncertainties.**   None of the factors in the risk management equation is absolute. No threat is infinitely capable and always lucky. No system is without vulnerability. No countermeasure is completely effective. Risk management requires the realistic assessment of uncertainties, erring on neither conservative nor optimistic sides.

Table 9-1 provides a matrix to assess the level of security you may need to implement, based on the level of concern about the information to be protected and the potential consequences of a confidentiality breach.

Level of Concern / Suggested Authentication Method	Qualifiers
High-classified / Use of encryption methods along with authentication	If loss of integrity at your site will affect confidentiality, the requirements for integrity is high and must be met.
High / Use of encryption methods and associated authentication methods	Absolute accuracy required for mission accomplishment (for example, electronic commerce); or expected dollar value of loss of integrity is high.
Medium / Use of authentication methods	High degree of accuracy required for mission accomplishment (personal information being catalogued, health environments), but not absolute, or expected dollar value of loss of integrity is not high.
Low / Use of password protection	Reasonable degree of accuracy required for mission accomplishment (database applications, search engines); or expected dollar value of loss is low.
Very Low / May not require security measures other than integrity of data	No particular degree of accuracy required for mission accomplishment (informative pages, minimum interaction with user).

Table 9-1.   Level of Integrity to Be Implemented

Data Security

Remember, web servers are obedient but they are dull. Because they will not think on their own, they don't know the difference between the firewall administrator and a hacker (well, we probably wouldn't know either). Anything placed into the web server's document root directory is exposed and unprotected if you don't find a way to protect it.

Therefore, be careful when configuring your web server. When you load it with a bunch of optional features and services, you can make it even more prone to data security risks. Check Point's Security Servers will go some way in preventing attacks or unwanted visitors, enhancing data security. It also will help you to cope with the holes generally opened by dangerous features present in so many web services. The operating system underlying the web server is also a vital aspect in determining how safe the server is against a hacker's attack.

Along with considering the operating system, you should be careful with the features that each operating system combined with the web server has to offer. There are potentially dangerous features that you should turn off, especially if you do not need them. The following is a list of features to which you should pay special attention:

- **Automatic directory listings**   The more a hacker knows about your system, the higher the chance it will be tampered with. Of course, automatic directory listings can be very convenient, but hackers can have access to sensitive information through them. For example:

- EMACS backup files containing CGI scripts
- Control logs
- Directories with temporary files and so on

Be aware that turning off automatic directory listings won't stop hackers from grabbing files whose names they guess correctly, but at least it makes the process more difficult.

- **Symbolic links following**   There are servers that extend the document tree with symbolic links. Although convenient, this can become dangerous if the link is added to a sensitive area such as /etc.

- **Server side includes**   One of the major security holes is the "exec" form of server side includes. It should be turned off completely or made available only to trusted users. Apache allows you to turn it off by entering this statement in the directory control section of access.conf: Options IncludesNoExec.

- **User-maintained directories**   Although it might be useful to allow users to maintain directories at the server, or even to add documents to it, you must trust the users if you are allowing user-maintained directories. If the organization is extremely security sensitive, then only authorized staff or nominated individuals would receive the information. After checking it, they would update the directory, hence reducing the risk of abuse but obviously increasing the administration overhead in achieving a business task.

Another way to protect data is through the use of SSL, which uses a public-key encryption to exchange a session key, which is used to encrypt the http transaction, between the client and server. Because each transaction uses a different session key, even if a hacker decrypts the transaction, the server's secret key will still be protected.

You will not be compromising data security by sharing directories between a FTP daemon and your web daemon. However, no remote user should be able to upload files that can later be read or executed by your web daemon. Otherwise, a hacker could, for example, upload a CGI script to your FTP site and then use a browser to request the newly uploaded file from your web server, which could execute the script, totally bypassing security! Therefore, limit FTP uploads to directories that cannot be read by any user.

As you can see, deploying a firewall, even one as comprehensive and feature rich as VPN-1/FireWall-1 NG, is not all that is required to secure your enterprise. For those seeking to achieve defense in depth, a lot more work is required. However, help is at hand, Check Point provides a number of add-on products that extend the capabilities of the base product to address these areas. Check out UserAuthority and its WebAccess plug-ins on the Check Point website, www.checkpoint.com. For further information on SmartDefense see Chapter 22.

VPN-1/FireWall-1 NG Policy Editor

The Policy Editor has a number of features to make working with the Security Policy easier. These features include masking (or hiding) rules, viewing hidden rules, querying the Rule Base, disabling rules and negating cells. VPN-1/FireWall-1 NG applies rules in order from top to bottom; this helps the security engineer by adhering to the number one principle for good security practice: keep it simple. A simple, easily understood Security Policy is a key factor in the success of VPN-1/FireWall-1 NG.

The Security Policy can be easily installed and uninstalled. In this chapter, we'll examine the uninstallation processes; we will also show how careful structuring of the Security Policy can improve the performance of VPN-1/FireWall-1 NG.

MASKING RULES

When creating, deleting, or troubleshooting rules, it is useful to focus on the part of the Rule Base you are making changes to. This can be done more effectively if you limit the view of the Rule Base to just the parts you need to work with. Masking or hiding rules allows you to do this. The rules are still there, they are just hidden from view; they are still installed when the policy is installed.

To view hidden rules use the View Hidden in the Rules | Hide menu, as shown in Figure 9-1. A thick colored horizontal line indicates the presence of a hidden rule or rules.

To view a hidden rule, select View Hidden from the Rules | Hide menu or press CTRL+ALT+H. The hidden rule will be shown in a different color to distinguish it, as shown in Figure 9-2.

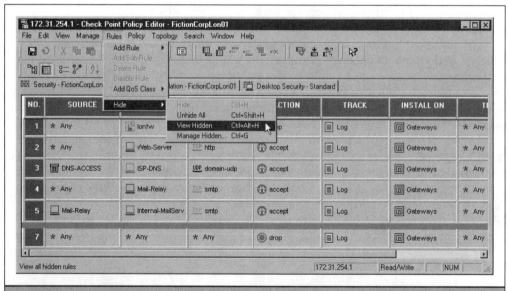

Figure 9-1.   Viewing hidden rules from the menu option

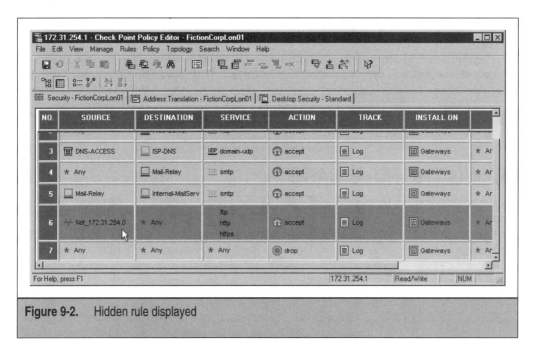

Figure 9-2.   Hidden rule displayed

To remove the hidden status of all rules completely, from the Rules | Hide menu, select Unhide All, as shown in Figure 9-3. This restores the rules to the normal view.

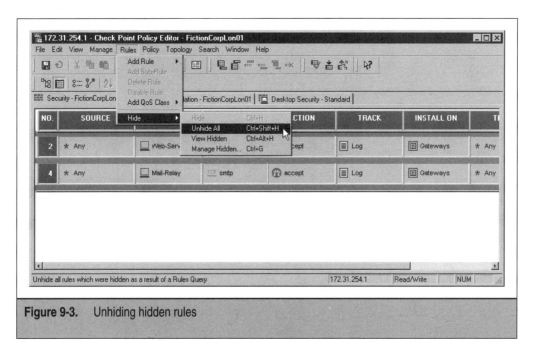

Figure 9-3.   Unhiding hidden rules

To hide a rule, you can right-click with the mouse on the number of the rule and choose Hide, or you can select the rule and press CTRL+H.

The Manage Hidden option on the Rules | Hide menu allows you to save and retrieve sets of hidden rules, as shown in Figure 9-4. This feature defines sets of hidden rules that can be recalled each time you need them within the Policy Editor. To save a set of hidden rules, first hide each of the rules you want hidden. Next, select Rules | Hide | Manage Hidden from the menu or press CTRL+G.

QUERYING THE RULE BASE

Rules can also hidden by querying the Rule Base. From the main menu, select Search | Query Rules. The Rule Base Query Editor is displayed, as shown in Figure 9-5.

Queries can be built to hide rules that are outside the scope of the query. To create a new query, click the New button. The Rule Base Query Editor is displayed, as shown in Figure 9-6. Type the name of the query and click New to add a new clause for the named query.

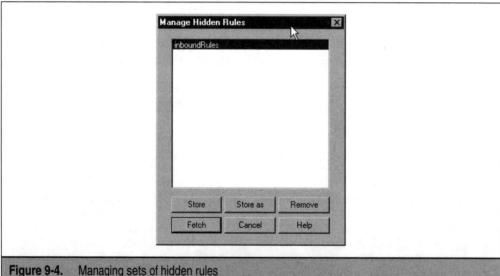

Figure 9-4.   Managing sets of hidden rules

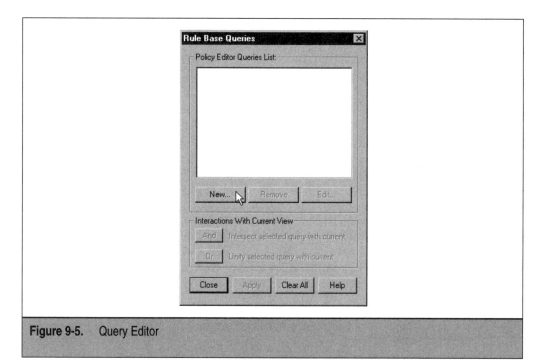

Figure 9-5.   Query Editor

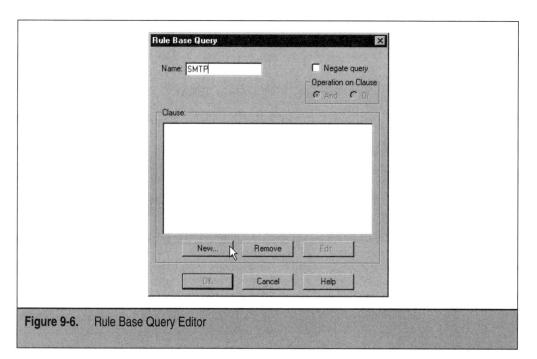

Figure 9-6.   Rule Base Query Editor

The Rule Base Query Clause window, shown in Figure 9-7, allows you to add a clause for the query. In this case, the Fiction Corporation security engineer wants to examine all rules regarding SMTP access. From the Column pull-down menu, select Services. Next, from the Not in List list box, select SMTP and click Add. Select the Explicit check box to limit the criteria to just those objects that are specified rather than those included in other composite objects such as groups or networks.

Click OK to close the clause window and click OK again to close the Rule Base Query window. Click Apply in the Rule Base Queries window to apply the query, as shown in Figure 9-8.

The effect of this query is to hide all rules that do not have SMTP explicitly defined as an object in the services column. The results on the Fiction Corporation Rule Base for London can be seen in Figure 9-9.

The Query Editor is a useful tool for working with large Rule Bases. As shown in Figure 9-7, there are several options to define a query. In the Query Editor, the column selection can be any or all columns and multiple clauses can be defined and combined using AND or OR. Compare this to the Policy Editor window, in which only one column can be used per Rule Base Query Clause. This gives it a high degree of flexibility and makes it useful for troubleshooting. Also note that each query clause can be negated by

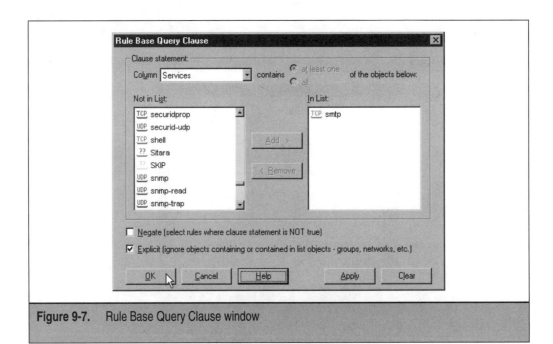

Figure 9-7.   Rule Base Query Clause window

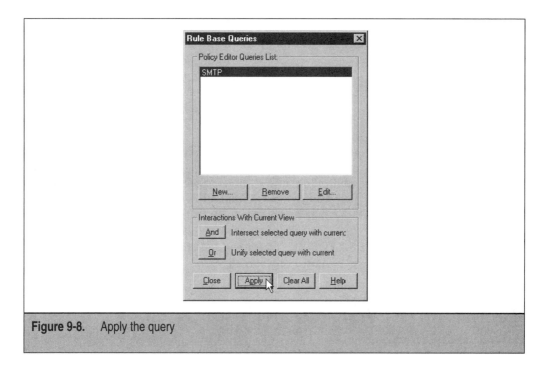

Figure 9-8.   Apply the query

checking the Negate check box. Negating a query with more than one clause combined with an AND is the same, for instance, as saying:

```
NOT (service=SMTP) AND (src=internal_mailserver or Mail-Relay)
```

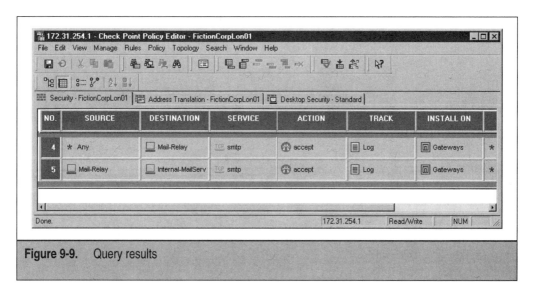

Figure 9-9.   Query results

This would have the effect of hiding all those rules that are a match for both criteria and nothing else. A negated OR, on the other hand, would match a rule that matched one or more of the clauses.

For those firewall administrators accustomed to querying databases, the Query Editor will seem totally natural; for the rest of us, it is worth practicing to become familiar with its capabilities.

NAMING SECTIONS

Feature Pack 3 (FP3) adds the ability to name sections in the Rule Base, as shown in Figure 9-10. This is another neat usability feature that allows you add a section name then fold away all the rules under that section name by collapsing the section with the minus button.

To add a section title, right-click the rule number and choose Add Section Above or Below; then enter the title in the entry box and click OK.

TRACKING AND REVISION CONTROL

FP3 enhances the management of policies further by adding revision control to the Smart Dashboard. From the File menu, select the Database Revision Control option. A dialog opens that allows you to create, restore, and remove database revisions, as shown in Figure 9-11.

Use the Create button to create a back up of the existing database.

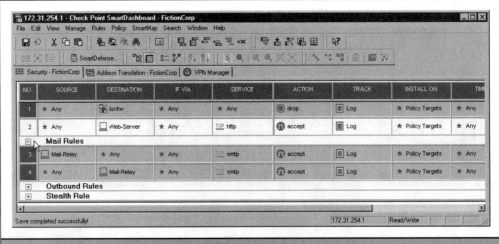

Figure 9-10.   Named sections

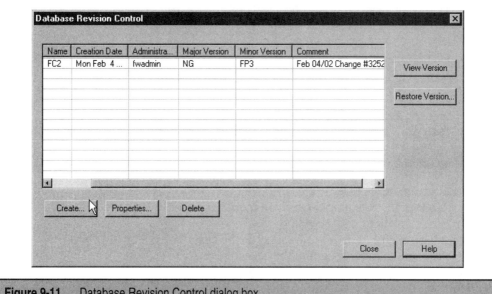

Figure 9-11. Database Revision Control dialog box

NOTE *All* policies are backed up in the policy package. It is the database itself that is stored, *not* the individual Policy you are currently working with.

If you have multiple enforcement points and are in the habit of saving a distinct policy for each and using the Install On field in the Rule Base to specify which gateway a particular policy relates to, then *all* the policies for *all* the gateways managed by this management server will be contained in the saved revision.

This is a very practical feature but should only be used for major changes. Backing out of individual Rule Base changes is easy as long as you remember to use the Comments field in the rules as you add rules. We often use this simply to add the change number to a new or modified rule because this gives us an instant reference back to our change control system.

NOTE Change control systems allow the management of system changes. Change numbers attach to particular change requests as they're placed on the system and approved for action. If you are a firewall administrator, change control is probably part of your daily life; if it's not, it probably should be.

You can restore the complete database either with the current installed user database or with the previous version contained in the revision. If you choose to restore a revision with the current user database, conflicts can arise. For instance, if you add a user to a new object and the object did not previously exist, an error will be shown regarding the conflict during restoration.

DISABLING RULES AND NEGATING OBJECTS

The ability to disable a rule and negate an object provides two powerful features that enhance the ability to troubleshoot and maintain a structured and efficient Security Policy.

Disabling Rules

To disable a rule, right-click the rule number and choose Disable Rule. A large red cross is placed in the rule number, as shown in Figure 9-12. The rule is only disabled after the Security Policy is installed.

This is very useful for troubleshooting the Security Policy; it provides a way of temporarily removing a rule so that the consequences can be observed. The rule could then be reinstated (enabled) again or changed as necessary. To enable a disabled rule, right-click the number of the rule. A check mark appears against the Disable Rule option, as shown in Figure 9-13. To deselect the rule, select Disable Rule again. Don't forget to reinstall the Security Policy after re-enabling rules.

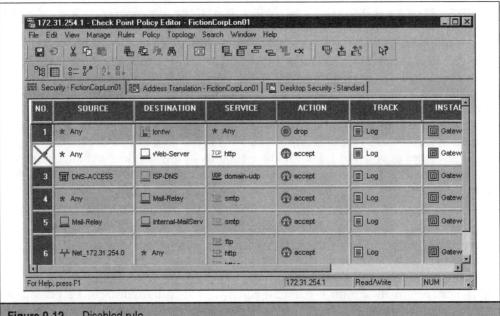

Figure 9-12. Disabled rule

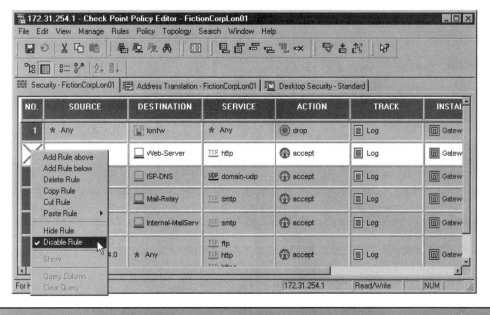

Figure 9-13. Enabling a disabled rule

Negating Objects

The ability to negate objects is an extremely powerful feature of VPN-1/FireWall-1 NG Security Policy Editor. Using a negated object can often save using many other rules to achieve the same result in the Security Policy. This improves the efficiency of the Security Policy and the performance of the firewall.

A negated object provides the logical NOT to any given object and essentially turns the rule on its head.

Negating an object is the opposite of specifying a specific source, destination, or service, and allows exceptions to rules lower down in the Security Policy. Care should be taken, however, as more specific rules should be placed higher up in the Security Policy than the more general rules below. To negate an object, right-click the object and select Negate, as shown in Figure 9-14.

Fiction Corporation has a Hot Desk area for visiting business partners to allow them to connect to their own systems, such as web-based e-mail and other services. However, Fiction Corporation would rather not allow these visitors the same access to the web server on their DMZ that the rest of their employees have. Figure 9-15 shows a rule inserted in the Rule Base that prevents visitor access to the Fiction Corporation DMZ while still allowing Internet access.

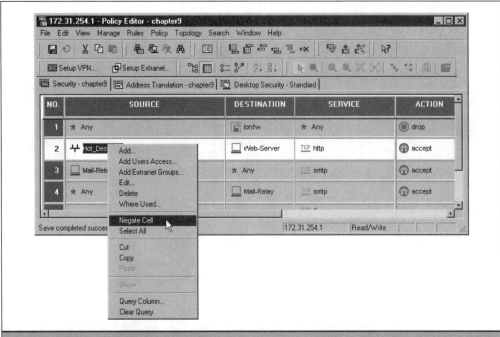

Figure 9-14.   Negating an object in the Rule Base

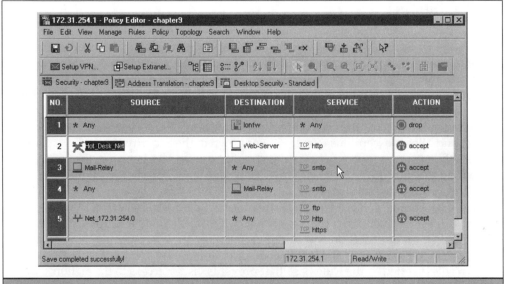

Figure 9-15.   Example of using the Negate object feature

UNINSTALLING THE SECURITY POLICY

Uninstalling a Security Policy removes it from the enforcement point. Once a Security Policy is uninstalled, the gateway acts as though no firewall were installed. However, VPN-1/FireWall-1 NG prevents the gateway from *forwarding*, or routing traffic, without a policy in place so that the network is not open to attack.

To uninstall the policy, from the Policy menu, select Uninstall or click the Uninstall Policy button. Deselect any enforcement points by clicking in the check boxes against the enforcement point names that you do not wish to uninstall the policy from and click OK, as shown in Figure 9-16.

When the Security Policy has been uninstalled, close the Uninstall Policy information screen by clicking Close, as shown in Figure 9-17.

IMPROVING PERFORMANCE WITH THE SECURITY POLICY

As already stated, VPN-1/FireWall-1 NG evaluates rules from top to bottom. This makes Rule Base order an important factor in the performance of the firewall. The most heavily

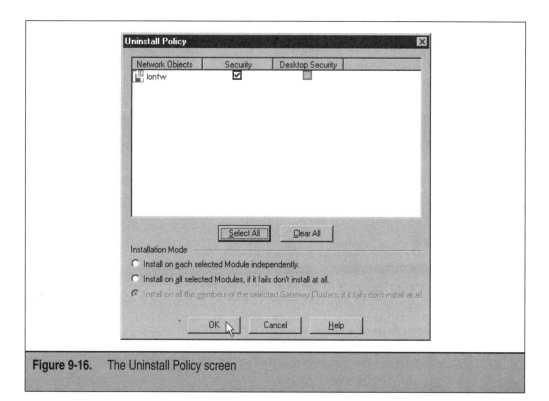

Figure 9-16. The Uninstall Policy screen

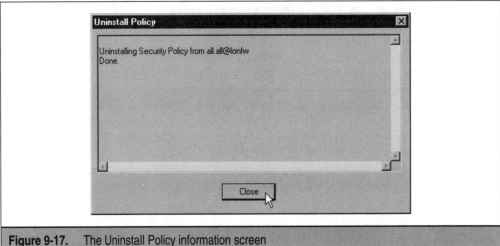

Figure 9-17.   The Uninstall Policy information screen

used rules should be placed as high up in the Rule Base order as is possible, taking into account the necessary order of rules such as the Stealth Rule and the User Authentication Rule. The latter must precede the Stealth Rule; otherwise, the Stealth Rule would prevent the User Authentication Rule from accessing the firewall, which it must do in order to function. In Chapter 8, you saw the rule allowing inbound access for HTTP to the web server was placed higher in the order than the mail relays SMTP rule and other rules, but lower than the Stealth Rule. Also, rules that are more generic should be kept as simple as possible so that the firewall can process the packets quickly.

Using the Accounting option in the Track section of each rule degrades system performance considerably—13 percent for Solaris and 10 percent for Windows. Only use the Accounting option for short periods of time and on low volume traffic rules.

Performance can be improved by limiting rules to those that are required. For instance, when creating outbound access rules, such as the internal network to any HTTP/HTTPS and FTP in the Fiction Corporation Rule Base, don't add services for Real Audio unless it is needed. Only add services that are actually going to be processed by the rule in question and not services that are hardly ever going to be used. Put those lower down in the rule base, in their own rules.

A WORD ABOUT VISUAL POLICY EDITOR

Check Point provides a Security Policy visualization tool for VPN-1/FireWall-1 NG Management Console platforms: Visual Policy Editor. This tool provides a detailed, graphical map of an organization's security deployment. In addition to providing better controls and improved security, Visual Policy Editor is much easier to use than the Policy Editor, because it draws a comprehensive picture of an organization's security deployment including firewalls, VPNs, servers, networks, routers, and the relationships between those objects. Such features enable security managers to validate the integrity of their Security Policy prior to deployment.

As shown in Figure 9-18, the Visual Policy Editor, unlike some mapping tools, does not need to search through the network to discover these objects. Instead, it is able to draw the map by using information already captured as part of the Security Policy definition process. This provides security managers with visual feedback that shows their environment as they have defined it.

Furthermore, the tool allows maps to be drawn that are not simply a static picture but enables security managers to search for objects and edit them in the map. For example, the IT security group of Fiction Corporation could search for a particular subnet. Visual Policy Editor would highlight the subnet in the diagram, drawing a box around it, which would make it easy to verify that the subnet appears in the right location and includes the right network nodes. The tool also allows security professionals to select objects in the diagram and edit them, allowing changes to be made as soon as issues are identified.

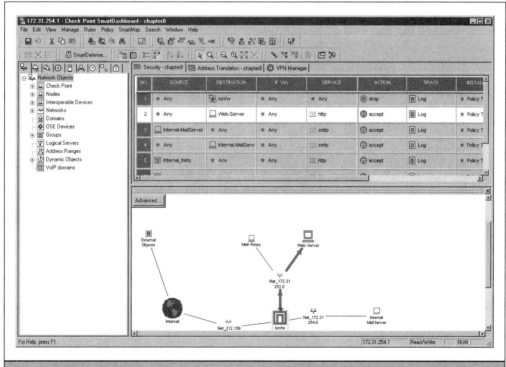

Figure 9-18.   Visual Policy Editor provides security managers with visual feedback that shows their environment as they have defined it.

Rule Settings Simulator

One of the most powerful features of the Visual Policy Editor is its ability to illustrate the effect of security rules. Rules are diagrammed on the Visual Policy Editor's map, with the source of a rule (for example, a subnet) coded in one color, the Destination (for example, a server) coded in another color, and the Action (for example, encrypt) color-coded in yet another. Finally, arrows indicate the direction of traffic flow, making it easy to see what the rule is securing. By seeing the effect of security rules on their deployment, security managers are able to ensure that the correct Security Policy is in place.

CHECKLIST: KEY POINTS IN WORKING WITH THE SECURITY POLICY

The following is a checklist for the key points in working with the Security Policy:

- ☐ Assess Fiction Corporation's security.
- ☐ List the masking rules.
- ☐ List the features in the Policy Editor.
- ☐ Use the Policy Editor to maintain a clear view of the rules you are working with, such as masking rules and querying the Rule Base.
- ☐ Show how the Disable Rule option can be used for troubleshooting the Rule Base.
- ☐ Show how negating objects assists in providing granular control over the Security Policy.
- ☐ Uninstall the Security Policy.
- ☐ Identify the effects (on the corporation) of uninstalling the Security Policy.
- ☐ List the performance considerations for the Rule Base.
- ☐ Maintain VPN-1/FireWall-1 NG's high performance through the careful consideration of rules.

CHAPTER 10

Log Viewer and System Status Viewer

You can record events, including acceptance and rejection of packets, in a log file. The Log Viewer (called SmartView Tracker in Feature Pack 3) is used to view the data in the log. Each event is logged according to the Rule Base Track field, or the policy or object properties. The Management Server is responsible for sending the log data to the Log Viewer for display. The System Status Viewer (known as SmartView Status in Feature Pack 3) provides real-time alerting and a management view of installed modules along with their status; this provides a health monitor and alerting function for VPN-1/FireWall-1 NG. The health monitoring capabilities include module communication and traffic flow statistics.

The VPN-1/FireWall-1 NG Log Viewer filters and searches the log in a variety of different ways so that you can quickly and efficiently extract the information you need.

You can issue an alert when VPN-1/FireWall-1 NG rejects or accepts a packet. The alert can take several forms. You can display a pop-up message on the System Status Viewer, send a mail message to some predetermined address, or issue an SNMP trap. In the Control Properties/Logging and Alerting window, you can specify any OS command to be executed. All alerts are also logged.

This chapter will guide you through the Log Viewer and System Status Viewer features.

LOG VIEWER

In addition to showing each event caused by the Rule Base Track field and properties, the Log Viewer also shows system events such as the installation or uninstallation of the Security Policy. The Track field column allows actions to be specified such as Alert or Log. These are then acted upon if that specific rule is invoked.

Furthermore, VPN-1/FireWall-1 NG's graphical Log Viewer provides real-time visual tracking, monitoring, and accounting information for all connections logged by VPN-1/FireWall-1 NG Enforcement Points. The Log Viewer Audit Log records administrator actions such as changes to object definitions or rules. This can dramatically reduce the time needed to troubleshoot configuration errors. Administrators can perform searches on or filter log records to quickly locate and track events of interest. In the case of an attack or otherwise suspicious network activity, administrators can use the Log Viewer to temporarily or permanently terminate connections from specific IP addresses.

The optional Reporting Module enables administrators to transform the detailed VPN-1/FireWall-1 NG logs into actionable management reports, presenting information in simple, intuitive tables and graphs. Predefined and custom report templates can be applied to generate reports. The rest of this chapter takes you through the Log Viewer architecture and shows how to efficiently use the Log Viewer and System Status Viewer for troubleshooting and monitoring your firewalls.

Log Viewer Architecture

The kernel-side FWD (FireWall Daemon) on the Enforcement Point takes log fragments produced by the VPN-1/FireWall-1 kernel components into a single log record. This log record is stamped with a Log Unification Unique ID (LUUID).

The server-side FWD—the Management Server or the Log Server—puts the log entries in the database (fw.log). The log record of the event is then available to the Log Viewer. A single connection is represented by one entry in the Log Viewer. The unification engine's job is to update the log entry fields in the Log Viewer.

Launching the Log Viewer

To launch the Log Viewer, go to Start | Programs | Check Point Management Clients. Select the Log Viewer; the login screen appears as shown in Figure 10-1.

Alternatively, if any of the management clients are currently loaded, you can use the Window | Log Viewer menu selection to start the Log Viewer, in which case your user credentials are automatically passed through to the client and you don't need to log in again.

Viewing Log Data

The Log Viewer allows you to navigate through the log file and lets you control what information is displayed. Each column has a header that describes the data it displays. Different views contain different headers that can be manually turned on and off as desired. The predefined views for Firewall, General, VPN-1, Account, Floodgate, and so on, are available on the Toolbar menu. The kind of information displayed includes source address, destination address, and service. In addition, when running the Log Viewer to show live connections, the Active Connections View can be used to monitor ongoing connections.

Security Managers can use Log Viewer in Active Connection mode to view current active connections, in real-time, as they pass through the VPN-1/FireWall-1 NG Modules. These live connections are then stored and handled in the same way as ordinary log records but are kept in a special file that is continuously updated as connections start and end. Thus, all the standard Log Viewer features, such as selection and search engine, can monitor current network activity.

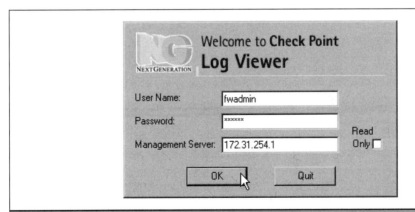

Figure 10-1.   Log Viewer login screen

Across the top of the Log Viewer, data fields or columns are displayed in the selected view. To see a column menu, right-click anywhere within the columns, as shown in Figure 10-2.

The column menu provides a number of functions:

- **Hide**   Hides the current column

- **Selection**   Provides selection criteria for the column and shows only those entries that match

- **Find**   Locates an entry in the log that matches the criteria for that column

- **Width**   Changes the width of the column

- **Show Details**   Shows any details of the selection

NOTE   Not all of the toolbar buttons have corresponding menu items. The toolbar buttons will display their function as you move the mouse pointer over them.

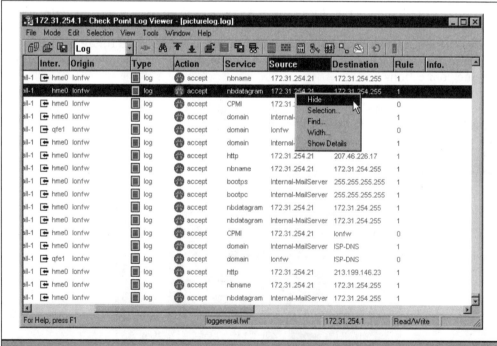

Figure 10-2.   Column Menu

Log Types

There are several different log types; each with its own predefined view using selection criteria. Each selects the level of detail appropriate to the product or service it represents. You can customize these and save them for future use.

- **General Predefined Selection**   Displays all log types
- **Firewall Predefined Selection**   Displays FireWall-1 details
- **VPN-1**   Displays VPN-1 details
- **Account Predefined Selection**   Displays accounting details (see the section "Accounting")
- **FloodGate-1 Predefined Selection**   Displays QoS/Floodgate-1 details
- **Virtual Link Monitoring Predefined Selection**   Displays end-to-end details
- **SecureClient Predefined Selection**   Displays SecureClient details

Accounting

VPN-1/FireWall-1 NG allows the firewall administrator to monitor accounting data on selected connections. For each connection handled by the rule, an Accounting Log entry is created, which includes the usual fields as well as the connection's duration, the number of bytes, and the number of packets transferred.

The Accounting Log records are generated when the monitored connection ends so they can be viewed in the Log Viewer. Care should be taken when choosing the Account option in the Track field because it can have a serious impact on the performance of the firewall. It is best to use this for limited periods of troubleshooting and examining data transfer times and bandwidth requirements. If you need to manage your bandwidth, check out FloodGate-1 on the Check Point website: Floodgate-1 introduces Quality of Service (QoS)–style bandwidth management to VPN-1/FireWall-1 NG.

Log Viewer Modes

The Log Viewer has three different modes available from the drop-down menu on the toolbar, as shown in Figure 10-3.

Each mode has a predefined selection view of the log data.

- **Log Mode**   The default shows all security related events.
- **Active Mode**   Shows currently active, open connections. The active connection window displays the following:
  - **Elapsed**   Duration of the connection
  - **Bytes**   The number of bytes transferred
  - **Start Date**   The date at which the connection began
  - **Conn. ID**   The connection ID

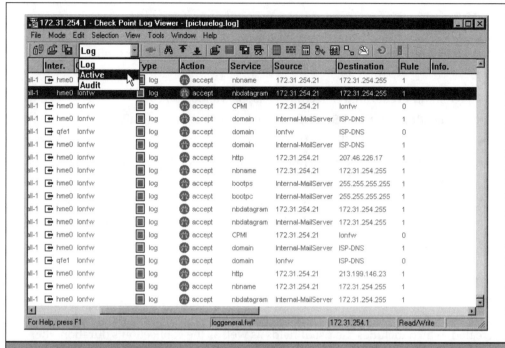

Figure 10-3.   Accessing the available Log Viewer modes

- **Audit Mode**   Displays only audit entries in the Log Viewer. This allows you to track changes made to Rule Base objects and general Policy Editor usage. The Audit window displays the following:
  - **Object Name**   The name of the object
  - **Object Type**   The object type, workstation, network, and so on
  - **Object Table**   The table in which the object is categorized
  - **UID**   The user ID of the object
  - **Administrator**   The administrator of the object
  - **Machine**   The host from which the administrator logged in
  - **Fields Changed**   Changes made to the field of the object
  - **Container Changed**   Changes made to the Rule Base
  - **Oper.**   Operations performed on the object

Navigating and Searching

There are a few ways to navigate through the Log Viewer. You can use the scrollbars to scroll; you can use the up- and down-arrows or the PAGE UP and PAGE DOWN keys, or you can use the Edit menu to select Find | Go to Top or Go to Bottom.

To find a specific record in the log file, either right-click the column you wish to search in or, from the Edit menu, select Find, as shown in Figure 10-4.

If you use Edit | Find, a dialog asks you which column you wish to search, as shown in Figure 10-5.

When you select the column, the appropriate screen is shown for input of the search string. For example, if you choose the Date column, the Find Date dialog box is shown. Enter the desired search criteria and click OK, as shown in Figure 10-6.

To search for a string in all columns, select the All Columns checkbox at the bottom of the Columns to Find screen, as shown in Figure 10-5. This option is only available if you access Find from the Edit menu.

After you enter the search pattern into the Find dialog box, select in which direction you want to search: Forward, Backward, or From the Top.

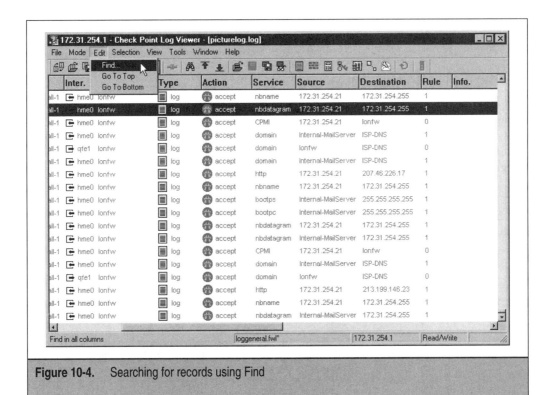

Figure 10-4. Searching for records using Find

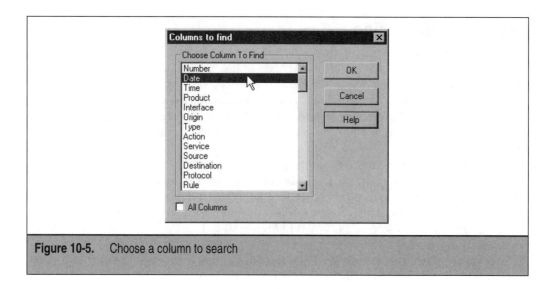

Figure 10-5. Choose a column to search

You can also go directly to the top or bottom of the Rule Base by selecting Edit | Go To Top or Go To Bottom. Both these options are also available directly from the toolbar by selecting the up or down arrow icons.

Specifying Selection Criteria

To specify a selection criteria, either right-click the column to which you want to apply a selection criteria and choose Selection from the pop-up menu, or choose the Selection | Customize option from the main menu. From the Column Options and Current Selection Criteria window, click the column you wish to apply selection criteria to; then click the Selection button at the bottom of the window, as shown in Figure 10-7.

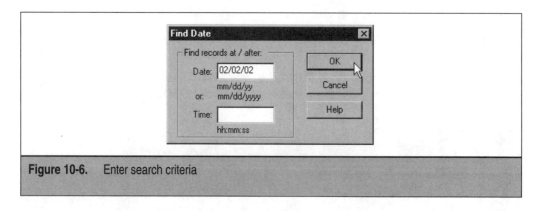

Figure 10-6. Enter search criteria

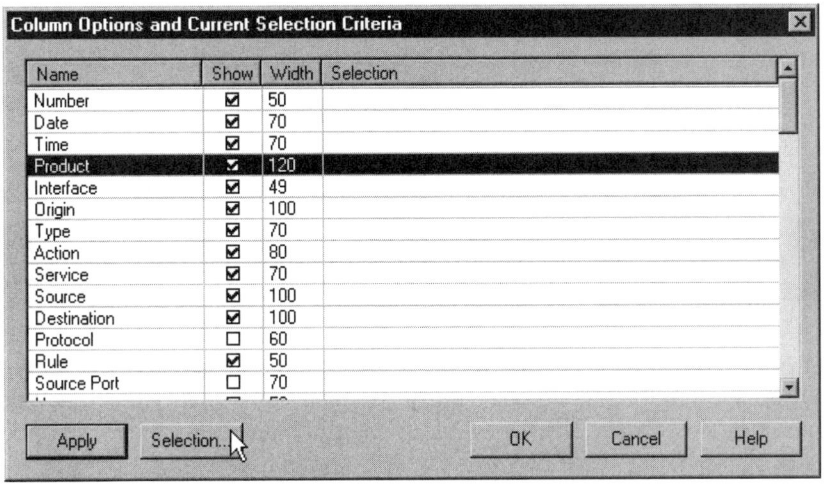

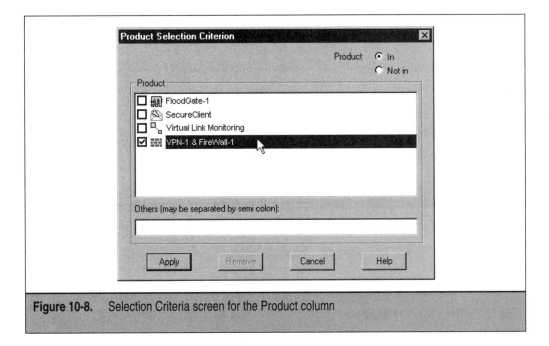

Figure 10-7. Column Options and Current Selection Criteria window

If you use the right-click method, the appropriate selection criteria entry dialog is loaded automatically. You can add as many selection criteria as you like. The selection criteria for the Product column is shown in Figure 10-8.

Figure 10-8. Selection Criteria screen for the Product column

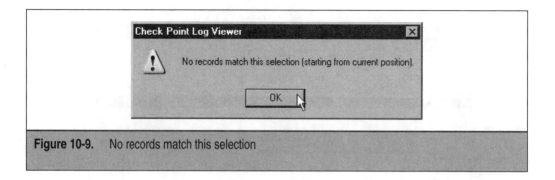

Figure 10-9.   No records match this selection

Once applied, only entries matching all the selection criteria will be displayed from the current position in the log; all other entries will be hidden. Any new log record that meets the criteria will also be displayed. If no records match the criteria, you will see the dialog box shown in Figure 10-9.

To make sure no previous records match above the current position, use the scroll bar to scroll back up the log.

Applying an active selection criterion is a valuable feature of the Log Viewer. It means you can focus on specific traffic as it comes to the firewall. This aids troubleshooting because so many new entries are constantly being created for the log that trying to examine them all visually as they scroll past is impossible.

Certain options affect viewing while using the selection criteria. On the Selection menu choose Options, as shown in Figure 10-10.

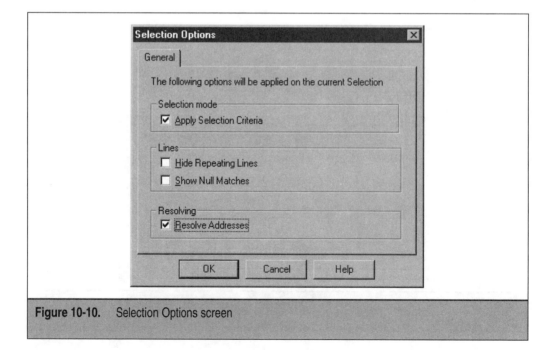

Figure 10-10.   Selection Options screen

The viewing options are as follows:

- **Apply Selection Criteria**   Applies any selection criteria already defined
- **Hide Repeating Lines**   Does not show any lines of data that differ only by date and time
- **Show Null Matches**   Displays null matches that are neither included or excluded from the current selection criteria
- **Resolve Addresses**   Shows host and domain names resolved from DNS or the hosts file

Note that resolving addresses can be detrimental to the speed and performance of the Log Viewer.

Log File Management

The File menu contains the log management functions:

- **New**   Saves and writes the current log file to disk with the current date and time in the filename and opens a new log file. Only one log file can be open at a time.
- **Open**   Opens another log file from the same management or log server.
- **Purge**   Deletes *all* entries in the current log file.
- **Save**   The current selection criteria is applied and only those entries that match the criteria are saved. All entries are saved if no criteria is applied.
- **Print**   Only the entries that match the current selection criteria are printed; if no selection criteria is applied, all entries will be printed.
- **Export**   The current log entries are saved to a text file.
- **Switch**   Allows the log file to be switched. A new log is started and the old log is renamed with the current date and time.

The Export option available from the File menu allows you to export the log data to a text file if required. The selection criteria applied at the time is also used when the log entries are exported. This is very useful because it allows a subset of entries from the log to be used in reports and for troubleshooting; you don't have to export the entire log and process the information before you find the entries you are interested in.

REDUCING THE NOISE IN LOGS

It is often desirable to reduce the amount of data logged by VPN-1/FireWall-1 NG by adding rules to the Rule Base that explicitly exclude data from being logged. These types of rules are referred to as noise rules; they prevent traffic that has no relevance and would otherwise fill up the logs with useless information from being logged.

Why Is It Called a Noise Rule?

Probably because of "signal to noise ratio", a term used to describe the amount of interference compared to the strength of a signal in electrical engineering; signal being useful and noise a distraction.

Table 10-1 shows an example of a noise rule. In this example, the Fiction Corporation firewall administrator has decided that he would like to remove all NetBios traffic and broadcasts from the Log file. Noise rules are useful for protocols that create a lot of broadcast packets. NetBios packets are particularly prolific and should only occur on the internal network. However, it should be noted that such a rule would prevent NetBios from traversing the firewall *completely*. If you require some NetBios connections to be allowed, you can add more specific rules above the noise rule. Noise rules work well to reduce the amount of traffic that is included in the logs but care must be taken with them or your Security Policy may not operate as you intended. Generally you need to place noise rules as high as possible in the Rule Base so they are handled quickly.

The NBT group, as shown in the Service field in Table 10-1, is a predefined group that contains the three NetBios protocols used in Microsoft networks. It may be desirable to specify Any in the source field if you do not wish to log these protocols no matter where they originate. You can add as many services as you like to the noise rule to reduce the amount of logged traffic.

Blocking Connections

The ability to terminate an active connection is provided in two different ways:

- Block Intruder
- Block Request

To use the Block Intruder function to block an active connection that has been identified as suspicious, select the log entry to block while in the active mode, then choose Block Intruder from the Tools menu or use the Block Intruder icon on the toolbar. The Block Intruder dialog box has several options, as shown in Figure 10-11:

- **Block Only This Connection** The selected connection is blocked and any further attempts to establish a connection between the same source to the same destination address and port will be blocked.

Source	Destination	Service	Action	Track
Internal_Nets	Any	NBT	Drop	-None

Table 10-1. Noise Rule

- **Block Access from This Source**   The selected connection is blocked and all further attempts to establish a connection from this specific source address will be denied.

- **Block Access to This Destination**   The selected connection is terminated and all further attempts to establish a connection to the same destination address will be denied.

- **Blocking Timeout**   Select Indefinite to block all further access or select For *xx* Minutes to block the connection for a given number of minutes, after which attempted connections will succeed.

- **Force This Blocking**   Specify a single Enforcement Point (such as Only on lonfw) at which to force blocking, or specify On Any VPN-1 & FireWall-1 to force blocking on all gateways or hosts defined on the Log Server.

To use the Block Request feature, do not select an entry in the active mode of the Log Viewer. Instead, select Tools | Block Intruder. The Blocking Request by Connection ID dialog box requests the Connection ID, as shown in Figure 10-12. Enter the Connection ID of the required connection and click OK. The connection will remain blocked until you choose Tools | Clear Blocking.

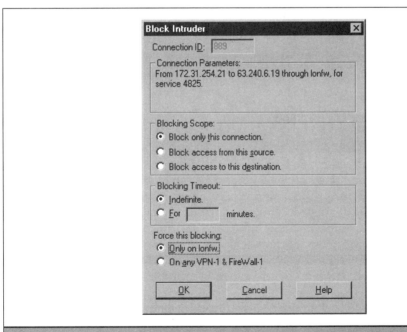

Figure 10-11.   Block Intruder dialog box

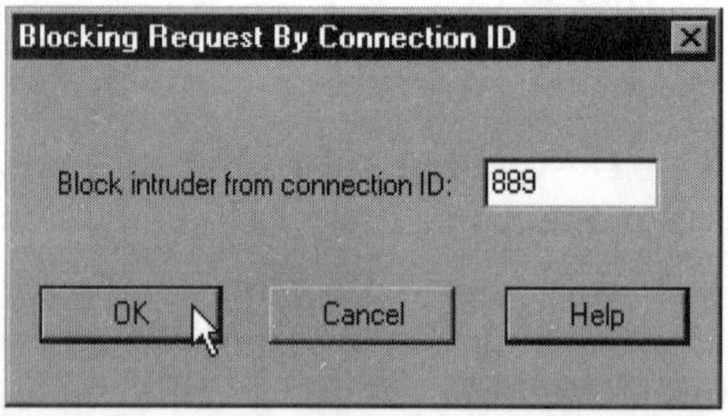

Figure 10-12. Blocking Request by Connection ID dialog box

ACTIVITY LOGGED AS RULE 0

IP spoofing is a technique in which an intruder attempts to gain unauthorized access by altering a packet's IP address to make it appear as though the packet originated in a part of the network with higher access privileges. For example, a packet originating on the Internet may be disguised as a local packet. VPN-1/FireWall-1 NG has integrated protection and logging against this type of attack. This kind of activity is logged under Rule 0, as is SYNDefender. In Feature Pack 3 (FP3), SmartDefense also logs as Rule 0 and can integrate the SYNDefender function. Items logged as Rule 0 are done so as they are part of a configuration in the global or object properties (including SmartDefense) and are applied to packets before *all* the rules in the Rule Base, as created by the administrator.

SMARTVIEW TRACKER (FP3)

Feature Pack 3 (FP3) changes the look and feel of the Log Viewer as well as its name. The Query menu has replaced the Selection menu, and the predefined views are shown in a separate pane, the Query Tree, on the left side. Custom queries can also be accessed from the Query Tree. In Figure 10-13, you can see the new SmartView Tracker with the Query Properties pane displayed. The Query Property pane allows you to make selection criteria (or filters, as they are now known) in the same way selecting Customize from the Selection menu did. You can right-click any of the fields and choose Edit Filter to add or modify selection criteria.

Once you have created a new query you can save it, and it can be recalled from the custom log queries in the Query Tree.

Feature Packs up to and including FP3 also introduce a number of new predefined views to SmartView Tracker.

- **SmartDefense** Displays attacks detected
- **UA WebAccess** Displays access to web servers via WebAccess plug-ins

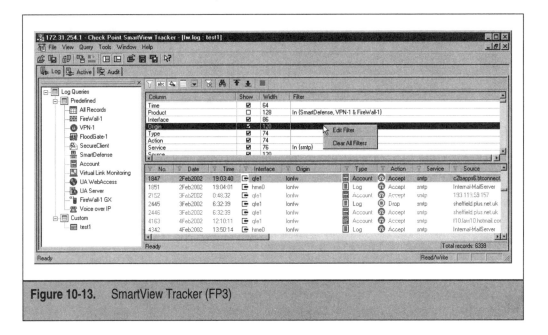

Figure 10-13.   SmartView Tracker (FP3)

- **UA Server**   Display user authority server logs
- **FireWall-1 GX**   Displays wireless 2.5G and 3G network security information
- **Voice over IP**   Displays voice over IP information

Log File Maintenance

Feature Pack 3 also extends the automated log file maintenance. Figure 10-14 shows the options for manipulating the log file, which have been extended.

You can choose to switch the log at a specific time or when the file reaches a certain size. Disk Space Management options allow you to choose whether you measure disk space in megabytes or as a percentage. You can set a minimum free disk space amount that will cause old log files to be deleted until the minimum disk space setting is restored. You can also specify not to delete log files from the last *n* days, although setting this can cause disk space not to be recovered under the Required Free Disk Space setting. The Advanced button allows you to specify a script to run before deleting log files. You can also set a minimum free disk space requirement and specify an alert if this minimum is reached. Finally, you can specify that logging should be stopped if free disk space falls below a given amount. If this option is set, you can optionally make the firewall reject all connections once this occurs. This option is a bit extreme, but from a security perspective it would be a valid thing to do if you can no longer log activity on a firewall; it would certainly get the attention of the administrator because of the number of support calls that they would be likely to receive!

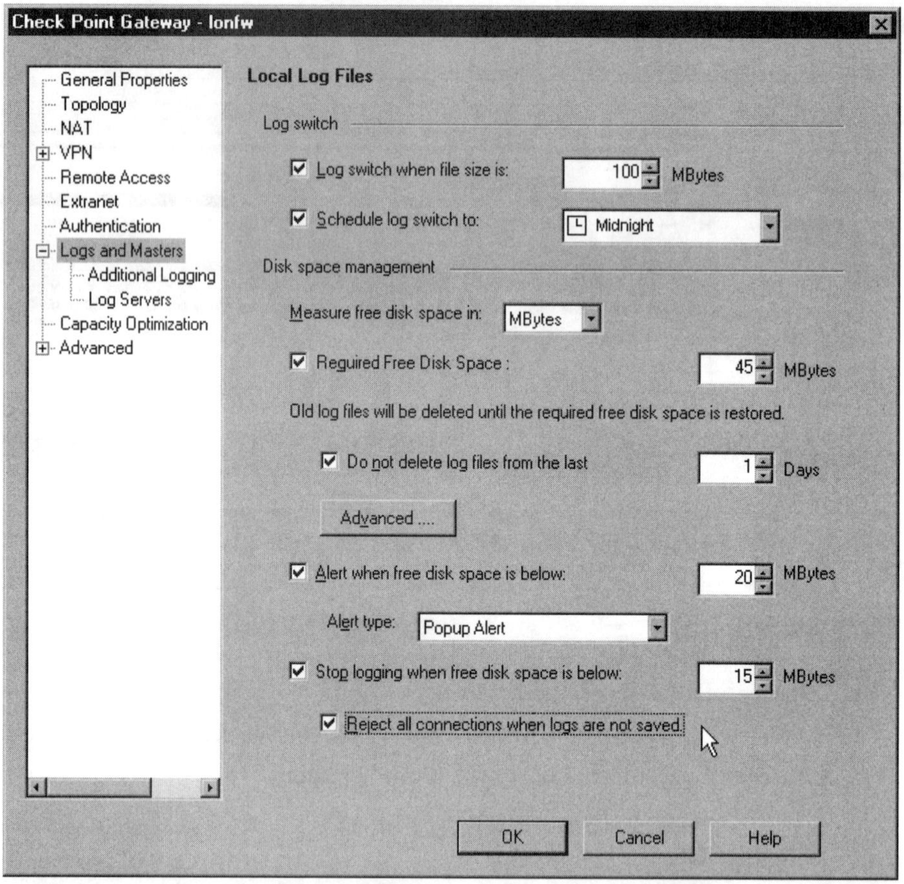

Figure 10-14.   Logs and masters

Despite its extremity, the option to stop logging shows that Check Point has adhered to one of the fundamentals of good security practice: *fail safe*. This simply means that if something does go wrong the product should not fail open, leaving the company vulnerable to a breach even if it's due to lack of logging information. Although causing the firewall to refuse connections simply because the disk space fills up might seem reactionary, remember that the data in the logs is as important to provisioning security as the Rule Base itself; its value should not be underestimated when it comes to securing your network.

SYSTEM STATUS VIEWER

The System Status Viewer displays communications and traffic flow statistics and a snapshot of all Check Point products. It also enables real-time monitoring and alerting. In addition, it presents a snapshot of all third-party products using OPSEC-partner modules.

Launching the System Status Viewer

To launch the System Status Viewer, choose Start | Programs | Check Point Management Clients | System Status Viewer or, from another Check Point management client, select Window | System Status Viewer. As with the other management clients, you only need to log in if you have not done so already to one of the other management clients.

Working with the System Status Viewer

The System Status Viewer contains several sections:

- **Modules View**   Shows all modules and their status in a hierarchical tree with the management servers shown above the modules that they manage.
- **Details View**   Shows the details of the selected module.
- **Critical Notifications**   Displays all problematic modules.

Figure 10-15 shows the System Status Viewer window.

Modules View

The Modules View displays the module hierarchy and status information in the following four columns:

- **Modules**   Displays the modules in a hierarchical structure
- **IP Address**   Shows the IP address of the module
- **Status**   Shows the status of the module
- **Updated**   Shows when the status was last updated

You can change the size of the columns by dragging the column's right border in the header. Sort order can be changed by clicking each heading.

Modules Status

There are two types of status: Workstation Status and Application Status. Workstation Status shows the available workstations running VPN-1/FireWall-1 NG components; Application Status shows the modules installed on those workstations.

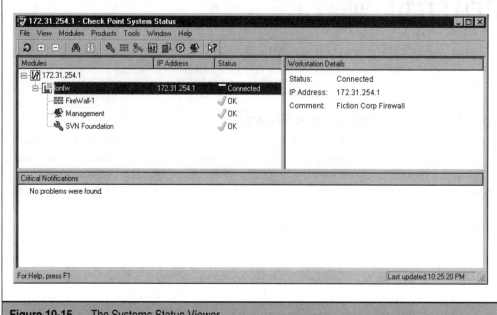

Figure 10-15. The Systems Status Viewer

Workstation Status displays the following messages:

- **Waiting**   From starting system status to the first status message received (30 seconds max).

- **Connected**   The workstation has been reached.

- **Disconnected**   The workstation cannot be reached.

- **Untrusted**   Secure internal communication failed. The workstation could be contacted but the management server is not the master of the module installed on the workstation.

Applications Status displays the following messages:

- **Waiting**   From starting system status to the first status message received (30 seconds max).

- **No Answer**   The machine cannot be reached, or there is no Check Point agent installed on it.

- **Untrusted**   Secure internal communication failed. The workstation could be contacted but the management server is not the master of the module installed on the workstation.

- **No Module**   There is no module installed on this machine, or the module is installed but corrupted.

- **Problem**   A module is installed and responding to status checks, but its status is problematic.

- **OK**   A module is installed on this object and is responding to requests from the management server.

Product Details Windows

Information on a per-product basis is available directly from the toolbar for easier viewing. Choose the product view by moving the mouse over the toolbar and clicking the required product view. The Product views available are SVN, FireWall-1, VPN-1, FloodGate-1, HA Details, OPSEC, Management, UA WebAccess, Policy Server, and Log Server.

Critical Notifications

The System Status Viewer uses the Critical Notifications window to help administrators locate modules with problems. Double-click any module in the critical Notifications Window to display further details.

SMARTVIEW STATUS

Feature Pack 3 (FP3) introduces the new SmartView Status monitor, as shown in Figure 10-16. With this monitor, you can now add predefined alerts for certain conditions that may affect the firewall.

These alerts can be set as Same as Global, Custom, or None on a per workstation basis. The default is for all workstations to be set as Same as Global. You can set the Global System Alert Definition from the System Alert | Global Menu.

The Global System Alert definition dialog is shown in Figure 10-17.

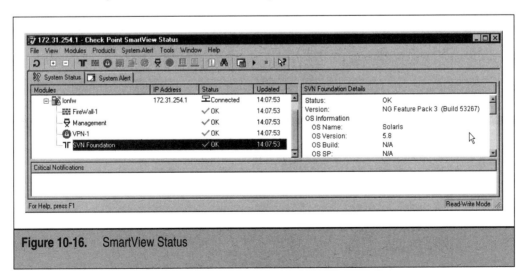

Figure 10-16.   SmartView Status

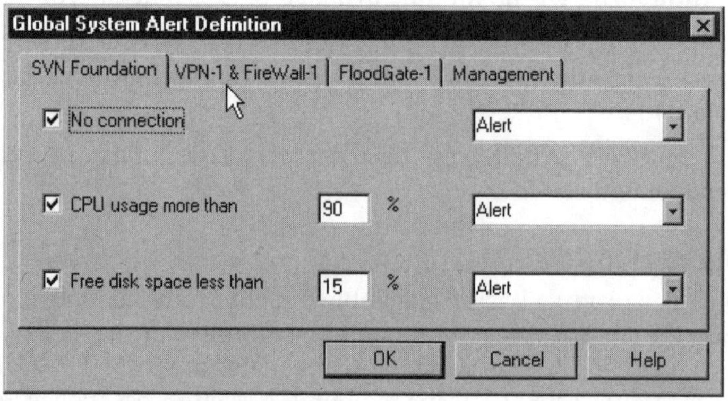

Figure 10-17. Global System Alert Definition dialog

You can define alerts for the SVN Foundation, VPN-1/FireWall-1 NG, FloodGate-1, and Management. As you can see in Figure 10-16, the options for SVN Foundation are as follows:

- No Connection
- CPU Usage More Than x%
- Free Disk Space Less Than x%

For each of these, you can set the desired track option from the drop-down list and optionally enter a percentage to alert where required. The VPN-1/FireWall-1 NG and FloodGate-1 alert definitions are as follows:

- No Policy Installed
- Policy Name Has Been Changed
- Policy Has Been Installed

The Management tab has just one option: to alert if synchronization failed.

In SmartView Tracker, you also have the ability to turn off receiving alerts. This is useful if too many alerts are being generated due to some condition and you need to disable the pop-ups while you investigate the problem. This can be done from the System Alert | Start/Stop menu options. Don't forget to turn them back on when you're done investigating the problem!

INTEGRATION WITH ENTERPRISE NETWORK MANAGEMENT

VPN-1/FireWall-1 NG provides integration of multiple alert options, including e-mail notification and SNMP traps for integration with SNMP-based network management systems such as HP OpenView, or IBM's NetView 6000. A user-defined alerting mechanism is also available to integrate with paging, trouble-ticketing, and help desk systems that provide a great deal of flexibility in how security alerts are integrated into current management systems.

CHECKLIST: KEY POINTS IN LOG VIEWER AND SYSTEM STATUS VIEWER

The following is a checklist for the key points in Log Viewer and System Status Viewer:

- [ ] Use the VPN-1/FireWall-1 NG Log Viewer to examine the log and to filter and search the log in a variety of ways.
- [ ] List the steps that are required to launch the Log Viewer.
- [ ] Use Log Viewer and System Status Viewer to monitor traffic and the status of the firewall.
- [ ] Identify the numerous searching and selection features that make Log Viewer a very powerful tool for analyzing all aspects of the firewall security policy in operation.
- [ ] Show how Security Manager can use Log Viewer in an active connection mode to view current active connections in real-time as they pass through the VPN-1/FireWall-1 NG Modules.
- [ ] List the column menu functions.
- [ ] List the seven different log types.
- [ ] List the three different Log Viewer modes.
- [ ] Identify the ways to navigate and search through the use of the Log Viewer.
- [ ] List the steps that are required to display the selection criteria or selected entries.
- [ ] List the log management functions contained in the File menu.
- [ ] Show how the System Status Viewer receives alerts and other critical monitoring information regarding VPN-1/FireWall-1 NG and its various modules.

☐ List the steps that are required to launch the System Status Viewer.

☐ Define IP spoofing.

☐ Use VPN-1/FireWall-1 NG to provide integration of multiple alert options, including e-mail notification and SNMP traps for integration with SNMP-based network management systems such as HP OpenView, or IBM's NetView 6000.

CHAPTER 11

Tracking and Alerts

VPN-1/FireWall-1 NG provides an extremely flexible and extensible tracking and alerting system that allows firewall administrators to integrate it into existing network monitoring and management platforms. This level of extensibility is typically unavailable from most firewall vendors.

Firewall administrators can create custom alert handlers. This provides far greater control over alerting—firewall administrators can choose as much or little detail as they like. Some intelligence can be built in to alert handlers by using different priorities and associated actions. For example, you may want to send a message to an SNMP (Simple Network Management Protocol) if spoofing is detected on an external interface. However, if spoofing is detected on an internal interface, you may prefer to write the information to a file.

TRACKING

Tracking takes place when an action is placed in the track column of a rule. When a packet is received, the rule that processed the packet will take the action defined in the track column. The possible actions are none, log, account, alert, SNMP trap, mail, or user-defined (1-3). As well as defining a track option in the Rule Base, certain objects such as resource objects also define a track option. For example, Figure 11-1 shows the process of creating an SMTP mail definition. The parameters are defined, and Alert is selected under Exception Tracking. Some tracking options will create just a log entry, viewable in the Log Viewer, while other tracking options will generate a log entry and trigger an executable. The executable can be used to send an SNMP trap, an e-mail, or any other function. This provides a method for the administrators to extend the capabilities of VPN-1/FireWall-1 NG alerting into anything they like. It is simply a matter of developing the code (C, C++, Perl, Unix shell scripts) to handle the function that you want it to perform.

Alert Commands

VPN-1/FireWall-1 NG logs show a complete history of traffic that has passed through the firewall (as long as you have not chosen to exclude it from the logs by choosing None as the tracking option) whereas alerts are provided for real-time messaging. Administrators may need to direct alerts to NOC/SOC (Network Operations Center/Security Operations Center) staff at the time the alerts occur so that some action can be taken according to agreed procedures. Pop-up, mail, and SNMP alerts can be defined and then applied to any of the predefined tracking properties of a Security Policy. User-defined alerts are executables or scripts created for the purpose of extending the alerting mechanism.

The various alert command options are as follows:

- **Pop-up Alert** The pop-up alert command goes to the System Status viewer, you can specify a replacement command to be executed.

- **Mail Alert**   The mail command to be run to perform the delivery of a mail alert can also be defined by the administrator.

- **SNMP Trap Alert**   The command to be run when an SNMP Trap is specified as the tracking option in a rule, the administrator can also define this command.

- **User-Defined Alert (1-3)**   The Operating System (OS) command to be executed when User-Defined (1-3) is specified as the track option in a rule, must be defined if required.

Specifying an alternate command for the standard pop-up alert command is not recommend because you may cause a complete loss of alerting to the System Status viewer (SmartView Status in FP3) client if this option is used. It is recommended that you use one of the user-defined methods instead.

Mail alerts can be very useful for sending notifications of alert conditions to support personnel. The default setting sends e-mail to root on the system where the

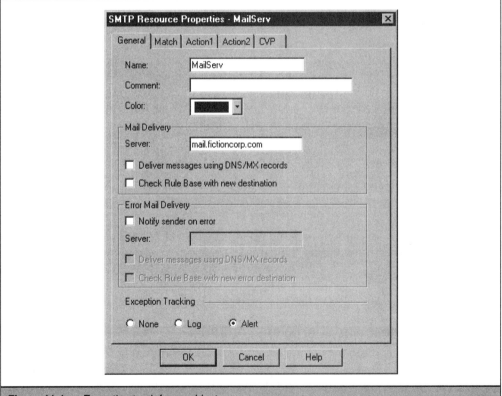

Figure 11-1.   Exception track for an object

firewall is installed. You can change this to allow messages to be sent to your internal mail server so that access is not required to the firewall in order to receive these messages. The following example shows how this is done for Fiction Corporation.

```
internal_sendmail -s alert -t 172.31.254.100 -f lonfw@fictioncorp.co.uk
fwadmin@fictioncorp.co.uk
```

This example sends e-mail to the fwadmin account on Fiction Corporation's internal mail-server (172.31.254.100). The -s option specifies the subject for the e-mail, the -t option specifies a mail server address, and the -f option specifies who the mail is from. This is an arbitrary text string, but it is useful in letting the recipient know which management server the message is coming from if you have a few. Finally, the mail recipient or recipients are specified. Whenever you use the mail track option, a notification will be sent to this e-mail account when the rule is applied. The command itself is an internal command and cannot be used from the command line.

SNMP (Simple Network Management Protocol) traps can also be sent using the SNMP track option by configuring the internal_snmp_trap command line to specify the host that the trap should be directed to. The internal_snmp_trap command is internal to VPN-1/FireWall-1 NG in the same way as the internal_sendmail command is and cannot be used from the command line.

You can replace both the mail and SNMP trap commands with commands of your own if required, in effect this means you can use these as user-defined alerts as well.

You can use user-defined scripts and executables to alert when complex conditions are met. You can also generate different types of alerts that are dependent upon different conditions. The scripts or executables are placed on the Management Server in the $FWDIR/bin directory. To generate your own alerts, you add the name of the user-defined script to the Policy Properties, Log and Alert, Alert Commands tab in the User-Defined Property field, as shown in Figure 11-2. There are three user-defined alerts that can be used. From Feature Pack 2 (FP2), you can choose any of the three user-defined alerts in the Track field of the Rule Base; prior to FP2 only the first one could be selected.

You can set up user-defined tracking options by checking the Run User-Defined Script check box and then entering the name of the script to run in the Command field. When you have entered the scripts or programs you want to use for user-defined alerts, you can select the appropriate user-defined alert in the Track field of the Rule Base or the Log and Alert Properties tab, as detailed in the next section.

The Alertd Process and Alert Commands

The alertd process is responsible for executing the alert commands. This takes place on the Management Server where the logs are written. The Enforcement Module is responsible for detecting the alert and informing the Management Module of the event.

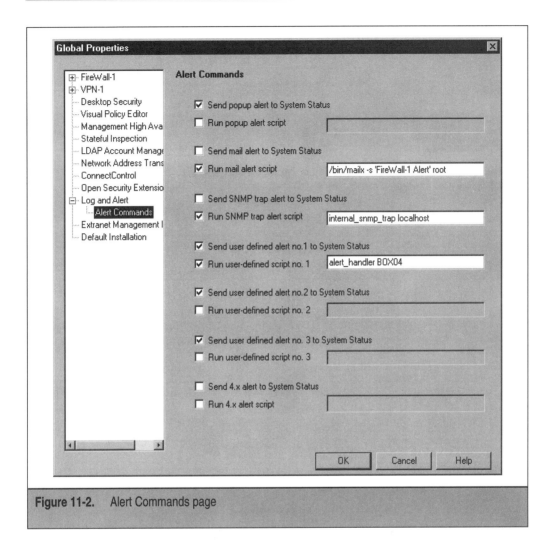

Figure 11-2.   Alert Commands page

This means if logging is being directed to another server an alert command can be run twice for each event triggered.

Track Options

You can configure any specific action defined for each of the Track options by choosing the suitable item from the drop-down list, as shown in Figure 11-3. If you intend to use any of the three user-defined alerts you need to define them, as described in the previous section.

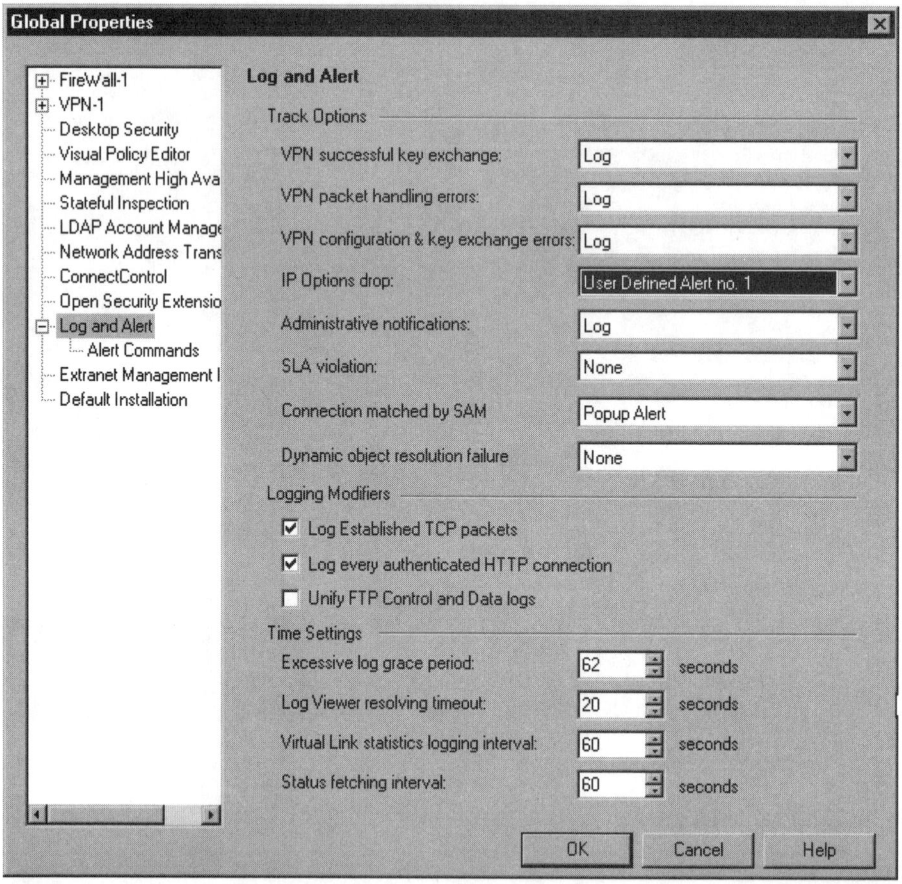

Figure 11-3. Log and Alert page

From this window you can define system-wide logging and alerting parameters for various operations as follows:

- **VPN successful key exchange**   Controls logging successful VPN key exchange events. This is when a key is exchanged between VPN Gateways.

- **VPN packet handling errors**   Controls logging encryption or decrypting errors. A log entry contains the action performed (either Drop or Reject), and the type of error such as scheme or method mismatch.

- **VPN configuration and key exchange errors**   Choose whether to log or alert for VPN configuration errors and key exchange errors; for example, when a user attempts to establish encrypted communication with a network object within the same encryption domain.

- **IP options drop**   Controls logging when a packet is received that has anything set in the IP Options field of the IP header. An option such as source routing, contained in the IP Options field, represents a security threat. VPN-1/ FireWall-1 NG always drops these packets. This option allows you to choose to issue an alert or create a log entry when such a packet is encountered.

- **Administrative notifications**   Controls the action to be taken when an administrative notification such as when a certificate is about to expire occurs.

- **SLA violation**   Controls virtual link notifications for SLA violation, such as when the CIR (Committed Information Rate) falls below the set SLA threshold. Virtual links are outside the scope of this book.

- **Connection matched by SAM**   The Suspicious Activity Monitor integrates third-party OPSEC (see www.opsec.com) Suspicious Activity Detection applications with VPN-1/FireWall-1 NG. This option allows you to choose how to monitor any detected suspicious activity.

- **Dynamic object resolution failure**   Controls the action to be taken when a dynamic object cannot be resolved on the enforcement point.

Logging Modifiers

Logging modifiers specify how logging should take place. Note that in Feature Pack 2 onward only the Log Every Authenticated HTTP Connection option is available.

- **Log Established TCP Packets**   Logs TCP packets for previously established TCP connections or packets whose connections have timed out.

- **Log Every Authenticated HTTP Connection**   Logs all authenticated HTTP connections independently.

- **Unify FTP Control and Data Logs**   Puts together log entries for both components (data and control) of a single FTP connection.

Time Settings

The following four options relate to timeouts for Log Viewer. In our experience, unless there is a specific issue, these are best left at their default values:

- **Excessive log grace period**   Specifies the timeout between consecutive log records created for similar packets.

- **Log Viewer resolving timeout**   Specifies the timeout for displaying the log page without resolving names and shows only IP addresses.
- **Virtual link statistics logging interval**   The frequency with which SLA statistics will be logged.
- **Status fetching interval**   Specifies how often the Management Server queries the VPN-l/FireWall-l NG, FloodGate, and other modules it manages for status information. Any value between 30 to 900 seconds can be selected.

Community Default Rule (FP3 Only)
In Feature Pack 3 (FP3), the Community Default Rule enables logging between VPN Communities where the action is to accept encrypted traffic between them.

CHECKLIST: KEY POINTS IN TRACKING AND ALERTS
The following is a checklist for the key points in Tracking and Alerts:

- ☐ Monitor the activity and alerts of the firewall from the supplied Management Console applications.
- ☐ Show how VPN-1/FireWall-1 NG tracking and alerting allows for extensibility and tuning for integration with enterprise network management and monitoring solutions to support NOC/SOC (Network Operations Center/Security Operations Center) support staff.
- ☐ Show how VPN-1/FireWall-1 NG tracking and alerting allows extensive tailoring for logging and alerting.
- ☐ Use System Status and Log Viewer (see Chapter 10) to provide in-depth coverage of the product required to monitor activity and receive alerts.
- ☐ Define tracking.
- ☐ Modify the default mail command to send alert e-mails to support staff.
- ☐ Modify the Log and Alert page and the Alerts Commands page of the Global Properties window to set up user-defined tracking.
- ☐ Define system-wide logging and alerting parameters.
- ☐ Identify logging modifiers, time settings, and the community default rule and how they affect logging.

CHAPTER 12

VPN-1/FireWall-1 NG Authentication

Authentication through the firewall gives you the ability to grant user access to systems and services, making it a crucial element of a secure infrastructure. VPN-1/FireWall-1 can use an authenticated user in a rule the same way you can use an object with a defined IP address as a source or communication initiator.

Three types of authentication are available: user, client, and session. In this chapter, we will look at all three and the scenarios where each is appropriate.

After we have discussed the types of authentication, we will use Fiction Corporation's internal firewall, which you have already installed in Chapter 6, to segregate the financial systems from users of the Fiction Corporation HQ. The financial systems contain highly sensitive information and require a higher level of security than the main office network.

SUPPORTED AUTHENTICATION SCHEMES

VPN-1/FireWall-1 NG supports a number of authentication schemes for managing user accounts both internally and externally:

- **S/Key**   Users are challenged to enter the value of requested S/Key iteration.

- **OS Password**   Users are challenged to enter their OS Password.

- **VPN-1/FireWall-1 NG Password**   Users are challenged to enter their VPN-1/FireWall-1 NG password on the gateway.

- **SecurID**   Users are challenged to enter the number displayed on the Security Dynamics SecurID card.

- **AXENT Defender**   Users are challenged for the response as defined by the AXENT server.

- **TACACS**   Users are challenged for the response as defined by the TACACS or TACACS+ server.

Users can be defined with any supported scheme. The supported scheme must be selected in the Authentication section of the workstation properties for the firewall object. Users can have different passwords on different gateways (for example, if the authentication scheme is OS Password), but they can have only one authentication scheme for all gateways operated by a single management server.

CREATING USERS AND GROUPS

User and group administration for internal and external authentication services requires the creation of a user template, a group, and the actual users for that group.

A user template allows for quick and easy entry of users into the VPN-1/FireWall-1 NG user database. A template establishes default properties for each user that will be created.

To create a user template, select the Manage | User menu item. The User screen will appear as shown in Figure 12-1.

Click the New button and select Template from the drop-down list. In the Login Name field, type the name of the template user; for example, a finance template might be named Finance_Users.

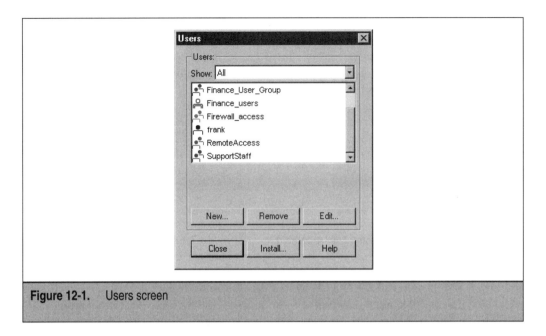

Figure 12-1.   Users screen

Configure all of the tabs to set the default values required for this user template.

Individual users cannot be used directly in a rule; VPN-1/FireWall-1 NG uses user groups to define rules. It is therefore necessary to create a user group so you can establish a Rule Base entry for authentication. To create a new group, click New from the Users screen and select Group. To continue with our finance example, type **Finance_Users_Group** and add the required users. Once the group is created, you can amend the Finance Users template to include the users in this group.

You are now ready to create as many users from the template created as required. In the example, we used VPN-1/FireWall-1 NG Password as the authentication scheme. You can just as easily use any internal or external authentication scheme, even when using advanced user management features such as LDAP directory integration.

To create new users for the Finance_Users_Group, click the New button from the Users screen and select User by Template | Finance_Users. If the template was defined correctly, all you have to do is set the passwords for each individual user.

After creating users, the User Database needs to be installed on the VPN-1/FireWall-1 NG Modules. You can do this by opening the Policy menu and then selecting Install User Database, or by clicking the Install button on the Users screen, as shown in Figure 12-1 (when a Policy is installed, the user database is also updated).

EXTERNAL AUTHENTICATION SERVERS

You may be wondering if you need to create every user for the VPN-1/FireWall-1 NG user database when using an external authentication system such as SecurID, in effect performing twice the administration work. The answer is, not necessarily. There is a shortcut: you can create a single user definition on the firewall that can be used with *all* external authenticated users. Creating a *local user would allow *all* users defined in the external authentication systems user database to be used with the firewall without having to define each user twice. The *local account is a special username that the firewall recognizes when created as a user. It tells the firewall to ask the external authentication source if the user name and password are valid. The firewall itself is not required to know the actual username it has been asked to authenticate, it merely passes the request on and receives an answer back. However, this solution has a drawback: if the external system (for instance, SecurID—ACE server) is not dedicated to providing its users to just the firewalls, you will inadvertently open access for anyone who, for whatever reason, has been issued an account and a SecurID token on that ACE Server. If you intend to take advantage of this capability, make sure to dedicate the ACE Server resource for use with the VPN-1/FireWall-1 NG alone.

NOTE   Only one *local account can be created.

STEALTH AUTHENTICATION

VPN-1/FireWall-1 NG will always ask for a password, whether or not it recognizes the user credentials—this is stealth authentication at work. This helps to prevent brute force attacks by preventing the attacker from gaining any insight into the user database. The first leg of the communication must be allowed for the user to authenticate, but the subsequent connection by the gateway to the end destination is not started until successful authentication has occurred. The default for the number of unsuccessful attempts to authenticate is three, after which the connection is terminated.

USER AUTHENTICATION

User Authentication uses the VPN-1/FireWall-1 NG Security Servers to intercept an intended communication and authenticate the user before they can communicate to the destination device. User Authentication does not require any additional software or procedures on behalf of the client or user. The user is challenged for a password using the service they started the connection on, as long as it is a supported service. The supported services are HTTP, Telnet, FTP, and Rlogin. Authentication is performed once per connection. This type of authentication is fairly transparent for users and does not require any special training or knowledge to use. However, it can be intrusive because "per connection" means a single web page could initiate numerous authentication challenges. Because the connection is mediated by VPN-1/FireWall-1 NG Security Servers, the client connection is made to the gateway, and the gateway makes a connection to the server. Therefore, the server sees the communications as coming from the gateway, not the client.

Care needs to be taken with the Rule Base because the authenticating Security Server first checks to see if the connection would be allowed by a less restrictive rule. Should one exist, the user will be granted a connection via that rule and may not have to authenticate.

To add a rule for User Authentication, add a new rule and, in the Source field, select Add with User Access. Optionally, select Location: Restrict To and choose a network from which the communication is restricted. User Authentication Rules can be created below the Stealth Rule. A rule for User Authentication to the Payroll server would look like the one defined in the following table.

Source	Destination	Service	Action	Track	Time
Finance_User_Group@any	Payroll_server	Telnet	User Auth	Log	any

When you create a user from a template, you can specify a source and destination that applies to the user, and a source and destination definition is also applied to a rule. If both or either the rule and the user have been specified, you can choose how to handle the conflict by right-clicking the Action field and choosing Edit Properties from the drop-down menu. The Properties window is shown in Figure 12-2.

User Authentication Rule Properties

In the Source and Destination fields, you can either choose Intersect with User Database or Ignore User Database. If you ignore the user database, the rule will take no account of the settings for source or destination in the user definition. If you choose to intersect with the user database, then the rule will apply to source or destination only where the rule and the user definitions overlap.

If a time specification is given to the user and the rule, the user will be allowed to use the rule only when both the users permitted access and the rules permitted access overlap. For instance, if the user was defined as being allowed access only between 9 AM and 5 PM and the rule was allowed access from 11 AM until midnight for some specific resource, the user would only be able to connect between 11 AM and 5 PM.

You can also specify how to handle the authentication track for successful login attempts by choosing the Track option in the Security Policy Global Properties Authentication screen (Authentication Failure Track). Otherwise only unsuccessful login attempts will show in the logs.

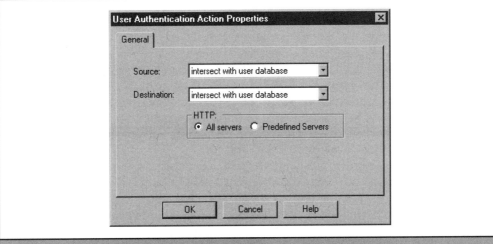

Figure 12-2.   User Authentication Action Properties

CLIENT AUTHENTICATION

Client and Session Authentication provide support for any type of service to be authenticated. This gives the security administrator the ability to grant access to specific IP addresses, applications, and users on a per session basis after successful authentication.

Client Authentication rules grant access to the client's IP address after successful authentication. This is done on a per-session basis and is nonintrusive to the user: once authentication is established, no more requests to reauthenticate will be sent until the logout, timeout, or number of sessions is reached. User Authentication is generally considered more secure because authentication occurs for a user on a per-connection basis. As with most security, a trade-off is made between functionality and security; getting this balance right is part of the job of the security administrator.

The user initiates manual Client Authentication directly with the firewall gateway using either Telnet on port 259 or HTTP on port 900. After entering their username and password, they are authenticated or, rather, their IP address is, and they can then create a connection to the servers and service(s) defined by the rule.

The Client Authentication rule for the finance users would look like the one shown in the following table.

Source	Destination	Service	Action	Track	Time
Finance_User_Group@any	Payroll_server	Telnet	Client Auth	Log	any
any	Lon2fw	any	Drop	Log	any

It is important to remember to place the rule above the Stealth Rule, or users will not be able to authenticate with the gateway.

Client Authentication Rule Properties

The properties of the rule define, among other things, how sign-on is to be accomplished by either the standard or the specific method. Standard sign-on allows access to all services and servers (destinations) that the rule permits and specifically requires reauthentication for any server or service other than the ones listed at the time of sign-on. If specific sign-on is forced, the user must enter a valid combination of server and service, or sign-on will fail. To edit the rule properties, right-click the Client Auth action in the rule and choose Edit Properties. The Client Authentication Action Properties window is shown in Figure 12-3.

Choosing Log under Successful Authentication Tracking option, as shown in Figure 12-3, logs all successful authentications. The Limits tab allows you to configure the timeout and number of sessions for the rule.

When you create a user from a template, you can specify a source and destination that applies to the user, and a source and destination definition is also applied to a rule. If both or either the rule and the user have been specified, you choose how to handle the conflict by right-clicking the Action field and choosing Edit Properties from the drop-down menu.

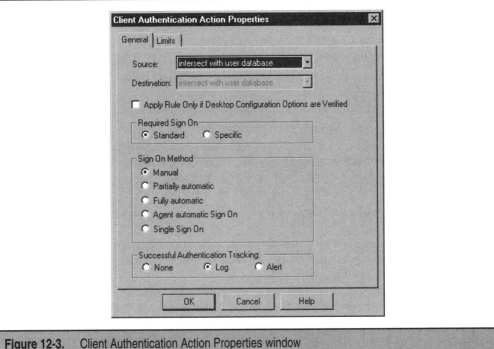

Figure 12-3.   Client Authentication Action Properties window

Sign-On Methods

As you can see in Figure 12-3, various methods are available for signing on for the Client Authentication scheme. The default setting is manual. The following are other methods available for signing on:

- **Manual**   The user must initiate the Client Authentication session on the gateway, in one of the following ways:
    - Telnet to port 259: the user begins a Telnet session on port 259
    - HTTP to port 900: the user initiates the session through a web browser. The requested URL must include the gateway name and the port number, such as

      ```
      http://lon2fw:900
      ```

- **Partially Automatic**   Provides that, if a connection matches the rule, and the service is an authenticated service (Rlogin, Telnet, HTTP, FTP), the user is signed on after successful User Authentication.

- **Fully Automatic**   If a connection using any service matches the rule, the user is signed on after they are authenticated by the VPN-l/FireWall-l NG Session Authentication Agent. (If the service is an authenticated service, the user is still signed on through the User Authentication mechanism.) This option requires a VPN-l/FireWall-l NG Session Authentication agent on the client.

- **Agent Automatic Sign On**   Provides transparent Client Authentication for all services. Users are signed on through the VPN-l/FireWall-l NG Session Authentication Agent. If authentication is successful, access is granted from the IP address that initiated the connection. Agent Automatic Sign On requires that a VPN-l/FireWall-1 NG Session Authentication Agent be installed on each client.

- **Single Sign On**   Check Point's address management feature provides transparent network access. In this method, the VPN-l/FireWall-l NG consults the user IP address records to determine which user is logged on at a given IP address.

SESSION AUTHENTICATION

Session Authentication requires a session agent running on the host computer that is to access an authenticated service. Access privileges are granted to a user and not an IP address as in the case of Client Authentication.

Session Authentication works by detecting the connection to the destination. The Inspection Module connects to the Session Authentication Agent. The Session Authentication Agent then prompts the user for their credentials. If the authentication is successful, the VPN-1/FireWall-1 NG module allows the connection to pass through the gateway.

Session Authentication works on per-session basis in a similar way to Client Authentication, but requires the installation of the Session Agent on the client computer. The Session Agent is a utility that is provided with VPN-1/FireWall-1 NG.

The Session Authentication rule for our finance users is shown in the following table.

Source	Destination	Service	Action	Track	Time
Finance_User_Group@any	Payroll_server	Telnet	Session Auth	Log	any

Session Authentication Rule Properties

Session Authentication Properties are available by right-clicking the Action column for the Session Auth rule. The source and destination properties are the same as for both User and Client Authentication, as detailed earlier in this chapter.

FICTION CORPORATION EXAMPLE

The security administrator for Fiction Corporation has deployed an internal VPN-1/FireWall-1 NG Enforcement Module to segregate the Finance servers from the main Head Quarters network. As discussed in Chapter 6, most fraud conducted by using computers happens within an organization. Therefore, the security administrator has elected to take stronger measures to protect the company's financial systems. The diagram in Figure 12-4 shows the internal structure of the Fiction Corporation network.

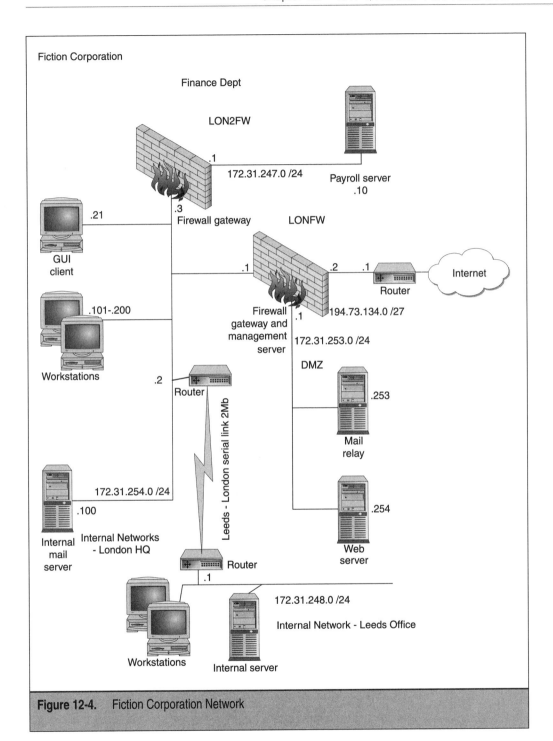

Figure 12-4. Fiction Corporation Network

As you can see, the Finance firewall Lon2fw has been put in place, and users in the HQ network must pass through it to create a connection to the Payroll server.

It would be desirable to enable accounting too, so that user access will be tracked for all connections to the Payroll server as well as maintaining strict control over who can access this system via authentication. To achieve this, the rules shown in Figure 12-5 are required on the Finance firewall.

Rule 1 in Figure 12-5 shows access required for the internal support staff who need access to administer the Payroll server. Client Authentication has been used here because the administration package uses ports other than those supported for User Authentication and because support staff are more readily trained in techniques that nontechnical users would have difficulty remembering. Rule 2 is the standard Stealth Rule used to protect the firewall itself, and Rule 3 shows User Authentication access for the Finance user group. The final rule is the standard Drop and Log rule.

USERAUTHORITY

Check Point UserAuthority brings your web and network applications into one centrally managed security framework by leveraging Check Point's proven networking, encryption, and authentication technologies. UserAuthority transparently integrates "best of breed" authentication mechanisms into your applications, enabling intelligent authorization decisions based on a connection's security context: user identity and profile information, encryption and authentication parameters, networking information and desktop security parameters. UserAuthority is the "security glue" that binds web and network applications to users, Check Point VPN-1/FireWall-1 NG, and OPSEC applications, creating a Secure Virtual Network (SVN) for your enterprise.

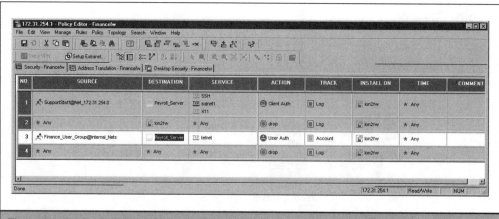

Figure 12-5. Finance Firewall Rule Base

UserAuthority Web Plug-In

Consider a web application, for example Outlook Web Access (OWA), using Basic Authentication (user name and password), where the VPN-1/FireWall-1 NG Security Policy specifies that a user who accesses the application must be authenticated using a digital certificate. If the user authenticates successfully, UserAuthority provides the application with the user name and password that it expects, greatly enhancing the application's security.

Other Applications and UserAuthority

Other applications can use the UserAuthority OPSEC API (UAA) to leverage the Check Point infrastructure and perform secured Single Sign-On and Secured Authorization based on networking and security information retrieved from VPN-1/FireWall-1 NG.
   Check out www.opsec.com for a list of OPSEC certified applications and partners.

CHECKLIST: KEY POINTS IN VPN-1/FIREWALL-1 NG AUTHENTICATION

The following is a checklist for VPN-1/FireWall-1 NG Authentication:

- ☐ Define User, Client and Session Authentication options.
- ☐ Define authentication.
- ☐ Implement authentication.
- ☐ List the extended capabilities of VPN-1/FireWall-1 NG.
- ☐ List the limited number of services that User Authentication provides a secure nonintrusive method for.
- ☐ Install the Session Agent to be installed on the client.
- ☐ Provide another layer of security for internal systems through the use of authentication.
- ☐ List the supported authentication schemes.
- ☐ Create Users and Groups.
- ☐ Identify external authentication servers.
- ☐ Define Stealth Authentication.
- ☐ Define user authority.

CHAPTER 13

Network Address
Translation (NAT)

All systems connected to the Internet require a unique address. Every IP address and IP network on the Internet is routable; hence, any system that is visible on the Internet can communicate with any other system. Unfortunately, there are a finite number of available IP addresses that can be allocated. In the early days of the Internet, organizations were given an entire IP class A, B, or C network range. This led to the real danger of IP address depletion, and organizations are now allocated a limited range of IP addresses—normally a subnet or a handful of addresses for Internet-connected systems.

Organizations may have many thousands of systems on their internal networks, and this limited allocation is not enough to give every system a unique Internet-valid IP address or registered IP address. This IP address allocation limit created a need to ensure that all internal systems can still connect to resources on the Internet even if they don't have a valid IP address.

Network Address Translation (NAT) addresses this issue by substituting a system's actual IP address with a registered or valid IP address. NAT is configured between the inside network (local network) and the outside network (a public network such as an ISP or the Internet—the outside network can also be another company, such as when two networks merge after an acquisition). NAT translates the internal local addresses into globally unique IP addresses, allowing data to flow into the outside network.

Therefore, NAT translates the local nonunique (that is, illegal to use on the Internet) IP addresses into legal, registered Internet IP addresses before placing packets from the local network to the Internet or other outside network. Figure 13-1 illustrates how the Fiction Corporation Mail Relay (which was configured in Chapter 8) has its source address translated into a registered (or legal) IP address that is routable on the Internet by the Fiction Corporation firewall.

NAT is usually handled in one of two ways: directly substituting an internal invalid IP address with a valid IP address, which is known as a static mapping; or using a single valid IP address for multiple outbound connections from an internal network, which is known as Port Address Translation or hide NAT (discussed later in the chapter). Static translation occurs when you manually configure an address table with IP addresses. A specific address on the inside of the network uses an IP address, manually configured by the network administrator, to access the outside network. This allows for multiple internal hosts to utilize a single IP address.

NOTE Check Point's hide NAT is generally known in the networking industry as Port Address Translation (PAT) because a single valid IP address uses a combination of the source port and the source IP address to create a unique entry within a table. This entry uniquely identifies each connection even if multiple connections come from the same host so that return packets are correctly sent back. The theoretical limit for connections using hide NAT is over 65,000.

VPN-1/FireWall-1 NG supports both forms of NAT. All registered IP addresses are allocated by regional organizations that track and maintain allocations for Internet-

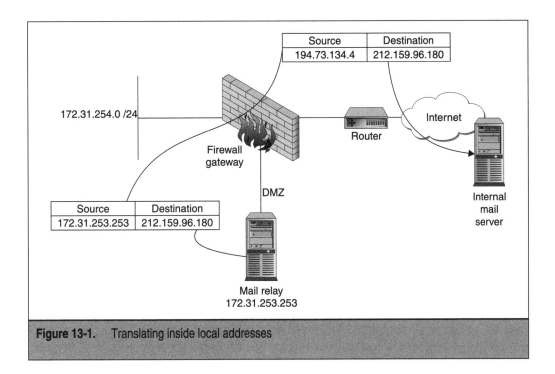

Source	Destination
194.73.134.4	212.159.96.180

172.31.254.0 /24

Firewall gateway

DMZ

Router

Internet

Internal mail server

Source	Destination
172.31.253.253	212.159.96.180

Mail relay
172.31.253.253

Figure 13-1.   Translating inside local addresses

connected systems for a geographic area. Table 13-1 shows the organizations that you are required to contact to obtain registered IP addresses when installing an Internet firewall.

It is common for your ISP to obtain these addresses for you, but if you have a special requirement or require a large number of addresses, you must contact these organizations and justify why you need the required IP addresses.

Organizations	Area of Coverage
American Registry for Internet Numbers (ARIN)	North America South America The Caribbean Sub-Saharan Africa
Réseaux IP Européens (RIPE NCC)	Europe Middle East Parts of Africa
Asia Pacific Network Information Center (APNIC)	Asia Pacific

Table 13-1.   Organizations That Allocate Registered (Valid) IP Addresses

IP ADDRESS ISSUES

Internetworking devices such as firewalls and routers implement NAT following the RFC 1631 guidelines for translating internal non-Internet-visible IP addresses into Internet-visible registered IP addresses.

There are two important IP addressing issues to consider when connecting an organization's internal network to the Internet:

- IP address conflicts
- Efficient use of registered (or valid) IP addresses

IP Address Conflicts

An organization's internal network is typically built of multiple IP networks that are connected by routers. Routers hold routing tables that show the path from any system to any other system through the internetwork (a collection of IP networks connected by routers). When a client system sends a request to communicate with a system that is not on its local IP network, the packet is sent to the default gateway, which is typically a router or firewall enforcement point. This gateway examines its routing tables to decide where to send the packet. If the destination is on a directly connected IP network, the gateway sends an ARP request to find the MAC address of the destination system and then forwards the packet. If the system is via another gateway, the local gateway sends the packet to the next gateway in the processing path. If the packet is destined for an unknown network, it is forwarded to a Gateway of Last Resort, which, for Internet-connected networks, is a firewall.

Therefore, a problem occurs when network administrators have chosen network addresses that are active on the Internet for all or a portion of the internal network. This problem causes any traffic destined for those addresses on the Internet to be sent to the internal network instead of to the firewall under the Gateway of Last Resort static routing entry. This rules out communication with any device on the Internet for which you have used the same network address internally.

The solution is to use RFC 1918 IP addressing guidelines for all internal networks. Table 13-2 lists the three IP network ranges RFC 1981 offers that are not used on the Internet.

Most firewall administrators use these private address ranges and then use NAT to convert them to registered or valid addresses where Internet communications are required. The NAT is implemented on firewalls at the perimeter of the network.

Let's assume that an organization chooses a random range of IP addresses to use on its internal networks without following Internet conventions. The internal addresses conflict with addresses that are legally in use on the public Internet and registered to another organization.

With NAT, the organization may be able to access Internet resources even though the destination IP address does not fall within the same range as an internal IP network. If anyone tries to access a public resource on the Internet that has an IP address in the range of an internal IP address, that resource will be inaccessible. Figure 13-2 shows what

Network	Range
Class A	10.0.0.0–10.255.255.255
Class B	172.16.0.0–172.31.255.255
Class C	192.168.0.0–192.168.255.255

Table 13-2.   IP Address Network Ranges

happens when there is an address conflict with registered IP addresses. Packets will never reach the intended system because the router in Figure 13-2 assumes that the destination is on a locally connected network.

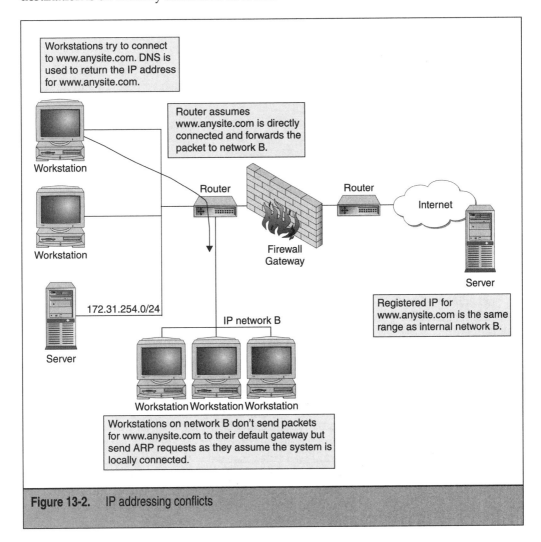

Figure 13-2.   IP addressing conflicts

EFFICIENT USE OF REGISTERED IP ADDRESSES

It is unnecessary and impractical to have a registered IP allocated for each internal system that needs to communicate with the Internet. Administrators generally allocate an individual IP address for each system that needs to be accessible from the Internet (static NAT) and utilize a single registered IP address for systems that need to access the Internet but need not be visible themselves (hide NAT). This allows thousands of internal systems to connect to resources on the Internet using a single registered IP address.

VPN-1/FireWall-1 NG implements transparent, fully RFC 1631-compliant Address Translation, which allows the use of either invalid internal IP addresses or historically allocated IP addresses that don't conform to Internet conventions to access Internet-based resources.

VPN-1/FireWall-1 NG implements two Address Translation modes:

- **Static NAT**   Each invalid address is translated to a corresponding valid address.
- **Hide NAT**   Many invalid addresses are translated into a single valid address and dynamically assigned ports are used to distinguish between the invalid addresses.

Static NAT

There are two modes of Static Address Translations as implemented by VPN-1/FireWall-1 NG:

- Static source mode
- Static destination mode

Static source NAT translates internal source IP addresses to registered (valid) source IP addresses and is used when internal systems initiate a connection to Internet resources. Rule 1 in Figure 13-3 shows how NAT works during a static source NAT session.

Static destination NAT translates valid addresses into internal addresses and is used when connections are initiated from external Internet systems to internal hosts. Rule 2 in Figure 13-3 shows how NAT works during a static destination NAT session.

Hide Mode

Hide NAT is used for connections from internal networks, with multiple invalid internal IP addresses being hidden behind a single valid IP address. Hide mode uses dynamically assigned port numbers to distinguish between internal hosts.

In the case of the Rule Base you built in Chapter 8 for Fiction Corporation (see Figure 13-3), you will notice there are two rules that were automatically created for the hide NAT defined for network 172.31.254.0 255.255.255.0. Rule 5 ensures that the internal address of the firewall gateway is not translated because this would result in the gateway being unable to communicate with an internal machine. Rule 6 translates

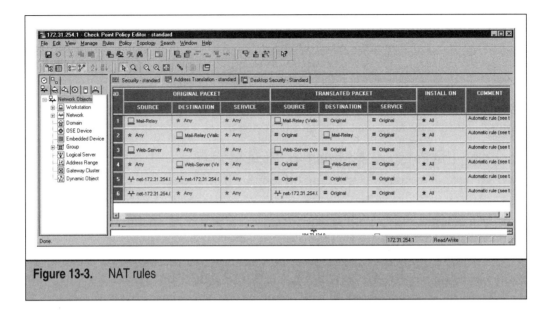

Figure 13-3. NAT rules

all traffic from the network object 172.31.254.0/255.255.255.0 to any other destination to the hide address. In the example selected, an imaginary address was used. This is common practice for VPN-1/FireWall-1 NG, but a special hide address of 0.0.0.0 could also have been chosen.

Using an address of 0.0.0.0 or using Manual Address Translation by defining a group as the source for the hide NAT and putting multiple network objects into that group are two ways of supporting hide NAT for multiple networks.

NOTE   The IP address of a gateway's external interface must never be hidden.

In hide mode, source port numbers are modified by VPN-1/FireWall-1 NG to uniquely identify internal hosts. The port numbers are assigned from two pools:

- 600 to 1023
- 10,000 to 60,000

VPN-1/FireWall-1 NG uses port numbers in the first pool if the original port number is less than 1024. It uses the second pool if the port number is greater than 1024. VPN-1/FireWall-1 NG tracks the port numbers assigned so that the original port number is restored for the return packets. Each new outbound connection is assigned a new port number.

NOTE   Hide mode is used only for outbound connections.

Hide Mode Limitations

Hide mode does not allow connections to be initiated to the internal hidden hosts from hosts on the outside. However, this limitation is actually considered one of hide mode's strengths because it secures the internal network against unauthorized access.

Hide mode cannot be used for protocols where the port number cannot be changed, nor can it be used when the external server must identify the clients by their IP address, because all the clients have the same valid IP address.

Choosing the External Address for Hide Mode

There are several techniques for hiding the internal IP addresses:

- Hide behind the IP address of the gateway's external interface
- Hide behind an imaginary IP address
- Hide behind 0.0.0.0

Hide Mode Using the Gateway's External IP Address

If you hide behind the external IP address of the gateway, no routing table changes need to be made because the perimeter router will already be configured to route traffic to the external IP address of the gateway. This is not recommended, however, as there may be problems with shadowed connections. For example, a user on the gateway might Telnet to an external server and get allocated a specific port, and another user on an internal network might Telnet to the same server and get the same port allocated by the VPN-1/FireWall-1 NG module on the gateway. This would cause returning packets to the first client from the external Telnet server to be incorrectly sent to the internal host, where they would be dropped.

Using a Valid Imaginary IP for Hide Mode

Most administrators tend to utilize an imaginary IP address that is in the same network range as the gateway's external IP address. This was the standard method utilized in VPN-1/FireWall-1 versions prior to NG and prevented the issue of *shadowed connections*. Shadowed connections are a conflict between an internal connection and connections direct from the gateway.

Using 0.0.0.0 as the Hide Address

If 0.0.0.0 is used as the hide address, then internal IP addresses will be hidden behind the IP address of the gateway's destination server-side interface. This can be useful if there are several networks connected to the firewall, and reduces the complexity of the NAT Policy.

ADDRESS TRANSLATION AND ROUTING

To implement NAT, you must ensure that a return packet intended for a host with an invalid IP address using hide mode is routed correctly back to that host. There are a number of methods of ensuring that return packets reach the internal host:

- **Static routes on the Internet router** This requires a configuration change on the perimeter router to have a static route to direct return traffic intended for the valid IP address to the firewall gateway's external interface where it is processed.

- **VPN-1/FireWall-1 automatic proxy ARP** The gateway will respond to ARP (Address Resolution Protocol) requests for the imaginary hide mode IP address. Normally, when a packet destined for the gateway reaches the perimeter router, the router sends out an ARP request to obtain the MAC address of the gateway. Proxy ARP ensures that the firewall gateway responds to the ARP for the valid address so the packet is sent directly to the firewall gateway.

NOTE VPN-1/FireWall-1 NG supports the Automatic ARP configuration property not available in earlier versions of the software. This feature is accessed from the Global Properties NAT tab.

- **Manual proxy ARP** Manual ARP configuration, the way VPN-1/FireWall-1 had to be configured in previous versions, mapped the valid IP address to the MAC address of the gateway's external interface. This is not required on Unix platforms but the Windows platform still requires Manual ARP.

- **Unix proxy ARP configuration** The format of the Unix proxy ARP command is as follows:

```
Arp -s <IP address> <MAC address> pub
```

Unix VPN-1/FireWall-1 NG administrators who use this approach often add a startup script placed in /etc/rc2.d with execute permissions that contain multiple ARP mappings when the gateway is booted; otherwise, a reboot clears the entries.

TIP To view published ARP entries on a Unix system use the command # `arp -a | grep` `SP`. Entries marked SP are static and published.

- **NT proxy ARP configuration** Windows NT does not support the startup scripts, so Check Point has defined a special file called local.arp that should be created in \$FWDIR\state (see Chapter 5 for an explanation of $FWDIR). Each line in the file should have the following format:

```
<IP Address> <MAC address>
```

CAUTION Automatic ARP is not supported on the Windows platform, so a local.arp file must be created and stored in $FWDIR\conf.

NETWORK ADDRESS TRANSLATION (NAT) RULES

VPN-1/FireWall-1 NG has NAT rules that make up part of the Security Policy. When the London Fiction Corporation Rule Base was created in Chapter 8, you were asked to add valid addresses for Fiction Corporation objects using the NAT tab for each workstation object defined. This created automatic NAT rules that were added to the Address Translation tab of the Security Policy.

Anatomy of a NAT Rule

A NAT rule consists of four sections: Original Packet, Translated Packet, Install On, and Comment. Install On and Comment are used in the same way as the Security Policy rules.

When the object Mail-Relay was created in Chapter 8 with an invalid IP address of 172.31.253.253, you gave the object a valid IP address of 194.73.134.4 by selecting the NAT tab and doing the following:

- Checking the box for Add Automatic Address Translation
- Selecting Static as the Translation Method
- Assigning the Valid IP address as 194.73.134.4
- Leaving Install On as All

This created two entries in the NAT rules. The first entry is a static source NAT, which translates an internal invalid IP address to a valid IP address. Automatic Address Translation always creates two rules for static NATs. The accompanying NAT rule is always a static destination mode NAT rule that translates valid addresses to invalid addresses.

Unless Perform Destination Translation on the Client Side is enabled in the NAT section of Global Properties, it should be noted that for each static destination NAT, a static route entry is required on the operating system. This is because VPN-1/FireWall-1 NG needs to know where to send the packet when a static destination NAT occurs. The format of this command is as follows:

- **NT**   Route add 194.73.134.4 172.31.253.253 255.255.255.255 1
- **UNIX**   Route add 194.73.134.4 mask 255.255.255.255 172.31.253.253 metric

---

NOTE   When the source, destination, or service section of the Translated Packet field of a NAT rule has the keyword Original inserted, it tells VPN-1/FireWall-1 NG not to perform NAT on that part of the packet header.

Network Address Translation Properties

There is a set of configurable options on the Network Address Translation tab of the Global Properties window, as shown in Figure 13-4.

Automatic Rules Intersection

If this option is checked and more than one NAT rule matches a connection, the rules are said to be intersected.

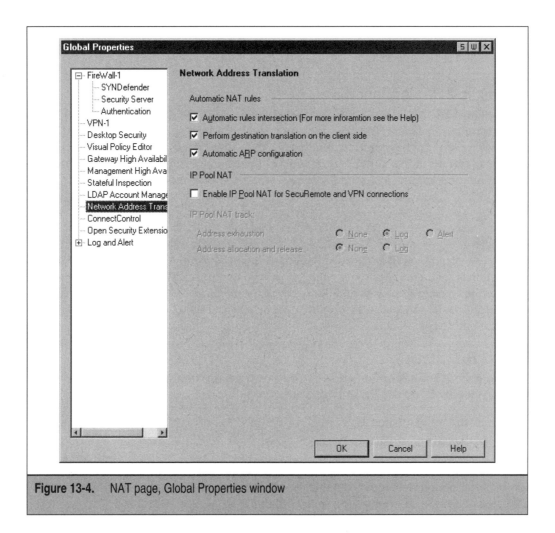

Figure 13-4.   NAT page, Global Properties window

Perform Destination Translation on the Client Side

In VPN-1/FireWall-1 NG, this option ensures that you do not have to maintain tables of static routes, as was the case in earlier versions of the software. If Perform Destination Translation on the Client Side is not enabled, Address Translation takes place in the gateway after internal routing but before transmission, so packets may get routed out of the wrong interface.

For new installations, Perform Destination Translation on the Client Side is enabled by default. It is important to note that if an upgrade is performed from earlier versions of VPN-1/FireWall-1, the option is disabled to maintain compatibility.

NOTE   If Perform Destination Translation on the Client Side is checked, the Automatic Rules Intersection setting is ignored.

Automatic ARP Configuration

VPN-1/FireWall-1 NG has the new feature of Automatic ARP configuration so that ARP requests for a translated (NAT) machine, network, or address range are answered by the gateway without having to manually configure files on the gateway as required by previous versions of the software. Previously, if you were using the ARP command in Unix or maintaining the local.arp file in NT, you'd use the following command:

```
fw ctl arp Displays the VPN-1/FireWall-1 NG modules ARP proxy table.
```

IP Pools

IP pools are a range of IP addresses that are routed to the gateway. When an encrypted connection is made to the gateway, the gateway substitutes an IP address from the IP pool for the source address. When the return packets reach the gateway, it restores the original source IP address and forwards the packets to the source. This is typically used for SecuRemote connections.

IP Pool NAT Track

The IP Pool NAT Track option allows various actions for logging or alerting to be taken when managing IP pools. The options are

- Address Exhaustion Track
- Address Allocation and Release Track

These options can be set to either log and generate alerts or none. It can be useful for troubleshooting purposes to enable the log option and monitor how addresses are allocated and released.

ADDRESS TRANSLATION AND ANTI-SPOOFING

Anti-spoofing examines the source IP address of a packet entering the gateway. The source IP address is checked to see that the incoming packet has not been modified to make it appear that the packet originated from an internal network.

Anti-spoofing is performed correctly for objects for which Automatic Address Translation is enabled. To avoid the potential pitfalls of NAT and anti-spoofing, let's examine how Address Translation takes place:

- For a client-initiated connection, NAT is performed on the packet just before the packet leaves the interface closest to the server.

- For a packet sent from the server, NAT is performed on the packet just after entering the interface closest to the server.

Anti-spoofing functions correctly in a NAT environment except when Static Destination Mode is being used. When NAT is performed on the server side, a conflict between anti-spoofing and NAT can occur. A conflict can occur when either manually defined rules are being used or Automatic Address Translation is used but Perform Destination Translation on the client side is not enabled in the NAT tab of Global Properties window.

To prevent a conflict from occurring between NAT and anti-spoofing if either of these scenarios are used, we recommend that a group object is created and the translated External IP addresses required are added to this group. This group should contain both defined networks that are reached via the firewall's internal interface. Figure 13-5 shows the group object Internal_nets with both networks added.

This group should now be added to the Internal Interface of the VPN-1/FireWall-1 NG gateway, as shown in Figure 13-6. Select the firewall object and edit the internal interface from the topology option.

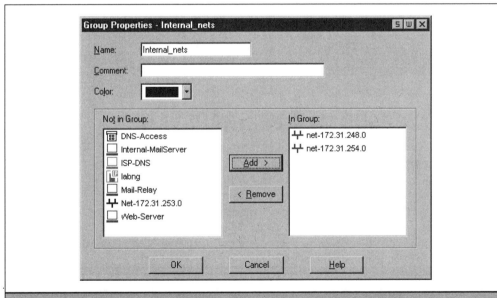

Figure 13-5.   Creating a group object for Internal_nets

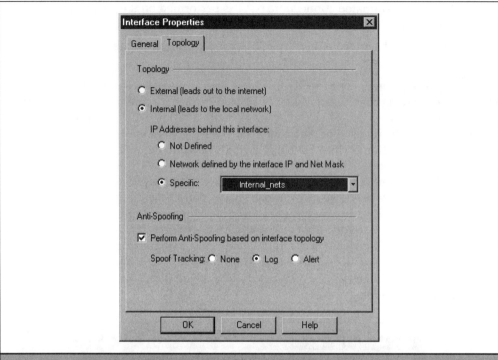

Figure 13-6. Adding a group for anti-spoofing to the internal interface

AUTOMATIC VERSUS MANUAL TRANSLATION

Automatic Address Translation is suitable for most installations of VPN-1/FireWall-1 NG. In Chapter 8, Fiction Corporation had Automatic Address Translation rules defined by opening an object's NAT tab and defining a valid IP address. Both static source and static destination NAT rules were automatically defined.

There are instances when Automatic Address Translation is not desirable and when more complete control over NAT is required. Manual NAT allows you to restrict NAT to specific destination IP addresses. You can use conditional NAT depending on the services used, or just translate the ports required.

Because you don't want NAT to take place when Fiction Corporation users are trying to access resources on the DMZ, you need to create a No NAT rule. This is quite common and usually involves creating a group object with the networks that the firewall is protecting and then creating a rule that ensures that both the source and destination of the translated packet are marked Original. This will ensure that no NAT takes place. Figure 13-7 shows the NoNAT object being created for Fiction Corporation.

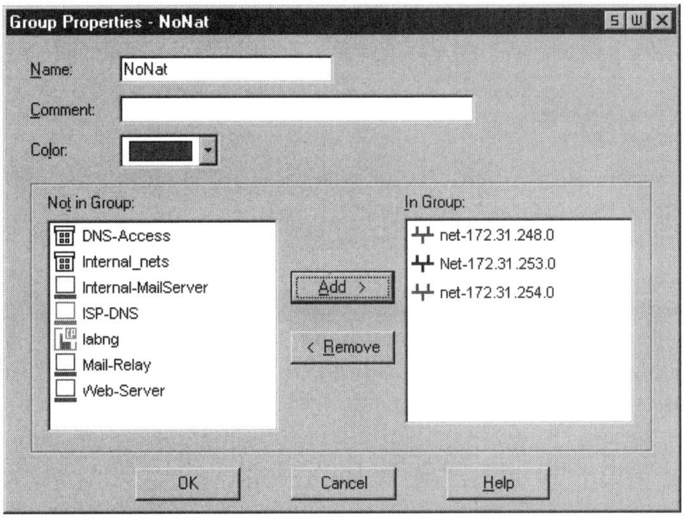

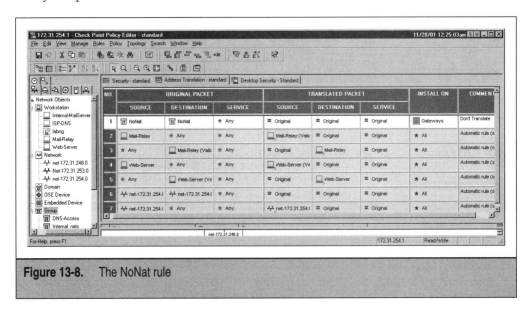

Figure 13-7.   The NoNAT object

You will create a rule that prevents Address Translation when the internal nets connect to the DMZ, or vice versa, as shown in Rule 1 in Figure 13-8. This rule should always be placed at the start of the Address Translation rules.

Figure 13-8.   The NoNat rule

> **NOTE** Automatic Address Translation rules are all in a block, and it is not possible to insert manual rules between them. All manual rules should be inserted before Automatic Address Translation rules.

OVERLAPPING NAT

There are circumstances in which a technique known as overlapping NAT has to be configured to allow two networks to connect. If two networks on either side of a firewall gateway use the same address space, for example, 172.16.254.0 255.255.255.0, then overlapping NAT has to be configured to allow communications between the two networks. Examine the example shown in Figure 13-9.

A scenario like this is quite common when a company connects a WAN link to a business partner and finds there is an address conflict. Users in the Fiction Corporation internal network who wish to communicate with users in the business partner network (DMZ) will use the 172.16.1.0/24 network as a destination. Users in network DMZ who wish to communicate with users in network A will use the 172.16.2.0/24 network as a destination.

The VPN-1/FireWall-1 Module will translate the IP addresses differently on each interface, as follows:

- **Interface inside** Inbound source IP addresses will be translated to virtual network 172.16.2.0/24; outbound destination IP addresses will be translated to network 172.16.254.0/24.

- **Interface DMZ** Inbound source IP addresses will be translated to network 172.16.254.0/24; outbound destination IP addresses will be translated to network 172.16.1.0/24.

For overlapping NAT to work correctly, some settings need to be configured in Objects_5_0.c with the dbedit utility:

- **enable_overlapping** NAT true
- **overlap_nat_dst_ipaddr** The overlapping IP addresses (before NAT). In the example configuration, this would be 172.16.254.0 for both interfaces.
- **overlap_nat_src_ipaddr** The IP addresses after NAT. In the example configuration, this would be 172.16.2.0 for interface inside, and 172.16.1.0 for interface DMZ.
- **overlap_nat_netmask** The net mask of the overlapping IP addresses. In the example, 255.255.255.0.

Detailed information is available in the Check Point manuals and on the VPN-1/FireWall-1 NG media CD in PDF format.

There are some limitations to overlapping NAT and you should be sure to check the current product documentation so these limitations do not affect your installation. If you are not using VPN and Security Servers with overlapping NAT, or if you are

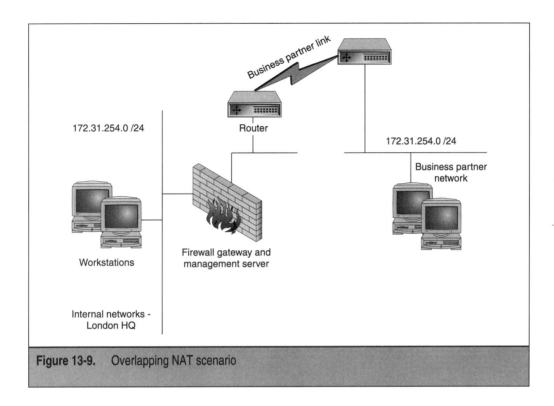

Figure 13-9. Overlapping NAT scenario

using PASV FTP and not the FTP port command, then overlapping NAT will work. Otherwise it is best not to perform this on a single gateway. In a scenario where you encounter these limitations, one workaround is to NAT at each network locally so packets arriving at the firewall gateway are already using a different IP address.

A final comment on overlapping NAT is that, even though you are using the same address space as the other network, if a host on the business partner network has exactly the same IP address, packets will never arrive at your gateway.

CHECKLIST: KEY POINTS IN NETWORK ADDRESS TRANSLATION (NAT)

The following is a checklist for Network Address Translation (NAT):

☐ Define how Network Address Translation (NAT) works with VPN-1/ FireWall-1 NG.

☐ List the different techniques for configuring NAT.

☐ Illustrate Automatic Address Translation.

- ☐ Configure NAT correctly to work with VPN-1/FireWall-1 NG's anti-spoofing feature.
- ☐ Utilize the manual NAT to establish greater control.
- ☐ Understand when there is a need for manual NAT in a more complex installation.
- ☐ List the AP address issues.
- ☐ Use registered (or valid) IP addresses efficiently.
- ☐ List the Network Address Translation rules.
- ☐ Define Address Translation and anti-spoofing.
- ☐ Define Address Translation and routing.
- ☐ Compare Automatic Translation to Manual Translation.
- ☐ Discuss complex NAT sceaiight!narios.

Check Point
VPN-1/FireWall-1 NG
Administration

Table of Contents

Automatic Address Translation

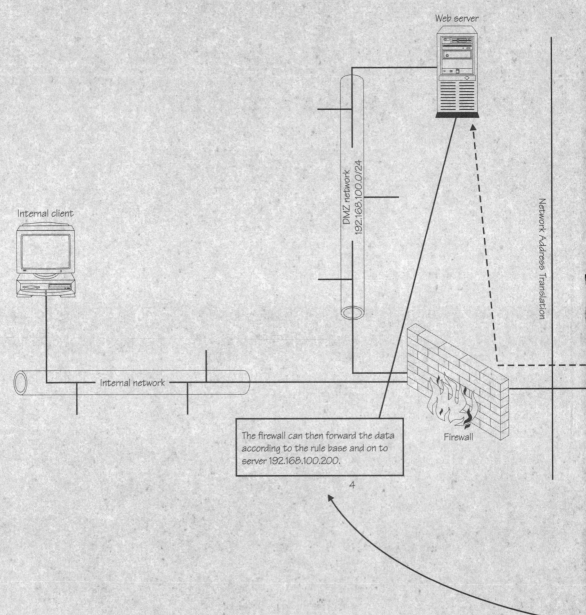

Web server

DMZ network
192.168.100.0/24

Internal client

Network Address Translation

Internal network

The firewall can then forward the data
according to the rule base and on to
server 192.168.100.200.

4

Firewall

Using Network Address Translation (NAT) on the client side and Automatic Address Resolution Protocol (ARP) configuration
in VPN-1/FireWall-1 NG.
VPN-1/FireWall-1 NG reduces the amount of necessary configuration when using Automatic NAT. FireWall-1 NG automatically provides Proxy
ARP entries for addresses on which NAT has been performed and performs destination NAT on the client side of the connection, removing the
necessity of adding Proxy ARPs and static routes for addresses on which NAT has been performed.
To enable this new feature, check Perform Destination NAT on the Client Side and Automatic ARP Configuration in the Policy, Global Properties,
Network Address Translation tab. If a firewall has been upgraded to VPN-1/FireWall-1 NG, these options default to disabled.

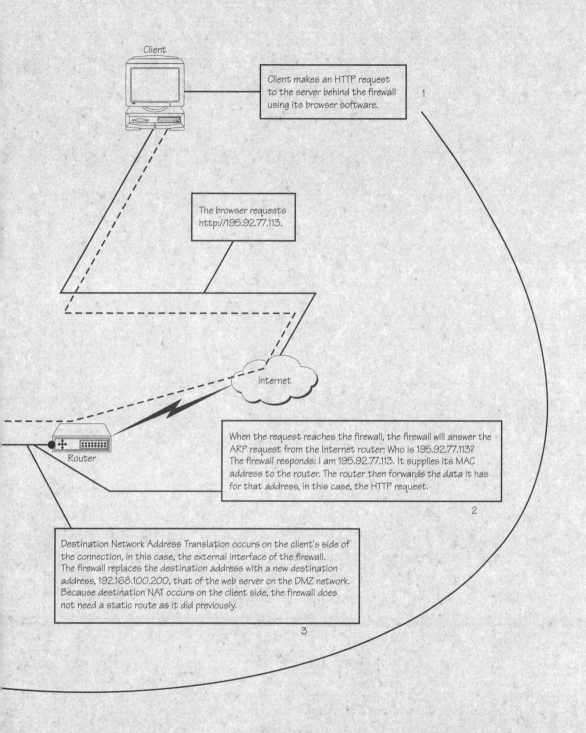

Client

Client makes an HTTP request to the server behind the firewall using its browser software.

1

The browser requests http://195.92.77.113.

internet

When the request reaches the firewall, the firewall will answer the ARP request from the Internet router: Who is 195.92.77.113? The firewall responds: I am 195.92.77.113. It supplies its MAC address to the router. The router then forwards the data it has for that address, in this case, the HTTP request.

2

Router

Destination Network Address Translation occurs on the client's side of the connection, in this case, the external interface of the firewall. The firewall replaces the destination address with a new destination address, 192.168.100.200, that of the web server on the DMZ network. Because destination NAT occurs on the client side, the firewall does not need a static route as it did previously.

3

Rapid Intranet VPN Deployment Using Distributed Management Model

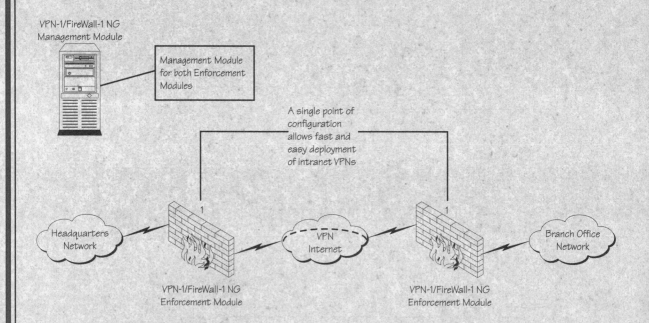

VPN-1/FireWall-1 NG
Management Module

Management Module
for both Enforcement
Modules

A single point of
configuration
allows fast and
easy deployment
of intranet VPNs

1

1

Headquarters
Network

VPN-1/FireWall-1 NG
Enforcement Module

VPN
Internet

VPN-1/FireWall-1 NG
Enforcement Module

Branch Office
Network

VPN-1/FireWall-1 NG can be deployed in a standalone or distributed model.
In the distributed model, the Management Module runs on a separate server to the Enforcement Module. An Enterprise Management License allows you to manage many Enforcement Modules from a single management platform. The diagram shows how a company can rapidly deploy branch office VPN using centralized management.

Remote Access VPN Using SecuRemote and SecureClient

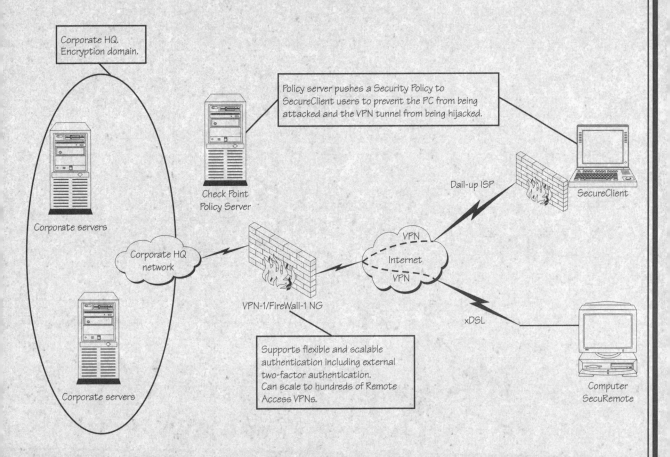

Corporate HQ.
Encryption domain.

Policy server pushes a Security Policy to
SecureClient users to prevent the PC from being
attacked and the VPN tunnel from being hijacked.

Corporate servers

Check Point
Policy Server

Corporate HQ
network

SecureClient

Dail-up ISP

VPN-1/FireWall-1 NG

VPN
Internet
VPN

xDSL

Corporate servers

Supports flexible and scalable
authentication including external
two-factor authentication.
Can scale to hundreds of Remote
Access VPNs.

Computer
SecuRemote

VPN-1/FireWall-1 NG can provide a highly cost effective and secure method of remote access using low cost, widely available, ISP dial-up, xDSL and cable connectivity.

Extending Check Point VPN-1/FireWall-1 NG Using OPSEC Partner Products

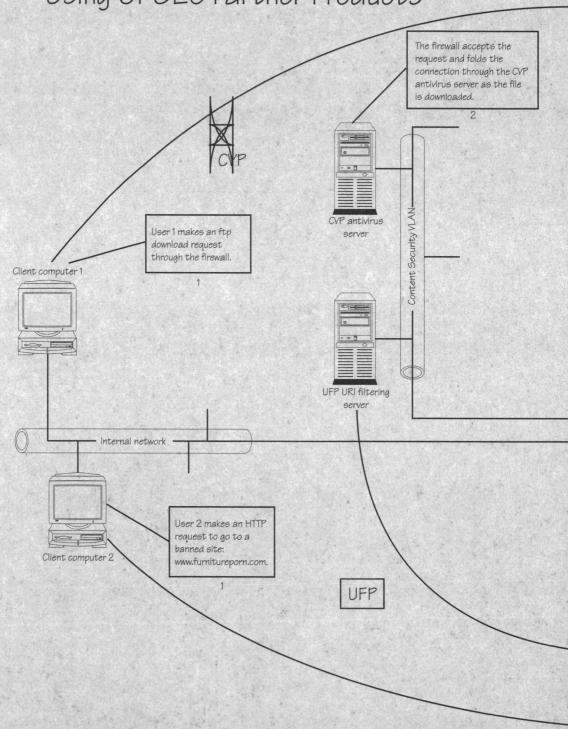

The firewall accepts the request and folds the connection through the CVP antivirus server as the file is downloaded.

2

CVP

User 1 makes an ftp download request through the firewall.

1

Client computer 1

CVP antivirus server

Content Security VLAN

UFP URI filtering server

Internal network

User 2 makes an HTTP request to go to a banned site: www.furnitureporn.com.

1

Client computer 2

UFP

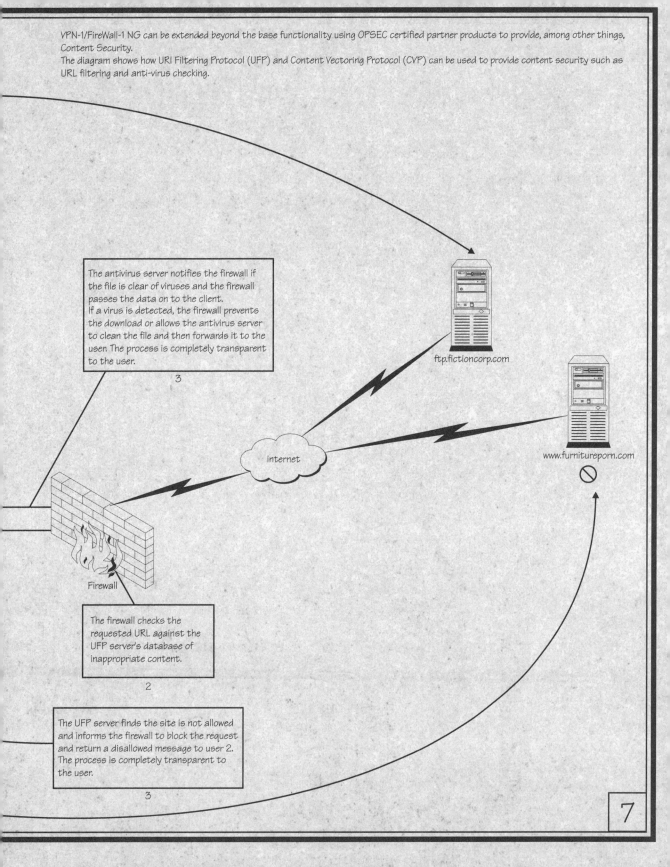

VPN-1/FireWall-1 NG can be extended beyond the base functionality using OPSEC certified partner products to provide, among other things, Content Security.
The diagram shows how URI Filtering Protocol (UFP) and Content Vectoring Protocol (CVP) can be used to provide content security such as URL filtering and anti-virus checking.

The antivirus server notifies the firewall if the file is clear of viruses and the firewall passes the data on to the client.
If a virus is detected, the firewall prevents the download or allows the antivirus server to clean the file and then forwards it to the user. The process is completely transparent to the user.

3

ftp.fictioncorp.com

www.furnitureporn.com

internet

Firewall

The firewall checks the requested URL against the UFP server's database of inappropriate content.

2

The UFP server finds the site is not allowed and informs the firewall to block the request and return a disallowed message to user 2. The process is completely transparent to the user.

3

7

Dynamic or Hide Mode
Network Address Translation (NAT)

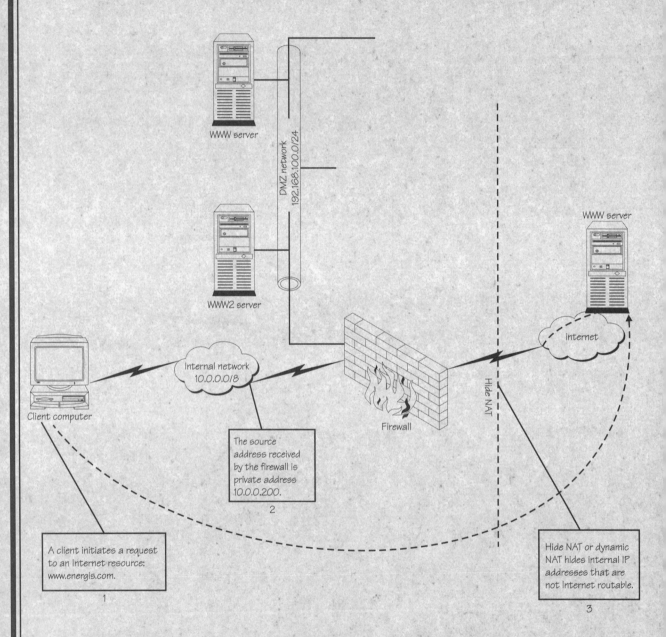

WWW server

DMZ network
192.168.100.0/24

WWW2 server

WWW server

internet

Internal network
10.0.0.0/8

Firewall

Hide NAT

Client computer

The source address received by the firewall is private address 10.0.0.200.

2

A client initiates a request to an Internet resource: www.energis.com.

1

Hide NAT or dynamic NAT hides internal IP addresses that are not Internet routable.

3

Dynamic or hide mode NAT can be enabled using three methods. New in VPN-1/FireWall-1 NG, you can use the IP address 0.0.0.0 to hide behind. This works by substituting the firewall's server-side interface when a client makes a connection. This has the advantage of being transparent should an interface be changed later. Alternatively, you can still use the external address of the firewall explicitly or another address from your registered address range.

You can identify hide mode in the Policy Editors Address Translation tab by the small H attached to the bottom of the icon.

CHAPTER 14

Load Balancing

When it comes to handling lots of visitors, corporations have learned that the quality of service a web server provides to end users typically depends on two parameters—network-transfer speed and server-response time. Network-transfer speed is mainly a matter of your Internet-link bandwidth, while server-response time depends upon resources: fast CPU, lots of RAM (especially for parallel-running processes), and good I/O performance (especially for disk and network traffic).

What can a corporation do when these resources are exhausted and their servers are struggling against heavy traffic? They could install more RAM on existing machines, or perhaps replace the CPU with a faster one. They could also use faster or dedicated SCSI controllers and disks with shorter access times (perhaps a RAID system with a huge cache). Software could be tuned as well; they could adjust operating-system parameters and web server settings to achieve better performance.

Or a corporation can address the problem with an alternative approach: improve performance by increasing the number of servers. This involves an attempt to distribute the traffic onto a number of web servers. Aside from the technical hurdles, this is an interesting approach because the servers don't need to be large-scale machines—medium-scale hardware works just fine.

Initially, a company might have one server behind a firewall for Internet-connected users to access. A single web server is a single point of failure as well as a point of congestion when a website becomes popular.

To alleviate this problem, VPN-1/FireWall-1 NG load balancing redirects traffic and distributes it among several servers. This reduces the load on any one server. Load balancing helps you to manage traffic flow from one firewall to multiple servers.

This chapter will build on the hosted firewall installation you performed in Chapter 7 and introduce load balancing for Fiction Corporation's business class website, which has two web servers that require load balancing.

THE NEED FOR LOAD BALANCING

The Internet is fast becoming a business-critical medium that delivers important information and has to support an ever-increasing number of client connections. Many commercial websites cannot afford to rely on a single server. This can result in poor response times or connection time-outs under peak load. Unreliable connectivity can result in customer dissatisfaction and decreased revenues or lost business opportunities.

VPN-1/FireWall-1 NG has an add-on module called ConnectControl (licensed separately) that has advanced traffic control functionality to ensure the highest degree of network connectivity and optimal server response times. With ConnectControl, a single server providing web or any other service can be replaced with a logical pool of servers that share a common IP address. Connection requests are load balanced across multiple servers. Network users experience noticeably improved response times, and it is transparent to users. ConnectControl offers businesses the opportunity to use a number of inexpensive servers rather than continually having to purchase more powerful and expensive systems to keep pace with increased demand.

It should be noted that in a real-world scenario, a good network design for hosting multiple web servers would include a range of resilience features to ensure maximum uptime, such as dual firewall enforcement gateways, dual switches, and dual homed servers with network card teaming. For business critical solutions, we have deployed solutions that also include multisite load balancing.

HOW LOAD BALANCING WORKS

Load balancing works by allowing several servers to share and distribute the network load.
VPN-1/FireWall-1 NG achieves this by creating a Logical Server on the firewall. The Logical Server has a unique IP address through which packets are routed for load balancing. Traffic directed to this Logical Server is then load shared among the physical servers in a logical server group. Using Address Resolution Protocol (ARP), VPN-1/FireWall-1 NG load balancing ensures packets destined to the IP address of the Logical Server are passed to the appropriate physical server. Figure 14-1 shows how load balancing works. Using a specific load balancing method, VPN-1/FireWall-1 NG routes the packet to a specific physical server.

TIP   ARP is used by the Internet Protocol (IP) network layer protocol to map IP network addresses to the hardware addresses used by a data link protocol. The protocol operates below the network layer as a part of the OSI link layer and is used when IP is used over Ethernet.

LOAD BALANCING ALGORITHMS

When a client connection request to a Logical Server's IP address reaches the firewall module, the VPN-1/FireWall-1 NG load balancing algorithm determines which physical server will service the request. There are five load balancing algorithms in VPN-1/FireWall-1 NG. Each algorithm prevents any server from handling a disproportionate volume of traffic.

The VPN-1/FireWall-1 NG load balancing algorithms are detailed in Table 14-1.

Algorithm	Description
Server load	Determines the load of each physical server. Server load requires a Load Measuring Agent to be installed on each server.
Round trip	Determines round trips between the firewall and each physical server. The firewall pings each server three times and averages the round trip time. The server with the lowest average gets the packet.
Round robin	Chooses the next physical server in the server group.
Random	Chooses the physical server randomly. This method is not recommended by the authors. This does not allow for even load distribution.
Domain	Chooses the physical server based on domain name. This only applies to HTTP load balancing.

Table 14-1.   Load Balancing, Algorithms

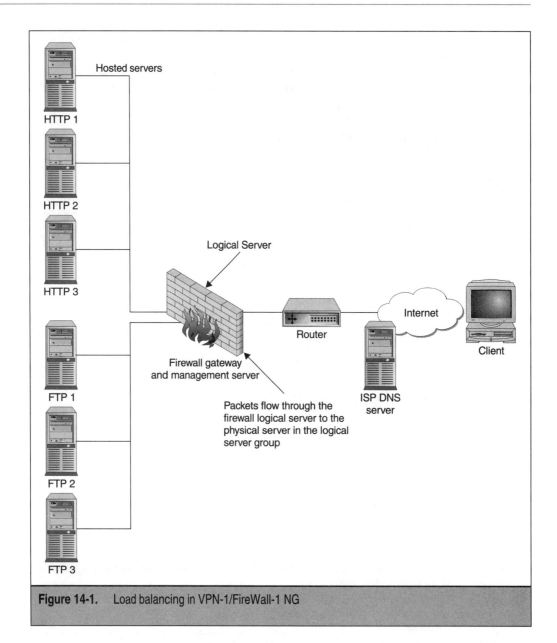

Figure 14-1. Load balancing in VPN-1/FireWall-1 NG

LOGICAL SERVER TYPES

VPN-1/FireWall-1 NG provides a management system that accelerates and manages the processing of work on firewall server farms. The application enables users to run parallel jobs, dispatch tasks, gather results, maintain a library of standard files, and configure and monitor the system.

HTTP

When HTTP is chosen under Server Types in the Logical Server Properties window, VPN-1/FireWall-1 NG detects any service request for a Logical Server and redirects the request to the load balancing module on the firewall. The load balancing application notifies the client that the request is being redirected to the destination physical server, which is selected based on the load balancing algorithm used. The rest of the session is conducted between the client and the destination physical server without the intervention of the load balancing module.

Other Load Balancing

Other load balancing places entries in the VPN-1/FireWall-1 NG address translation tables for a connection. Other load balancing allows a server's IP address to be a Logical Server's address from a firewall to a client, and a physical server's IP address from a server to the firewall. Each HTTP connection is then handled separately, and the connection may be redirected to different servers. This may cause problems in some cases; for example, in an application where a user fills in a number of HTTP forms and a single server is expected to process all the data.

Non-HTTP Load Balancing

When a non-HTTP service request is received—FTP for example—the client starts an FTP session on the FTP Logical Server, and VPN-1/FireWall-1 NG uses a special address translation mechanism similar to a reverse hide. VPN-1/FireWall-1 NG modifies the IP address of the incoming packets. If a back connection is opened, the connection is correctly established between the server and client automatically. The source IP address of the packets is changed back to the Logical Server's IP address for outgoing packets.

Load Balancing Algorithms and Their Use

VPN-1/FireWall-1 NG load balancing algorithms determine which physical server will handle the new communication request. The VPN-1/FireWall-1 NG load balancing algorithms prevent any server from handling a disproportionate volume of traffic. In the case of the Server Load algorithm, each incoming connection request is directed to the server with the lightest load.

Server Load and Round Trip are two of the HTTP load balancing algorithms. The main difference between the two is that Server Load uses VPN-1/FireWall-1 NG load measuring, requiring that the VPN-1/FireWall-1 NG Load Measuring Agent be installed on the physical servers, and Round Trip does not.

In a service provider environment, if you are offering a customer full managed servers, incorporating the Load Measuring Agents into the standard customer server build is easy and provides end-to-end visibility of the whole solution. The corporate customer has the same advantage. However, if you are a managed security provider then Round Trip is probably the best option because it does not require you to place code on systems that may have taken your customer months to stabilize.

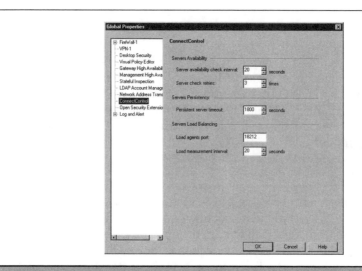

Figure 14-2. ConnectControl properties

ConnectControl Properties

The ConnectControl properties are set using the Global Properties Setup Window. To access this window, from the Management Console, select Policy | Global Properties | Connect Control, as shown in Figure 14-2.

The ConnectControl properties are listed in Table 14-2 with their descriptions.

Load Measuring Agent

Load Measuring Agent is the VPN-1/FireWall-1 NG load balancing component. Check Point provides a sample Load Measuring Agent application for installation on servers on which VPN-1/FireWall-1 NG is not installed and provides a protocol for users who wish to write their own agents.

Property	Description
Server Availability Check Interval	The interval, in seconds, in which the module will ping a physical server to determine if it is available
Server Check Retries	The number of consecutive failures for a server check before the module considers the server to be unavailable
Persistent Server Timeout	The length of time connections are redirected to the same physical server when Persistent Server mode is enabled for a Logical Server in the Logical Server Properties option
Load Agents Port	The port the Load Measurement Agent uses to communicate
Load Measurement Interval	The intervals at which the Load Measurement Agent measures the load

Table 14-2. ConnectControl Properties

Server Load Algorithm

The Server Load algorithm queries all physical servers in a Logical Server group to determine which is the best to handle a communication request. A Load Measuring Agent must be installed on each physical server. Figure 14-3 shows how the Server Load measuring algorithm distributes communication requests.

There are three steps in the Server Load algorithm process:

1. A client sends an HTTP communication request to a Logical Server.

2. The load balancing application queries traffic on the HTTP physical servers using the Server Load algorithm. The load balancing application then sends a redirect to the client with the IP address of the chosen physical server, the one with the lightest load.

3. The client communicates directly with the physical server, assuming the server is using persistent-server mode.

Round Trip

The Round Trip algorithm uses Ping to determine the time of the round trips between the firewall and each physical layer server, and chooses the server with the shortest round-trip time.

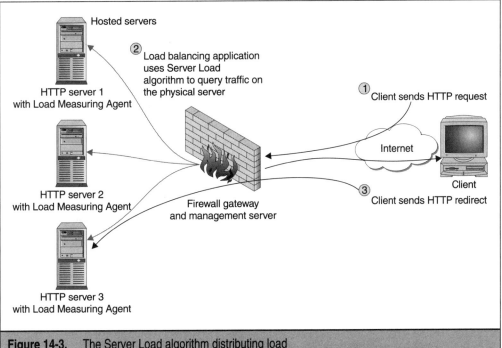

Figure 14-3.   The Server Load algorithm distributing load

Round Robin

Round Robin is a sequential algorithm, which means requests are directed to servers in sequential order and VPN-1/FireWall-1 NG chooses the next server in the list. The Round Robin algorithm assumes that all physical servers are equally capable of servicing connection requests, regardless of location or server load.

If a server fails or is unreachable, the application ceases directing connections to that server until it is available. The firewall pings the servers and, if one does not reply, the firewall will not send a request to that server. If, however, a server goes down but still replies to a ping, the firewall module will continue to direct connections to the server.

Random

The Random load balancing algorithm chooses a server at random. That is, when all other network variables are deemed equal, the algorithm directs connection requests to servers on a random basis.

Domain

With the Domain algorithm, VPN-1/FireWall-1 NG chooses the closest server based on domain names. This algorithm is useful outside a network, such as when a domain name identifies the location of a remote device.

NOTE This method is not recommended as it creates a noticeable delay to HTTP requests because of the reverse DNS lookups required.

SETTING UP LOAD BALANCING ALGORITHMS

To configure load balancing, you are going to build on the VPN-1/FireWall-1 NG installation carried out in Chapter 7 for the Nokia Appliance platform. Fiction Corporation wants two servers to be hosted behind the Nokia firewall and they want load balancing. The diagram for the Fiction Corporation–hosted servers is shown in Figure 14-4.

REAL WORLD LOAD BALANCING CONFIGURATION

We will now go through a step-by-step process to begin load balancing using VPN-1/ FireWall-1 NG in the real world. Fiction Corporation has been allocated a network range of 194.73.134.96/27. To load balance two servers for HTTP, three valid IP addresses are required: one IP address for the logical server and one IP address for the each of the web servers.

1. To create the web server objects, launch the Management Console and connect to the firewall. Now create workstation objects for the two web server objects as follows:

Name:	Web01
IP address:	172.31.249.100
Valid IP:	194.73.134.100

Name:	Web02
IP address:	172.31.249.101
Valid IP:	194.73.134.101

2. To create the web server group, group both Web01 and Web02 into a group called WebServers. Your object windows should look like those in Figure 14-5.

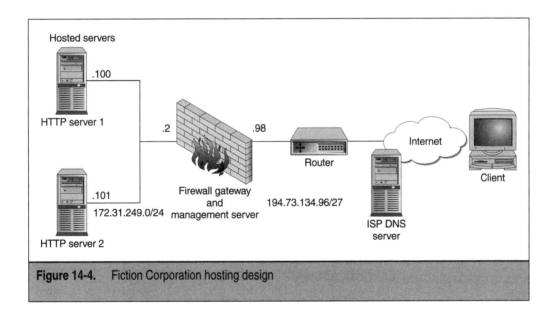

Figure 14-4.   Fiction Corporation hosting design

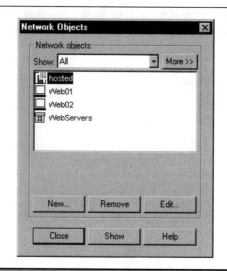

Figure 14-5. Fiction Corporation hosted objects

3. Define the Logical Server object with the Round Robin algorithm with Persistent Server mode turned on using the following information:

Name:	HTTP_LS
Valid IP:	194.73.134.102
Server Type:	HTTP
Server Group:	WebServers
Persistent Server Mode:	On
Balance Mode:	Round Robin

4. To define a Logical Server, click the new button on the Network Objects screen and the new menu appears as shown in Figure 14-6.

5. Select the Logical Server option from the New menu, and the Logical Properties screen appears, as shown in Figure 14-7. Complete the screen with the information as defined for logical server in Step 3 then check Persistent Server Mode, click Persistence by Service and Balance Method, Round Robin.

6. Click OK to save the new Logical Server object.

7. To build a Rule Base for load balancing, you need to first create a Cleanup Rule in the empty Rule Base. Select Rules | Add Rule | Top.

8. Above the Cleanup Rule, create the rule for access to the Logical Server as detailed in the following table.

Source	Destination	Service	Action	Comment
Any	HTTP_LS	HTTP	Accept	Load Balancing Rule
Any	Any	Any	Drop	Cleanup Rule

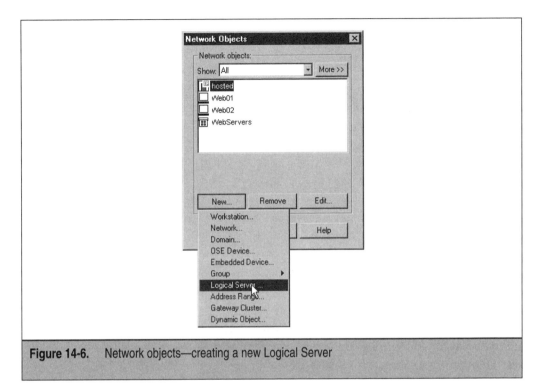

Figure 14-6. Network objects—creating a new Logical Server

The completed Rule Base should look like Figure 14-8.

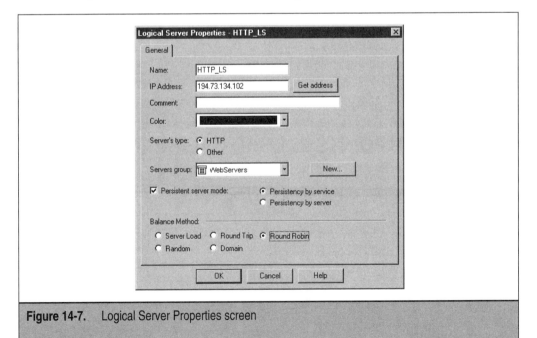

Figure 14-7. Logical Server Properties screen

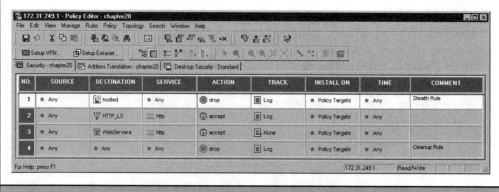

Figure 14-8. Load Balancing Rule Base

Installing and Testing the Policy

The Policy can be installed and tested. For details on Policy Installation, see Chapter 8. Note that in an actual deployment, Fiction Corporation would need more rules for allowing management access from their corporate sites for server updates and content uploads, but for the purpose of defining load balancing alone, the rules shown here are all that is required.

Connect Control Feature Enhancements

Feature Pack 1 included some enhancements to Connect Control including the extension of support for all protocols, not just TCP and UDP, for use with Logical Server rules. SSL is also now supported in HTTP mode.

VPN-1/FireWall-1 NG timeouts and frequency values have been opened up so they can be configured under the Connect Control option in Global Properties of a Security Policy, as shown in Figure 14-9.

CHECKLIST: KEY POINTS IN LOAD BALANCING

The following is a checklist for the key points in load balancing:

☐ Define the need for VPN-1/FireWall-1 NG load balancing.

☐ Define ConnectControl.

☐ Show how ConnectControl offers advanced load balancing.

☐ List all of the options for load balancing.

☐ List all of the simple Ping-based checks.

☐ List all of the load measurement components.

☐ Monitor server application availability via other management tools.

☐ Identify why the load measurement agent would serve no purpose in the monitoring of server application availability.

☐ Explain why Round Trip time would suffice in the monitoring of server application availability.

☐ Define Load Balance Method—Server Load, Round Trip, Round Robin, Random, and Domain.

☐ Configure load balancing so that it is tailored to the requirements of a particular deployment.

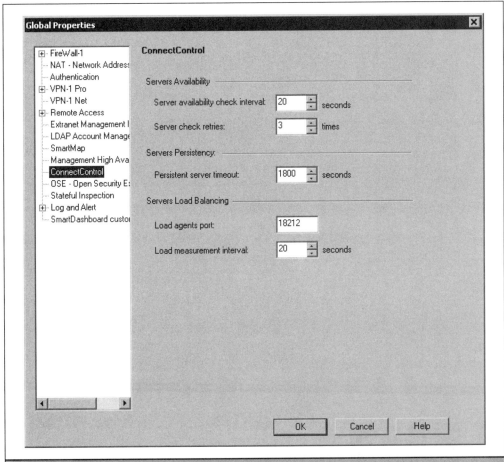

Figure 14-9.   New configurable ConnectControl properties

CHAPTER 15

Content Security and Content Vectoring Protocol

Most businesses are concerned about protecting the corporate network against virus infections and the amount of time employees can spend surfing the Internet for non-work-related information. Check Point provides Content Security via the VPN-1/FireWall-1 NG Security Servers.

Content Security is an integral part of VPN-1/FireWall-1 NG and does not require any additional servers. Check Point, however, has a large number of third-party developers called OPSEC (Open Platform for Security) partners who have developed products that integrate with VPN-1/FireWall-1 NG via the Content Vectoring Protocol (CVP).

To illustrate how Content Security is configured with VPN-1/FireWall-1 NG, this chapter will introduce a CVP server to Fiction Corporation's London site and go through the steps of configuring VPN-1/FireWall-1 NG for CVP operation.

ROLE OF THE SECURITY SERVER

VPN-1/FireWall-1 NG Security Servers provide a wide range of integrated security that can be expanded by using OPSEC partner software and VPN-1/FireWall-1 NG Security Servers. Security Servers improve network security with several features, including:

- Virus protection
- Content Security
- Authentication
- Java blocking
- ActiveX blocking

There are a large number of third-party applications available that integrate with Check Point VPN-1/FireWall-1 NG. A current list of supported applications is available on the Check Point OPSEC website at www.opsec.com.

NOTE Check Point takes OPSEC certification very seriously, and partner applications are thoroughly tested before being given the OPSEC-certified approval.

EXTENDING DATA INSPECTION WITH CONTENT SECURITY

Content security extends the scope of data inspection to the highest level of a service's protocol, achieving highly tuned access control to network resources. VPN-1/FireWall-1 NG provides Content Security for the following connections, using VPN-1/FireWall-1 NG Security Servers and resource object specifications:

- HTTP
- FTP
- SMTP

A VPN-1/FireWall-1 NG resource specification defines a set of entities, which can be accessed by a specific protocol. You can define a resource based on HTTP, FTP, and SMTP. For example, you may define a URI resource whose attributes are a list of URLs and the HTTP and FTP schemes. The resource can be used in a Rule Base the same way as a service, with the standard logging and alerting methods available for monitoring.

For each connection that is established through the VPN-1/FireWall-1 NG Security Server, the administrator is able to control specific access according to fields that belong to the specific service. When a resource is specified, the Security Server will divert the connection to a CVP server, or a URI Filtering Protocol (UFP) server.

When a rule specifies a resource in the service field of the Rule Base, the VPN-1/ FireWall-1 NG Inspection Module diverts all packets on the connection to the corresponding Security Server, which performs the required Content Security inspection. If the connection is allowed, the Security Server opens a second connection to the final destination, as shown in Figure 15-1.

The administrator can control specific access, according to fields that belong to the specific service for each connection established through a VPN-1/FireWall-1 NG Security Server. The major benefit enabled by the Content Security feature is that CVP checks for files transferred and URI filtering. When a resource is specified, the Security Server diverts the connection to either a CVP or UFP server:

- **Content Vectoring Protocol (CVP)**   A CVP server reports on the contents of files by examining either inbound or outbound data packets prior to establishing a connection.

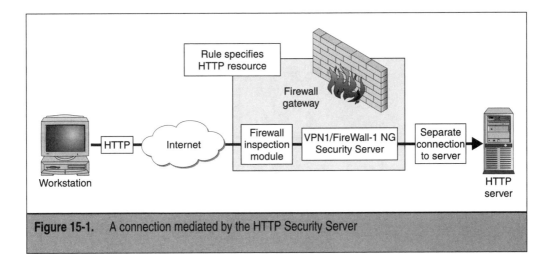

Figure 15-1.   A connection mediated by the HTTP Security Server

- **URI Filtering Protocol (UFP)**   A UFP server maintains a list of URLs and their categories. The URL filtering protocol protects against specific destinations on the Internet. This Security Server can determine user rights, including the ability to visit a particular website or download certain files. Some of the OPSEC-certified applications maintain lists in excess of 1.5 million sites in a variety of categories.

VPN-1/FireWall-1 NG has the capability to perform URL filtering without additional software, but this integrated functionality is not scalable. Check Point recommends that no more than 50 restricted site URLs are configured, due to the entries having to be manually maintained. In practice, when deploying Content Security or URL filtering, we tend to bypass this feature and use CVP-based products that integrate with VPN-1/FireWall-1 NG.

Figure 15-2 shows what happens when a VPN-1/FireWall-1 NG Security Server passes a file to a Content Vectoring server for inspection during an FTP session.

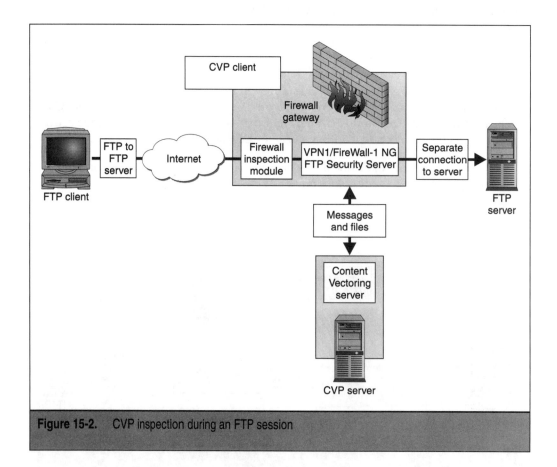

Figure 15-2.   CVP inspection during an FTP session

Content inspection during an FTP session, as detailed in Figure 15-2, occurs in the following order:

1. VPN-1/FireWall-1 NG determines that the Content Vectoring server must be invoked. The relevant rule for the connection specifies a resource that includes CVP checking.

2. The FTP server connects to the Content Vectoring server and initiates the CVP.

3. The FTP Security Server sends the file to be inspected to the Content Vectoring server.

4. The Content Vectoring server inspects the file and returns a Validation Result message, notifying the FTP Security Server of the result of the inspection.

5. The Content Vectoring server optionally returns a modified version of the file to the FTP Security Server.

The FTP Security Server takes the action defined for the resource, either allowing or disallowing the file transfer.

Content Vectoring Protocol (CVP)

VPN-1/FireWall-1 NG does not have any integrated antivirus software. The Security Server allows the VPN-1/FireWall-1 NG gateway to transfer packets to another server running an OPSEC-certified virus scanner. This method uses Content Vectoring Protocol (CVP) to transfer packets to and from an OPSEC virus scanning server.

CVP uses TCP port 18181 to communicate with the CVP server. When a file transfer is initiated, the VPN-1/FireWall-1 NG Security Server redirects the packets to the CVP server running the antivirus scanner. The virus scanner determines if there is a virus and returns the file to the VPN-1/FireWall-1 NG gateway if it is virus-free. These servers may be integrated with HTTP, FTP, and SMTP transfers.

Using CVP Security Servers for virus scanning assists network security in several ways:

- Eliminates viruses from being downloaded from FTP or HTTP transfers

- Prevents malicious script viruses from entering the e-mail system

- Off-loads the scanning process to another server and maintains the high performance of the VPN-1/FireWall-1 NG gateway

The CVP servers should be placed either on the DMZ or a private segment with the VPN-1/FireWall-1 NG gateway, as shown in Figure 15-3, using Fiction Corporation as an example. This allows fast, secure connections between the CVP servers and the VPN-1/FireWall-1 NG gateway. You will notice that the Mail Relay is no longer required because SMTP virus scanning will now be performed as the SMTP packets pass through the firewall.

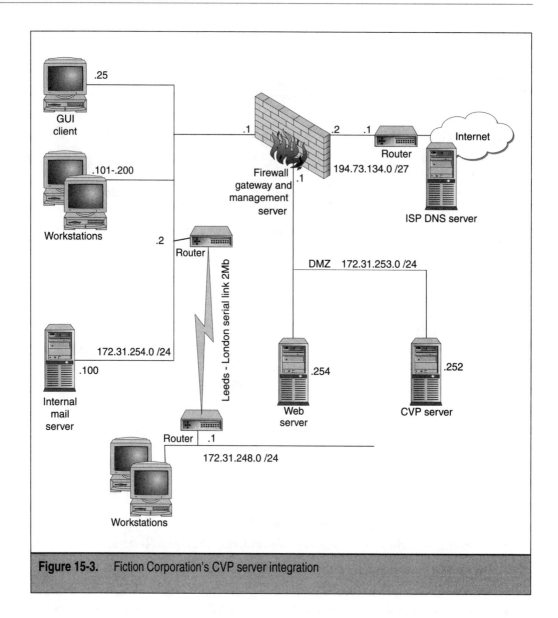

Figure 15-3. Fiction Corporation's CVP server integration

Antivirus inspection reduces the vulnerability of hosts and gateways. With the use of an external antivirus module or a CVP server, the antivirus option can check all files transferred for HTTP, FTP, and SMTP.

Implementing Content Security (Aladdin Systems eSafe)

You will now create a CVP server to offer SMTP, HTTP, and FTP Content Security through all methods (Get, Put, Post, and so on). Adding content filtering to VPN-1/FireWall-1 NG using Aladdin Knowledge System eSafe Gateway Software will be discussed. It is important that you examine the OPSEC partner's product specific documentation and release notes to ensure a successful implementation because there are differing requirements depending on which third-party vendor's products are chosen.

The Aladdin eSafe Gateway Software provides proactive, multitiered Internet Content Security for gateway and mail servers, protecting the entire enterprise from:

- Viruses, Trojans, worms, blended threats, and other malicious code that destroys or steals digital assets
- Spam that reduces productivity, wasting bandwidth and space
- Security exploits in corporate e-mail servers and e-mail clients
- Inappropriate and nonproductive material including the optional URL Filtering module, which utilizes the SurfControl database of inappropriate sites
- The misuse of company resources

Installing a CVP Server

Using Aladdin Systems documentation, configure the Aladdin eSafe Gateway Software by supplying IP addresses and activating the license. We will concentrate on the Check Point CVP configuration in the next section. To obtain information about the eSafe product visit the website at http://www.ealaddin.com or http://www.esafe.com and select the support and downloads section where documentation and evaluation software to work through the example in this chapter is freely available.

Increasing the Default Mail Message Size

VPN-1/FireWall-1 NG by default restricts mail messages to 1MB in size when using CVP applications. Most organizations frequently send much larger messages but some prefer to restrict the size for management purposes. For Fiction Corporation, you will increase the default to 5MB as shown in Figure 15-4. To perform this operation, select the gateway object and expand the Advanced option in the list and adjust the mail message size as shown.

Creating a CVP Object

Launch the VPN-1/FireWall-1 Policy Editor. Under Manage | Network Objects, define the CVP server as a workstation object with the following information, as shown in

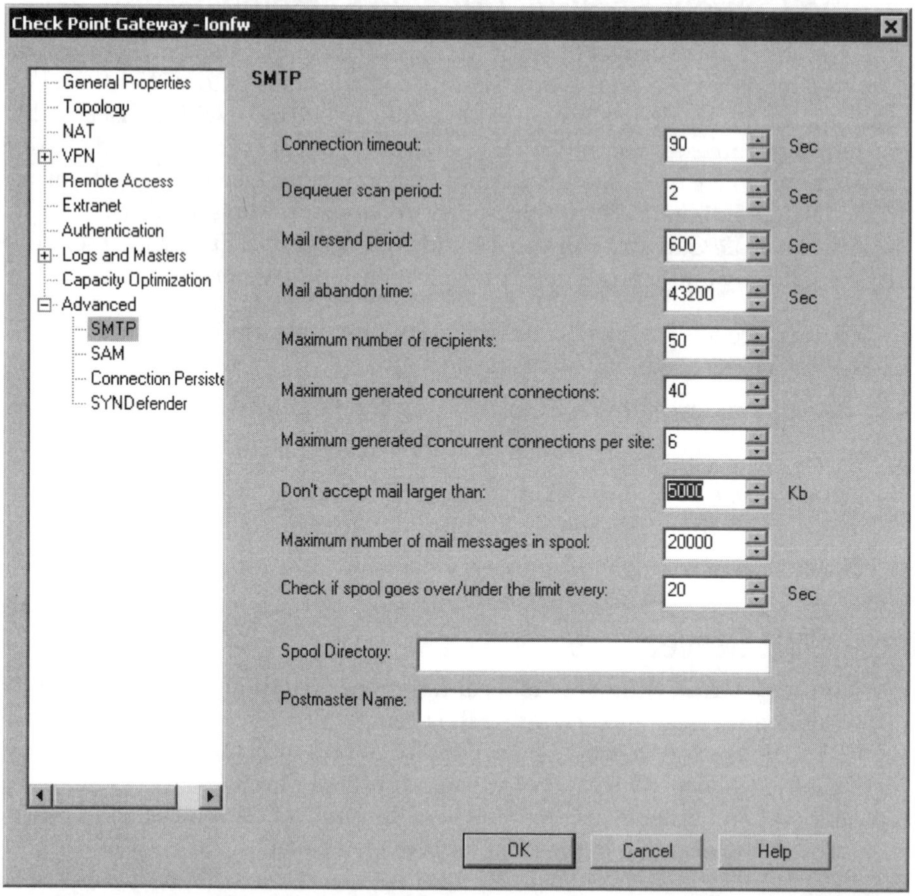

Figure 15-4. Increasing the default mail message size

Figure 15-5. Select the NAT option from the left pane and enter a Static NAT using the IP address shown.

Name:	esafe01
IP Address:	172.31.253.252
Color:	Blue
NAT	Static
NAT IP	194.73.134.5

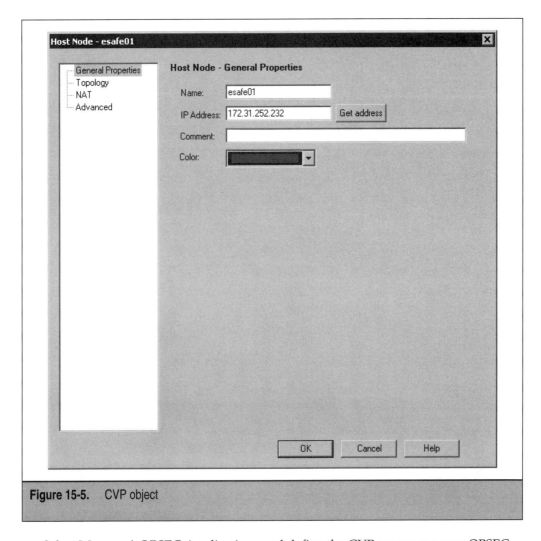

Figure 15-5. CVP object

Select Manage | OPSEC Applications and define the CVP server as a new OPSEC application by clicking New and selecting OPSEC Application. Under the General tab, enter the following information and select OK, as shown in Figure 15-6.

Name:	CVP-Gateway
Color:	Blue
Host:	Select the esafe01 object created previously
Vendor:	Select Aladdin_Knowledge_Systems
Product	ESafe_Protect_Gateway
Version	3.0
Server Entities	Check the CVP box

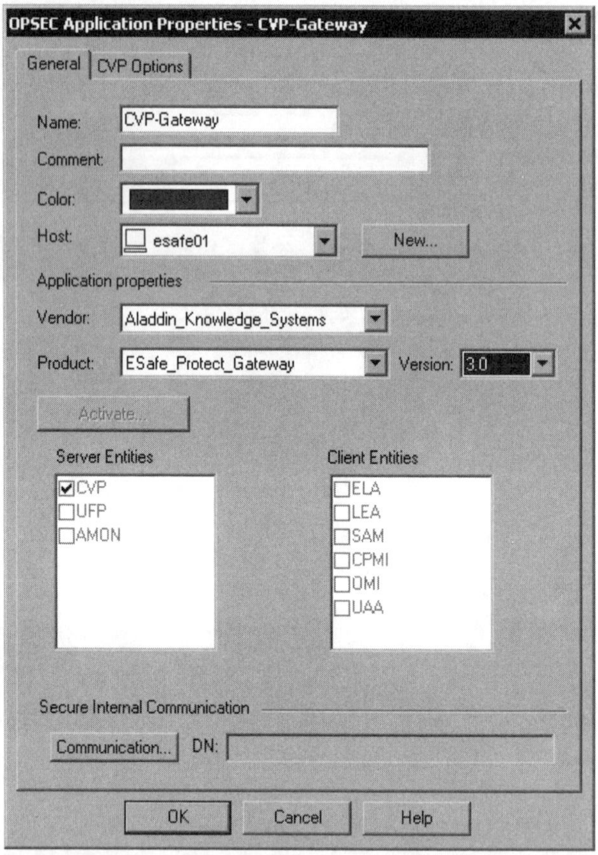

Figure 15-6. OPSEC application General tab

Now click the CVP Options tab. If the CVP product was designed for VPN-1/
FireWall-1 4.x, click the Use Early Versions Compatibility Mode check box and click
the appropriate radio button to choose the type of authentication required, as shown
in Figure 15-7. Select Clear (OPSEC) because the server is secure on the Fiction
Corporation DMZ. Select the OK button to save the object. SSL-based authentication
is available for communication between the firewall and the OPSEC application if required.

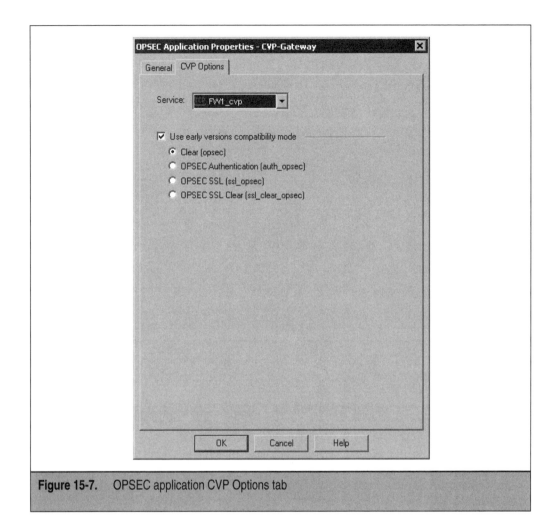

Figure 15-7. OPSEC application CVP Options tab

Creating an FTP Resource

Now you are going to define an FTP resource. Under Manage | Resources, select the General tab to define a new FTP resource. In the Name field, enter FTP-Resource. In the Exception Track section, select Log, as shown in Figure 15-8.

Select the Match tab, ensure that the path field has an asterisk, and check both the GET and PUT check boxes, as shown in Figure 15-9.

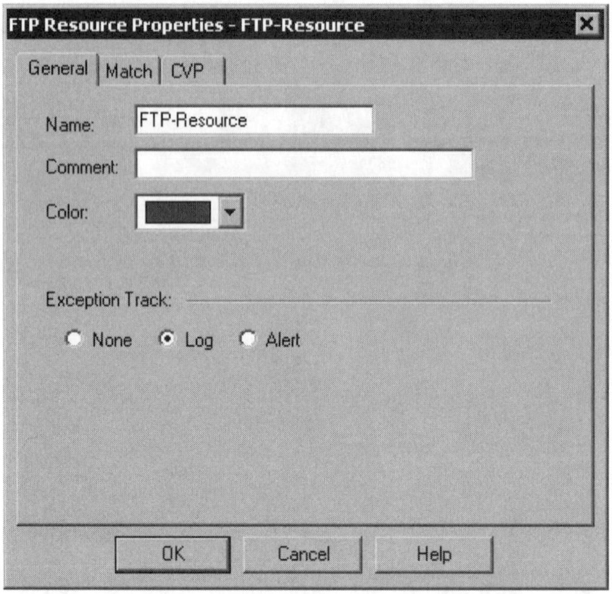

Figure 15-8. FTP Resource General tab

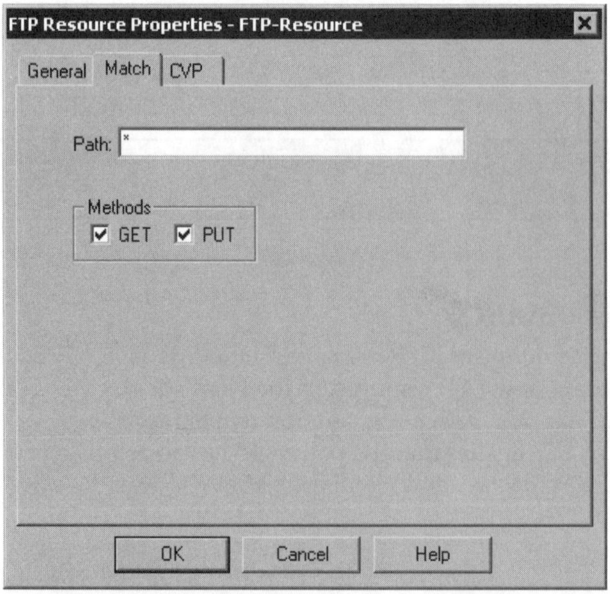

Figure 15-9. FTP Resource Match tab

Select the CVP tab. Check the Use CVP (Content Vectoring Protocol) check box and choose CVP-Gateway from the CVP Server menu, as shown in Figure 15-10. Ensure that CVP Server Is Allowed to Modify Content and Return Data After Content Is Approved are selected as shown. Click OK to return to the Resources List.

Creating a URI (HTTP) Resource

Select New URI from the Resources List and check that the following information is entered, as shown in Figure 15-11:

Name:	HTTP-Resource
Connection Methods:	Transparent and Proxy
Exception Track:	Log
URI Match:	Wild Cards

Select the Match tab. Unless you are experienced in using Content Security, we recommend you check all the boxes and enter an asterisk (*) in all the text fields, as shown in Figure 15-12.

Under the CVP tab, check Use CVP and select the CVP-Gateway object. Check the Send HTTP Headers to CVP Server check box and ensure that Send HTTP Requests to CVP Server is deselected, as shown in Figure 15-13. Click OK to return to the Resources List.

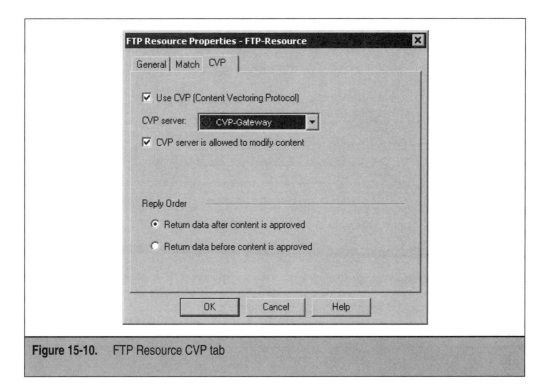

Figure 15-10.   FTP Resource CVP tab

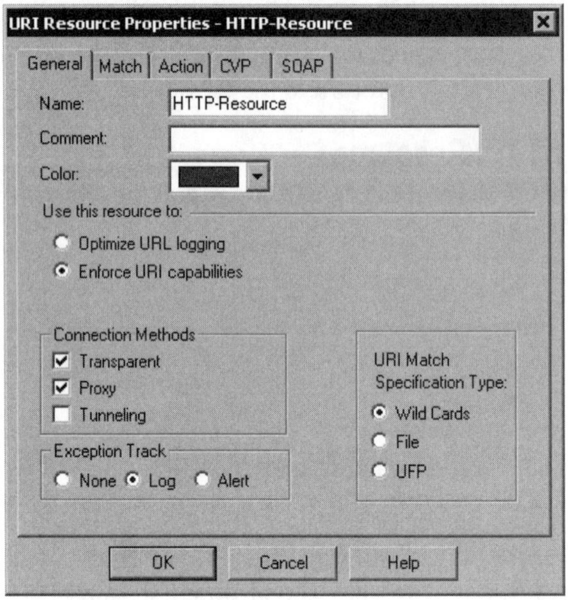

Figure 15-11. URI Resource General tab

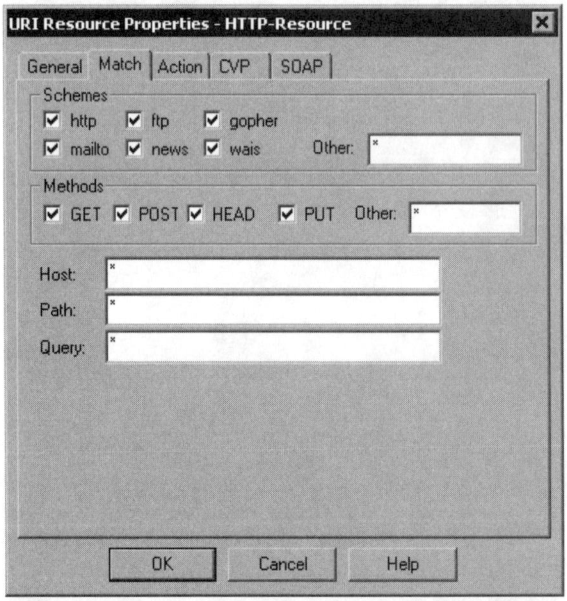

Figure 15-12. URI Resource Match tab

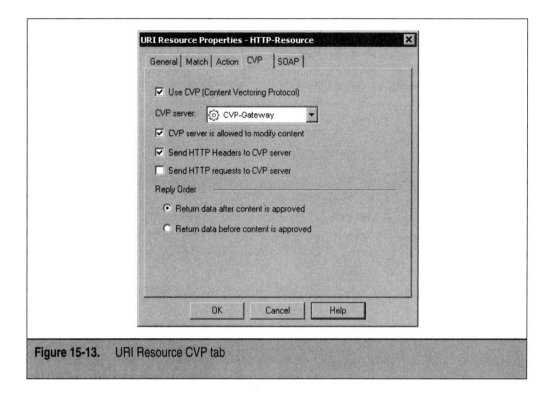

Figure 15-13. URI Resource CVP tab

Creating an SMTP-Out Resource

For SMTP, two resources need to be created: the first for SMTP outgoing traffic and the second for inbound SMTP. Select New SMTP from the Resources List and enter SMTP-Out in the Name field. Select Log under Exception Tracking, as shown in Figure 15-14.

> **CAUTION** Entering the Mail Server address within the Mail Delivery section can cause some OPSEC applications to loop. Check the OPSEC partner's documentation.

Select the Match tab and enter an asterisk (*) in both the Sender and Recipient fields, as shown in Figure 15-15. This is the general setting that most firewall administrators use. If you are a advanced user, you can customize these settings, but they are poorly documented by Check Point—our recommendation is to stick with using the asterisk, which will inspect everything.

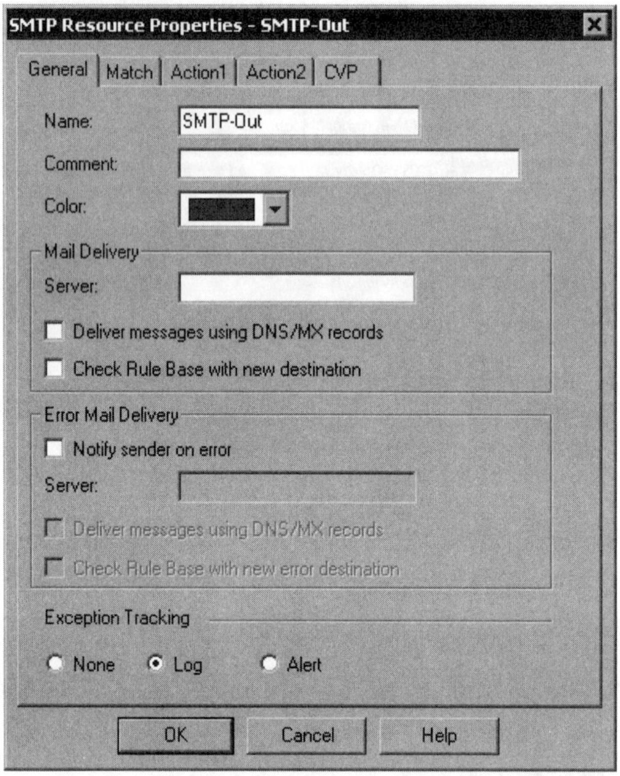

Figure 15-14. SMTP-Out Resource General tab

Select the Action2 tab and change the Do Not Send Mail Larger Than field to a value that is acceptable to your business. As shown in Figure 15-16 for the Fiction Corporation example, we selected 5000KB, because the default of 1000KB does not meet our requirements. This limit will be enforced by the VPN-1/FireWall-1 Security Server.

The Action1 tab is not required for configuration of the eSafe gateway product.

Figure 15-15. SMTP-Out Resource Match tab

NOTE If the value shown in Figure 15-16 differs from the Don't Accept Mail Larger Than value as shown in Figure 15-4, the smaller of the two values will be used.

Under the CVP tab, check Use CVP and, in the CVP server listbox, choose the CVP-Gateway object. Make sure you check Send SMTP Headers to CVP Server, as shown in Figure 15-17. CVP Server Is Allowed to Modify Content and Return Data After Content Is Approved should also be selected.

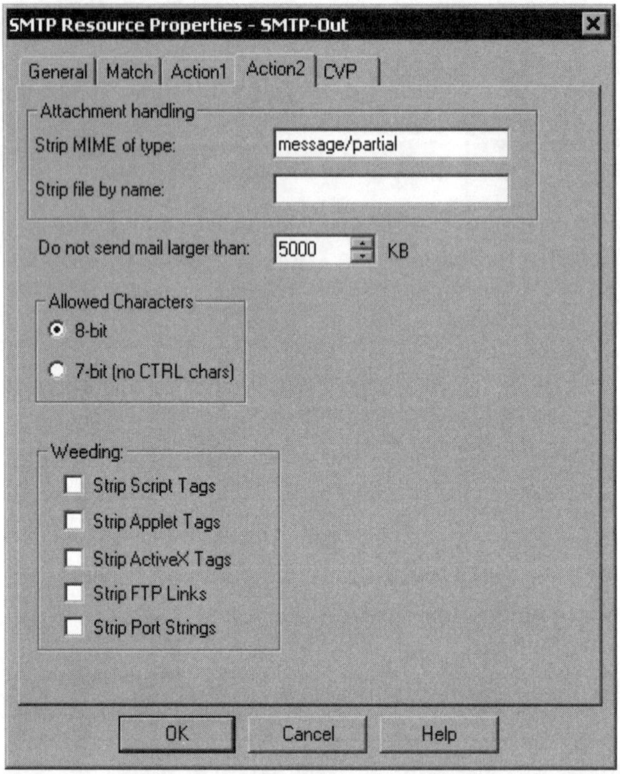

Figure 15-16. SMTP-Out Resource Action2 tab

Click OK to return to the Resources List. If you did not type in message/partial as shown in Figure 15-16, you will be shown the Policy Editor dialog box, which will ask you whether to strip MIME of type message/partial. Select Yes, and this will be inserted into the object definition.

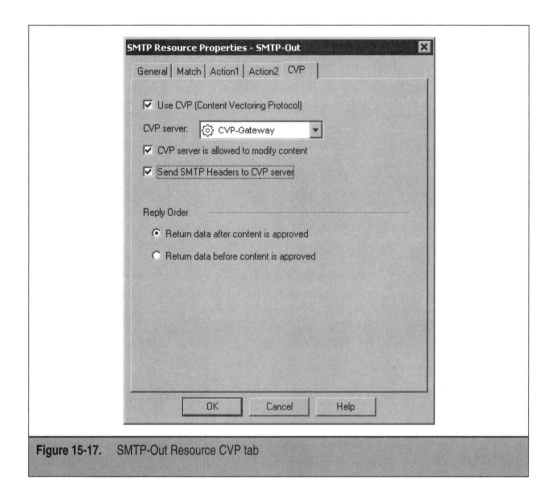

Figure 15-17.   SMTP-Out Resource CVP tab

Creating an SMTP-In Resource

You will now define a second SMTP resource. Defining two resources allows you to limit the SMTP traffic to your domains and prevents spammers from using your organization as a relay for spam.

Select New and SMTP as the resource from the options presented. Name this resource SMTP-In and select Log under the Exception Tracking section, as shown in Figure 15-18.

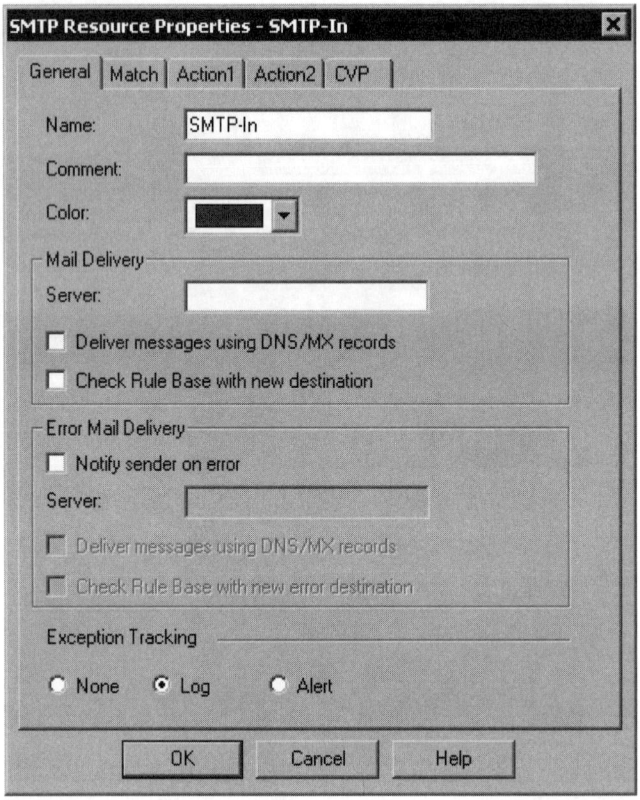

Figure 15-18. SMTP-In Resource General tab

Select the Match tab and enter an asterisk (*) in the Sender field and an asterisk with your domain in the Recipient field (for example, *@yourdomain.com). In the example shown in Figure 15-19, we specified *@fictioncorp.com. This ensures that the mail server will accept only messages destined for the Fiction Corporation domain and prevents the mail server from being used as a relay for spam.

TIP Multiple domains must be placed in curly brackets ({}) in the format {*@domain1.com,domain2.com}. This is useful where an organization uses multiple Domain Name System (DNS) names.

Figure 15-19.   SMTP-In Resource Match tab

Select the Action2 tab and enter *message/partial* in the Strip Mime of Type field. Type in the size of message allowed in the Do Not Send Mail Larger Than field, as shown in Figure 15-20. Under Allowed Characters, leave the default value of 8-bit selected.

The Action1 tab is not required for configuration of the eSafe gateway product.

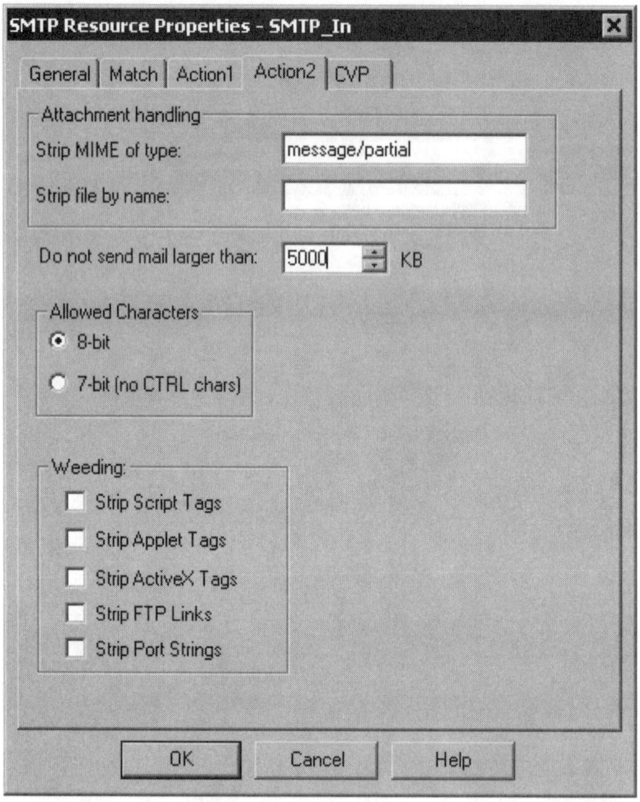

Figure 15-20. SMTP-In Resource Action2 tab

Under the CVP tab, check Use CVP and choose the CVP-Gateway object as the CVP server. Check Send SMTP Headers to CVP Server, as shown in Figure 15-21. Leave all other settings as shown in Figure 15-21, as these are defaults.

You have now defined resources for FTP, HTTP, and SMTP. The Resources list should look like Figure 15-22.

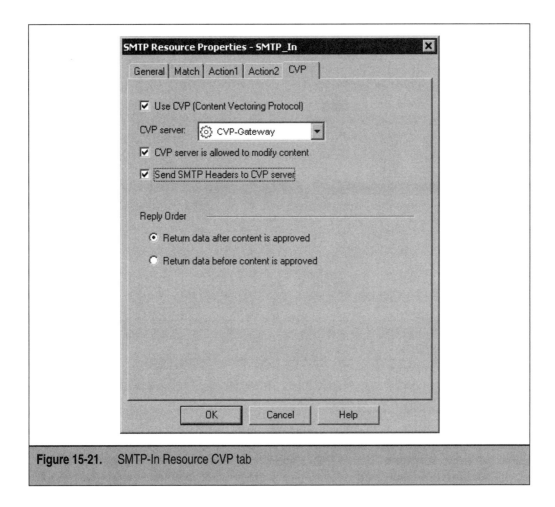

Figure 15-21. SMTP-In Resource CVP tab

Adding Rules for Content Security

We are now going to amend the Fiction Corporation London Rule Base to incorporate Content Security–specific rules. Often organizations install VPN-1/FireWall-1 NG and then decide at a later stage to add Content Security. We have deliberately designed the chapters to reflect this situation; you will have to analyze the original Rule Base and amend it to enable Content Security, just as you would in the real world.

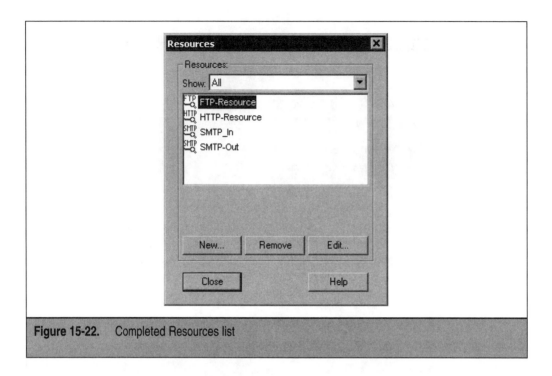

Figure 15-22. Completed Resources list

Planning Rule Base Changes

There are some key points to consider when working with Content Security rules. Let's examine a table of the rules first, as detailed in Table 15-1. When building a Rule Base, make a point of planning it first. This is good practice because it allows you to check your Rule Base logic and shuffle rules about until you are satisfied before working with what, in many cases, is a live firewall gateway.

The first two rules in Table 15-1 can be combined into a single rule for performance, but for initial debugging it is better to treat them as separate rules. The Content Security rules should be placed at the top of the Rule Base unless there are specific rules that need to be applied prior to the Content Security rules. We will work through such an example during the process of updating Fiction Corporation's London Rule Base.

Aladdin eSafe Caveats

Open the SMTP port for the eSafe Gateway machine as a Source. This is necessary to allow it to send e-mail alerts. For additional security, limit the destinations to the Mail Server(s) to which e-mail alerts will be sent (defined in eConsole under Administration | Alerts | Alert Recipients).

Source	Destination	Service	Action	Comment
esafe01	Internal-MailServer	SMTP	Accept	eSafe alerts
esafe01	Any	Domain-UDP FTP	Accept	eSafe Updates
Internal-MailServer	Any	SMTP with SMTP-Out	Accept	Use CVP for SMTP outbound
Any	Internal-MailServer	SMTP with SMTP-In	Accept	Use CVP for SMTP inbound
Internal_Nets	Any	FTP with FTP-Resource	Accept	Use CVP for FTP outbound
Internal_Nets	Any	HTTP with HTTP-Resource	Accept	Use CVP for HTTP outbound

Table 15-1. Plan of CVP Rule Base

Open ports 21 (FTP) and 53 (DNS) for the eSafe Gateway machine as a Source at the firewall to allow the eSafe Gateway machine to get updates from the eSafe update site.

Econsole can either be installed on the same segment as the eSafe gateway or, if connecting via a firewall, a rule needs to be created as follows:

Source	Destination	Service	Action	Comment
Econsole Workstation	eSafe Gateway	UDP 43891 UDP 43892 UDP 43893	Accept	Allows Econsole to talk to FW-1

NOTE eConsole is a Windows-based configuration console for the Aladdin appliance.

First, study the current Fiction Corporation Rule Base, as shown in Figure 15-23, and examine what changes are required.

Preparing the Rule Base

You should note that the Internal Mail Server will require a registered (or valid IP) address because Mail Servers on the Internet will be trying to send mail directly to this server which will be vetted by your SMTP resource with the SMTP-In rule.

To prepare the Rule Base completely, perform the following tasks:

- Remove the SMTP rules.
- Remove the HTTP and FTP rules.
- Supply a public IP address for the Internal-MailServer.
- Add the two rules for the esafe01 object above the Stealth rule.

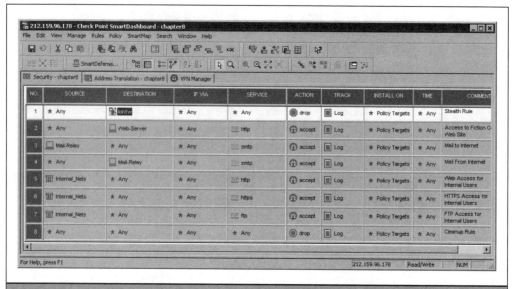

Figure 15-23. Fiction Corporation's initial London Rule Base

The prepared Rule Base is shown in Figure 15-24.

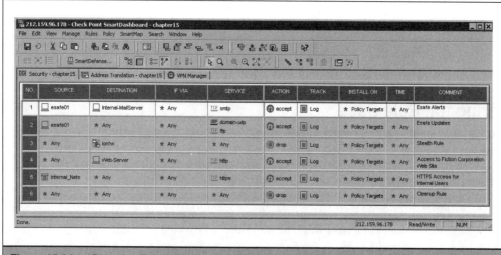

Figure 15-24. Preparing Fiction Corporation's Rule Base

Adding the Content Security Rules

Now you will work through the rules you defined in Table 15-1. Remember that these rules should be added at the top of the Rule Base. Start with the first rule in the table, which is the SMTP-Out.

Select the No. column, right-click in the 2 field, and select Add Rule | Below, to add a new default rule after the esafe rules of the Rule Base. Select Internal-MailServer as the source and Any as the destination. In the Service column, right-click and select Add with Resource from the pop-up menu, as shown in Figure 15-25.

In the Service with Resource dialog, as shown in Figure 15-26, select smtp under Service and select SMTP-Out under Resource.

Finish off the rule by selecting accept in the Action column and adding a comment saying Outbound SMTP. Repeat this procedure for each of the other rules in Table 15-1, making sure that the correct Service is selected. The completed Rule Base should look like Figure 15-27.

Editing $FWDIR\objects_5_0.C

The changes discussed in this section are specific to the Aladdin Knowledge Systems eSafe Gateway Software. It is important to consult vendor notes if using other OPSEC partner products.

VPN-1/FireWall-1 NG handles objects files differently from version 4.*x*. In the past, there was an objects.C file on both the module and the management servers. VPN-1/FireWall-1 NG has an objects file on the module and a new file, objects_5_0.C, located on the Management Station. Note that a new objects.C file gets created and

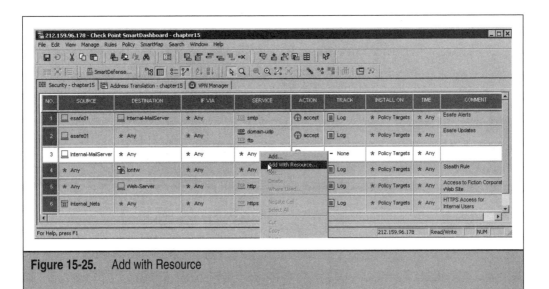

Figure 15-25. Add with Resource

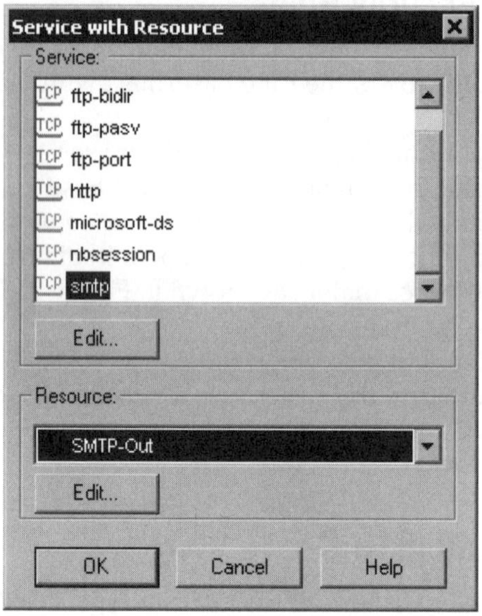

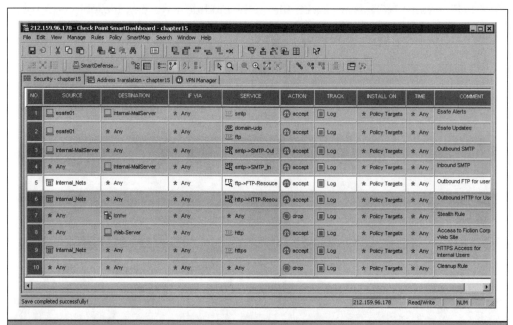

Figure 15-26. Service with Resource

Figure 15-27. Fiction Corporation's Rule Base with Content Security Rules

pushed to the module each time a policy is installed! Thus, editing the objects.C file on the module or the management server is no longer needed or desirable because the change will be lost the next time you install a new policy or restart the Management Server.

When installing eSafe Gateway for CVP, you need to edit the objects_5_0.C file on the VPN-1/FireWall-1 Management Server to include the attributes in the example below. The objects_5_0.C file should be edited on the VPN-1/FireWall-1 Management Station only.

The easiest and most efficient way to edit the objects_5_0.C file is to use Check Point's dbedit utility. The dbedit utility is designed to replace the error-prone manual editing of the objects_5_0.C file and to allow searching of the file based on type and attribute. Additionally, the use of this tool maintains the audit trail for changes to the database, another new feature of VPN-1/FireWall-1 NG.

To make the necessary changes:

1. Close all VPN-1/FireWall-1 NG GUI clients.

2. Back up the original FWDIR/conf/objects_5_0.C to another partition or folder.

3. From a command line, run dbedit. (To learn about the dbedit command options, issue the command dbedit -h.)

4. Enter a resolvable host name or IP address when prompted.

5. Enter the username and password of the VPN-1/FireWall-1 administrator when prompted.

6. Enter each attribute on a separate line as listed in the following example. If you use the recommended values for the attributes (as shown in the example), you can prepare a text file and add it using the *filename* parameter (if you create a text file named ngcvp.txt, use the command dbedit –f ngcvp.txt). If you choose to edit manually, use the quit command to exit.

Example with Recommended Values

Important Note: NG does not recognize some version 4.x commands, such as http_sup_continue true.

- modify properties firewall_properties smtp_encoded_content_field true
- modify properties firewall_properties smtp_rfc821 false
- modify properties firewall_properties http_disable_content_enc true
- modify properties firewall_properties http_disable_content_type true
- modify properties firewall_properties http_use_host_h_as_dst true
- modify properties firewall_properties http_force_down_to_10 1
- modify properties firewall_properties http_avoid_keep_alive true
- modify properties firewall_properties http_max_header_length 8000

- modify properties firewall_properties http_max_url_length 8000
- modify properties firewall_properties http_check_request_validity false
- modify properties firewall_properties http_check_response_validity false
- modify properties firewall_properties http_cvp_allow_chunked true
- modify properties firewall_properties http_weeding_allow_chunked true
- modify properties firewall_properties http_block_java_allow_chunked true
- modify properties firewall_properties http_allow_ranges true
- modify properties firewall_properties http_buffers_size 32768
- modify properties firewall_properties http_allow_content_disposition true
- modify properties firewall_properties http_enable_uri_queries false

Saving Your Changes

To save your changes without exiting dbedit, issue the command update properties firewall_properties. To save your changes and exit dbedit, issue the quit command. To exit dbedit without saving your changes, press CTRL+C.

Reinstall the Security Policy (open the VPN-1/FireWall-1 GUI and click Install).

Database Tool (FP3 Only)

The Database Tool is a GUI utility that is a CPMI client whose purpose is to edit the objects file on the Management Server (mainly to change the properties that cannot be edited through SmartDashboard). The file is downloadable or can be obtained from your Check Point authorized reseller. This tool is a lot easier than working with command-line utilities or manually editing objects_5_0.C. This utility supports version NG FP3 and above only.

The zipped file includes three files:

- GuiDBedit.exe
- GUIDBEDIT.HLP
- GuiDBedit.CNT

To start using this utility, copy these files to the Check Point Management Clients directory (example: C:\Program Files\CheckPoint\SmartClients\NG FP3\program) and then run GuiDBedit. Enter the information required to connect to the Management Server, as shown in Figure 15-28.

To change the settings, select Table | Global Properties | Properties and double-click firewall_properties in the right pane, as shown in Figure 15-29. You can now search for and double-click on the appropriate properties in an easy-to-use GUI tool.

Figure 15-28. Database Tool

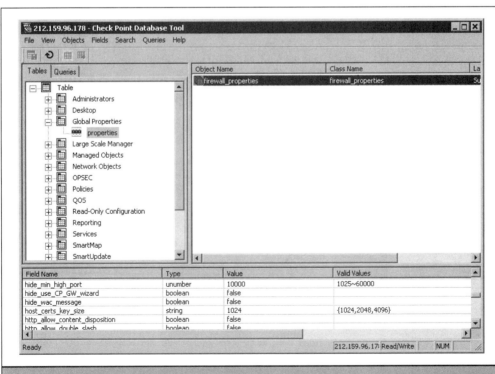

Figure 15-29. Firewall properties

Database Tool Attributes

Table 15-2 lists each of the attributes, with a brief description of its purpose, that are required to be tuned for CVP configuration when using eSafe gateway software.

Attribute	Purpose
:smtp_encoded_content_field (true)	Prevents incorrect parsing of headers by the firewall's MIME-stripper, which causes attachments to be stripped and replaced by a numbered ATT file containing the text **<<MIME ATTACHMENT STRIPPED>>**. This mainly occurs with MS Office files whose file names contain non-English encoding (German, Swedish, Hebrew, etc.).
:smtp_rfc821 (false)	Enables the SMTP Security Server to handle e-mail received from e-mail clients that do not use the RFC 821 standard. Without this change, the SMTP Security Server will drop this type of e-mail.
:http_disable_content_enc (true) :http_disable_content_type (true)	Prevents the firewall from blocking encoded HTTP responses that pass through the Security Server.
:http_use_host_h_as_dst (true)	Forces the firewall to use the host name in the header, rather than the destination's IP address.
:http_force_down_to_10 (1) :http_avoid_keep_alive (true)	Downgrades HTTP1.1 protocol to HTTP1.0, thereby enabling the proxy-like operation used by CVP.
:http_max_header_length (8000) :http_max_url_length (8000)	Prevents the firewall from truncating long URLs. Truncation can prevent CGI pages from loading and cookies from being written.
:http_check_request_validity (false) :http_check_response_validity (false)	Allows Internet Explorer to browse URLs with characters that are not between ASCII 32 and 127. It does this by disabling the set of checks that the firewall performs on request and response headers. This enables the HTTP Security Server to handle HTTP 1.1 downloads that occur as byte ranges. This increases the size of the buffer in the HTTP Security Server.
:http_allow_content_disposition (true)	Allows the download of files from sites that list the file type in the Content Disposition field of the HTTP header.
:http_enable_uri_queries (false)	**Important Note: This attribute appears as** true **in the default objects_5_0.C file. You must therefore change the value in the existing attribute rather than adding a new line.** This prevents VPN-1/FireWall-1 from stripping ASCII encoding of special characters, such as %20 used in place of a space, thus solving the following problems that are expected to be resolved by Check Point's FP2: Cannot access www.hotmail.com when using an HTTP Security Server. Web pages are not displayed. VPN-1/FireWall-1 replaces %20 characters in a URL with spaces. GIF files disappear from a website when working with an HTTP Security Server. GIF file names arrive with spaces. *Note: This change is very general and can cause other, very specific Web queries to fail.*

Table 15-2.   VPN-1/FireWall-1 Attributes Required for eSafe

Completing the Installation

You have added the Content Security rules, but there are still points to discuss about the Rule Base, as shown in Figure 15-27. If the organization does not want all of its users to be subject to the Content Security rules, those exceptions have to be inserted above the default Content Security rules, as do rules for VPN traffic.

OPSEC partners will require you to amend some of the VPN-1/FireWall-1 NG configuration files—for example, the object file—but that is beyond the scope of this book. All OPSEC partners fully document any such changes if required. In our experience, it usually takes a little while for updated OPSEC partner documentation to arrive after the latest Feature Pack for VPN-1/FireWall-1 NG. For example, what worked in Feature Pack 2 won't necessarily work in Feature Pack 3, so some testing and lab trials are recommended.

CAUTION   VPN-1/FireWall-1 NG handles objects files differently from previous versions of the software. The objects.C file on the Enforcement Module should not be edited. Instead, the /$FWDIR/conf/objects_5_0.C file on the VPN-1/FireWall-1 NG Management Server should be edited to make any changes necessary. This is because each time the Security Policy is installed, a new objects.C file on the Enforcement Module is created.

CONTENT SECURITY CHANGES FOR FEATURE PACK 3

When Check Point released Feature Pack 3, three of the attributes that are required to be tuned for CVP to work correctly have moved to another configuration file called asm.C.

Instead of putting the following properties in as documented earlier in the chapter, replace the property in DBEdit with the alternative configuration command as listed:

1. `modify properties firewall_properties http_max_header_length 8000`

   should be changed to:

   ```
   modify asm AdvancedSecurityObject
   asm_active_protection:HTTP_security_server:http_max_header_length 8000
   ```

2. `modify properties firewall_properties http_check_request_validity false`

   should be changed to:

   ```
   modify asm AdvancedSecurityObject
   asm_active_protection:HTTP_security_server:http_check_request_validity false
   ```

3. `modify properties firewall_properties http_check_response_validity false`

   should be changed to:

   ```
   modify asm AdvancedSecurityObject
   asm_active_protection:HTTP_security_server:http_check_response_validity false
   ```

These settings are required for eSafe gateway software to work correctly when used with VPN-1/FireWall-1 NG Feature Pack 3.

CVP LOAD SHARING AND CHAINING

VPN-1/FireWall-1 NG enables a resource to invoke any number of CVP servers. Identical CVP servers can be configured to share the load among them. This load-sharing capability offers two benefits: performance is increased and, in the event of a CVP server failing, functionality is maintained. If your sole CVP server fails, a user attempting to connect to an Internet website, for example, would get the message, "Cannot connect to CVP Server" in their browser window. VPN-1/FireWall-1 NG uses the concept of grouping multiple CVP servers into groups that can be used in resource definitions. You can specify round-robin or random as the algorithms that will be used to load balance the CVP servers. Not only does this offer load balancing, it also ensures there is connectivity should a single CVP server fail.

CVP chaining is useful when each of the CVP servers performs a different function. The chaining process connects servers for the purpose of stringing functionality. This functionality is controlled via CVP Manager.

UPGRADING FROM VPN-1/FIREWALL-1 4.*x*

In our experience, OPSEC applications require different configuration settings and file editing because there is no one standard for all vendors or applications.

Check Point has included the upgrade_fwopsec command to upgrade OPSEC configuration information on the Check Point Management Server from pre-NG to NG format, based on the upgraded module information.

The command should be used only if the OPSEC default settings were changed in the VPN-1/FireWall-1 4.*x* configuration, which relates only to CVP, UFP, SAM (proxy), and CVP Load Sharing.

Care should also be taken to study release notes and installation notes from vendors because there can be two different installation procedures, depending on whether you are using VPN-1/FireWall-1 4.*x* or VPN-1/FireWall-1 NG.

To be supported fully by Check Point with VPN-1/FireWall-1 NG, applications are required to use the CVP API and not the old CVP protocol.

CHECKLIST: KEY POINTS IN CONTENT SECURITY AND CONTENT VECTORING PROTOCOL

The following is a checklist for the key points in content security and content vectoring protocol.

☐ List the features and functionality of VPN-1/FireWall-1 NG for Content Security.

☐ Perform URL filtering, stripping Java applets and ActiveX controls via Security Servers, by using VPN-1/FireWall-1 NG.

☐ List the key strengths of VPN-1/FireWall-1 NG.

☐ List all OPSEC partner applications specifically written for VPN-1/FireWall-1 NG.

☐ Integrate CVP-based Content Security into the Rule Base.

☐ Demonstrate CVP configuration using Aladdin Knowledge Systems' eSafe product.

☐ List all of the minor differences in configuration that reside in each OPSEC application.

☐ Read the OPSEC partner's documentation prior to configuring a CVP server.

CHAPTER 16

SYNDefender

SYN Flood attacks are a common Denial of Service (DoS) attack. They effectively reduce a server's capacity to perform useful work by filling up its backlog queue of pending connection requests with half-open connections. This can eventually crash the server or at least prevent it from servicing legitimate connections. The SYN attack takes advantage of the normal TCP connection establishment mechanism known as the three-way handshake.

Denial of Service attacks are characterized by an explicit attempt by attackers to prevent legitimate users of a service from using that service. Examples include attempts to do the following:

- "Flood" a network, thereby preventing legitimate network traffic

- Disrupt connections between two machines, thereby preventing access to a service

- Disrupt service to a specific system or person

- Prevent a particular individual from accessing a service

Not all service outages, even those that result from malicious activity, are necessarily Denial of Service attacks. Other types of attack may include a Denial of Service as a component, but the Denial of Service may be part of a larger attack.

Illegitimate use of resources may also result in Denial of Service. For example, an intruder may use your anonymous ftp area as a place to store illegal copies of commercial software (this is known as a "wares server," in hacker terminology), consuming disk space and generating network traffic.

VPN-1/FireWall-1 NG provides the SYNDefender component to stop SYN Flood attacks. In this chapter, we will examine the way TCP/IP performs its three-way handshake to initiate communications and how SYNDefender protects networks.

TCP THREE-WAY HANDSHAKE

The three-way handshake is used to establish a connection between the client and the server. TCP uses a method of connection establishment because it is a connection-oriented protocol. The client initiates a connection with the server and sends a TCP packet requesting communication with the server. The server responds to the client with an acknowledgement. The client then replies with its own acknowledgement to the server, and the communication process starts.

Normal Handshake

In a normal three-way handshake, the client acknowledges the servers SYN/ACK, and communication can begin because the connection is now fully established and synchronized, as shown in Figure 16-1.

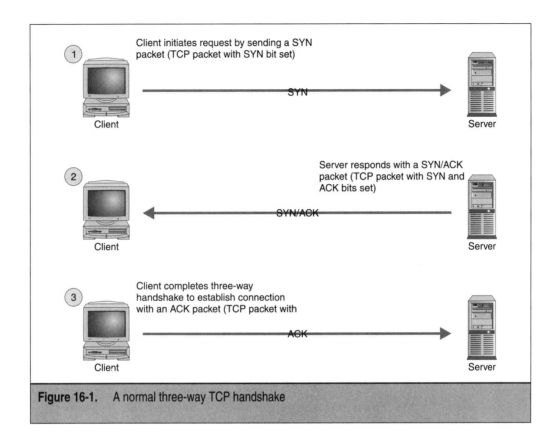

Figure 16-1. A normal three-way TCP handshake

Server programs, such as a web server, maintain a backlog queue for pending connections. This queue can usually accommodate about ten unacknowledged connection requests. For each SYN the server receives, it allocates some memory for the new connection and places it in the backlog queue until the connection is either established, reset, or timed out. Once the backlog queue is full, further connection attempts for the service will be dropped until space becomes available in the backlog queue.

SYN FLOOD ATTACK

As already stated, the SYN Flood attack is used to prevent the server service from responding to legitimate requests. This is achieved by exploiting the TCP protocols limitation in handling half established connections in the backlog queue, each of which remains in the queue until the timeout at around 75 seconds.

This means that a sustained attack can render the service unusable. The client sends a TCP packet with the SYN (Synchronize) flag set to signal its desire to communicate, the server responds with a SYN/ACK (Synchronize/Acknowledge). The final step to establishing a connection is that the client replies to this with another SYN packet. At this point, data transfer over the established connection can begin. This moves the connection out of the server's backlog queue pending list, and into the established connection state. Servers can handle many thousands of established connections.

However, during a SYN attack, the attacker *spoofs* their own source address to that of an unreachable host. This causes the server to try and contact the source of the SYN being sent to acknowledge it. The server will get no response when it tries to contact the host because the attacker has made sure the address they have chosen as their source address is not available on the Internet. This is a necessary step in the SYN Flood attack.

NOTE   If the hacker chose an address that was reachable via the Internet, that host would respond with an RST flag or reset because the host didn't initiate the request to which the target server was responding. An RST would move the connection out of the backlog queue and free the resource the hacker is trying to consume.

Because the server is trying to respond to a host that it cannot possibly get a response back from, it will keep trying to respond to these malicious requests without success. It cannot complete the three-way handshake and each request remains in the backlog queue until it times out the request after approximately 75 seconds. When enough of these requests are targeted at a server, the backlog queue buffers will fill up and the server will be unavailable to process real requests. It can even cause a server to crash!

An example of a SYN Flood attack that sends multiple SYN requests to a server is shown in Figure 16-2.

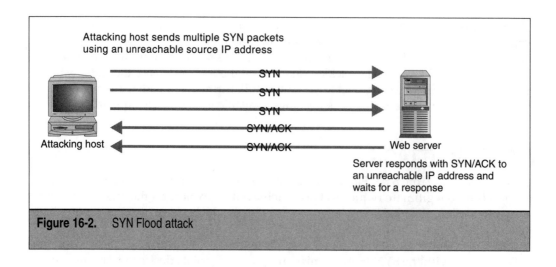

Figure 16-2.   SYN Flood attack

DENIAL OF SERVICE ATTACKS

Denial of Service (DoS) attacks can disable your computer or your network. Depending on the nature of your enterprise, this can effectively disable your entire organization. Some DoS attacks can be executed with limited resources against a large, sophisticated site. This type of attack is sometimes called an "asymmetric attack." For example, an attacker with an old PC and a slow modem may be able to disable much faster and more sophisticated machines or networks. For example, with a SMURF attack, the attacker sends only a small amount of traffic, but this is then amplified, and the target ends up receiving a very large number of packets—hence the asymmetric tag.

DoS attacks come in a variety of forms and aim at a variety of services. There are three basic types of attack:

- Consumption of scarce, limited, or nonrenewable resources
- Destruction or alteration of configuration information
- Physical destruction or alteration of network components

Of these types of attacks, the security manager is chiefly concerned with the first two and should be involved in providing guidance on how to secure the physical building and the technologies involved, such as card-swipe access for data centers and increasingly biometric access systems.

Consumption of Scarce Resources

To operate, computers and networks have certain requirements: network bandwidth, memory and disk space, CPU time, data structures, access to other computers and networks, and certain environmental resources such as power, cool air, and even water. All of these resources can be attacked or compromised.

- **Network connectivity**   Denial of Service attacks are most frequently executed against network connectivity. The goal is to prevent hosts or networks from communicating on the network. In this type of attack, the attacker begins the process of establishing a connection to the victim machine, but does it in such a way as to prevent the ultimate completion of the connection. In the meantime, the victim machine has reserved one of a limited number of data structures required to complete the impending connection. The result is that legitimate connections are denied while the victim machine is waiting to complete bogus "half-open" connections. A one-second SYN Flood attack can result in the server being unavailable to process requests for over a minute.

- **Reversing resources against you**   An intruder can reverse your own resources against you in unexpected ways. For instance, the intruder can use forged UDP packets to connect the echo service on one machine to the chargen service on another machine. The result is that the two services consume all available network bandwidth between them. Thus, the network connectivity for all machines on the networks of the targeted machines may be affected.

- **Bandwidth consumption**   An intruder may also be able to consume all the available bandwidth on your network by generating a large number of packets and directing them to your network. Typically, these packets are ICMP ECHO packets, but in principle they may be anything. Further, the intruder need not be operating from a single machine and may be able to coordinate or co-opt several machines on different networks to achieve the same effect.

Destruction or Alteration of Configuration Information

An intruder may also be able to alter or destroy configuration information that prevents you from using your computer or network. If an intruder can change the routing information in your routers, your network may be disabled. If an intruder is able to modify the registry on the machine, certain functions may be unavailable.

Physical Destruction or Alteration of Network Components

Physical security is an important component in guarding against many types of attacks in addition to DoS. You should guard against unauthorized access to computers, routers, network wiring closets, network backbone segments, power and cooling stations, and any other critical components of your network.

Defending Against DoS Attacks

Denial of Service attacks can result in significant loss of time and money for many organizations. We strongly encourage sites to consider the extent to which their organization can afford a significant service outage and take steps commensurate with the risk.

VPN-1/FireWall-1 NG has very good defense features, which are discussed in this section, but we encourage you to consider the following options with respect to your needs:

- Implement router filters as described in CERT's advisory at www.cert.org/advisories/CA-1996-21.html.

- If they are available for your system, install patches to guard against TCP SYN flooding as described in CA-96.21.tcp_syn_flooding. This will substantially reduce your exposure to these attacks but may not eliminate the risk entirely.

- Disable any unused or unneeded network services. This can limit the ability of an intruder to take advantage of those services to execute a Denial of Service attack.

- Enable quota systems on your operating system if they are available. For example, if your operating system supports disk quotas, enable them for all accounts, especially accounts that operate network services. In addition, if your operating system supports partitions or volumes (that is, separately mounted file systems with independent attributes), consider partitioning your file system to separate critical functions from other activity.

- Routinely examine your physical security with respect to your current needs. Consider servers, routers, unattended terminals, network access points, wiring closets, environmental systems such as air and power, and other components of your system.

- Use Tripwire or a similar tool to detect changes in configuration information or other files. For more information, see www.cert.org/tech_tips/security_tools.html.

- Invest in and maintain "hot spares"—machines that can be placed into service quickly in the event that a similar machine is disabled.

- Invest in redundant and fault-tolerant network configurations.

- Establish and maintain regular backup schedules and policies, particularly for important configuration information.

- Establish and maintain appropriate password policies, especially for access to highly privileged accounts such as UNIX root or Microsoft Windows NT Administrator.

Many organizations can suffer financial loss as a result of SYN attacks and may wish to pursue criminal or civil charges against the perpetrators.

USING SYNDEFENDER

SYNDefender provides three different defenses against SYN flood attacks:

- SYN Gateway (for versions prior to VPN-1/FireWall-1 NG)
- SYN Relay
- Passive SYN Gateway

The latter two solutions are integrated into the VPN-1/FireWall-1 NG Inspection Module.

SYN Gateway

SYN Gateway provides protection by responding to the server's SYN/ACK itself so the server can move the connection out of the backlog queue. It then waits to receive the genuine ACK from the client and forwards this to the server. The server disregards the second superfluous ACK because, as far as it is concerned, it has already received an ACK. If the client does not respond to the server's SYN/ACK within the firewall's timeout period, then the firewall sends the server a RST (reset) to close the connection. Servers are capable of handling many thousands of concurrent connections, whereas the backlog queue has very limited resources. In this way the backlog queue is protected—the only caveat is that the timeout period must be long enough to allow clients coming over slow links to connect. As you can see, the protection offered by SYN Gateway is an effective way of keeping the backlog queue free of pending connections and therefore protecting against this type of attack.

NOTE SYNDefender only works when IP forwarding is enabled.

Figure 16-3 shows how the firewall mediates the TCP three-way handshake to provide protection for your network.

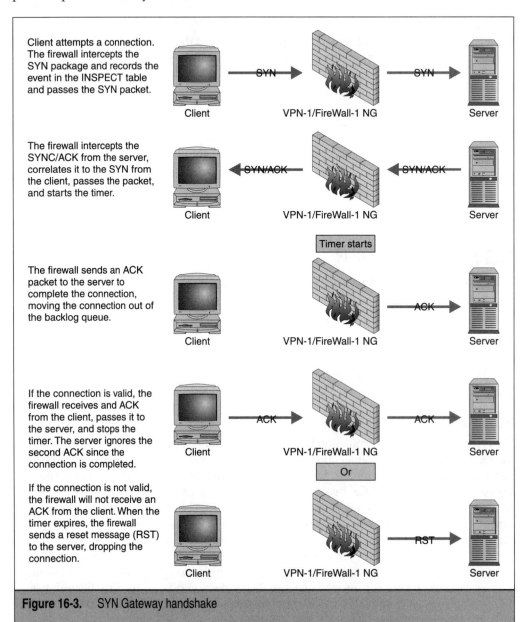

Figure 16-3. SYN Gateway handshake

SYN Gateway is an option in the Global Properties of the VPN-1/FireWall-1 NG policy, but it is only effective for previous versions. To configure the SYNDefender component in VPN-1/FireWall-1 NG, use the option for SYNDefender in the Workstation Properties window. VPN-1/FireWall-1 NG defines the SYNDefender settings for each firewall object locally rather than globally, as opposed to earlier versions of the software.

NOTE SYN Gateway is not available for VPN-1/FireWall-1 NG onward. The option for SYN Gateway in Global Properties is for managing previous versions of VPN-1/FireWall-1.

SYN Relay

SYN Relay makes sure the connection attempt is valid before it passes the server the connection. It does this by undertaking the three-way handshake with the client and making the request before passing it on to the server. This has the benefit of not involving the server with the inbound connection attempt until the firewall has made certain it is genuine. Despite being a high-performance kernel-level process, there is trade-off in a slight delay in connection establishment compared to SYN Gateway. This method is the most secure.

Figure 16-4 depicts the SYN Relay handshake.

Passive SYN Gateway

The Passive SYN Gateway option is similar to the SYN Gateway method except that VPN-1/FireWall-1 NG does not respond on behalf of the client to establish the connection. Instead, the pending connection remains in the server's backlog queue until either the firewall timeout is reached or the final ACK is received from the client. This does allow the backlog queue to grow, but the firewall timeout is much lower than the server's, and it can therefore reset the connection if no ACK is received. This prevents the queue from filling up and the resultant denial of service. This method has the advantage of not overburdening the firewall but is less secure than SYN Relay.

Figure 16-5 illustrates how VPN-1/FireWall-1 NG handles the Passive SYN Gateway handshake.

SYNDefender Properties

To use SYNDefender to protect against SYN Flood attacks, open the Workstation Properties screen for your firewall and select the SYNDefender tab, as shown in Figure 16-6.

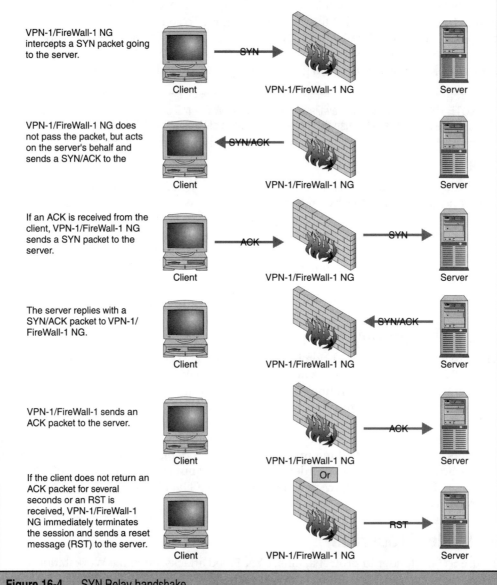

Figure 16-4. SYN Relay handshake

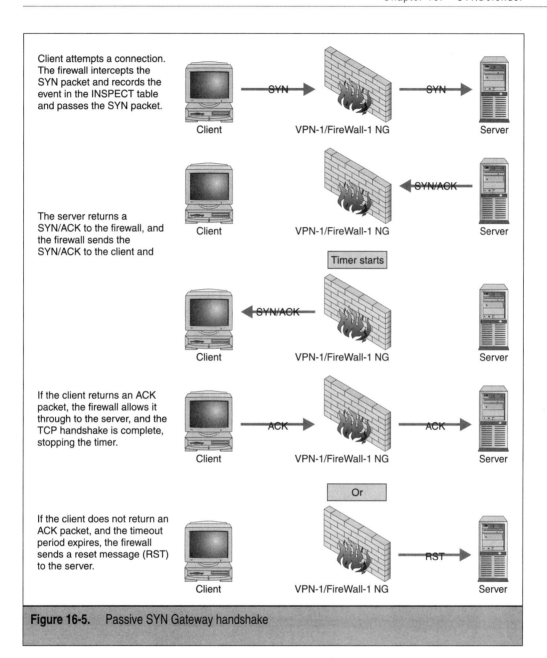

Client attempts a connection. The firewall intercepts the SYN packet and records the event in the INSPECT table and passes the SYN packet.

Client   VPN-1/FireWall-1 NG   Server

The server returns a SYN/ACK to the firewall, and the firewall sends the SYN/ACK to the client and

Client   VPN-1/FireWall-1 NG   Server

Timer starts

Client   VPN-1/FireWall-1 NG   Server

If the client returns an ACK packet, the firewall allows it through to the server, and the TCP handshake is complete, stopping the timer.

Client   VPN-1/FireWall-1 NG   Server

Or

If the client does not return an ACK packet, and the timeout period expires, the firewall sends a reset message (RST) to the server.

Client   VPN-1/FireWall-1 NG   Server

Figure 16-5.   Passive SYN Gateway handshake

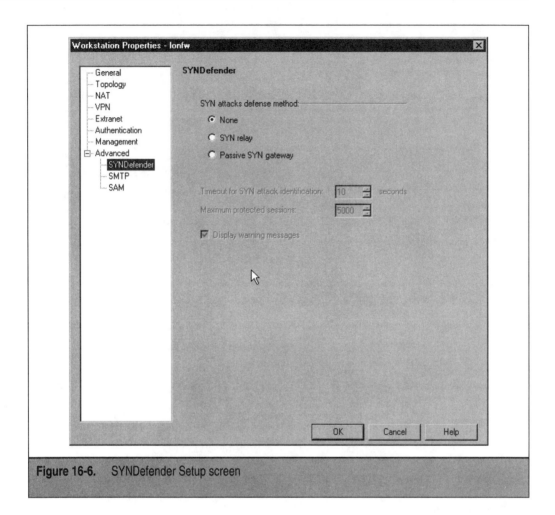

Figure 16-6. SYNDefender Setup screen

VPN-1/FireWall-1 NG has several methods of defense against SYN attacks. However, as noted previously, with the release of VPN-1/FireWall-1 NG, the SYN Gateway option is no longer available. The options are as follows:

- **None**   SYNDefender is not deployed
- **SYN Relay**   Deploys the SYN Relay method.
- **SYN Gateway**   Deploys the SYN Gateway method. As of VPN-1/ FireWall-1 NG, this option is not available from the workstation's Advanced | SYNDefender options. It is available for versions prior to VPN-1/FireWall-1 NG from Global Properties of the Security Policy.

- **Passive SYN Gateway**   Deploys the Passive SYN Gateway method.
- **Timeout for SYN Attack Identification**   Sets how long VPN-1/FireWall-1 NG waits for the ACK packet from the client before ending the connection attempt.
- **Maximum Protected Sessions**   Sets the number of entries in an internal connection table maintained by SYNDefender. Once the table is full, SYNDefender doesn't examine any new connections.
- **Display Warning Messages**   Prints warning messages to the system's console in Solaris, Nokia IPSO, or Linux and adds entries to the Application Event log in Windows NT, depending on which system you are using.

Guidelines for Deploying SYNDefender

SYNDefender is easily integrated into existing VPN-1/FireWall-1 NG installations. It provides strong protection against the TCP SYN attacks by intercepting all SYN packets and mediating the connection attempts before they reach the operating system. This prevents the target host from becoming flooded by these unresolved connection attempts, which causes the operating system and the host to stop receiving new connections. As a result, the host system is effectively insulated from the SYN Flood attack and Denial of Service condition that results.

However, as already stated, there are other methods available to the security engineer to defend against SYN Flood and other Denial of Service attacks, and you may want to consider these. Internal firewalls may not even require this kind of protection, as DoS attacks launched inside organizations are rare. You must examine the risk and make a judgment on the appropriate level of protection required.

SYN Relay provides the greatest level of protection, but it causes a slight delay in connection setup. Clients can usually tolerate this, but some may not.

FEATURE PACK 3 CHANGES

In Feature Pack 3 (FP3), SYNDefender capabilities can be overridden by the settings in SmartDefense. If you require backward compatibility with older Enforcement Modules (4.1), you cannot override the individual workstation properties for each NG Enforcement Module on the Management Server. Instead, you can set the global setting for all earlier versions in the SmartDefense TCP | SYN Attack screen. Each NG Enforcement Module must have the settings for SYNDefender set in the Workstation Properties. The SmartDefense TCP | SYN Attack configuration screen is shown in Figure 16-7.

If you do not have any Enforcement Module versions prior to NG to support on the Management Server, you can check the Override Modules' SYNDefender Configuration in SmartDefense. Click the Configure button to enter the parameters for SYNDefender, as shown in Figure 16-8.

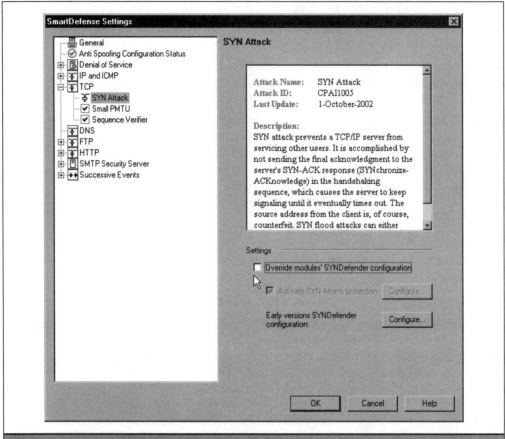

Figure 16-7. SmartDefense SYN Attack configuration

As you can see in Figure 16-8, you can now specify that SYN Attack protection be applied to an external interface only, saving the firewall additional and perhaps unnecessary work. Also, an Attack Threshold parameter is now available so you can specify the number of SYNs counted as SYN Flood attack. The Track Level option has also been added to allow you to track identified attacks, each individual SYN, or none.

Finally, as you may have noticed, all options regarding which method to use for SYN Attack protection have been removed! FP3 makes the decision for you; the attack detection threshold is used to switch the VPN-1/FireWall-1 NG into SYN Relay mode from the normal Passive SYN Gateway mode. This provides the advantages of both methods by using the appropriate one as the situation dictates.

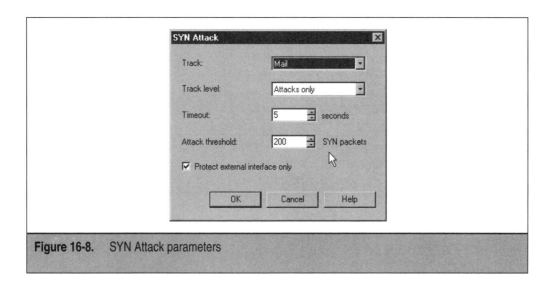

Figure 16-8. SYN Attack parameters

CHECKLIST: KEY POINTS IN SYNDEFENDER

The following is a checklist for the key points in SYNDefender:

- ☐ Identify the TCP three-way handshakes.
- ☐ Define a normal handshake.
- ☐ Show how TCP can be exploited to perform Denial of Service attacks.
- ☐ Define SYN Flooding.
- ☐ Define Denial of Service attacks.
- ☐ Research other methods for preventing DoS attacks.
- ☐ Show how the VPN-1/FireWall-1 NG's SYNDefender application can protect servers against Denial of Service attacks.
- ☐ List all of the slight differences between the initial and subsequent releases of VPN-1/FireWall-1 NG.
- ☐ Identify the SYN Flood attack.
- ☐ Show how to defend against SYN Flood attacks.
- ☐ Identify the SYNDefender methods.
- ☐ List all of the guidelines for deploying SYNDefender.
- ☐ Show how SmartDefense is used to configure global settings.
- ☐ Identify changes in Feature Pack 3.

CHAPTER 17

Encryption and Virtual Private Networks

By encrypting the communications on insecure public networks such as the Internet, VPN-1/FireWall-1 NG can be used to build site-to-site Virtual Private Networks (VPNs) that provide secure communications between two defined participants. VPN-1/FireWall-1 NG's encryption will be demonstrated in this book through the use of IKE (Internet Key Exchange) and VPN-1/FireWall-1 proprietary encryption (FWZ) encryption schemes.

In addition to supporting site-to-site VPNs, Check Point has developed SecuRemote/ SecureClient to build client-to-site VPNs. SecuRemote enables mobile and remote users to connect to an organization's corporate network through dial-up Internet connections. Users can connect either directly to the server, or through Internet Service Providers (ISPs). They can communicate sensitive corporate data as safely and securely as users that are located on the corporate network because the data is encrypted in transit. VPN-1/FireWall-1 NG also supports Clientless VPNs enabling clients using HTTPS through their browsers to create VPNs, but this is limited in functionality and not discussed in this book. Although for some e-commerce applications, administrators may want to explore this functionality.

This chapter will introduce the concept of VPNs from a theoretical perspective and focus on introducing the reader to the key terms and processes of how VPNs work. It is important background reading for anyone who is new to working with VPNs or who wants a refresher on the underlying processes.

HOW ENCRYPTION WORKS

Good security involves careful planning of a Security Policy, which should include access control and authentication mechanisms. These security strategies and procedures can range from a very simple password policy to complex encryption schemes. Encrypting the information of your company can be an important security method and provides one of the most basic security services in a network: authentication exchange. Other methods, such as digital signatures and data confidentiality, also use encryption.

When information is sent over a public network such as the Internet, the message passes through multiple routers, gateways, and other internetworking equipment before it arrives at a destination. There are many points where the data can be intercepted or altered; a false message can be sent that appears to have come from a trusted sender but does not. Let's put this into perspective: do you really want to entrust your business to the security of the ISPs and the many systems your data travels through from your network and its destination? We guess the answer is no, so we recommend that you play it safe and use encryption.

Network system administrators need to ensure the following:

- **Privacy**   No one but the intended parties can understand the communication.
- **Integrity**   No one has tampered with the communication.
- **Authenticity**   No one is sending false communication.

VPN-1/FireWall-1 NG protects communications on the Internet and enables an organization to build its own easy-to-maintain VPN using private and public network segments. VPN-1/FireWall-1 NG supports industry standard algorithms and protocols such as DES, 3DES, and IPSec/IKE. VPN-1/FireWall-1 NG also supports Public Key Infrastructure (PKI), which enables the use of digital certificates.

PRIVACY

Encryption is the transformation of readable data, or *clear-text*, into an unreadable form called *ciphertext*. VPN-1/FireWall-1 NG provides secured connections between end points by encrypting data so it may travel through unsecured networks.

Encryption works by encrypting data with encryption software and a secret key, which is known only to the sender and recipient. This shared key is used to decrypt the encrypted packet, as shown in Figure 17-1.

Encryption techniques that don't use any keys are very simple: they work by transforming and scrambling the information being encrypted. Although you might think this sort of algorithm is secure, they are easy to decipher. Once you learn the algorithm, you will be able to decipher the encrypted information.

VPN-1/FireWall-1 NG supports the following encryption schemes:

- Symmetric and asymmetric encryption
- Diffie-Hellman key management
- Digital certificates

Figure 17-1.   Encryption using a secret key

SYMMETRIC ENCRYPTION (SHARED KEY)

Two major types of encryption algorithms are private key encryption and public key encryption. A private key is also called a single key, secret key, symmetric key, or shared key encryption. A public key is called an asymmetric key. Symmetric encryption uses the same secret key to encrypt and decrypt data—that is, the same key value is used for both encryption and decryption.

With symmetric key encryption algorithms, only one key exists. To ensure security, you must protect this key: only you should know it. Kerberos, for example, is an authentication protocol that uses private key algorithms. Another characteristic of symmetric key encryption is that the keys used are usually small, making its algorithms computation relatively faster than asynchronous ones.

One of the main limitations of using symmetric key encryption is its distribution to everyone who needs it. The distribution itself must be secure or you could expose and compromise the key and, therefore, all the information encrypted with it. Thus, it is necessary for you to change your symmetric key encryption every so often.

If you have only symmetric key schemes available to you, we recommend you use it with digital signatures, as they are much more versatile and secure.

Symmetric encryption is primarily used for faster encryption performance. An example of symmetric encryption is shown in Figure 17-2.

In Figure 17-2, symmetric key encryption occurs in the following stages:

1. The clear-text message is encrypted using the shared key.

2. The encrypted packet passes through the insecure network.

3. On the remote gateway, the same shared key is used to decrypt the message.

Data Encryption Standard (DES)

The Data Encryption Standard (DES) is one of the most commonly used symmetric key algorithms. DES was developed by IBM and became a U.S. government standard in

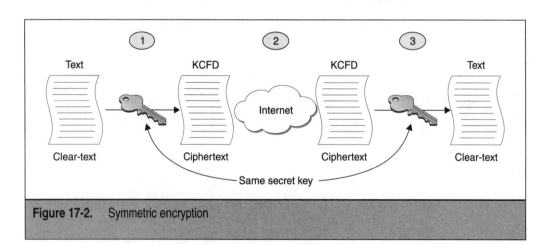

Figure 17-2. Symmetric encryption

1976. This is a well-known algorithm with a large implementation base in commercial and government applications. As mentioned earlier, Kerberos uses the DES algorithm to encrypt messages and create the private keys used during various transactions.

DES is very fast. According to RSA Labs, when DES is implemented entirely in software, it is at least 100 times faster than the RSA algorithm. But if implemented in hardware, DES can outperform the RSA algorithm by 1,000 or even 10,000 times because DES uses S-boxes, which have very simple table-lookup functions, while RSA depends on very-large-integer arithmetic.

DES uses the same algorithm for encryption and decryption. The key can be just about any 64-bit number. Because of the way the algorithm works, the effective length is 56 bits. NIST certified DES for use as an official U.S. government encryption standard but only for "less-than-top-secret secret material." Although DES is considered very secure, there are two known ways to break it:

- Through an exhaustive search of the keyspace, providing a total of 2^{56} (about $7.2*10^{16}$) possible keys, which would take about 2,000 years if you were to test one million keys every second

- Through sheer good luck

Until few years ago, DES had never been broken and was believed to be secure. But a group of Internet users, working together in a coordinated effort to solve an RSA DES challenge for over four months, finally broke the algorithm

```
"Strong cryptography makes the world a safer place."
```

The group used a technique called *brute-force*, in which the computers participating in the challenge tried every possible decryption key. There were over 72 quadrillion keys (72,057,594,037,927,936). When the winning key was reported to RSA Data Security, Inc. in June 1997, the group, known as DESCHALL (DES Challenge), had already searched almost 25 percent of the total possibilities. During the peak time of the group's efforts, 7 billion keys were being tested per second.

Symmetric Encryption Disadvantages

Symmetric encryption uses the same key for both encryption and decryption. This has some security implications that you should consider. The same key is used for both encryption and decryption of data. If anyone steals or learns the key, all currently encrypted data can be compromised. The normal practice is for the key to be communicated by direct face-to-face negotiation or a telephone call.

CAUTION   Do not send shared keys through unsecured networks such as the Internet. Use hand delivery, mail, fax, or phone to communicate the private key to the intended recipient.

Symmetric encryption is generally used when there is a requirement for a small number of keys to be managed. Administration becomes virtually impossible as the number of keys increases, so it is not recommended for large-scale VPN implementations. It should be noted, for example, that for 10,000 hosts, about 50 million keys would be required.

Public key (asymmetric) encryption systems solve these problems. With public key encryption, a key pair is composed of two mathematically related keys: a public key known to everyone and a private key known only to its owner. A message encrypted with one of the keys in a key pair can only be decrypted with the other key in the pair.

ASYMMETRIC ENCRYPTION

Asymmetric encryption, which, as just discussed, uses one key to encrypt a message and another to decrypt the message, is an encryption technology used for the following:

- Secure key exchange mechanisms
- Authentication
- Data-integrity checking

Some examples of public key encryption usage include:

- **Certificates**   Ensures that the correct public and private keys are being used in the transaction.

- **Digital signatures**   Provides a way for the receiver to confirm that the message came from the stated sender. In this case, only the user knows the private key and keeps it secret. The user's public key is then publicly exposed so that anyone communicating with the user can use it.

- **Plaintext**   Is encrypted with a private key that can be deciphered with the corresponding public key or even the same private key.

One of the main public key encryption algorithms is RSA, which was named after its inventors, Rivest, Shamir, and Adleman. These public key algorithms have advantages and disadvantages. Usually, the encryption and decryption of the algorithms uses large keys, often with 100 or more digits. That's why the industry has the tendency to resolve key management and computing overhead problems by using smart cards such as SecureID and so on.

Asymmetric encryption is also known as public/private key encryption because the encryption scheme uses two keys, a private key and a public key. These keys are created using the Diffie-Hellman key scheme, where one firewall's public key and another firewall's private key create a shared secret key. This shared secret key is used to verify and decrypt the incoming encrypted packet. Because different keys are used for encryption and decryption, they are called asymmetric keys.

Diffie-Hellman

Diffie-Hellman was the first public key algorithm (in 1976). Figure 17-3 illustrates the Diffie-Hellman scheme encryption:

1. Gateways in London and New York exchange their public keys.

2. Using Diffie-Hellman, London combines its private key with New York's public key to generate the shared secret key.

3. New York combines its private key with London's public key to generate the shared secret key.

4. Because the two gateways exchanging their respective public keys are the only parties that can generate the shared key, a two-way trust model is established, where no other party can create the shared secret.

Asymmetric cryptography is around 1000 times slower than symmetric cryptography and very processor intensive. The Diffie-Hellman protocol includes three predefined groups. Longer groups provide better security, but their computation requires more

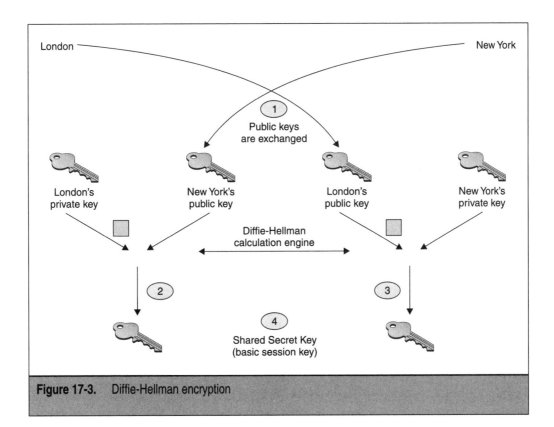

Figure 17-3.　Diffie-Hellman encryption

CPU resources. VPN-1/FireWall-1 NG allows you to expand the database of mathematical groups by adding customized groups.

The Diffie-Hellman Method for Key Agreement allows two hosts to create and share a secret key based on simple mathematics. The following steps detailed explain how this is calculated.

1. The hosts must get the *Diffie-Hellman parameters*: a prime number, *p*, which is an integer that is larger than 2; and a base number, *g*, which is an integer that is smaller than *p*. They can either be hard coded or fetched from a server.

2. The hosts each secretly generate a private number called *x*, which is less than $p - 1$.

3. The hosts generate the public key, *y*. They are created with the function:

   $$y = g\char`^x \% p$$

4. The two hosts exchange the public keys (*y*) and the exchanged numbers are converted into a secret key, *z*.

   $$z = y\char`^x \% p$$

5. *z* can now be used as the key for whatever encryption method is used to transfer information between the two hosts. Mathematically, the two hosts should have generated the same value for *z*:

   $$z = (g\char`^x \% p)\char`^{x'} \% p = (g\char`^{x'} \% p)\char`^x \% p$$

All of these numbers are positive integers. In the equations just performed, x^y means x is raised to the y power. The formula x%y denotes that x is divided by y and the remainder is returned (modulus).

Integrity

To ensure a message's integrity, in addition to using keys, a message is hashed. A *hash function* is a one-way mathematical function that maps variable values into smaller values of a fixed length. The smaller size of the hashed message maximizes network performance. The result of the hash function is called the *message digest*, and it is much smaller in size than the original message but unique to that message.

The process of creating a one-way hash function is shown in Figure 17-4. First, the original message is created. Next, the message is processed by the hash function and creates a new, much smaller version of the original message. The hash is simple and fast.

Using a one-way hash function is easy to use and irreversible. When the hash function is encrypted with the sender's private RSA key, the message digest becomes a digital signature and can be used for authenticating data integrity, as shown in Figure 17-5.

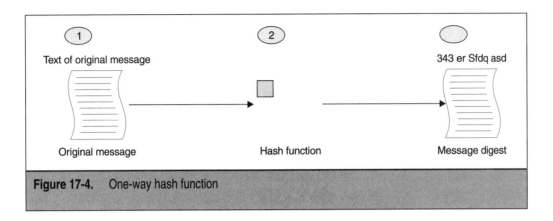

Figure 17-4.   One-way hash function

Authenticity

A digital signature is a code that is attached to an electronically transmitted message that identifies the sender and verifies that the message hasn't been tampered with in transit. Digital signatures use public key cryptography. To be effective, digital signatures must not be forged by someone else. These are provided via a third party or Certificate Authority (CA) that verifies the key authority.

VPN-1/FireWall-1 NG digital signatures use *RSA encryption* and *hash functions*. RSA is the public key cryptosystem that VPN-1/FireWall-1 NG uses to create and verify digital signatures. In contrast to Diffie-Hellman, RSA key pairs are used to encrypt and decrypt messages. Any information encrypted with the RSA public key can only be decrypted with the matching RSA private key, and vice versa. This is known as a one-way trust model because only the sender can generate the keys necessary to encrypt and decrypt the message, as shown in Figure 17-6.

In Figure 17-6, the hash value confirms the message's integrity and is also the pre-agreed text of the digital signature. It is possible to use some other pre-agreed text, but the hash value is convenient because it is different for each message and the content doesn't have to be agreed on beforehand.

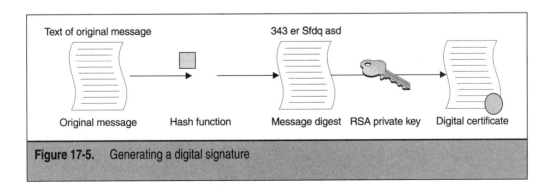

Figure 17-5.   Generating a digital signature

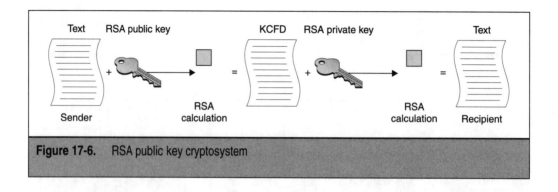

Figure 17-6.   RSA public key cryptosystem

NOTE   Digital signatures are especially important for electronic commerce and are key components of most authentication schemes.

Two Phases of Encrypted Communication

Public key encryption requires much more computational effort than private key encryption, so it is much slower. In practice, most encrypted communication sessions are usually divided into two phases:

1. A preliminary, short, key negotiation that is the exchange phase, secured by public key encryption, where a private key is negotiated or exchanged for encrypting the actual message. Internet Key Exchange (IKE) is a common key exchange method.

2. The main message encryption phase, in which the message is encrypted using the faster private key that was already negotiated in the first phase. Data Encryption Standard (DES) and CAST are commonly used encryption algorithms.

PUBLIC KEYS

Public keys form the basis for secure encryption, so there must be a reliable and secure method to obtain public keys. A Certificate Authority (CA) is a trusted third party from whom a public key can be obtained reliably, even via an insecure network such as the Internet. The CA certifies a public key by generating a certificate, as shown in Figure 17-7.

A digital signature acts as proof of the sender's identity. The certificate's security is based on the following:

- The difficulty of obtaining and reading the physical device that the certificate is stored on

- The secrecy of the access password

The certificate is often embedded in a token, which is either an encrypted disk file or a hardware device such as a smart card. The token has a password. Only someone

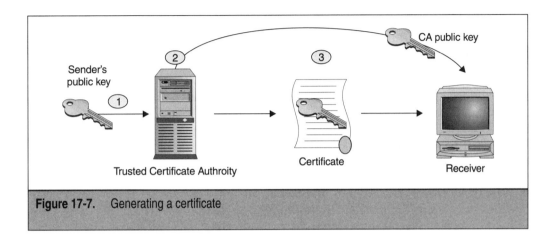

Figure 17-7. Generating a certificate

who physically has the token, file, or device in their possession *and* knows the password can use it.

A certificate can also be provided directly by the sender of a message. The receiver can verify the certificate using the same steps used in verifying any encrypted message, as discussed earlier. The sender proves their identity by sending a message, consisting of a digital signature encrypted with their private key, and their certificate, which includes their unique identifier, such as their LDAP DN (LDAP Distinguished Name) and IP address. LDAP is an acronym for Lightweight Directory Access Protocol.

After identities have been proven, each host or user can use the other's public keys with confidence because they are verified by certificates from a trusted CA. Usually public keys are used to negotiate a secret key for encrypting the actual message. In VPNs, certificates are also issued by encrypting entities, such as gateways, to identify themselves and supply their public keys to their peers.

CREATING CERTIFICATES

A user's certificate is created by a Certificate Authority (CA). There are several ways a user can acquire their certificate:

- The user creates a profile on their workstation using client software such as Check Point SecureClient. The profile is then stored on a diskette or on a hardware token to minimize the possibility of unauthorized access and misuse. The profile is further protected by an access password.

- The CA creates the profile file and then give it to the user. This method centralizes the creation of profile files but may be impractical due to geographically dispersed organizations.

- The user registers with the CA using a web browser and then exports the certificate and private key for use in other applications.

- The user creates a certificate registration request file, then transfers the file via mail or FTP to the CA. The CA approves the request and generates the certificate on a file, transferring it back to the user.

When a user leaves an organization or when a key is compromised (for example, a token is stolen or lost), the certificate must be revoked. The CA does this by issuing and distributing a Certification Revocation List (CRL). Before a certificate is accepted, the CRL should be checked to confirm that the certificate has not been revoked. The CRLs distribution point is usually a web server specified in the certificate.

To view the CA for a VPN-1/FireWall-1 NG gateway, select the gateway workstation object from the Management Console and select the VPN option from the Workstation Properties screen, as shown in Figure 17-8.

The CA is defined in the Certificate Properties screen. To view the Certificate Properties screen, select Add or Edit from the Certificate List, as shown in Figure 17-9. VPN-1/FireWall-1 NG management servers function as CAs for encrypting gateways.

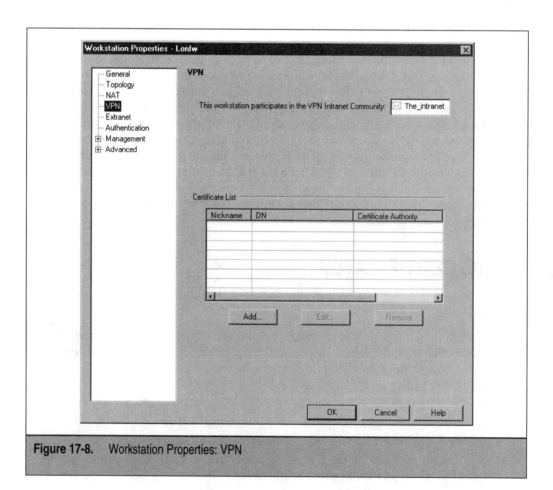

Figure 17-8. Workstation Properties: VPN

Figure 17-9.   Certificate Properties screen

VPN-1/FIREWALL-1 NG ENCRYPTION SCHEMES

Encryption schemes consist of the following:

- **Key Management Protocol**   For generating and exchanging keys
- **Encryption Algorithm**   For encrypting messages
- **Authentication Algorithm**   For ensuring integrity

Table 17-1 details the Encryption schemes VPN-1/FireWall-1 NG supports:

Key Management Protocol	Encryption Algorithm	Authentication Algorithm	Encryption is
IKE—Industry standard protocol for VPN key management	DES (3DES for key encryption), CAST, AES	HMAC-MD5 HMAC-SHA-1	Encapsulated; the traffic encryption is IPSec
FWZ—proprietary VPN-1/FireWall-1 NG encryption scheme	FWZ1, DES	MD5	In-place

Table 17-1.   Encryption Schemes

Encryption algorithms are VPN-1/FireWall-1 NG's method of determining how to encrypt data. VPN-1/FireWall-1 NG supports the following encryption algorithms:

- **FWZ-1**   Check Point's proprietary symmetric encryption algorithm using a 40-bit key. VPN-1/FireWall-1 NG FP2 and later do not support FWZ, neither does SecureClient, but SecuRemote still supports FWZ for backwards compatibility with earlier versions of VPN-1/FireWall-1.

- **DES**   A symmetric key encryption method that uses a 56-bit key. DES allows interoperability with other vendors' IKE-compliant firewalls.

- **Triple DES**   Encrypts under three different DES keys in succession, giving a key length of 168 bits for increased security.

- **Advanced Encryption Standard (AES)**   The new Federal Information Processing Standard (FIPS) publication that specifies a cryptographic algorithm for use by U.S. government organizations to protect sensitive (unclassified) information. Rijndael (pronounced Rain-Doll) is the AES algorithm. A key length of between 128 bits and 256 bits is supported.

- **CAST cipher**   Similar to DES. Faster than DES and triple DES but generally not as strong using the same key lengths. VPN-1/FireWall-1 NG supports 40-bit CAST.

INTERNET KEY EXCHANGE (IKE)

The Internet Key Exchange (IKE) protocol is a key management protocol standard that is used in conjunction with the IPSec standard, which in turn is an IP security feature that provides robust authentication and encryption of IP packets.

IPSec can be configured without IKE, but IKE enhances IPSec by providing additional features, flexibility, and ease of configuration for the IPSec standard. IKE is a hybrid protocol that implements the Oakley Key Exchange and Skeme Key Exchange inside the Internet Security Association and Key Management Protocol (ISAKMP) framework. ISAKMP, Oakley, and Skeme are security protocols implemented by IKE.

ISAKMP

The Internet Security Association and Key Management Protocol (ISAKMP) is the encryption standard of the Internet Engineering Task Force (IETF). The ISAKMP protocol provides a consistent framework for transferring keys and authenticating data, independent of the encryption and authentication mechanisms.

ISAKMP defines payload formats, the mechanics of implementing a key exchange protocol, and the negotiation of a security association. ISAKMP is implemented per the latest version of the ISAKMP Internet Draft (draft-ietf-ipsec-isakmp-xx.txt).

Oakley

Oakley (IKE—Internet Key Exchange) is a key exchange protocol that defines how to derive authenticated keying material. The protocol is used to establish strong cryptography-based keys used for encrypting data as follows:

- Defines how the users select the prime number groups for Diffie-Hellman key exchange
- Derives keys from the Diffie-Hellman keys or from an existing encryption key
- Allows IPSec to use secret key and certificate-based authentication

ISAKMP/Oakley

ISAKMP/Oakley, also known as IKE (Internet Key Exchange), allows VPN servers and clients to share encrypted key information. The systems must agree on how to exchange and secure information by forming a Security Association (SA) before that exchange can take place. The systems need to agree on how to encrypt and decrypt the data being sent.

To achieve this, ISAKMP and the Oakley Key generation protocols are combined. The ISAKMP protocol is the centralized manager of the SA between the server and client, while the Oakley protocol generates and manages the encryption keys used to secure the information.

The ISAKMP/Oakley process in done in two phases. Each phase uses the encryption and authentication agreed on by the two systems during initial negotiations.

Phase 1: ISAKMP SA Negotiation   In phase 1, the peers negotiate an SA that will be used for encrypting and authenticating phase 2 exchanges. Phase 1 involves long and CPU-intensive computations, so is executed infrequently. A cookie exchange mechanism precedes the computations in order to prevent Denial of Service (DoS) attacks. The negotiated SA includes the encryption method, authentication method, and keys. This SA is then used in the phase 2 negotiation. Phase 1 is used to protect the identity of the two systems connected; the steps in phase 1 are as follows:

1. Negotiate the four parameters of the SA:
   - The encryption algorithm: DES or 3DES
   - The hash algorithm: MD5 or SHA
   - The authentication method
   - The Diffie-Hellman group
2. The basic information needed to generate the shared secret key is exchanged (the Diffie-Hellman public key exchange), and the Oakley service generates the master key on each system to be used for the authentication step.

3. The systems try to authenticate the Diffie-Hellman exchange. The master key is used to authenticate the systems' identities. The identity information is hashed and encrypted to protect it using the keys generated from the Diffie-Hellman exchange.

4. If authentication occurs, phase 2 is initiated.

NOTE   VPN-1/FireWall-1 NG supports two modes for phase 1: aggressive mode (default), in which three packets are exchanged, and main mode, in which six packets are exchanged.

Phase 2: IPSec SA Negotiation   In phase 2, the SA negotiated in phase 1 is used by the peers to negotiate an SA for encrypting the IPSec traffic. Keys can be modified as often as required during a connection's lifetime by performing phase 2. Phase 2 provides additional protection by refreshing the keys to ensure the reliability of the SAs and prevent a man-in-the-middle attack. The steps in phase 2 are as follows:

1. The Policy Negotiation, exchanging:
   - The IPSec Protocol
   - The hash algorithm: DES or 3DES

   When the systems are in agreement, two SAs are established, one for inbound communications and one for outbound communications.

2. Oakley refreshes the key material, and new shared or secret keys are generated for authentication and encryption.

3. The SAs and keys are passed to the IPSec driver, and communication is established.

Tunneling-Mode Encryption

IKE uses tunneling-mode encryption, which works by encapsulating the entire packet and then adding its own encryption protocol header to the encrypted packet. You can envision tunneling-mode encryption as follows:

1. A message (data) is written and placed in an envelope.
2. The envelope has the destination and the return address written on the outside.
3. The addressed envelope is then placed inside another envelope that contains a different address and return address (that is, the encryption protocol header).
4. The envelope is mailed.

The main drawback to tunneling-mode encryption is that the packet size is increased. This increase can degrade network performance, but the security of the packet is increased. In our experience, we have had to adjust the Maximum Transmission Unit (MTU) of some client/server applications like Outlook and Exchange to prevent fragmentation of packets, as the size of the packet can sometimes exceed 1500 bytes. In DSL-based environments especially an MTU of 1458 seems the maximum for optimum performance.

FWZ VPN-1/FIREWALL-1 NG ENCRYPTION SCHEME

As discussed, under the VPN-1/FireWall-1 NG encryption scheme, a message is encrypted with a secret key derived in a secure manner from the correspondent's Diffie-Hellman keys, and the Diffie-Hellman keys are authenticated by a CA.

With FWZ, the TCP/IP packet headers are not encrypted to ensure that the protocol software will correctly handle and deliver the packets. Instead, the clear-text TCP/IP header is combined with the session key to encrypt the data portion of each packet so that no two packets are encrypted with the same key. A cryptographic checksum is embedded in each packet in normally unused bits in the header to ensure data integrity. Encryption is done in-place, with the packet length unchanged so efficiency is not compromised. The FWZ scheme does the following:

- Encrypts all data behind the IP and TCP headers
- Uses Reliable Datagram Protocol (RDP) to manage VPN session keys, encryption methods, and data integrity
- Gets certified Diffie-Hellman public keys from a trusted CA, the Check Point Management Server
- Supports a 40–56-bit FWZ-1 encryption key

In-Place Encryption

FWZ supports in-place encryption, encrypting the payload portion (data) of the packet and leaving the original TCP/IP headers intact. In-place encryption allows for better network performance because the packet size is not increased, whereas IKE encryption does increase the packet size, resulting in worse performance.

A drawback to using in-place encryption is that the headers remain intact, indicating the origin IP address and destination IP address. However, there is no performance degradation because the packet size has not changed.

ENCRYPTION SCHEME COMPARISON

Before encrypting data, it is important to decide on the best encryption scheme to use. VPN-1/FireWall-1 NG uses two encryption modes, depending upon the encryption scheme chosen:

- Tunneling-mode encryption: IKE
- In-place encryption: FWZ (Not supported in Feature Pack 2 or later)

Table 17-2 compares the features of the two encryption schemes.
Table 17-3 compares and contrasts the two encryption schemes.

Feature	IKE	FWZ
Portability	Standard	Check Point proprietary
Key management	Automatic, external PKI	Automatic
Number of keys is proportional to the...	Square of the number of correspondents	Number of correspondents
Packet size	Increased	Unchanged
Perfect Forward Secrecy (PFS)	Yes	Not available
Replay protection	Yes	Not available
Certificate Authority	Specified in the workstation properties	Local or remote VPN-1/FireWall-1 NG Management Station

Table 17-2. Comparison of Encryption Scheme Features

CERTIFICATE AUTHORITIES (CA)

As already mentioned in this chapter, a Certificate Authority (CA) is a trusted third party that can provide a public key even over an untrusted network such as the Internet. The CA certifies a public key by generating a certificate. The certificate's security is based on the following:

- The difficulty of obtaining and reading the physical device the certificate is stored on
- The secrecy of the access password

A CA issues certificates to entities, users or hosts, that these entities may then use to identify themselves and provide verifiable information to a peer gateway. A certificate might include a Distinguished Name (DN), public key, and IP address. After two entities exchange and validate each other's certificates, they can encrypt communication between them using each other's public keys.

IKE: Tunneling-Mode Encryption	FWZ: In-Place Mode Encryption
Supports all schemes except FWZ	Only supports FWZ scheme
Encrypts original IP and TCP headers	Does not encrypt IP or TCP/UDP headers
Adds new IP (first) header and IPSec (second) header in a packet	Does not increase packet size
Can be used in VPNs that use reserved IP addresses without needing address translation or proxying	Cannot be used in VPNs with reserved IP addresses

Table 17-3. Tunneling-Mode and In-Place Mode

This mechanism allows for a trust to be established even over an untrusted connection without having to pre-share keys via a secure mechanism (such as the telephone or in person).

In VPN-1/FireWall-1 NG, two kinds of entities can identify themselves using certificates:

- Encrypting gateways, when encrypting with other encrypting gateways or with SecuRemote clients
- SecuRemote clients and the site confirming each other's identities with certificates

Certificates are used in gateway-to-gateway encryption, when both gateways have public key signatures enabled in their IKE properties. Certificates are used in SecuRemote client-to-site encryption when the gateway has public key signatures enabled in the IKE properties, and the user has public key enabled in the IKE properties of the User properties.

Enabling and Trusting Certificates

Follow these steps to enable VPN-l/FireWall-l NG to use certificates:

1. Determine which CA to use, contact them, and load any specific software they require.
2. Define the CA to the VPN-l/FireWall-l NG.
3. Generate the certificates using the steps that apply to the specific type of CA.

The VPN-l/FireWall-l NG IKE implementation supports X.509 digital certificates provided by these Public Key Infrastructure (PKI) implementations:

- Check Point Certificate Manager
- OPSEC PKI vendor
- Entrust Technologies

For small networks, a single CA may be all that is needed. Larger enterprise networks that need to authenticate and encrypt their communications with different branches, vendors, and customers that use different CAs may need to use multiple CAs.

Enterprise network VPNs must be able to do the following:

- Acquire and recognize different certificates, such as Entrust and OPSEC PKI
- Trust more than one CA
- Acquire more than one certificate for an entity

NOTE An entity can only have one certificate from each CA.

Certificate Authority Hierarchy

In a CA hierarchy, when a CA's certificate is issued by another CA, only the highest-level trusted CA needs to be defined, even if there are other CAs higher up in the hierarchy. Certificates issued by a CA subordinate to a trusted CA are also trusted.

In Figure 17-10, Gateway A and Gateway B trust CA-US, and CA-NY's and CA-TX's certificates were both issued by CA-US. Therefore, Gateway A and Gateway B will also trust both CA-NY and CA-TX. If Gateway A has a certificate issued by CA-TX and Gateway B has a certificate issued by CA-NY, Gateway A and Gateway B will accept each other's certificates.

SecureClient CAs with Users

When a SecureClient user and a site authenticate using a certificate, the SecureClient trusts only the CA that signed the user's certificate. If the site's certificate is signed by a different CA, even if the gateway's CA is in the same hierarchy as the user's CA, the authentication will fail.

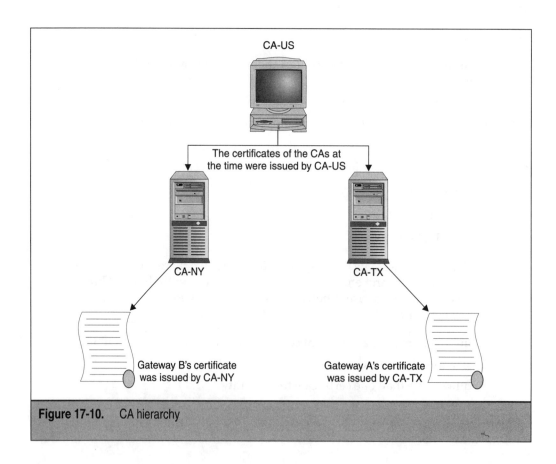

Figure 17-10.   CA hierarchy

Certificate Authority Deployment

The following sections describe typical deployment with VPN-l/FireWall-l NG and PKI components.

Internal Certificate Authority

In this configuration, the CA and Certificate Revocation List (CRL) repository are local servers managed by the administrator in headquarters. SecuRemote users do not have access to the LDAP servers and cannot download CRLs. The VPN-l/FireWall-l NG Management Station manages keys and certificates for the VPN-l/FireWall-l NG Modules, with the certification process itself involving interaction between the VPN-l/ FireWall-l NG Management and the CA.

In Figure 17-11, the two VPN-l/FireWall-l NG Modules create a VPN between them using certificates to authenticate one another. SecuRemote User Bob generates a key pair on his own, contacting the CA to receive his certificate. He then uses his key and certificate

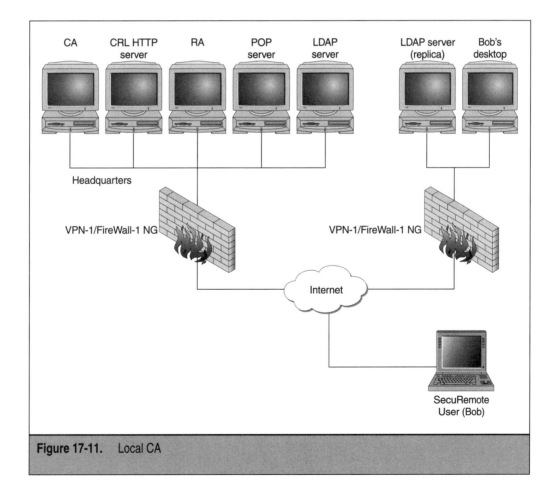

Figure 17-11.   Local CA

to establish a VPN between his remote PC and any of the offices. The SecuRemote software mandates that the CRL be sent to it. IKE negotiation will fail if a valid CRL is not sent to it as part of the negotiation.

Certificate Authority Service via the Internet

In this configuration, the CA and CRL HTTP server are accessed over the Internet.

Figure 17-12 shows a PKI where the CA and CRL repository are active servers, accessible over the Internet. The VPN-1/FireWall-l NG Management Station manages keys and certificates for the VPN-1/FireWall-1 NG Modules, with the certification process itself involving interaction between the VPN-l/Fire Wall-l NG Management Station and the CA.

In Figure 17-12, the two VPN-l/FireWall-1 NG Modules create a VPN between them using certificates to authenticate one another. SecuRemote User Bob generates

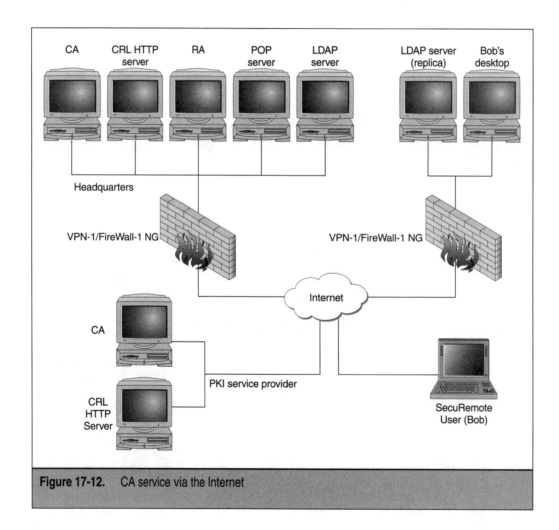

Figure 17-12. CA service via the Internet

a key pair on his own, contacting the CA directly, receiving a certificate. He can then use his key and certificate to establish a VPN between his remote PC and any of the offices.

IMPLEMENTING TWO-GATEWAY IKE ENCRYPTION CONFIGURATION

Fiction Corporation requires a VPN from New York for secure transmission of data over the Internet to the third party–hosted web servers within the secure hosting center in Leeds, England. Alternative options such as ISDN or using a private circuit from a service provider were discarded due to their high cost.

Users in New York wish to communicate securely with systems in Leeds from Network 172.31.251.0 /24 to update web content. Fiction Corporation's business requirements are best met by use of VPN-1/FireWall-1 NG capabilities to create a secure tunnel (a virtual private network, or VPN) over the Internet.

Let's examine Fiction Corporation's New York Rule Base (see Figure 17-13). It is a simple Rule Base allowing outbound access for the common protocols with a Stealth Rule and a Cleanup Rule in place.

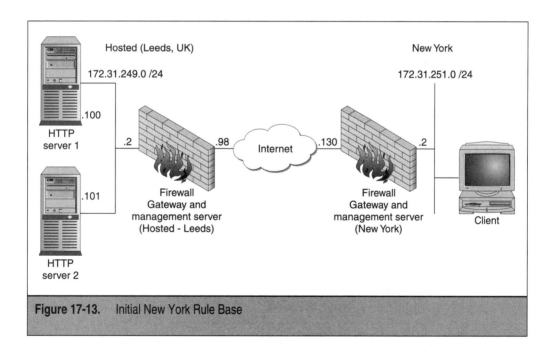

Figure 17-13.   Initial New York Rule Base

Configuring the NewYork Gateway

An encryption domain defines the networks that this gateway is responsible for protecting. To configure an encryption domain, select the Workstation object for NewYork and click Edit. Select the Topology option from the Properties list and, under the VPN Domain section, verify that All IP Addresses Behind Gateway is selected.

Select the VPN option from the Properties list and, in the Encryption Schemes section of the window, select the IKE option. Click the Edit button and the IKE Properties window appears.

Accept the default settings for the Support Key Exchange Encryption With and Support Data Integrity With sections of the screen.

In the Support Authentication Methods section of the window, select the Pre-Shared Secret option, as shown in Figure 17-14.

You have now completed the configuration on the NewYork gateway. You must now define and configure the hosted gateway as an external object to this Management Station. Define a workstation object with the following information:

Name:	Hosted
IP address:	194.73.134.130
Subnet Mask:	255.255.255.224
Color:	Red

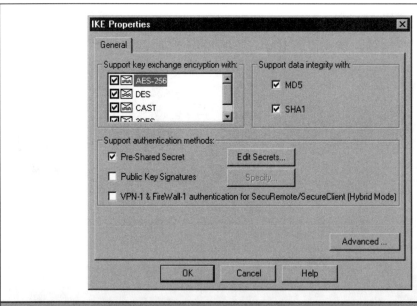

Figure 17-14.   IKE Properties window

Configure the General tab as shown in Figure 17-15. Under the Object Management section, make sure to select Managed by Another Management Server (External).

Configure the Hosted Gateway

You will now be required to connect to the hosted firewall and configure it with the following information:

1. Specify the encryption domain to be All IP Addresses behind Gateway Based on Topology.

2. Select the VPN tab and ensure IKE is selected.

3. Select Edit and ensure the settings match the definitions in Figure 17-13 that you defined for NewYork. The settings in this tab of Figure 17-15 must match those defined already in Figure 17-13 otherwise the VPN won't work correctly.

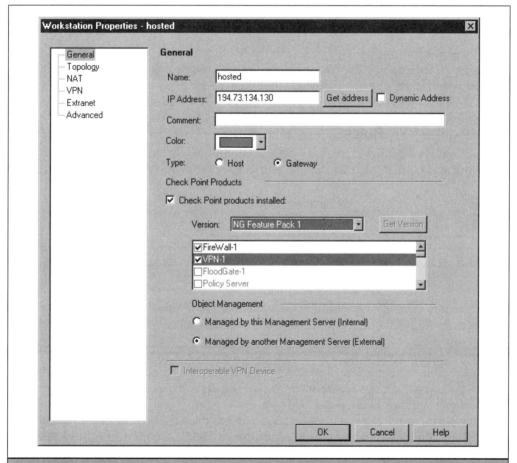

Figure 17-15. General tab of Hosted Gateway

You are now required to define an external object for the NewYork gateway on the hosted Management Server. Create a new workstation object for NewYork with the following configuration:

1. Specify the IP address and topology of the NewYork gateway.

2. For Type, select Gateway.

3. Select the check box for Check Point Products Installed.

4. In the list box, select the check boxes for both FireWall-1 and VPN-1.

5. Under Object Management, select Managed by Another Management Server (External).

6. Under the VPN tab, select IKE and click Edit. Configure the tab as shown in Figure 17-13.

7. Now select the Pre-Shared Secret option and highlight the hosted gateway shown. Select Edit to ensure the Pre-Shared Secret that was used on the NewYork Management Server.

Now you must configure the object in the Management Server to specify the IKE properties. Configure the Pre-Shared Secret by selecting it and clicking Edit Secrets. You are required to type in a password that you will be required to ensure on the hosted Management Server definitions, so make a note of it.

Creating the VPN Rules

On the New York gateway, create an object called VPN_Partners and put both NewYork and Hosted into this. Now create a rule as shown:

Source:	PN_Partners
Destination:	VPN_Partners
Service:	Any
Action:	Encrypt
Track:	Log

The newly created rule should appear as shown in Figure 17-16. It should be noted that rules for VPNs should be inserted above the Stealth Rule to ensure they function correctly.

Now right-click in the Action field on the Encrypt icon and select Properties. Verify that IKE is selected in the Encryption schemes defined field and click the Edit button to ensure the correct settings are defined. Accept the defaults and select OK. You are now able to verify and install the policy.

It should be noted that when configuring VPNs to third-party IPSec implementations, tuning the Data Integrity, Encryption Algorithm, and other settings may be required.

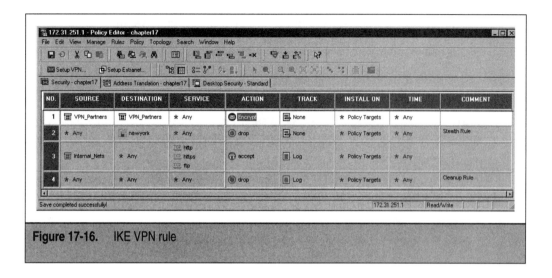

Figure 17-16. IKE VPN rule

VPN COMMUNITY

The management model enables the system administrator to directly define a VPN on a group of gateways. Each gateway and all or part of its protected domain constitutes a new entity referred to as a VPN site (not to be confused with a site defined for SecuRemote/ SecureClient). By grouping an unlimited number of VPN sites, the system administrator creates a VPN Community whose predefined properties are automatically applied to each community member.

A VPN Community is a collection of VPN sites and the enabled VPN tunnels among them. The structure of a VPN Community is automatically translated into an establishment of encrypted connections between its members. The administrator is relieved of the necessity to design and define encryption rules.

By defining a VPN Community, the administrator completes the VPN configuration. To create an all-encompassing security system, the administrator will be merely required to define access control. Because the new management model totally separates VPN as a secure connectivity platform from access control, no access control–related decision will affect the VPN Community, and vice versa.

Topology of a VPN Community

The topology of a VPN Community is the collection of VPN links enabled by the VPN Community. For instance, in a star topology, all the VPN connections from the satellites to the center of the community are enabled. Likewise, in a mesh topology, every VPN link between any pair of community members is enabled. It is important to note that the VPN topology has no effect on clear connections between community members. For instance, if enabled by access control policy, a clear connection between two satellites of a star topology in a VPN community will be allowed. There are two topologies available for VPN Communities:

- **Mesh**   Every VPN connection between any pair of members (VPN-1 gateways) is enabled in the community.

- **Star**   Any VPN connection between satellite gateways and central gateways in the community is enabled. Star topology can have two flavors:
    - Meshed center
    - No meshed center, that is, no VPN connection is enabled among the central gateways in the community.

The following principles are applied to VPN Communities:

- A network object can participate in multiple communities.

- A VPN link between any pair of VPN-1 gateways can be defined only once, thus it can be defined in a single VPN Community.

- In star topology, encrypted connection between two satellites cannot be established even if explicitly allowed by a rule. To create a VPN connection between these network objects, do one of the following:
    - Add them to another star-configured VPN Community, one as central, the other as a satellite
    - Add them to a mesh-configured VPN Community

Implementing Two-Gateway IKE VPN Community with Shared Secrets

With the release of Check Point VPN-1/FireWall-1 Feature Pack 1, 2, and 3, by default the Encrypt option has disappeared from the standard Security Policy screen and been replaced by VPN Communities. This section deals with the method for configuring VPNs using this new option.

You will create a VPN similar to the one in the section "Implementing Two-Gateway IKE Encryption Configuration," but you will use VPN Communities instead. This example has been fully tested as working on VPN-1/FireWall-1 NG Feature Pack 3. This will connect Fiction Corporation's London office to their hosted website at the Leeds location.

To configure VPNs, it is often best to draw out a table of the IP addresses and encryption domains concerned, as detailed in Tables 17-4 and 17-5.

Leeds Gateway		
Object Name	**IP address**	**Comment**
lonfw	194.73.134.2	London Gateway
Net_172.31.254.0	172.31.254.0 /24	London Network Encryption Domain

Table 17-4.   lonfw Gateway Properties

Configuring the lonfw Gateway

Objects for Net_172.31.254.0 and lonfw already exist on the lonfw firewall. Objects for the hosted gateway and Net_172.31.254.0 should be created first. To configure the VPN, first ensure that the objects are defined on the lonfw gateway as for Network 172.31.249.0 255.255.255.0 using the following information:

Name:	Net_172.31.249.0
IP address:	172.31.249.0
Subnet Mask:	255.255.255.0
Color:	Blue

1. Enable VPN-1 Pro on the local firewall module network object. Select Manage | Network Objects. In the Network Objects dialog box, select the local firewall object, lonfw as shown in Figure 17-17. An internal CA certificate will now be created and IKE properties set.

2. A dialog box with the message "Certificate Operation Succeeded" will be displayed. Click OK to continue.

Hosted Gateway		
Object Name	**IP address**	**Comment**
Hosted	194.73.134.99	Hosted Leeds Gateway
Net_172.31.249.0	172.31.249.0 /24	Hosted Gateway's Encryption Domain

Table 17-5.   Hosted Gateway at Leeds

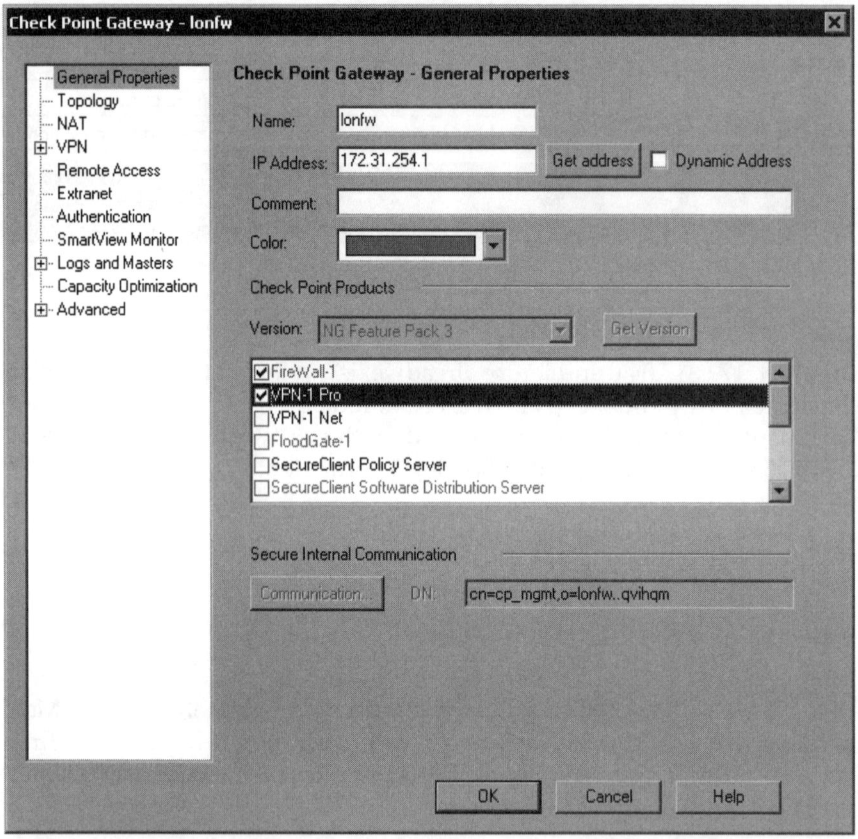

Figure 17-17. lonfw object

3. You will now define the Encryption Domain for lonfw. Ensure lonfw is highlighted and select Edit. Select Topology from the left pane and, under the VPN Domain section, select Manually Defined. From the pop-up list, select the Net_172.31.254.0 object as shown in Figure 17-18.

4. Select VPN from the left pane and under the VPN heading on the right, click the Add button. Add MyIntranet as shown in Figure 17-19. Click OK to accept changes.

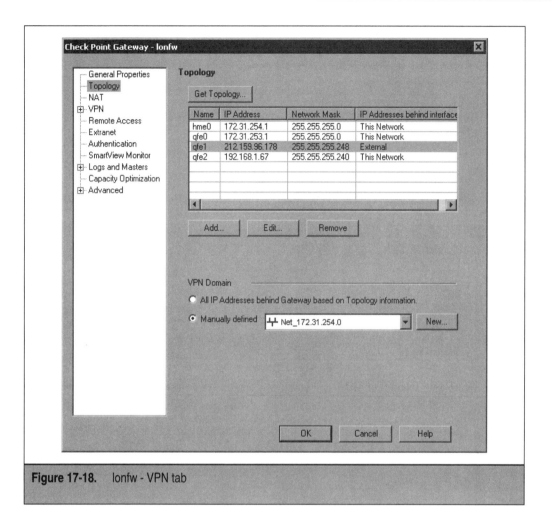

Figure 17-18. lonfw - VPN tab

5. You will now create the remote firewall, hosted. Select Manage | Network Objects. In the Network Objects dialog box, click New and select Check Point | Externally Managed Gateway. In the General Properties option, enter the following information:

Name:	Hosted
IP address:	194.73.134.99
Subnet Mask:	255.255.255.224
Color:	Red

In the Check Point Products section, select NG Feature Pack 3 from the Version drop-down list and ensure that the FireWall-1 check box in the Check Point Products section is selected, and check the VPN-1 Pro check box, as shown in Figure 17-20.

6. In the Topology Section, under the VPN Domain section, select Manually Defined and select Net_172.31.249.0.

7. Click OK in the Externally Managed Check Point Gateway dialog box to define the object. You have to do this before you can configure the VPN section. Re-open the hosted gateway object and select the VPN option from the left pane.

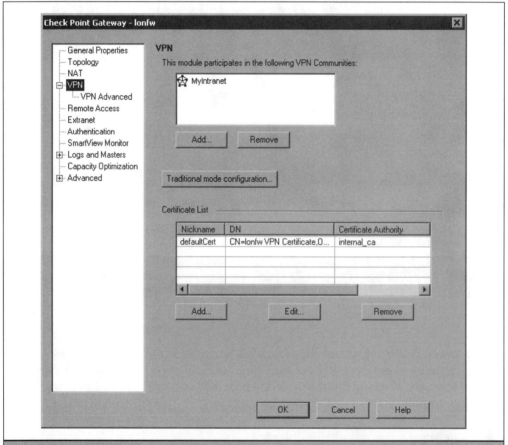

Figure 17-19. Hosted object properties

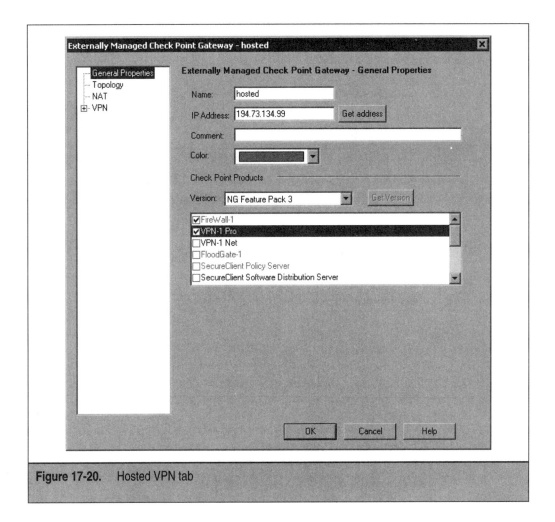

Figure 17-20.   Hosted VPN tab

8. Under the VPN option, select Add and select MyIntranet as shown in Figure 17-21. Click OK to continue.

9. You will now configure the MyIntranet VPN Community. Select Manage | VPN Communities. Select MyIntranet from the list and select Edit.

10. In the General properties in the Community Traffic Security Policy section, check the Accept All Encrypted Traffic check box.

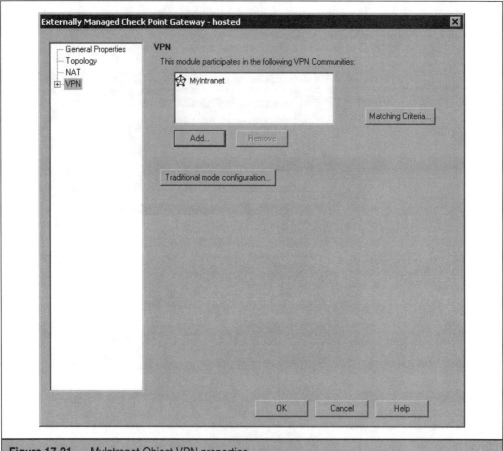

Figure 17-21. MyIntranet Object VPN properties

11. Select VPN Properties in the left pane and enter the following information, as shown in Figure 17-22.

> **IKE Phase 1 Properties**
> Perform Key Exchange Encryption with: DES
> Perform Data Integrity with: MD5
> **IPSec (Phase 2) Properties**
> Perform IPSec Data Encryption with: DES
> Perform Data Integrity with: MD5

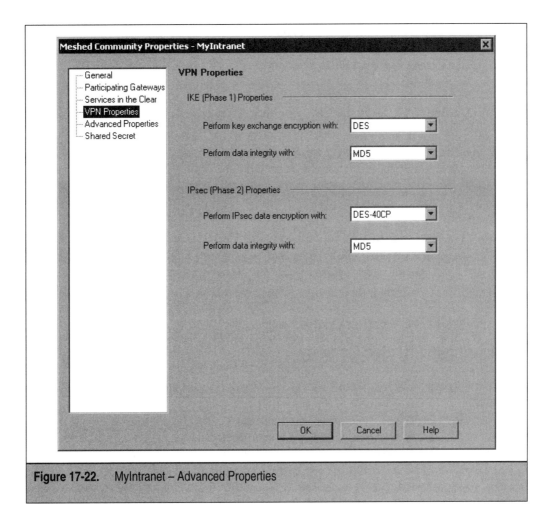

Figure 17-22.   MyIntranet – Advanced Properties

NOTE   It is recommended that in real-world deployments 3DES (168-bit encryption) be selected instead of DES (40- or 56-bit encryption) for IPSec Phase 1 and that AES-128 (128-bit encryption that is inherently stronger than the DES schemes) or stronger encryption be selected for IPSec Phase 2. DES has been cracked and is not generally considered secure, even though it took a concerted effort of many systems working together and four months to crack it.

12. Now Select the Advanced Properties from the left pane and configure the Advanced Properties using the following information, as listed.

    IKE (Phase 1)
    Use Diffie-Hellman Group: Group 2 (1024-bit)
    Renegotiate IKE Security Associations Every: 1440 minutes

Use Aggressive Mode: unchecked
IPsec (Phase 2)
Use Perfect Forward Secrecy: unchecked
Renegotiate IPsec Security Associations Every: 3600 seconds
Support Site to Site IP Compression: unchecked
Disable NAT Inside the VPN Community: checked

13. Select Shared Secret from the left pane. In the Shared Secret properties, check the Use Only Shared Secret for All External Members check box. In the Each External Member Will Have the Following Secret with All Internal Members in This Community window, select the Remote Firewall Module Network object (i.e., hosted). Click Edit and enter the shared secret (i.e., secret123). Click OK to save the object.

NOTE   The shared secret is a secret key that must match the one that will be defined on the other gateway. If both firewalls' secret keys match, communications will be accepted; if they do not, the connection will be rejected.

---

14. Install the Security Policy on the local firewall module.

Configuring the Hosted Gateway

The configuration required on the hosted gateway will be exactly the same as the steps carried out on the lonfw gateway, but the external gateway to be defined this time will be lonfw.

Objects for Net_172.31.249.0 and hosted already exist on the hosted firewall. Objects for the lonfw gateway and Net_172.31.254.0 should be created first. To configure the VPN, first ensure that the objects are defined on the hosted gateway as for Network 172.31.254.0 255.255.255.0 using the following information:

Name:	Net_172.31.254.0
IP address:	172.31.254.0
Subnet Mask:	255.255.255.0
Color:	Blue

1. Enable VPN-1 Pro on the local Firewall Module Network object. Select Manage | Network objects. In the Network Objects dialog box, select the local firewall object, hosted. An internal CA certificate will be created and IKE properties set.

   A dialog box with the message, Certificate Operation Succeeded will be displayed. Click OK to continue.

2. You will now define the Encryption Domain for hosted. Ensure hosted is highlighted and select Edit. Select Topology from the left pane and under the VPN Domain section, select Manually Defined. From the pop-up list, select the Net_172.31.249.0 object.

3. Select VPN from the left pane and under the VPN heading, click the Add button. Add MyIntranet and click OK to accept changes.

4. You will now create the remote firewall lonfw. Select Manage | Network Objects. In the Network Objects dialog box, click New and select Check Point | Externally Managed Gateway. In the General Properties option, enter the following information:

Name:	lonfw
IP address:	194.73.134.2
Subnet Mask:	255.255.255.224
Color:	Red

In the Check Point Products section, select NG Feature Pack 3 from the Version drop-down list, ensure that the FireWall-1 check box in the Check Point Products section is checked, and check the VPN-1 Pro check box.

5. In the Topology Section, under the VPN Domain section, select Manually Defined and select Net_172.31.254.0.

6. Click OK in the Externally Managed Check Point Gateway dialog box to define the object. You have to do this before you can configure the VPN section. Reopen the hosted gateway object and select the VPN option from the left pane.

Under the VPN option, select Add, select MyIntranet, and click OK to continue.

7. You will now configure the MyIntranet VPN Community. Select Manage | VPN Communities. Select MyIntranet from the list and select Edit.

8. In the General properties, in the Community Traffic Security Policy section, check the Accept All Encrypted Traffic check box.

9. Select the VPN Properties in the left pane and enter the following information:

   IKE (Phase 1) Properties
   Perform key exchange encryption with: DES
   Perform data integrity with: MD5
   IPSec (Phase 2) Properties
   Perform IPSec data encryption with: DES
   Perform data integrity with: MD5

10. Now Select the Advanced Properties from the left pane and enter the following information:

   IKE (Phase 1)
   Use Diffie-Hellman group: Group 2 (1024 bit)
   Renegotiate IKE security associations every: 1440 minutes
   Use aggressive mode: unchecked
   IPsec (Phase 2)
   Use Perfect Forward Secrecy: unchecked

Renegotiate IPsec security associations every: 3600 seconds
Support Site to Site IP Compression: unchecked
Disable NAT inside the VPN community: checked

11. Select Shared Secret from the left pane. In the Shared Secret properties, check the Use Only Shared Secret for All External Members check box. In the Each External Member Will Have the Following Secret with All Internal Members in This Community window, select the Remote Firewall Module Network object (i.e., lonfw). Click Edit and enter the shared secret (i.e., secret123). Click OK to save the object.

NOTE   The shared secret is a secret key that must match the one that will be defined on the other gateway. If both firewalls' secret keys match, communications will be accepted; otherwise, the connection will be rejected.

---

12. Install the Security Policy on the local firewall module

You have now learned how to configure a Site to Site Virtual Private Network using VPN Communities. You can add other gateways into the VPN Community and create a full mesh network in which all sites can use VPN tunnels to communicate by simply adding additional gateways to each gateway configuration. For example, say another site was required to participate in the VPN Community on both lonfw and hosted gateways. You would need to create another external Check Point External Gateway object for the additional site gateway and create two external gateways on the additional gateway, one each for lonfw and hosted.

EXTRANET MANAGER

An extranet is a private network that makes use of Internet/intranet technology to securely share information operations between organizations in an extended enterprise, which may include customers, suppliers, vendors, or other types of partners. It is typically behind a firewall that closes it off from the public and can be viewed as a part of a company's intranet extended to selected partners outside the company.

The Complexity of Extranet Management

The establishment of a large-scale extranet is a complex, often unintuitive process with substantial potential for error. Creating an extranet requires elaborate object and topology definitions. For every partner's every gateway, the encryption domain and the shared resources protected by the gateway must be defined. The larger the extranet, the more difficult and time consuming these processes become.

In the case of PKI-based extranets, the initial construction is further complicated by the setup of PKI configurations and the need for careful coordination between sides. Certificate Authority (CA) public keys and distinguished names must be exchanged,

CRLs must be transferred from side to side, and IKE properties must be coordinated—all without compromising the security of the networks involved.

Even after an extranet has been successfully configured, it requires constant maintenance, which can also be problematic. For every change in a partner's network, whether in the topology of the gateways, the IP addresses of objects, or security-related properties, all the other partners must update their configurations in accordance. It becomes less and less feasible to make these changes smoothly as the size of the extranet increases.

Check Point Extranet Management Interface

Extranet Management Interface addresses the problems of large-scale, PKI-based extranet deployments and significantly simplifies their creation and maintenance. By providing an easy, comfortable framework for defining and updating the topology and security information of imported objects, Extranet Management Interface makes coordination between partners in an extranet less complicated and more reliable. In addition, the integration of an internal CA in VPN-1/FireWall-1 NG reduces the amount of configuration required to establish a PKI-based extranet using Extranet Management Interface.

Licensing

Extranet Management Interface requires that one of the following three types of licenses be installed on your Management Server:

- One partner
- Up to five partners
- Unlimited partners

Licenses are additive, so that holding a license for one partner and another license for up to five partners will allow you to form an extranet with up to six partners.

Creating an Extranet

Implementation of Extranet Management Interface requires that all sides of an extranet have Check Point VPN-1/FireWall-1 NG installed with Extranet Management Interface enabled.

This section outlines the process of defining and implementing extranets using Check Point Extranet Management Interface, which will be described in further detail in the following sections. Note that each participant partner or entity in your extranet must follow this procedure if the extranet is to be implemented properly.

1. Set up an extranet community environment by doing the following:
   - Create at least one extranet-enabled gateway.

- Define the general properties of the extranet community.
- Define the network objects that will be exported to your extranet partners.

The relevant subsets of information regarding these objects or groups will be accessible to your partners through a VPN tunnel. In this part of the process, you essentially define a section of your network that you will share with each of your extranet partners. Once the exported objects have been defined, you may add or remove partners at any time. You may also add, remove, or modify the exported objects themselves.

2. Define your extranet partners and import their network objects.

Each of these partners will be able to import your exported network objects and use them in their respective Security Policy Rule Bases. Specific access to any of the objects you export will be determined by your own Rule Base settings. The process of defining extranet partners includes the establishment of trust through the exchange of Check Point Extranet Management Interface public keys and verification of their fingerprints. Each Extranet Management Interface fingerprint is calculated on the Management Server's Internal Certificate Authority and its Distinguished Name.

3. Integrate network objects imported from your extranet partners in the Security Policy Rule Base.

Extranet Resolution Protocol

After public keys have been exchanged and approved between partners, completing the initial Extranet Management Interface trust setup, extranet partners can initiate a certificate-based secured protocol to get each other's exported resources and topologies. These are derived from their extranet community definitions.

Each extranet-enabled gateway houses two Extranet Resolution Servers. One is the Public Key Distributor, and the other is the Extranet Objects Distributor.

Check Point's VPN product documentation contains detailed information about extranet configuration and management.

VPN ROUTING

VPN Routing is a new Feature Pack 3 option which is designed to fulfill the need for gateways to encrypt with each other indirectly via a central VPN-1 Module that acts as a VPN router. With this feature, you can decrypt traffic coming from one gateway and re-encrypt it to forward to another gateway. The functionality copies the architecture of Frame Relay networks for an easier migration from traditional networks to IP-based networks using IPSec VPN technology.

VPN routing offers simple configuration for branch offices by hiding them from the whole network while allowing full connectivity.

Full mesh configuration, in which you would like to enable redundancy between VPN-1 modules, so that if one module is incapacitate, the VPN traffic is automatically routed through a backup VPN-1 in an MEP (Multiple Entry Point) configuration.

Implementation of VPN Routing

To better understand the VPN routing feature, consider a scenario of an enterprise with a VPN-1 hub and two VPN-1 spokes. The two spokes should be able to open a tunnel to the VPN-1 hub. The two spokes should also be able to open a tunnel to each other but only indirectly via the hub. In other words, traffic from one spoke should be forwarded to the hub; it should then be decrypted and re-encrypted to be forwarded to the other spoke. Such a requirement could arise from the need to inspect the traffic between the spokes at the hub, or simply because the two spokes cannot form a direct network connection between them.

Before the VPN routing feature was available, the only way to enable connectivity between the two spokes was to create a direct VPN tunnel from one spoke to another. With VPN routing, two main capabilities have been added:

1. **Forwarding of VPN traffic is configurable.**   VPN traffic can be forwarded to another VPN-1 module that is not necessarily protecting the final destination. In the preceding example, VPN traffic may be forwarded from one spoke to the hub even if the final destination is protected by the other spoke.

2. **Forwarding encrypted traffic between VPN tunnels is possible.**   You can now decrypt VPN traffic and re-encrypt it to forward to the final destination.

The VPN routing feature allows the administrator to specify VPN "hops" similar to routing hops. Each VPN tunnel is opened to the next hop, decrypted and then re-encrypted to the next hop. When a spoke wishes to encrypt to another spoke, the next VPN hop is the hub (VPN router) that decrypts the data, enforces the Security Policy, re-encrypts the data, and sends it to the final destination—the second spoke.

Configuration of these VPN hops requires adding VPN routing rules to a routing table (vpn_route.conf file).

NAT AND VPN

VPN-1/FireWall-1 NG supports Network Address Translation to connect to another network that is using IP addresses in the same range as your own. For example, let's assume Fiction Corporation wants to connect to an external supplier whose internal network is also 172.31.254.0 255.255.255.0. By using Automatic Address Translation on both the supplier's VPN-1/FireWall-1 NG gateway and Fiction Corporation's gateway in conjunction with perform NAT on client side being checked, the configuration will work automatically without requiring the addition of Static Routes as was the case in prior versions of VPN-1/FireWall-1 NG.

CHECKLIST: KEY POINTS IN ENCRYPTION AND VIRTUAL PRIVATE NETWORKS

The following is a checklist for the key points in Encryption and Virtual Private Networks.

- ☐ Configure Virtual Private Networks (VPNs).
- ☐ List all of the differences between symmetric and asymmetric encryption.
- ☐ Create Certificate Authorities (CAs).
- ☐ Show how CAs are secure.
- ☐ Compare the differences between the Internet Key Exchange and Check Point's FWZ encryption schemes.
- ☐ Define the IKE standard.
- ☐ Define the FWZ standard.
- ☐ Show how IKE supports interoperability with other vendors' VPN products.
- ☐ Show how to use CAs.
- ☐ Identify what can be supported by using Public Key Infrastructure (PKI).
- ☐ List the steps required to implement a two-site IKE VPN.
- ☐ Define VPN Communities.
- ☐ List the steps required to implement a two-site IKE VPN using VPN Communities.
- ☐ Define the Feature Pack 3 VPN routing option.
- ☐ Discuss NAT and VPNs.

CHAPTER 18

SecuRemote and SecureClient

A key component of enterprise security is to provide it to increasingly mobile workers such as traveling sales staff or home workers. The challenges of offering secure access to confidential information require a seamless Security Policy across an enterprise that also incorporates mobile workers. Check Point has developed remote access VPNs and a remote access client to support the mobile or roaming access market.

SecuRemote and SecureClient provide the client-side application in a client-to-site VPN (Virtual Private Network). This provides users with a secure connection to remote services. These client-side applications provide users and administrators with a new model for remote access, replacing expensive dial-up NAS/RAS solutions with extremely flexible and cost efficient secure remote access to corporate networks.

But that's not all they can be used for. They can also be deployed inside the corporate network to provide greater security for critical systems by encrypting traffic on the corporate LAN.

SECUREMOTE/SECURECLIENT

VPN-1 SecuRemote/SecureClient uses client encryption technology. SecuRemote encrypts data before it leaves the remote user's computer, providing the "in transit" security.

Because SecuRemote and SecureClient work at the network layer, no modifications are required to the users' applications. Seamless integration of remote users is therefore possible just as though they were connected to the local network.

SecuRemote and SecureClient Differences

SecuRemote and SecureClient are the same except for one important difference: SecureClient supports a desktop Security Policy that is pushed down to the user's system. This extends VPN-1/FireWall-1 NG stateful inspection technology to the users inside (and outside) an organization. Although all communication is encrypted between the client and the remote access network, the possibility exists for the client to be compromised and for the VPN tunnel to be hijacked and used for nefarious purposes. The SecureClient mitigates this risk completely by allowing the administrator to control and log inbound and outbound connections to the SecureClient desktop. Now don't you wish you had that level of control with all the systems you administer? We do.

Table 18-1 shows where it is appropriate to use SecuRemote and SecureClient.

NOTE Sometimes the service provider for xDSL and cable Internet connections supplies a *NAT box*, which provides outbound-only Network Address Translation (NAT), effectively preventing inbound access. This can provide a reasonable level of security for the client.

As you can probably imagine, there are numerous other scenarios where SecuRemote and SecureClient could be used. You need to assess what level of risk is associated with each and determine if the client needs the added protection of a Security Policy enforced to the desktop or if encrypted data alone provides sufficient mitigation of risk.

Purpose	Use SecuRemote	Use SecureClient
Secure remote access with dial-up Internet account	No—the client can be attacked and the tunnel hijacked	Yes—laptop users get the benefit of low-cost dial access and a protected client through Policy Server
Extranet access from a partner organization from within another protected corporate network	Yes—the client is already protected inside your partner's network so there is no need to protect the client	Yes—if you cannot verify the security of your partner's network, you can assure yourself that the client is protected while connected to your extranet
Internal secure access to servers (see the section "SecureServer versus SSL" later in this chapter)	Yes—if protection for data in transit alone is sufficient	Yes—if there exists the possibility of attempts that will compromise the client and the risk cannot be tolerated
Secure Remote Access via Internet using xDSL or cable	Yes—if protection is provided at the client's network perimeter such as a NAT box or secured router	Yes—if client is used to connect directly to the Internet without any perimeter security

Table 18-1.   SecureClient/SecuRemote Differences

VPN-1/FireWall-l NG administrators use the standard Policy Editor for SecuRemote/SecureClient configuration. You can use the Policy Editor to control access once a client-to-site VPN is established just as you can for any other type of connection: features such as authentication, logging, and alerts can all be used just as with unencrypted connections.

SecureServer versus SSL

VPN-1/FireWall-1 NG SecureServer is a version of VPN-1/FireWall-1 NG designed to protect a single application server. It provides access control, client and session authentication, Network Address Translation, and logging and auditing for a single host. VPN-1/FireWall-1 NG SecureServer was called the Host Inspection Module in version 4.

SSL (Secure Sockets Layer) makes no claim to protect the systems and applications themselves, only the privacy, authentication, and data integrity of the communications. SSL is not unlike a network layer VPN solution, like the Check Point IPSec and FWZ VPNs, although it has specific pros and cons. For example, the primary benefit of SSL is that most browsers support it. The job of distributing and managing the client VPN is done when the browser is installed, as opposed to the out of band installation of SecuRemote. The downside, however, is that SSL is service specific (for example, it has no support for UDP services, and non-SSL TCP applications cannot use it), and it is not especially scalable or efficient. It also runs in user space, whereas IPSec IKE runs in the kernel.

SecureServer also protects the server itself from unauthorized network accesses, something SSL cannot do. SecureServer intercepts packets below the IP stack and allows for highly granular rules that users and IPs can access (SecureServer still supports Client and Session Authentication), thus protecting from classes of attacks such as dictionary attacks, Denial of Service (DoS) attacks, and exploits of nonmission critical services.

Using SecureClient in conjunction with SecureServer provides a method of deploying highly secure cooperative workgroups for local or remote users, something SSL alone falls far short of.

SECURE CONNECTIONS FOR FICTION CORPORATION FINANCE GATEWAY

The reason for using VPN technology inside a private network is to enhance the security of some internal systems—in this example, access to the Payroll server. The Payroll server at Fiction Corporation has been around a while and still uses old-fashioned Telnet for payroll workers to get a remote session. Using an encrypted connection to the Finance firewall ensures that no snooping or data capture can be used to reveal passwords or other sensitive information as the data traverses the network.

Figure 18-1 shows the network design for securing internal connections to Fiction Corporation's Payroll server.

To configure client-to-site VPN, you must specify an encryption domain in the Workstation Properties Topology tab, as shown in Figure 18-2. *Encryption domain* refers to the object or group of objects that has been selected for this gateway to protect.

It should be noted that in previous versions it was necessary to enable Respond to Unauthenticated Topology Requests in the Global Policy Properties setup of VPN-1/FireWall-1 NG, but this is no longer required unless you intend to support older versions of the client. Topology requests to the gateway are no longer in the clear and unauthenticated; instead, SSL is used to provide secured communication for topology requests.

Configure the firewall object's Workstation Properties on the VPN tab to reflect the preferred encryption scheme, IKE or FWZ. Edit the scheme properties and select the required options for IKE or FWZ. IKE supports pre-shared secret keys (that is, it uses users' passwords as SecuRemote/SecureClient pre-shared keys), PKI certificates, and hybrid mode. FWZ uses an internal Certificate Manager (a basic PKI scheme). You may choose both or either schemes, but make sure that the user-selected schemes are supported on the VPN-1 gateway that will be used with the connection.

Figure 18-3 shows the rule in the Policy Editor that is used to establish a VPN connection for the Fiction Corporation users of the Payroll server. We will expand upon this example in Chapter 19.

Although you have already created users for authenticated access to the Payroll server, you need to make some changes to allow those same Fiction Corporation users to use SecureClient to access the Payroll server.

Each user has a defined encryption method. This method will be used when the users attempt to establish a secure connection via SecureClient.

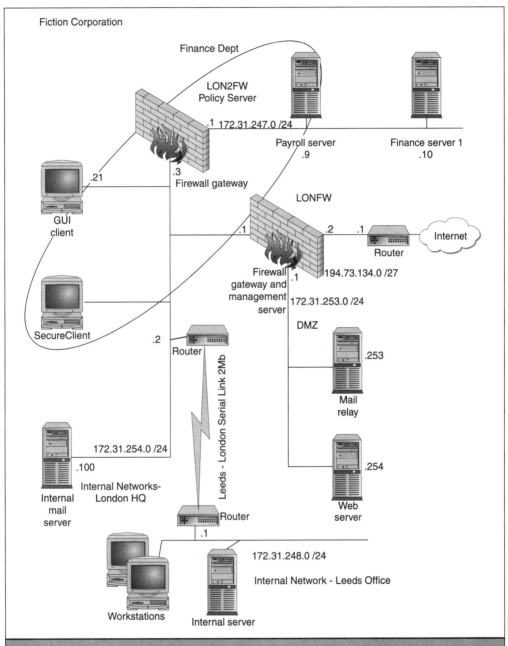

Figure 18-1. Fiction Corporation's Network

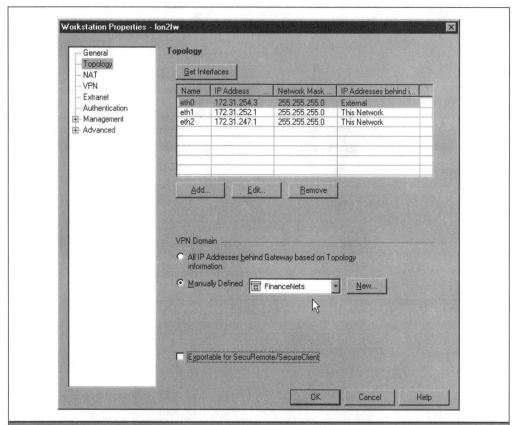

Figure 18-2. VPN encryption domain

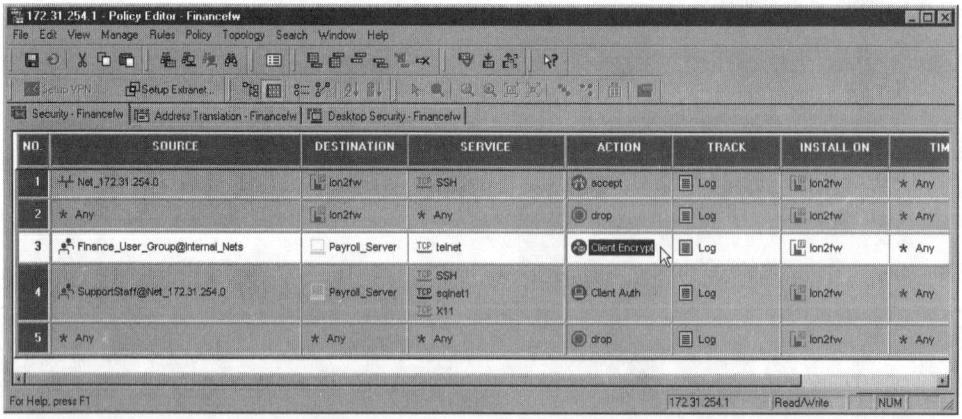

Figure 18-3. Rule to enable client-to-site VPN

IKE OR FWZ

The two encryption schemes, IKE (Internet Key Exchange) and FWZ (a Check Point proprietary key exchange method), vary in their capabilities and the strength of encryption provided.

IKE always encapsulates the packet. *Encapsulate* means the original packet is encrypted and placed in the payload of a new packet. This adds an additional overhead but allows packets to be routed over the Internet even if the source and destination addresses are private. You can also enable the Encapsulate Connections option for SecuRemote on the Workstation Properties tab for FWZ. If you don't do this, you can only use FWZ where addresses can be routed to and from, because only the payload of the packet is encrypted, and the source and destination address will remain per the original packet.

DNS name resolution also needs to be considered when deciding if you need to encapsulate the packet or not. For example, if the destination machine has a private unregistered IP address, who resolves its name? One solution is to configure the SecureClient's primary DNS as an internal DNS server that can resolve internal names with unregistered IP addresses. It is best to encrypt the DNS resolution of these internal names, but you will probably not want all DNS traffic to be encrypted because this would mean that every DNS resolution would require authentication, which could be a nuisance to users.

IKE can use AES (Advanced Encryption Standard, 256-bit), 3DES (Data Encryption Standard, 168-bit), and DES (56-bit). FWZ supports FWZ1 (a Check Point proprietary encryption algorithm that supports 40-bit key lengths) and DES.

All authentication methods supported by the gateway can be used by FWZ, but IKE can only use a VPN-1/FireWall-1 NG password as the pre-shared secret. However, Check Point has written an extension to IKE to allow all supported authentication methods to be used; the IKE hybrid mode gets around the limitation imposed on IKE.

Figure 18-4 shows the Users Properties Encryption tab. Select the required scheme, IKE or FWZ, as appropriate. Then click OK.

Users of Feature Pack 3 should note that FWZ support has now been removed from the product, as it was not widely used.

Hybrid IKE

Hybrid IKE extends the IKE scheme to support all the FireWall-1 authentication methods such as SecurID Cards, RADIUS, LDAP, or the VPN-l/FireWall-l NG Internal Password. IKE only supports FireWall-1 passwords as pre-shared secrets and certificates natively. This gives security administrators the ability to deploy strong two-factor authentication for remote access. This is highly desirable because it limits the risks of someone accessing your internal systems by guessing usernames and passwords. Two-factor authentication means something you have and something you know, for example, you have a SecurID key fob and you know your pin number. This provides superior security because either component alone cannot be used to gain access.

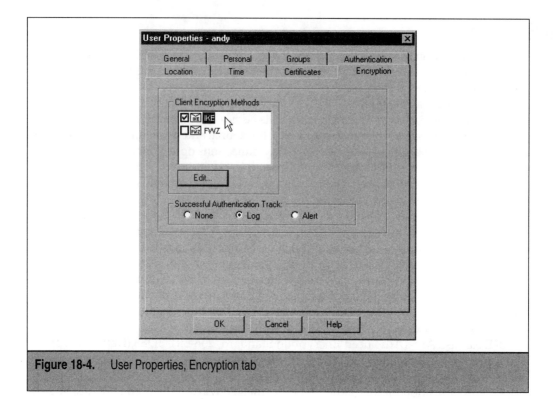

Figure 18-4. User Properties, Encryption tab

ROUTING CONSIDERATIONS

If you use multiple gateways, you need to consider routing and make sure that the return packet goes via the same gateway as the original packets were routed. You might do this so that one firewall handles just remote access while the other gateway handles general inbound and outbound traffic. This can be useful if you have two Internet connections and want to dedicate them to specific purposes. There are two ways of making sure that the traffic returns to the correct gateway. One way is to use NAT and hide all traffic behind the gateways address so the return traffic goes back to where it appears to originate from. The other way is to use IP Pools.

SECURE DOMAIN LOGIN

The Secure Domain Logon feature allows Windows SecuRemote/SecureClients to log on to a domain controller securely, protected by VPN-1/FireWall-1 NG, using both LAN and dial-up connections. If the feature is enabled, SecureClient is activated before the domain controller authenticates a domain logon. The next time you attempt to log in after a restart to the domain controller, a SecureClient User Authentication window will be displayed after you have entered the operating system credentials. The exchange of credentials and user profile between the workstation and domain controller will then be encrypted.

If you enable the Single SignOn feature, the username and password are stored, in encrypted form, and automatically retrieved from the Windows Registry. The User Authentication screen is therefore not displayed.

Secure Domain Logon can only be enabled if the machine is configured as part of a domain. Selecting Enable Secure Domain Logon from the Password menu enables Secure Domain Logon.

SIMPLIFIED MODE (FP2 AND ABOVE)

Feature Pack 2 introduced the simplified mode for VPN creation and the concept of VPN Communities. FP3 adds further refinements; all information and screen shots in this section relate to FP3. See Chapter 17 for further details on site-to-site VPN communities. The Remote Access community is a predefined community that allows the configuration of SecuRemote and SecureClient remote access. The *simplified* metaphor has been extended to allow you to quickly configure remote access. You can still use traditional mode, client-encrypt action in the Rule Base, but you must decide whether you want to use simplified or traditional mode when you create a new policy. You cannot mix both modes within the same policy. You can specify the default behaviour regarding creating a new policy in the Policy Global Properties, VPN-1 Pro tree item as shown in Figure 18-5.

If you have upgraded, you will need to create a new policy and select Simplified Mode, as the default will be to remain with Traditional Mode for upgraded systems.

Once you have chosen simplified mode, the VPN Manager tab is available to manage the creation of VPN communities. In Figure 18-6, you can see the single firewall lonfw providing remote access to a single group called Remote_Access. As already stated, the remote access community is already created for you—all you need to do is add the gateway and the user group to the community and specify access control restrictions in the Security Policy using the new If Via column heading.

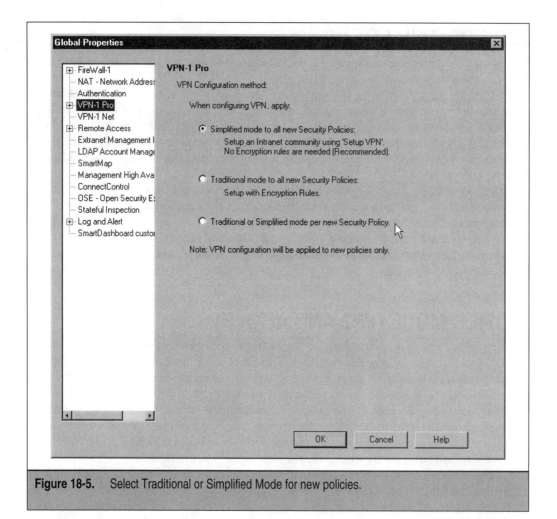

Figure 18-5. Select Traditional or Simplified Mode for new policies.

To add the gateway you wish to use for remote access to the Remote Access community, double-click the icon to open the Remote Access Community properties page, as shown in Figure 18-7. Select the Participating Gateways tree item and click Add.

Add the group by selecting Participant User Groups, and add the group as you did the gateway (you can choose New if you have not yet created the user group).

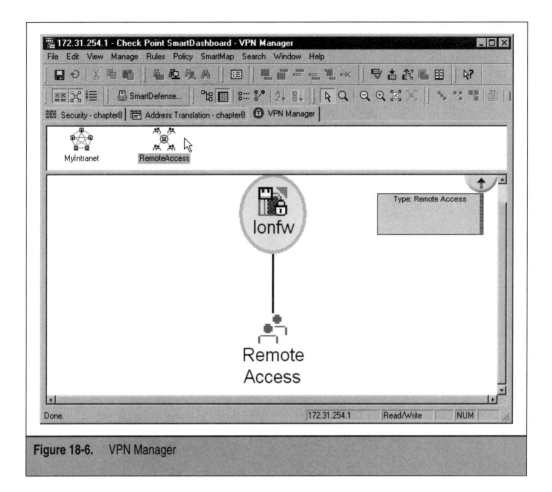

Figure 18-6.   VPN Manager

Finally, add a rule to the Security Policy to define access control for the remote access user groups who come in via the Remote Access community, as shown in Figure 18-8.

Members of the user group Remote_Access need to have the properties for IKE set as before in traditional mode, although this can now be overridden with a global setting available from the Remote Access VPN Advanced section of the Global Properties page, which can enforce settings on all users.

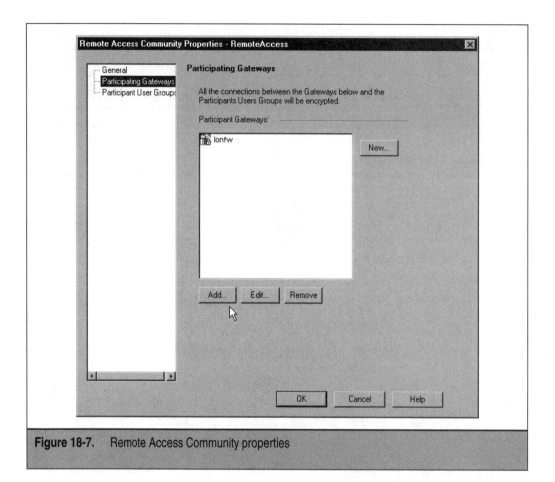

Figure 18-7. Remote Access Community properties

As you can see, simplified mode speeds up the creation of remote access services for use with SecureClient and SecuRemote, providing even more sophisticated capabilities with improved graphical configuration and ease of use.

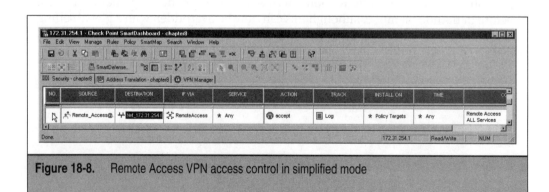

Figure 18-8. Remote Access VPN access control in simplified mode

CHECKLIST: KEY POINTS IN SECUREMOTE AND SECURECLIENT

The following is a checklist for what's new in SecuRemote and SecureClient:

☐ Deploy the SecureClient/SecuRemote to provide secured access to resources.

☐ Define SecuRemote/SecureClient.

☐ List the differences between SecureClient and SecuRemote.

☐ Compare differences between SecureClient and SecuRemote to the differences between Secure Server and SSL.

☐ Illustrate the advantages of the Check Point remote access solution.

☐ Use SecureClient/SecuRemote within a corporate network.

☐ Use SecureClient/SecuRemote across an insecure public access network such as the Internet.

☐ Show how extending the VPN-1/FireWall-1 NG stateful inspection to the desktop gives you complete mitigation of risk when you need to secure access to remote resources.

☐ List the more advanced configuration options available with SecureClient and SecuRemote.

☐ Identify SecuRemote/SecureClient operation.

☐ List the routing considerations.

☐ Define Secure Domain Logon.

☐ Define traditional mode versus simplified mode.

CHAPTER 19

Policy Server

The need for a firewall arises when there is concern about unauthorized access to internal systems, such as when an organization connects to the Internet or another public network. Over the years, a trend has emerged that clearly shows that more security-breaching incidents occur within an organization than come from outside. These incidents are often the most damaging in terms of financial loss, with hackers on the inside working with accomplices on the outside to defraud the business.

In Chapter 18, we looked at how client encryption technology used within SecuRemote can be used to provide enhanced security for internal systems as well as for remote access. Check Point's Policy Server was developed to protect the client desktops from both external and internal attack by pushing a Security Policy to the desktop of the SecureClient system. The SecureClient software uses the same client encryption technology as SecuRemote but enhances the security of the client by allowing a rule base to be applied and enforced on the client.

POLICY SERVER DEFINED

Firewall administrators can define a rule base for clients that are installed with SecureClient software. The Policy Server module provides the rule base to the client when it connects to the encryption domain. The Security Policy installed on the desktop prevents authorized connections from being compromised by controlling access to the local system in exactly the same way as the firewall provides protection from external networks. This is in effect, a personal firewall, for the users of laptop or desktop PCs installed with SecureClient software. The rule base or security policy for the client is defined centrally and distributed by the Policy Server Module. It is necessary to monitor whether the security policy has been successfully installed on the client system before you allow client connections. Checking to make sure the policy is installed and operating allows the administrator to prevent access to the protected network if there is a danger that the client can be attacked. This reduces the risk of a misconfigured client system presenting a security threat to the protected network.

To receive the benefits of a Desktop Security Policy and authenticated secure connections you will need:

- Policy Server software installed
- SecureClient software (licensed per client)

The installation of the Policy Server software can be accomplished at the same time you install the Enforcement Module, or you can install Policy Server later by rerunning the installation program. The prerequisites for software and hardware are the same as for the Enforcement and Management Modules. You will need to select SecureClient Policy Server in the General properties tab on your firewall object if you add the Policy Server software after initial installation.

You must have a Policy Server license to use the software.

SecureClient extends SecuRemote to allow a desktop user to download a Desktop Policy or rule base from the Policy Server.

SecuRemote is currently provided free of charge by Check Point. SecureClient is licensed and priced per client, as discussed in Chapter 18.

A single Policy Server provides just one Desktop Policy to all SecureClients in its domain. The Policy Server can be installed on the gateway on which it will be used or on a separate host with a VPN-1/FireWall-1 NG module installed on it.

NOTE   When SecureClient is used with a firewall that is not licensed for SecureClient (that is, one that does not have a Policy Server), the software will default to act as though it were SecuRemote.

In Figure 19-1, SecureClient can be used inside and outside the LAN. To reach the Finance network, SecureClient users must pass through the Finance gateway.

If a connection is made, the Finance gateway will attempt to load its Security Policy on the SecureClient remote user's PC. The Finance gateway will not allow an incorrectly configured SecureClient (one that does not have the correct policy loaded or has other protocols defined for any of its interfaces) to reach its internal encryption domain, which is Fiction Corporation's Finance network. Figure 19-2 shows how the Policy Server is configured in the network to protect clients attempting to access secured resources.

Policy Server Configuration

First, configure the Global Policy properties: open the Global Policy Properties window and click Desktop Security, as shown in Figure 19-3.

The Desktop Security page contains several configuration options:

SecuRemote/SecureClient

- **Respond to Unauthenticated Topology Requests (IKE and FWZ)**   This feature enables backward compatibility with earlier versions of SecuRemote/SecureClient. If you are using SecuRemote/SecureClient NG, you do not need to select this option. If you must support older versions of the client while migrating to NG, you should make sure this option is turned on. However, turning it on could allow an attacker to obtain information about your firewall, even if it only allows them to determine that you are running VPN-1/FireWall-1—this is more information than *we* would give out voluntarily. This option is only available in the base NG release and FP1— support for FWZ was removed in FP2.

- **Allow Cache Static Passwords on Desktop**   This allows static passwords to be cached on the desktop or client. SecuRemote/SecureClient users will not be required to reauthenticate until the next login if they're using OS and VPN-1/FireWall-1 NG internal passwords.

- **Encrypt DNS Traffic**   Use encryption for all DNS resolution of internal names.

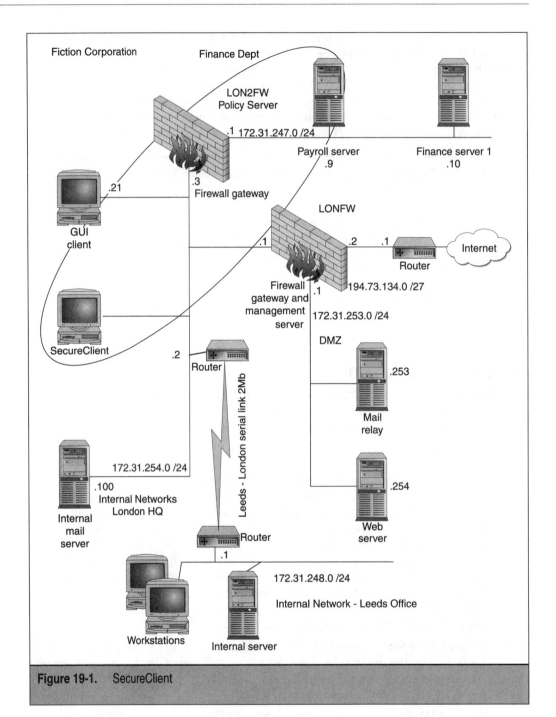

Figure 19-1. SecureClient

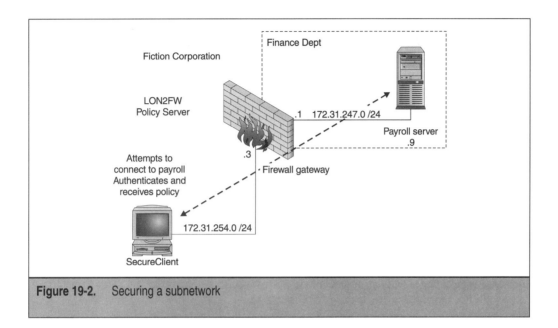

Figure 19-2.   Securing a subnetwork

Validation Timeout

- **Use Default Values**   If this option is selected, FWZ passwords will not expire, they remain valid until the next time the SecureClient machine is turned off or rebooted. Depending on the Allow Cache Static Passwords on Desktop option, users of hybrid IKE will not need to reauthenticate if this option is set. If Allow Cache Static Passwords on Desktop is not set, they will need to reauthenticate as one-time password users. The default is that passwords expire in 24 hours.

- **Validation Timeout Every *n* Minutes**   SecuRemote/SecureClient passwords become invalid after the time specified in the minutes field. If multiple sites are defined on SecureClient, the timeout for all sites will be the minimum of all the site timeout values.

NOTE   If you are using FP2 (Feature Pack 2) and above, these options have moved to Global Policy Properties | Remote Access tree item, as shown in Figure 19-4.

IKE Properties for SecuRemote/SecureClient

- **Use DH Group for IKE Phase I**   The default setting is Group 2. If required, select a different group from the drop-down list. This is for the IKE (Internet Key Exchange) SA (Security Association) as used with either of the remote access clients (SecuRemote/SecureClient).

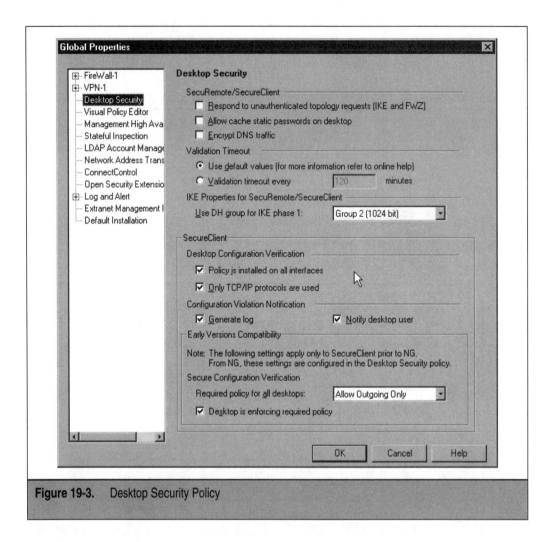

Figure 19-3. Desktop Security Policy

NOTE If you are using FP2 and above, the IKE Properties have moved to the Global Policy Properties I Remote Access I VPN—Advanced tree item.

Desktop Configuration Verification

Although you can disable desktop configuration verification which makes sure the client has a valid policy installed, amongst other verification checks, the default is for this option to be enabled. You should not disable it; if you do, users of SecureClient could disable the Desktop Policy locally and still gain access, putting their system and all of yours at risk. If the Desktop Policy is not installed, the SecureClient can be denied access to the remote encryption domain. This requires that you use the Policy I Global Properties I Desktop Security option or, on FP2 and above, Policy I Global Properties I Remote Access I Secure Configuration Verification options be enabled. Turning the

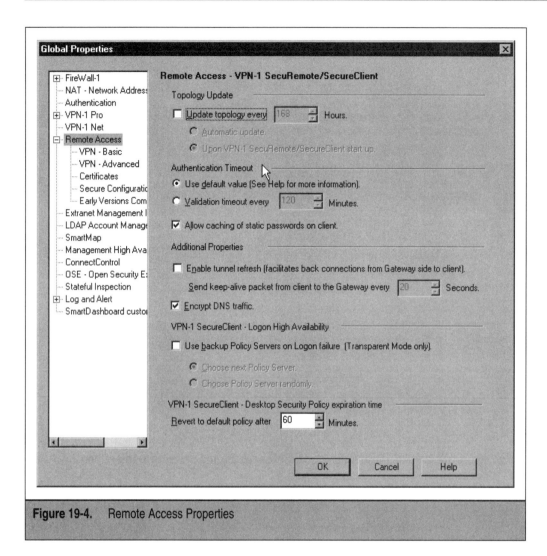

Figure 19-4.   Remote Access Properties

Secure Configuration Verification option off will allow SecureClients access without checking for a Desktop Policy on the SecureClient system. Note that this option provides the checking capability for the firewall; you can additionally prevent a connection if the Desktop Policy cannot be verified.

- **Policy Is Installed on All Interfaces**   If selected, checks that the policy is installed on all interfaces; disallows access if is not.

- **Only TCP/IP Protocols Are Used**   This checks for unsupported, non-TCP/IP protocols such as NetBEUI and disallows access if any are installed. Security can only be enforced using TCP/IP. If other protocols are installed on the SecureClient system, these may provide a back door through which the system could be compromised.

NOTE   The Desktop Configuration Verification properties have moved in FP2 and above to the Policy | Global Properties | Remote Access | Secure Configuration Verification tree item; they are now referred to as Secure Configuration Verification (SCV). Also in FP2 and above, another option is available: Apply Secure Configuration Verification on Simplified Mode Security Policies. If you are using the simplified mode VPN Communities, as discussed in Chapter 18, you should select this option to apply SCV to the Remote Access Community. This option enforces the use of Desktop Policies on *all* SecureClient systems— an improperly configured SecureClient will not be able to connect.

Configuration Violation Notification

- **Generate Log**   A log entry will be created if the either of the options specified in the Desktop Configuration Verification (Secure Configuration Verification in FP2 and above) cannot be verified. This will contain the name of the user, the IP address of the host, and the reason the verification failed. This option should be selected so that information regarding a failure of Desktop Configuration Verification will be logged.

NOTE   Users of FP2 and above will find the option for Generate Log now reads Generate Log on Client. If you click the Help button for this screen, you will see the option described as Generate Log on Alert. It might be better written as Generate Log on Client Alert, as this is what this option does. The wording is likely to be changed in FP4.

NOTE   The Configuration Violation Notification properties have moved in FP2 and above to the Policy | Global Properties | Remote Access | Secure Configuration Verification tree item.

The messages that can be logged in the VPN-1/FireWall-1 Management Module (or Customer Log Module) for the Policy Server are described in Table 19-1.

Logged Message	Reason
Old SecuRemote	The user is using an old version of SecuRemote that is not supported by SecureClient.
Lost Policy	The user has been removed from the group of users authorized to have a policy.
No Policy	The desktop has no Desktop Policy.
Wrong Policy	The Desktop Policy is different from the Policy Server assigned to the desktop.
Not all network adapters are protected, and you are using a non-IP protocol, which is not protected	The desktop has an unprotected network adapter and is using a non-IP protocol.
Not all network adapters are protected	The desktop has a non-IP network adapter.
Non-IP protocol in use	A network adapter on the desktop is using a non-IP protocol and is not protected.

Table 19-1.   Logged Verification Failure Messages

- **Notify Desktop User**   If, upon login, a SecureClient's SCV (Secure Configuration Verification) fails for any reason, a message will be passed to the user of the SecureClient system indicating the reason for failure; the possible messages are described in Table 19-2.

Early Versions Compatibility

- **Required Policy for All Desktops**   In VPN-1/FireWall-1 version 4.1, a single simple Desktop Security Policy could be installed for SecureClient. This option allows firewall administrators to set one Desktop Policy for all pre-NG SecureClients within this Policy Server's domain. You could choose one of four policies:

- **No Policy**   Allow all communications to and from the SecureClient.

- **Allow Outgoing and Encrypted**   Allow both outgoing connections and encrypted communications from the SecureClient (these options are both as described in the next two policies).

- **Allow Outgoing Only**   Allow only SecureClient-initiated outbound connections.

- **Allow Encrypted Only**   Allow only encrypted communications to or from the SecureClient. If the SecureClient resides in the encryption domain of a gateway, all communications that remain in the gateway's domain are trusted and treated as though encrypted.

Logged Message	Reason
Internal Error	An internal computer error on the desktop PC caused SecureClient to malfunction.
The Security Policy on your computer has been removed	A nontrivial policy has changed to Allow All.
The Security Policy on your computer has changed	A policy has been changed from Allow All or Disable Policy to no policy.
You are not authorized to have a policy	The user logged in to a Policy Server from which they are not authorized to download a policy.
You are using an inappropriate policy. Load a new policy from your Policy Server	VPN-1/FireWall-1 NG detects that the user's Desktop Policy is different from the global policy defined by the module's Management Server.
Failed to load a policy to your desktop	The Policy Server has failed to load a policy to the desktop.
Not all network adapters are protected, and you are using a non-IP protocol, which is not protected	The desktop has an unprotected network adapter and is using a non-IP protocol.
Not all network adapters are protected	The desktop has a non-IP network adapter.
You are using NetBEUI, or another non-IP network protocol, which is not protected	A network adapter is using a non-IP protocol and is not protected by SecureClient.

Table 19-2.   SecureClient Verification Failure Log Messages

CLIENT ENCRYPTION RULES

Client Encryption rules for SecureClient are created in the security Rule Base and are the same as SecuRemote rules: they define the connection that matches the rule based on source, destination, and service, where source is a user group and the action is Client Encrypt. This defines that a specific group of users should first be authenticated and that their traffic should be encrypted to the gateway and the rule applied to control access. See Chapter 18 for further information on using both traditional Client Encrypt rules and the new Feature Pack 2 "simplified" mode of operation.

To make sure a SecureClient is granted access only if the client is verified as meeting all the requirements for Secure Configuration Verification, right-click Client Encrypt and choose Edit Properties. On the Security Rule Base Client Encrypt Properties screen, check the Apply Rule Only if Desktop Configuration Options Are Verified check box. A SecureClient connecting under a rule must also install the Desktop Policy, which is defined on the Policy Server it is connecting to, or it will not be permitted access. To get to the Client Encrypt Properties screen in the Security Rule Base tab, right-click and choose Properties in the Action column of the Client Encrypt rule.

DESKTOP SECURITY RULE BASE

The Policy Server, Desktop Policy Rule Base allows the administrator to create a Rule Base that will be applied to SecureClients. The Rule Base defines the connections that match the rule based on source, destination, and service. The first rule is applied, and the specified action is taken. Logging and alerting can be used if specified in the Track field. Alerts will be sent to the Policy Server and from there to a Log Server at the next SecureClient logon. Logs may be viewed on the client using the SecureClient Log Viewer application.

Each rule must be assigned to at least one user group. The Users Group specifies the users who will download their Desktop Security Policy from the Policy Server. Internal user groups can be used as well as those groups defined on an LDAP (Lightweight Directory Access Protocol) server.

A rule is either inbound or outbound in the Desktop Security Policy Rule Base. If the rule is inbound, it applies to traffic going to the user's SecureClient machine. This is particularly important because it denotes connections that can be made to the client system while it is connected via the VPN. This is because a system could be hijacked and the VPN tunnel could then be used by an attacker to gain access to internal systems. If a rule is outbound where the source is the user group, this applies to connections that are initiated from the SecureClient system.

- If a user's group is defined in the Source Field, the rule is outbound.
- If a user's group is defined in the Destination column, the rule is inbound.

Two windows are provided to make it easier to add inbound and outbound rules, one for each. Rules applied to the specific group the Policy Server supports are enforced while the SecureClient is connected; rules applied to All Users remain enforced once the client is disconnected. Split tunneling is managed using a rule to permit unencrypted outbound connections from the client; if this is applied to All Users, it remains after the client disconnects from the remote site. *Split tunneling* denotes that a client can access other network services at the same time as using an encrypted connection with the remote site. Most users prefer this method because it allows them to access the Internet and other locally connected services (such as network print servers) while accessing the corporate network.

Receiving Desktop Policies

The Policy Server receives its Desktop Policy when you install the VPN-1/FireWall-1 NG Rule Base on the modules in the network. The Desktop Policy is then available to the SecureClient system when it attempts to make a connection. The SecureClient system will receive a policy when the user makes either an explicit or implicit login.

- **Explicit login**   An explicit login takes place if a SecureClient user logs in to a Policy Server to download a new or updated Desktop Policy. This is initiated by the desktop user.

- **Implicit login**   An implicit login takes place if a SecureClient user does not have an installed policy and tries to communicate through a Policy Server. The Policy Server will attempt to install a Desktop Policy on the desktop. The Policy Server initiates this.

Intermediate Firewalls and Address Translation

If there are any intermediate firewalls along the path connecting the SecureClient and the Policy Server, you need to configure the other firewalls to allow connections to pass between the SecureClient and the Policy Server, as shown in Figure 19-5.

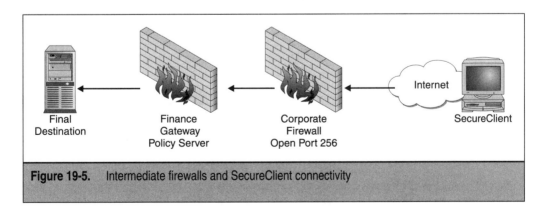

Figure 19-5.   Intermediate firewalls and SecureClient connectivity

If an intermediate firewall in the path between the SecureClient and the Policy Server translates the SecureClient's IP address so the Policy Server does not see the SecureClient's real IP address (see Chapter 13 for information on how NAT works), the SecureClient will not function properly. An intermediate firewall must be able to allow addresses to pass through unaltered by NAT. You may need to give special consideration to using routed public address space on the internal network in these circumstances.

THE SECURECLIENT GUI

The SecuRemote interface differs from the SecureClient interface in a couple of ways: it adds a new toolbar icon and a new Policy menu option (see Figure 19-6).

The following are the Policy menu options:

- **Disable Policy**   This option can be removed only by the administrator because it disables the Desktop Policy Firewall. Administrators can prevent the Disable Policy from being available by editing the userc.C file as shown here:

```
:options
        :manual_slan_control (false)
```

If a user chooses Disable Policy from the menu, a warning message is displayed. If you confirm by clicking Yes, the desktop Security Policy will be removed. You can log in again to the Policy Server or click Disable Policy again to toggle it back on. If you have an active encrypted session, choosing Disable Policy will only take effect after you restart SecureClient.

- **Log in to Policy Server**   This submenu allows desktop users access to Policy Servers. First select a site, then select Log in to Policy Server, and a window will display a list of Policy Servers available at the site. Select one from the list and log in using your credentials as usual.

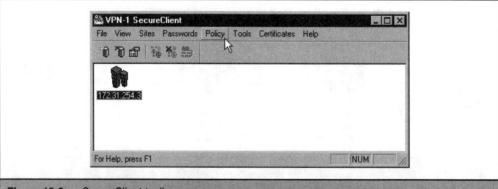

Figure 19-6.   SecureClient toolbar

Getting Site Topology

A SecureClient must obtain the topology of the site before a connection can be made. A fresh installation of SecureClient has no site topology information in the userc.C file. Either the user must download the site topology information, or the administrator can do it once on a machine installed with SecureClient and then copy the userc.C file to new installations. This is a good option because it saves the administrator from having to depend on the users to do it correctly.

The userc.C file can then be distributed to all SecureClient users. Although it is not recommended for users, the userc.C file can be edited with a standard text editor for customization by the firewall administrator.

You can define a site by entering the IP address and download the topology by clicking the Update button on the Site Definition screen.

NOTE   For versions prior to FP2, exportable for SecuRemote must be enabled on the General Properties page of the gateway you are connecting to. This exports the site topology and makes it available to the SecuRemote/SecureClient software, FP2 and later versions no longer require this step.

Passwords

The first time a user attempts to connect to a site, they must enter their username and password. After the initial connection is authenticated, the username and password will be held securely in the SecureClient daemon; the information is not written to disk for security reasons. Once authenticated, the user credentials are provided automatically for each subsequent connection request by the client, until SecureClient is restarted or the client rebooted.

On the first attempt to connect, you will be prompted to enter your logon credentials. This causes a delay in the first connection attempt, which in turn often causes the requested TCP/IP service to timeout while you are still entering your username and password. To prevent this, there are two ways a user can set a password for a site before attempting to make a connection: they can either choose the Set Password option or enable Single Sign-on. The Set Password option allows the password to be set and stored (securely), ready for use when a connection is attempted, thus avoiding the timeout. The Single Sign-on method stores your details securely on the system and ties them to your logon credentials that are supplied when you log on to your computer. These are then ready for use whenever you log on to your system. Single Sign-on is only appropriate if you have just one site defined for remote access.

Single Sign-on (SSO) is configured, enabled, and disabled from the SecureClient Password menu, as shown in Figure 19-7.

SecureClient Considerations

Changing your computer's network configuration after installing SecureClient means you will need to reinstall the software again.

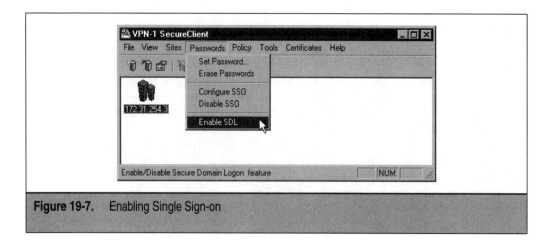

Figure 19-7. Enabling Single Sign-on

If you have more than one network adapter, SecureClient can be bound to all adapters. If you add another network adapter after you install SecureClient on Windows 98, you will have to reinstall so that the SecureClient software binds to the new adapter. If you use Windows NT or 2000, SecureClient can bind dynamically when the system is rebooted.

The latest SecureClient software supports the Microsoft Windows XP operating system. See the most current information on the Check Point website (www.checkpoint.com).

If you have modified your network configuration by removing SecureClient adapters, you can reinstall these adapters without reinstalling SecureClient by selecting Rebind Adapters from the Tools menu.

Uninstalling SecureClient

You should not attempt to uninstall SecureClient manually by deleting files and removing shortcuts; instead, use the following steps to access the Add/Remove programs feature in Windows:

1. Deactivate the SecureClient daemon by selecting Stop from the File menu.
2. Open the Windows Start menu.
3. Select Settings | Control Panel.
4. Select the Add/Remove Programs icon or option, depending on the version of Windows you are running.
5. Select Check Point SecureClient NG.
6. Click the Add/Remove button.
7. Click OK.

FICTION CORPORATION

Fiction Corporation's Finance gateway, lon2fw, is being used to restrict internal communication into the finance network. An Enforcement Module and a Policy Server module are both installed. In Chapter 12, we examined how the gateway could be used to authenticate users who had a legitimate need to access the Finance servers. In this chapter, we'll examine for the first time the next logical step in securing the Finance Department's systems, which provide authenticated and encrypted connectivity to prevent the clear-text nature of the Telnet sessions to the Payroll server from being intercepted or snooped. While SecuRemote could be used to accomplish this, it would still leave a hole in the security because the client system itself is left open to attack, and the potential exists for the VPN tunnel to be hijacked should the client be compromised.

You may remember that in Chapter 12 we defined finance users and a finance group, as shown in Figure 19-8.

Because the users and groups are already defined, you do not need to modify them for use with client-to-site VPN tunnels.

The Policy Server policy required for finance users' access protects the client from inbound connections while keeping the traffic between itself and the gateway private by using VPN encryption.

Each client may need to initiate unencrypted sessions to the local network and externally to the Internet. You could define each outbound connection specifically, but this may turn out to be an administrative burden. The most important thing is that inbound connections to the system are controlled, so that the connection cannot be hijacked. Figure 19-9 shows a policy that allows all outbound connections and drops

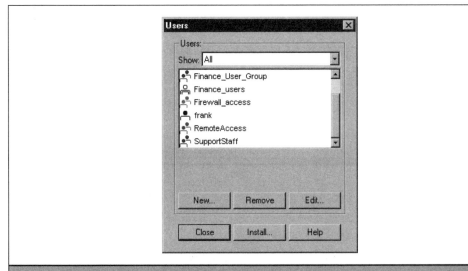

Figure 19-8.   Finance users and groups

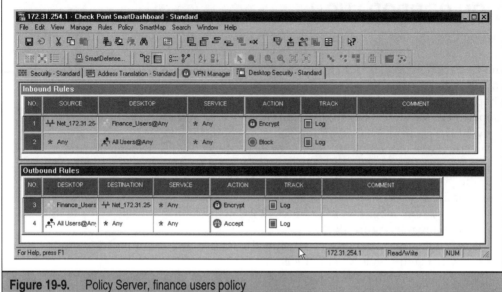

Figure 19-9. Policy Server, finance users policy

all (and logs) inbound connections. In this way, the administration requirements are minimized and the policy achieves its objective. Connections are permitted for encrypted traffic to and from the client machine.

It should be noted that the Policy Server has two default implied rules. The first allows all outbound connections; the second blocks all inbound connections. However, neither of these rules is visible and neither provides any logging. It is therefore advisable to explicitly define these rules both for clarity and to effect logging of the connections.

SECURITY CONFIGURATION VERIFICATION

You have already seen how SCV is used to verify a client has the required Desktop Policy installed and that only those networking protocols that SecureClient can protect (TCP/IP) are configured. However, SCV has capabilities beyond this and can perform checks on the client to validate that the latest antivirus software is installed. It can also check the version of Internet Explorer, check that a process is running or not running, check that the user is a member of a group, and check that a particular level of hotfix security patch is applied to the OS. These and other checks are built in to SecureClient in version FP3 (Feature Pack 3). The SCV Policy is located in the $FWDIR\conf\local.scv file and can be edited manually. Alternatively, an SCV Editor application, SCVEditor, is available from Check Point.

SECURECLIENT FOR MOBILE DEVICES

Check Point has developed a version of SecureClient for the growing market of PDA's (Personal Digital Assistants). SecureClient for PocketPC 2002 provides organizations with a single unified capability for integration of PDAs into enterprises. Businesses are rapidly embracing varied computing platforms and wireless connectivity. Wireless connectivity has so far shown weaknesses in the vendor-supplied security measures, and SecureClient is an ideal mechanism with which to provide the additional security these devices need. If you are considering deployment of wireless networking, you need to consider the risks associated with it and make sure network security is maintained along with the adoption of this highly flexible technology.

CHECKLIST: KEY POINTS IN POLICY SERVER

The following is a checklist for the key points in Policy Server.

- ☐ Define the VPN-1/FireWall-1 NG Policy Server.
- ☐ Install the Policy Server.
- ☐ Identify SecureClient functionality.
- ☐ Define the SecureClient GUI.
- ☐ Show real-world deployment examples for customers using Policy Server.
- ☐ Deploy the Policy Server component of Check Point VPN-1/FireWall-1 NG.
- ☐ Identify the client-to-site VPN security connection.
- ☐ Show how the Policy Server extends Check Point's stateful inspection technology to the desktop.
- ☐ Identify the Rule Base.
- ☐ Define Security Configuration Control.
- ☐ Define SecureClient for mobile devices.
- ☐ Deploy VPN-1/FireWall-1 NG VPN technology throughout an enterprise and beyond.

CHAPTER 20

High Availability Module

Any company that is serious about e-commerce will want to ensure that resilient network architecture is put into place to maximize service availability, and Fiction Corporation is no exception. Since Chapter 14, when a load-balancing web solution was installed for them at a U.K.-based ISP, Fiction Corporation has added VPN connectivity for their developers based in New York. Now management has realized that the hosted solution requires resilience in the firewall architecture to ensure a single firewall outage does not disable the service.

Check Point has an answer for these requirements in the form of redundant management servers and gateway clusters. Because of budgetary constraints, Fiction Corporation has decided that redundant management servers can be deployed at a later stage for increased resilience, but the gateway does need to be somewhat resilient.

NOTE Check Point has supported redundant management servers since the initial release of VPN-1/FireWall-1 NG. More information is available in the Check Point documentation and technical white papers.

This chapter will build on the hosted firewall installation example in Chapter 14 and introduce high availability for Fiction Corporation's business-class website to complement the load balancing solution already put in place in Chapter 14.

THE NEED FOR HIGH AVAILABILITY

Many commercial websites cannot afford to rely on a single point of failure. We have deployed solutions for dozens of customers who have selected resilient switches, dual-homed Internet feeds, clustered or load-balanced servers, and resilient firewall architectures. Unreliable connectivity can result in customer dissatisfaction and can mean decreased revenues or lost business opportunities.

VPN-1/FireWall-1 NG has an add-on module called High Availability Module (licensed separately) that offers an active standby high availability option. This still allows only one gateway to be the active firewall at any given time, but should the primary or active firewall fail, the standby takes over and ensures service continuity.

HOW HIGH AVAILABILITY WORKS

The High Availability Module configures two or more VPN-1/FireWall-1 NG gateways to act as backups for each other. If one of the gateways fails for any reason, the other gateway takes over the connections to minimize connection or service loss.

Communication between high availability cluster members is carried out by Cluster Control Protocol which operates on TCP Port 8116. Figure 20-1 shows the architecture of a high availability cluster.

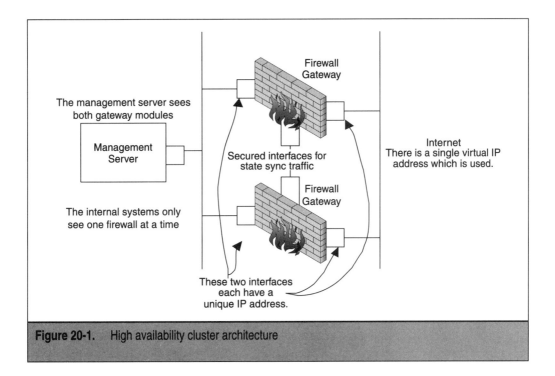

Figure 20-1. High availability cluster architecture

Synchronization

Check Point VPN-1/FireWall-1 NG modules keep track of state information for all connections in special tables. The synchronization mechanism ensures that all gateways in a cluster have the same information about connections. Therefore, if a gateway goes down, other gateways are aware of the state of current connections and seamless failover can occur.

Secured Interfaces

An interface is considered secured if a connection through that interface can be trusted (for example, if the interfaces on the same network are connected with a cross cable or dedicated hub). Because an intruder is unable to send packets on that connection, a secured interface can be safely used to transmit synchronization and high availability information.

In a high availability configuration, each machine should have at least one secured interface. Additional secured interfaces are recommended for backup purposes. If these secured interfaces are configured, a VPN-1/FireWall-1 NG module will accept state change commands only on those interfaces. If there are no secured interfaces, the synchronization feature will not work.

Enabling Check Point High Availability

The high availability feature is part of the standard VPN-1/FireWall-1 NG installation. It should be installed only in a distributed configuration, in which the Management Server and the VPN/FireWall NG modules are installed on different machines.

CONFIGURING HIGH AVAILABILITY

To configure the high availability parameters on Unix platforms, run the cpconfig program and select Enable Check Point High Availability/State Synchronization. On Windows NT/2000, select the check box labeled Enable Check Point High Availability/State Synchronization in the High Availability tab of the Check Point Configuration Tool window.

In the Fiction Corporation Rule Base there is already a workstation object for Hosted. You must add a workstation object for hosted2, which will be the secondary gateway, with the following information:

Workstation name:	Hosted2
IP Address:	194.73.134.99
Subnet Mask:	255.255.255.224
Color:	Red

Ensure that the object is defined as a gateway and that the correct Check Point products are installed.

You now need to create a gateway cluster object to incorporate the two gateway workstation objects. Select New from the Network Objects dialog and select Gateway Cluster.

In the General page of the Gateway Cluster Properties window, create a new gateway cluster called Hosted_Cluster and assign it a unique IP address of 194.73.134.100, as shown in Figure 20-2. Check High Availability Module under Check Point Products Installed. The CP High Availability page will become enabled.

In the Check Point High Availability page, define Cluster Mode, Gateway Recovery, and Failover Tracking parameters as shown in Figure 20-3.

Select High Availability for Cluster Mode, not Load Sharing. (Further information on load sharing is available in Check Point manuals.) With high availability, the primary machine alone handles traffic, with the secondary machine taking over only in the event of a failover.

There are two settings in the Upon Cluster Failure section:

- **Maintain Current Active Gateway**   If the primary machine passes control to the secondary machine, control will be returned to the primary machine only if the secondary machine fails.

- **Switch to Higher Priority Gateway**   If the secondary machine has control and the primary machine is restored, control will be returned to the primary machine.

Fiction Corporation selected Switch to Higher Priority Gateway so switchover will be automatic, but in some organizations this will not be preferred. For example, if there has been a switch to the secondary unit you may not want to risk switching back to a suspect unit automatically, because you might want to investigate the reason it was switched first.

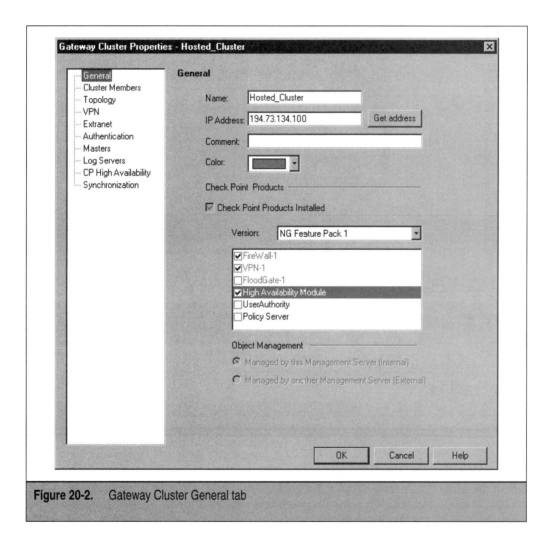

Figure 20-2.   Gateway Cluster General tab

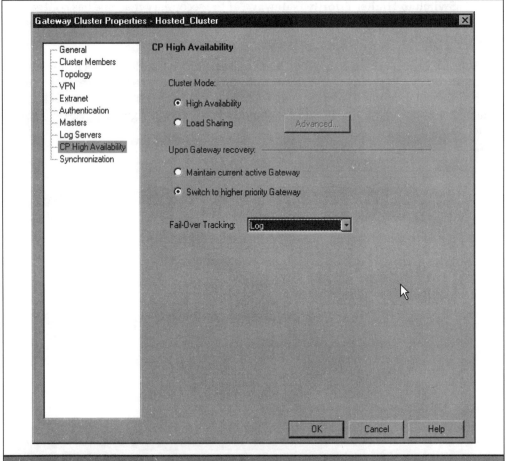

Figure 20-3. Gateway Cluster Properties (High Availability page)

Failover Tracking

Set Failover Tracking to Log. This will enter events in the Event Log so you can be informed when there is a failure or transition to the secondary gateway.

Adding Cluster Members

Select the Cluster Members option and add the two gateways to the cluster objects. Note that when a gateway is added to the cluster object, the following information is overridden by the cluster object:

- Topology—VPN domain
- VPN

- Authentication
- Account units
- Masters
- Log servers

Synchronization

The Synchronization tab, as shown in Figure 20-4, defines a synchronization network. For this you normally use 10.99.99.0 /24 (/24 is often used as an abbreviation in networking circles to denote 255.255.255.0) because it is almost never used elsewhere in a network. This network should be a real network with a dedicated firewall interface for state traffic

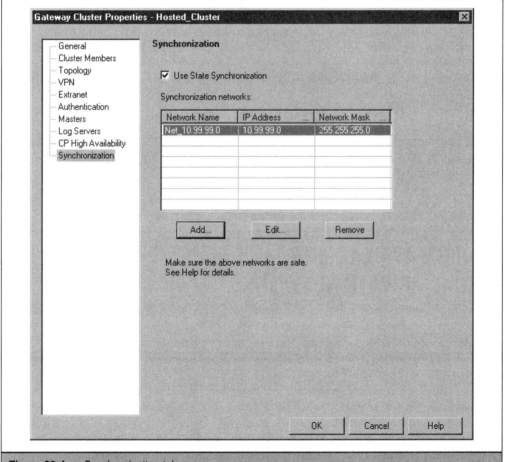

Figure 20-4.   Synchronization tab

to be sent over. A crossover cable is usually sufficient for this, but a hub or switch can be used as long as the network is not carrying other traffic.

The Use State Synchronization check box is selected by default. If you choose not to use this feature, deselect the check box. If State Synchronization is not enabled, existing connections will be closed when failover occurs.

TIP   Win NT and Windows 2000 machines require another reboot after the policy installation because MAC addresses were changed.

AUTOMATIC MAC ADDRESS CONFIGURATION

Check Point's high availability solution is based on several machines using the same IP address and MAC address. The configuration of the IP addresses is a preliminary step that should be taken before configuring the high availability. The MAC addresses of the shared interfaces are configured automatically on all platforms. The shared MAC address (which will be configured on each machine) is usually, but not necessarily, the MAC address of the first configured machine—that is, the machine that was the first to be installed or the first to be upgraded.

On Solaris and Linux, the MAC address assignment is performed transparently after the policy installation.

On Windows NT and Windows 2000, every machine whose MAC address has been changed should be rebooted.

Installing a new cluster is similar to upgrading clusters except that the Management Server and VPN-1/FireWall-1 NG modules should be installed, not updated.

TIP   On Unix platforms (Solaris, Linux), run the script /wrappers/unix/ha_config_amon. This will display all the interfaces and problem notifications on the cluster in the System Status Viewer.

USING HIGH AVAILABILITY
IN VIRTUAL PRIVATE NETWORKS

When implementing high availability, the VPN-1/FireWall-1 NG modules should be defined as members of a gateway cluster to synchronize connections and other important information required for VPN Single Entry Point implementation between the VPN-1/FireWall-1 NG modules. You also need to ensure that the same Security Policy is installed on all the VPN-1/FireWall-1 NG modules.

For further information about configuring the VPN-1/FireWall-1 NG modules as members of a cluster, see the Check Point Virtual Private Network Guide. In a Check Point high availability configuration, the gateway cluster's IP address (defined in the General page of the Gateway Cluster Properties window) should be the nonunique IP address facing the Internet that the gateways share. The IP address of each of the gateways in the cluster should be defined as the unique address facing the Management Server.

NOKIA FIREWALL APPLIANCE

The Nokia Firewall Appliance uses Virtual Routing Redundancy Protocol (VRRP) monitored circuits for high availability clusters that do not require the High Availability option to function. It should be noted that using Check Point high availability in this configuration will add only the application monitoring functionality to the active-standby failover available with VRRP monitored circuits.

NOTE If you are using VRRP, make sure to enable the ifwd daemon on both modules.

CAUTION When using high availability in a switched network, you must ensure that there is no rate limiting on broadcasts because this could cause state synchronization to fail or become unreliable.

HIGH AVAILABILITY ENHANCEMENTS

Feature Pack 1 simplifies configuration of synchronization by moving it to the GUI; you no longer have to edit a configuration file.

With Feature Pack 2, State Synchronization–load sharing has been introduced, in addition to high availability, in the ClusterXL product. Synchronization overhead has been significantly reduced.

Feature Pack 3 Enhancements

ClusterXL is a license option for VPN-1/FireWall-1 NG. In addition to an Enforcement Module license, a central license on the SmartCenter Server is also required with one of the following SKUs:

- CPMP-CXL-HA-1-NG (for a single cluster)
- CPMP-CXL-HA-U-NG (for an unlimited number of clusters)

ClusterXL must only be installed in a distributed configuration in which the SmartCenter Server and the cluster members are on different machines. ClusterXL is currently available for Windows NT, Windows 2000, Solaris, and Linux. Some of the feature enhancements are as follows:

- Cluster and cluster member objects in the SmartDashboard are much easier to define, following an extensive redesign of the objects.
- The state of the cluster members can be controlled from the Status Manager. The state of a cluster member can be changed to Up or Down with no need to access the cluster member modules.
- A new high availability mode (New CPHA) enables remote management and a one-click transition to load sharing mode. New CPHA mode uses unique unicast IP addresses and MAC addresses, rather than sharing the IP and MAC address among the cluster members.

- New CPHA mode and the load sharing modes now use multicasts instead of broadcasts for the clustering protocol. This significantly reduces cluster protocol traffic in the network.

- The Security Policy is now fetched first from another cluster member. If no other cluster member is available, the policy is fetched from the management. This ensures that the policy in the cluster will be consistent.

- VLANs are now supported on Linux platforms, including SecurePlatform NG FP3 and Red Hat 7.2.

CHECKLIST: KEY POINTS
IN HIGH AVAILABILITY MODULE

The following is a checklist for the key points in a high availability module.

- ☐ Define VPN-1/FireWall-1 NG high availability.
- ☐ Define the need for high availability.
- ☐ Show how high availability works.
- ☐ Configure high availability.
- ☐ Define Automatic MAC address configuration.
- ☐ Use the separately licensed module that offers advanced high availability.
- ☐ Implement solutions from OPSEC partners that offer clustering and high availability.
- ☐ Implement additional alternate solutions from Check Point high availability.
- ☐ Use high availability in Virtual Private Networks.
- ☐ Show how the Nokia Firewall Appliance works.
- ☐ Define Cluster XL.
- ☐ Consider Feature Pack 3 enhancements.

CHAPTER 21

Troubleshooting

The book so far has covered all aspects of the Check Point VPN-1/FireWall-1 NG product and how to correctly implement these components to produce a working solution. However, based on our experience there are times when methodical troubleshooting is required.

If you are a consultant, you may find yourself in a situation where a customer already has a VPN-1/FireWall-1 NG installation that is either not meeting the customer's requirements or is failing to operate correctly in some way. This situation is a chance for you to demonstrate your expertise and ensure that you receive the customer's future business, as well as a chance to get satisfaction from resolving issues.

If you have implemented VPN-1/FireWall-1 NG and it does not work as expected, you need a methodology for troubleshooting to resolve issues and ensure the business has a secure and reliable VPN-1/FireWall-1 NG implementation.

We will start by looking at VPN-1/FireWall-1 NG debugging tools and then move on to methodologies with some tips on where to look for specific problems.

VPN-1/FIREWALL-1 NG DEBUGGING TOOLS

VPN-1/FireWall-1 NG features many debugging commands and functions. The main commands will be looked at in this section.

Environment Variables

Two environment variables should be set to allow VPN-1/FireWall-1 NG to locate its base directories. $FWDIR is discussed in the installation Chapters 4, 5, 6, and 7, under the section entitled "Locating the Installation Directories." $CPDIR is new to NG and is the base directory for locating the SVN Foundation or shared components. $CPDIR/bin contains the programs that enable Secure Internal Communications (SIC); see Chapter 3 for further information on SIC.

If $FWDIR is not set when you log on to the firewall or Management Server, you will need set it manually. On UNIX, the installation creates a symbolic link named fw in the /etc directory to point to the actual installation directory. Therefore, the quick and easy way to set the environment variable is to use the following command:

```
# FWDIR=/etc/fw ; export FWDIR
```

To check where the symbolic link points, use the following command in the /etc directory:

```
# ls -ld fw
lrwxrwxrwx   1 root     other        13 Feb 15 09:20 fw -> /opt/CPfw1-53
```

No such shortcut exists for locating the $CPDIR, CP Shared directory. However, once you have located the real $FWDIR directory as just shown, you can locate the $CPDIR directory using the following commands:

```
# cd /opt
# ls -ld CP*
drwxr-xr-x  12 root      other        512 Feb  4 10:01 CPclnt-53
drwxr-xr-x  10 root      other        512 Feb 15  2002 CPfw1-53
drwxrwx---   3 root      other        512 Feb 15  2002 CPshared
drwxr-xr-x   9 root      other        512 Feb 15  2002 CPshrd-53
```

To set the $CPDIR environment variable use this command:

```
# CPDIR=/opt/CPshrd-53 ; export CPDIR
```

If you log on as the same user that was used to install the firewall, you will probably notice that the $FWDIR and $CPDIR environment variables are set for you each time you log on. This is because the installation edited the .profile in the home directory of the user that was used to install the system and added the following line:

```
. /opt/CPshared/5.0/tmp/.CPprofile.sh
```

This line executes the .CPprofile.sh shell script to set the environment variables each time you log on. You can add this command to your own profiles (or any number of users) to do the same thing.

If the $FWDIR and $CPDIR variables are not set, command-line VPN-1/FireWall-1 NG commands will fail to operate.

TIP Sometimes even though the $FWDIR variable is set, the commands you type yield unexpected results or the syntax of the command appears to be wrong. This is caused by the $FWDIR variable being set to the previous installation of VPN-1/FireWall-1 on a system that has been upgraded. Make sure you change any profiles on the system once the upgrade has taken place.

It useful to add the $FWDIR/bin directory to the path environment variable so that you do not have to keep typing the full path each time you want to issue a command. In the UNIX environment you can add the $FWDIR/bin directory to your path by typing the following command:

```
# PATH=$PATH:$FWDIR/bin ; export PATH
```

UNIX commands and environment variables are case sensitive and the path variable must be uppercase to be recognized.

fw ctl pstat

This command is used to show a snapshot of kernel memory available and verify if packets are encrypting and translating. Statistics are flushed after a reboot, or after the fwd daemon is restarted. This command can be useful in determining if sufficient memory is available to the fw-1 kernel.

A Word About Daemons

You may notice the term *daemon*, pronounced dee-muhn, has appeared throughout the book. In mythology, a daemon was "an attendant power or spirit." In computer terminology, it has come to represent an application that runs continuously for the sole purpose of servicing periodic requests made to it by other applications. It has become a convention to name the service and append a *d* (for daemon), for example, syslogd and httpd.

---

fw ctl debug

This command is a kernel module debugging tool for VPN-1/FireWall-1 NG Enforcement Modules. It has many options and can enable you to see what exactly is being done inside the kernel module. The following table shows the available fw ctl debug commands and their definitions.

Command	Description
All	Uses all commands. This option is not recommended. The amount of data is huge and it is nearly impossible to retrieve useful information. On some platforms it can crash the system because the operating system will try to write massive amounts of data to the console.
Cookie	Shows all cookies in the data structure holding the packets. Cookies are useful to avoid the problems that arise from the various methods that operating systems use to handle packets. This is not related to HTTP cookies. VPN-1/FireWall-1 NG utilizes cookies as packet fragments for consistency between operating systems.
Crypt	Prints all encrypted/decrypted packets in clear-text and ciphertext. The algorithms and keys in use are also printed.
Driver	Shows access to the kernel module as log entries.
Filter	Shows the packet filtering performed by the kernel module and all data loaded into the kernel.
Hold	The holding mechanism—shows all packets being held, released, or installing a filter on an interface.
If	Displays all interface-related information, such as accessing the interface or installing a filter on an interface.
Ioctl	Shows all the ioctl or Input/Output Control messages, such as communication between the kernel and the daemon and loading and unloading of VPN-1/FireWall-1 NG.
Kbuf	Shows all kbuf-related information, such as RDP when encrypting. The kbuf is the kernel buffer memory pool. The encryption keys use these memory allocations.
Id	Shows all the reads and writes to the tables. This generates lots of logging.
Log	Shows everything related to calls in the log.
Machine	Shows the actual assembler commands being processed. This results in heavy log generation.
Memory	Shows the memory allocations of VPN-1/FireWall-1 NG.
Misc	Shows all items not shown in other commands.
Packet	Shows all the actions performed on a packet such as accept, drop, or fragment.

Command	Description
Q	Shows information regarding the driver queue.
Tcpseq	Prints the TCP sequences being changed when using NAT.
Xlate, xltrc	Prints the NAT-related information (changing IP addresses) where the xlate switch is the basic and most commonly used switch. Xltrc provides additional information by showing the actual process of going through the NAT Rule Base for each packet, mostly on FTP and Telnet connections.
Winnt	Shows special information on the NT operating system.
Synatk	Shows all information regarding SYNDefender.
Domain	Shows DNS queries.
Install	Shows driver installation information.
Profile	Prints the number of packets filtered and the amount of time spent on them.
Media	Makes level information on Windows NT using frames not packets.
Align	Gives information regarding the decoding of the H.323 data in H.323 data connections.
Ex	Gives information about dynamic table expiration.
Balance	Gives information about load balancing of logical servers.
Chain	Gives information about cookie chains.

To use the command to start debug mode, use the following syntax with one of the commands from the previous table:

```
# fw ctl debug [command]
```

To stop debugging, use the following command:

```
# fw ctl debug 0
```

You can use this command for a number of diverse reasons, including performance baseline measurements and troubleshooting.

fw tab Command

This command displays the content of INSPECT tables.

```
Fw tab [-all | -conf conf_file] [-a] [-s] [-u | -mnumber] [-t table] targets
```

Table 21-1 shows the command parameters and their definitions.

Parameter	Definition
-all	Executes on all targets specified in the default system configuration file ($FWDIR/conf/sys.conf).
-conf conf_file	Executes on the targets specified in conf_file.

Table 21-1.   fw tab Parameters

Parameter	Definition
-a	Displays all tables.
-s	Uses short format: host name, table name, table ID, and its number of elements.
-u	Doesn't limit the number of displayed entries.
-m number	For each table, displays only its first number of elements (default is 16).
-t tname	Displays only tname table.
-f	From FP1, displays output in decimal instead of hexadecimal.
Targets	Executes on the designated targets only.

Table 21-1.   fw tab Parameters *(continued)*

The following command shows how to list the connections table with decimal output:

```
# fw tab -t connections -f
```

This command results in the following output (one connection shown):

```
21:32:02        172.31.254.1 >     ----------------------------------(+);
Direction: 0; Source: 172.31.254.21; SPort: 1199; Dest: 172.31.254.1; DPort: ssh;
Protocol: tcp; CPTFMT_sep: ;; Type: 114689; Flags: 8405120; Rule: 2; Timeout:
3600; Handler: 0; Uuid: 3c7a949b30000ac1ffe017b6; Ifncin: 1; Ifncout: 1; Ifnsin: -
1; Ifnsout: -1; Bits: 0000000000000000; Expires: 3596/3600; product: VPN-1 &
FireWall-1;
```

Without the -f switch, the command results are returned in hexadecimal.

The fw tab -t connections -s command can be used to see approximately how many entries are currently in the connections table; the default is for this table to be limited to 25,000 entries. If the number returned is approximately 25,000 you should increase the connections table limit.

Debug Mode for FWD and FWM

These two VPN-1/FireWall-1 NG daemons can be placed in debug mode for troubleshooting either Management Module or firewall daemon problems. Debugging the FWD process is useful for troubleshooting NAT, security server and kernel issues. The FWM process is responsible for communication between the various clients (SmartDashboard, SmartView Tracker, and so on) with the Management Server.

- There are two methods of instigating debugging mode with either of these modules:
- Stop the fwd/fwm process and restart it in debug mode.
- Start debug logging while the fwd/fwm process is running.

Running the Process in Debug Mode

The fwd -d -n syntax is for a management server on its own. For a management server with enforcement point or enforcement point only, use the fwd -d or fwm -d syntax as shown here:

To start debug mode

- Run fwstop
- Run the required daemon in debug with either fwd –d or fwm -d
- Run fwstart in a new telnet window

You will need to use two Telnet sessions to the server to be able to run the fwstart command in another window because once the fwd or fwm process is started manually it will run in the previous Telnet session window. When you have finished using debugging, type CTRL+C in the fwd or fwm debug window to stop the daemon running. You should then restart all firewall services by running the following commands:

```
# fwstop ; fwstart
```

If you need to send the output of the debug session to a file, you can use the same commands but redirect the output. Those familiar with Unix systems will know that you use the greater than (>) symbol to do this; however, in this case, the daemons write their output to standard error not standard output, so you must use 2> to redirect standard error to a file:

```
# fwd -d 2>/tmp/foo.txt
```

Activating Debug Mode with fwd and fwm Running

You can use the fw debug command to place either of the running fwm or fwd processes into debug mode. This is useful if it is not convenient to stop and start services on the firewall, for instance, when you are troubleshooting a live system.

The syntax for starting and stopping a debug for either fwd or fwm is as follows:

```
Fw debug [fwd | fwm] on | off
```

Debug information is captured in the $FWDIR/log/fwd.elg or $FWDIR/log/fwm.elg log files, depending on which daemon you are debugging.

Debugging the CP Daemon Process

The CP daemon controls the SVN Foundation, also known as the CP Shared components. If you need to troubleshoot policy installation, Secure Internal Communication (SIC) or OPSEC partner product communication, you can run the cpd process in debug mode.

To enable debug logging for the CP daemon, use the following procedure:

1. Open a Telnet/secure shell window.

2. Configure the following environment variables:
   - `OPSEC_DEBUG_LEVEL=3` (used for OPSEC related issues)
   - `TDERROR_ALL_ALL=3` (used for general cpd issues)

3. Stop the CP daemon with the following command:

   ```
   # $CPDIR/bin/cpd_admin stop
   ```

4. In the same window, run one of the commands shown in the following CPD debug options table:

Command	Output
`cpd`	Redirects output to $CPDIR/log/cpd.elg. Prints brief status messages to the console.
`cpd -d`	Displays debug output of the command to the console
`cpd -d 2> [filename]`	Redirects debug output to the specified filename

5. Use CTRL+C to stop debugging in the window.

6. Stop and restart the CP shared and firewall services with the following command:

   ```
   # cpstop ; cpstart
   ```

cpinfo Utility

The cpinfo utility produces an extremely long list of configuration information, system settings and stats using OS and VPN-1/FireWall-1 commands. The environment variable $FWDIR must be set for cpinfo to operate. If you ever call Check Point support, you will most likely be asked to run cpinfo, capture the output to a file, and send it to them. It contains enough to set the background information for Check Point's technical support teams, who otherwise would have to ask you a very long list of questions. To run cpinfo and capture the output to a file, use the following command:

```
# cpinfo >/export/home/fwadmin/fwinfo.txt
```

Running cpinfo can generate quite a lot of processor and disk usage; make sure you run it at a suitable time so that the firewall does not become overstressed. It is advisable to compress the file before sending it off, as the file produced can be quite large, and being text it will compress quite effectively.

Note that cpinfo is not installed with the product. You will need to download a copy from the Check Point website. Installation is very straightforward: just uncompress the file and copy it to your $FWDIR/bin directory. On Unix systems, you must set the file attributes to executable with the following command:

```
# chmod 755 cpinfo
```

USING THE POLICY EDITOR IN *local MODE

When troubleshooting a policy, for example, if you are a consultant who needs to examine or model a customer policy, obtain copies of the files listed in Table 21-2 and copy them to the new names highlighted. These should then be placed in the Policy Editor or SmartDashboard program directory. You can enter *local in the management server field when starting the Policy Editor. The *local option is used to simulate a management server on the local workstation running the management client. In Feature Pack 3 (FP3), you can check the SmartDashboard check box for demo mode instead of using *local.

Remember, if you are using a customer's or your own company's Rule Base locally, the security of your laptop or workstation becomes very important, and Rule Bases should be considered highly confidential information.

Using local mode can be very useful for educational, documentation, and simulation purposes. Note, however, that you cannot verify a policy in local or demo mode.

VPN DEBUGGING

You can obtain debugging information for VPN (Virtual Private Network) and IKE (Internet Key Exchange) by turning on debugging using the following commands:

```
# vpn debug on
# vpn debug ikeon
```

The former command enables debugging information to be sent to both ike.elg and vpnd.elg log files in the $FWDIR/log directory. The latter command logs only IKE debug information. This debug technique is useful for showing the negotiation process for encrypted tunnels.

Original Filename	New Filename
rulebases_5_0.fws	rules.fws
objects_5_0.C	objects.fws
objects_graph.md1	objects_graph.md1
setup.C	setup.fws
fgrulebases_5_0.fws	fwrules.fws
1crulebases_5_0.fws	cerules.fws
s1prulebases_5_0.fws	slprules.fws

Table 21-2. Files Required for *local

The commands shown in the following table can also be useful when troubleshooting VPN connections.

Command	What It Does
vpn ver	Displays the version of VPN software.
vpn drv off	Causes all VPN tunnels to be disconnected.
vpn drv on	Forces a renegotiation of IKE from phase 1.

You can use the vpn drv off command to disconnect all tunnels; this will prevent communication from taking place between all VPN connected sites. Then use the vpn drv on command to allow tunnels to reconnect and start a new IKE negotiation from phase 1.

THE METHODOLOGY FOR TROUBLESHOOTING

To effectively troubleshoot VPN-1/FireWall-1 NG, you should follow the steps outlined in this section.

Obtain a Network Design

The first and most crucial step in troubleshooting is to have a network diagram that details the scenario where VPN-1/FireWall-1 NG is deployed. The diagram should include IP addresses, subnets, and IP routes.

Obtain the Security Policy

A copy of the VPN-1/FireWall-1 NG Security Policy should be obtained, including object definitions, Network Address Translation rules, and any desktop security rules. If necessary, back up the $FWDIR/conf directory so it can be restored to a temporary replacement server. This is always a good idea before making changes.

Examine the Technical Issue

The problem should be fully documented; for example, is the issue specific? Can it always be reproduced?

Make Sure the Implementation Is Correct

It is crucial that you understand how VPN-1/FireWall-1 NG functions if you want to effectively troubleshoot more complex issues such as a failure in secure internal communications or issues with VPN certificate keys. Chapter 3 is a good starting point for a thorough understanding of the components and how they interact.

Utilize Available Resources to Obtain a Solution

Check Point offers software subscription and support contracts that entitle users to upgrades and hot fixes.

If you purchased your VPN-1/FireWall-1 NG product through a reseller or consultant, they usually have direct access to Check Point's Secure Knowledgebase and can check if the issue is known and whether there is a documented resolution. They can also initiate a support call with Check Point engineers, who are experts at resolving technical problems with VPN-1/FireWall-1 NG.

In addition, there are a variety of Internet resources that are available to all users. One of the most famous Internet resources for VPN-1/FireWall-1 is www.phoneboy.com. This website contains lots of technical information and even has an article by the authors of this book about VPNs between VPN-1/FireWall-1 NG and third-party firewalls.

Check Point has several newsgroups that allow anyone to subscribe and post information on issues they are having; these newsgroups are valuable reading for common issues.

Document the Issue and Solution

Once an issue has been resolved, it should be fully documented, especially for a consultant, because other customers may have the same issue. We maintain our own detailed Knowledge Base, which has proven invaluable to resolving customer issues.

MAKE SURE THE SERVER IS UP AND RUNNING

If, when trying to log on to the Management Server using the Policy Editor or SmartDashboard, you get the error message, "Connection cannot be initiated. Make sure that the Server '<SmartServer IP address>' is up and running." (as shown in Figure 21-1), it could be that the Management Server has stopped, but it is often simply that the client workstation's IP address does not appear in the GUI Clients list. Run cpconfig on the Management Server and add the client's IP address to allow it to connect to the Management Server.

IP ROUTING

The most common issues with VPN-1/FireWall-1 NG are often routing issues. An organization finds that users on some subnets can get Internet access but users on other subnets cannot. For example, if an organization installs multiple routers and adds multiple IP subnets as shown in Figure 21-2, the firewall needs to know about the next-hop (the directly connected router) to send packets to for each subnet.

In Figure 21-2, the firewall will require two additional routing entries. A static route for network 172.16.2.0 255.255.255.0 via Router A and another static route for network 172.16.3.0 via Router B. It will not need a specific router entry for network 172.16.1.0 255.255.255.0 because it is a directly connected network.

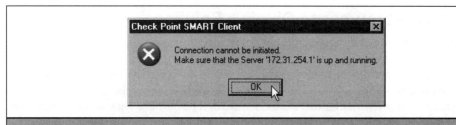

Figure 21-1. SmartDashboard error

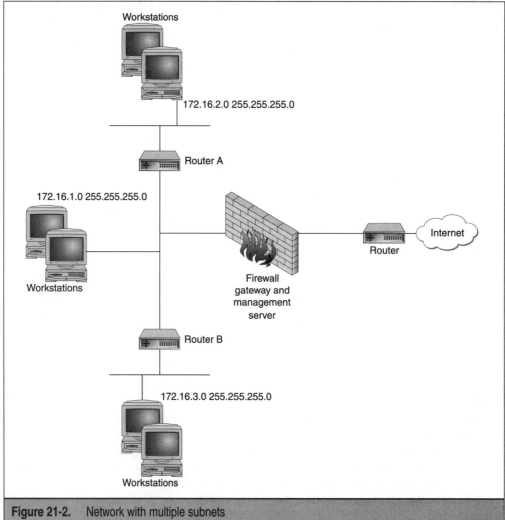

Figure 21-2. Network with multiple subnets

Good network design plays an important part in ensuring that a large organization with multiple subnets minimizes the administration required to support a multiple subnet environment. For example, ensuring that subnets are contiguous simplifies the routing tables on VPN-1/FireWall-1 NG.

An example of contiguous subnets is shown here:

172.16.1.0 /24
172.16.2.0 /24
172.16.3.0 /24

This translates into a summary entry on VPN-1/FireWall-1 NG of 172.16.0.0 /16 that allows a single routing entry to support all three subnets. This is a technique known in routing circles as *route summarization* or *route aggregation*. Route summarization capability is often found in advanced routing protocols. All routing protocols as supported by your platform can be used with VPN-1/FireWall-1 NG.

To troubleshoot routing entries for internal users, create a rule to allow ICMP from internal users to the firewall. Next, to see where the problem is, perform Traceroute and ICMP tests from the workstations that are having problems.

To view the routing table on a Windows NT/2000–based gateway, perform the command:

```
c:\>route print
```

To view the routing table on a Unix-based system, perform the command:

```
# netstat -rn
```

SECURE INTERNAL COMMUNICATIONS

Secure Internal Communications (SIC) is the new method for how Check Point components will communicate with each other in Check Point VPN-1/FireWall-1 NG. It is based on SSL with digital certificates. This is presented in this chapter as a useful reference because it is a new feature of VPN-1/FireWall-1 NG.

When you install the management station, you will create a Certificate Authority (CA). This CA will issue certificates for all components that need to communicate with each other. For example, a distributed VPN-1/FireWall-1 NG Module will need a certificate from the Management Station prior to downloading a policy to this module (or even licensing this module remotely via the new license method).

Remember, the Management Station must be able to communicate to the Remote Module before you can remotely apply the Check Point license from the Management Station.

If you get the "Failed to Connect to Module" error message, a number of things could be wrong:

- There could be connectivity issues from the Management Station to the VPN-1/FireWall-1 NG Module.

- CPShared may not be installed on the VPN-1/FireWall-1 NG Module.

- The VPN-1/FireWall-1 NG Module may not be listening on the proper ports for the SIC communications.

Let's troubleshoot the VPN-1/FireWall-1 NG Module:

First, check the network port that SIC is trying to listen on with the netstat command. It should be listening on port 18211. On UNIX type the following command.

```
# netstat -a | grep 211
```

The Windows version of the command is shown in Figure 21-3.

To reset your OTP, use the cpconfig utility. In Windows, use Start | Programs | Check Point Management Clients | Check Point Configuration NG on the VPN-1/FireWall-1 NG Module. In Unix, use cpconfig and enter menu item number 5, as shown in Figure 21-4.

Remember to use the same password on the Management Station that you define within Figure 21-4.

After you initialize the OTP again, try and initialize the object at the Management Station.

If you don't see the host listening on this port, perform a stop of the VPN-1/FireWall-1 NG service by typing **cpstop** at the command line.

There is a common infrastructure component called CPShared with Check Point NG. This component is located under C:\Program Files\CheckPoint\CPShared\5.0. There is a subdirectory called bin that has all of the commands for this shared component. To stop and start the shared component infrastructure, use the commands CPSTOP and CPSTART, respectively. An excellent troubleshooting program for this communications is the CPD application—see the "VPN-1/FireWall-1 NG Debugging Tools," section

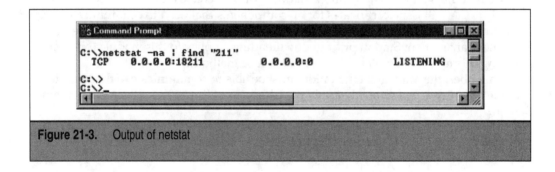

Figure 21-3.   Output of netstat

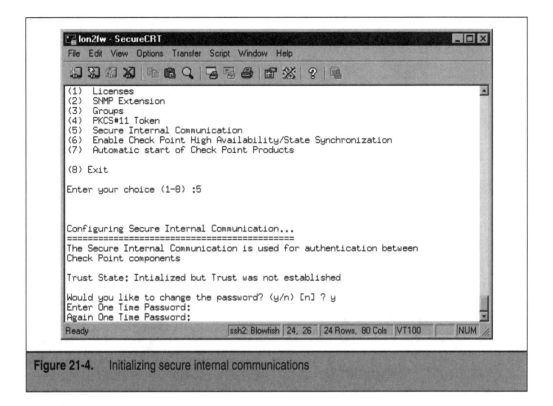

Figure 21-4. Initializing secure internal communications

earlier in this chapter. To troubleshoot the SIC communications between the Management Station and the VPN-1/FireWall-1 NG Module, perform the following steps on the VPN-1/FireWall-1 NG Module.

1. First, stop the cpd process on the module with the following command:

   ```
   # $CPDIR/bin/cpd_admin stop
   ```

2. Next, put the module into debug mode by running the CPD application with the -d flag.

3. Now try and initialize the VPN-1/FireWall-1 NG object on the Management Station by selecting the Initialize button in cpconfig, as shown in Figure 21-5.

4. If the OTPs are in sync, you should see Trust Established displayed on the Management Station. On the VPN-1/FireWall-1 NG Module, you will see the output as shown in Figure 21-6.

5. If the VPN-1/FireWall-1 NG Module already has a certificate, as shown in Figure 21-7, re-initialize the OTP, so that the Management Station can issue the correct certificate to this VPN-1/FireWall-1 NG Module.

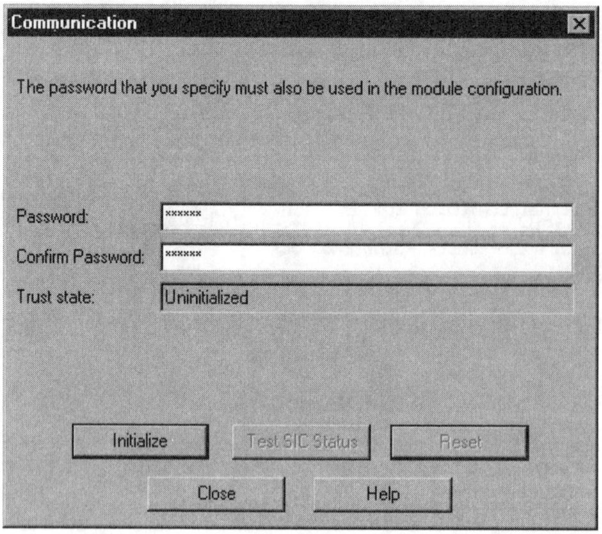

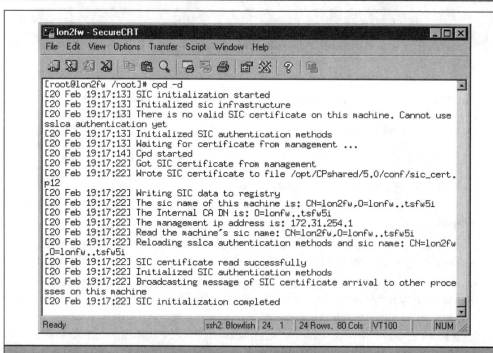

Figure 21-5. Reinitialize the Management Module SIC communication

Figure 21-6. CPD in debug mode shows SIC initialization

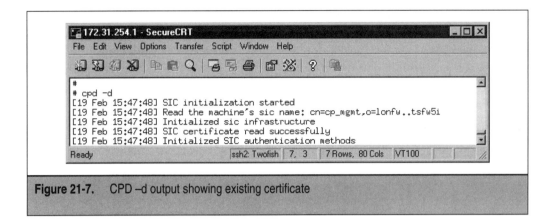

Figure 21-7.   CPD –d output showing existing certificate

6. In this particular case, SIC has already been initialized on this module but is unable to communicate with the Management Station. You have to reset the OTP to get another certificate from the Management Station, as shown in Figure 21-8.

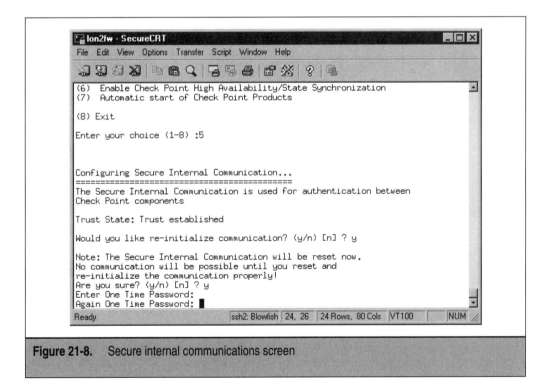

Figure 21-8.   Secure internal communications screen

7. A warning screen will appear to remind you that the OTPs must be the same on the Management Station object and the VPN-1/FireWall-1 NG Module. Select Yes and enter the OTP on the VPN-1/FireWall-1 NG Module.

8. Next, restart the CPShared processes by issuing the commands cpstop and cpstart, or press Y to allow the CP Config program to do this for you, as shown in Figure 21-9.

9. Next, try to initialize the object at the Management Station. You should see the screen shown in Figure 21-10.

NETWORK ADDRESS TRANSLATION

As opposed to previous versions (4.x and below), in VPN-1/FireWall-1 NG the server's address in a connection can be translated on the network interface closer to the client (that is, the "inbound" interface of the first packet). This can be determined in the Network Address Translation (NAT) page of the Global Properties window in the Policy Editor.

If the VPN-1/FireWall-1 NG installation is a clean build, NAT occurs on the client side. Essentially, VPN-1/FireWall-1 NG translates the packet and then routes it. However,

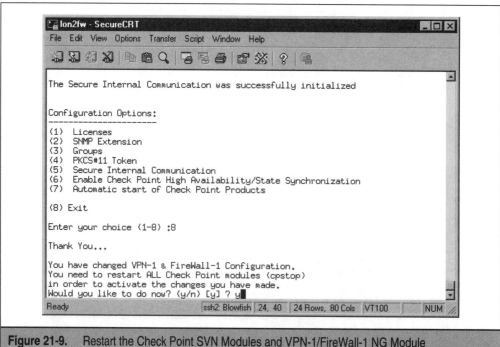

Figure 21-9. Restart the Check Point SVN Modules and VPN-1/FireWall-1 NG Module

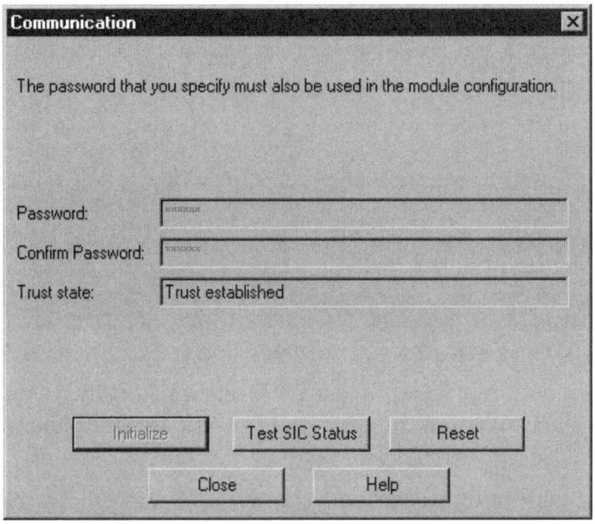

Figure 21-10. Trust Established screen

if you upgraded from VPN-1/FireWall-1 4.*x*, the gateway will route first and then NAT. This is why VPN-1/FireWall-1 4.*x* required static routes to support address translation. If you performed an upgrade, you will be required to provide static routes from the registered IP address to the internal real IP address. A common problem is that in this scenario, an administrator has configured everything correctly except for defining a static route. This causes the internal server to not respond to external connection requests.

Applications That Do Not Support NAT

There are a number of application-layer protocols that do not support NAT. This is because they encode the IP address in the data segment of the packet, and once NAT takes place the two addresses no longer match up. We have found that web hosting application developers have occasionally used the same technique and this has caused the application not to work with NAT.

Make sure developers are aware of the limitations imposed by NAT; otherwise, you may find that you will need to change the network design to use registered addresses on the DMZ and have your service provider route to your firewall for that subnet.

See the section on "Hard-Coded IP Addresses" later in this chapter, which describes another situation that can result in change to your network design brought about by application design issues.

CONTENT VECTORING PROTOCOL TROUBLESHOOTING

Once Content Vectoring Protocol (CVP) is configured, an error can stop all access, because if traffic redirected through a resource does not pass HTTP, the users will not be able to access external websites. Instead, they'll see an error on their browser saying "access denied."

To effectively troubleshooting CVP issues, follow this procedure:

1. Verify the rule is properly configured.

2. Verify that the resource is properly configured. It is always important to examine the release notes and documentation to ensure that if you are using an OPSEC partner's product, it has been correctly implemented.

3. If the resource redirects traffic to a CVP service, edit the resource, disable the CVP server, and reinstall the policy. If traffic passes via the rule now that CVP is not being used, the problem may be with the CVP server.

4. Contact the vendor of the software on the CVP server and troubleshoot the CVP server.

5. If the edited rule doesn't allow traffic to pass, remove the resource from the rule and replace the resource with the appropriate service for that resource. For example, replace HTTP resource with HTTP.

6. Install the policy. If traffic passes via the rule, re-create the resource without the CVP server, place the resource in the rule, and install the policy.

7. If traffic passes via the rule with the resource, activate the CVP server in the resource and install the policy.

8. Verify that traffic passes via the rule.

TOO MANY HOSTS

Customers who have installed VPN-1/FireWall-1 NG can sometimes get the error "too many internal hosts." In addition, traffic is processed very slowly and the operating system can hang. The log is full of errors.

There are many possible causes for these errors:

- The number of nodes behind the firewall may be greater than permitted by the license.

- The external.if file may not contain the name of the external interface of the firewall.

- Internal objects, which use NAT statically, may be misconfigured.

- Routing tables may not be properly configured.

- Automatic Private IP Addressing (APIPA) on Windows may be configured.

The first step to resolving this issue is to troubleshoot the EXTERNAL.IF file:

1. Copy the name of the interface.

2. Stop the firewall with the command cpstop.

3. With a text editor, create the file $FWDIR/conf/external.if.

4. Paste the name of the external interface in the file.

5. Start the firewall with the command cpstart.

To remove the errors, perform the following steps:

1. Stop the firewall with the command cpstop.

2. Remove the files with the following commands:

    ```
    # rm $FWDIR/conf/fwd.h
    # rm $FWDIR/conf/fwd.hosts
    ```

3. From the command prompt, run the following command:

    ```
    # fw tab -t host_table -x
    ```

4. Start the firewall with the command cpstart.

NOTE   The command fw lichosts -n will show the IP addresses detected by the firewall and counted against the license. Improper configuration of the route tables, objects that use NAT statically, or internal routers will result in the output of the fw lichosts command showing IP addresses that are not members of the internal network.

If the errors persist, examine the NAT rules:

1. Open the Policy Editor GUI and go to Manage | Network Objects.

2. Select the object on which NAT is being used statically, and choose Edit.

3. Verify that the General tab contains the actual internal IP of the box and not the external IP to which it may be converted using NAT on an intermediate gateway.

4. Check the route table. The static route on the firewall module should be the virtual IP (routable) address to the real IP (internal) address of the object on which NAT is being used.

5. If the route is correct, but for some reason the NAT rule doesn't apply, check the NAT Rule Base and correct it so the correct NAT rule is applied. This will ensure that the firewall doesn't count the external IP of the object.

If there is another path from the external network into the internal network, some connections that originated on the outside may be coming into the internal network via that path. Correct the routing or increase the number of licensed hosts.

APPLICATION RELATED ISSUES

The following sections are a selection of the types of problems that can be encountered if the developers have not taken into account that a firewall can introduce specific challenges to application development.

Hard-Coded IP Addresses

In some bespoke applications that our customers have developed, the IP address of the server is hard coded as its registered IP address. In this scenario, when the server is placed behind a firewall, the server address is changed. When, for example, an application tries to connect to the local server by using the public IP, the packet is sent to the firewall, which cannot successfully use NAT to send it back to the internal IP.

The solution is to either recode the application or get the developers to use the fully qualified domain name of the server. On the local server, this can be mapped to the real IP address by using the host file to resolve this issue. Or, instead, have the ISP route a block of IPs to the firewall and use a registered address DMZ. It should be noted that this has implications for security because an attacker could potentially learn more about your inside networks than you might wish.

TCP Timeouts

Some applications open connections and then maintain these connections as open even when the connection state is idle. This results in the firewall dropping the connection, but the application still thinks the connection is open. This usually requires a restart of the application. From our work with ISPs and hosting solutions, we know this to be a very common problem.

VPN-1/FireWall-1 NG can be configured to increase its default TCP timeout to allow for a greater period of idle connectivity, or the application can be written to send periodic keepalives to ensure the gateway does not timeout the connection. This is typical of SQL-type applications.

FTP Connection Timeout

FTP traffic can sometimes timeout. If you find this happening and want to increase the timeouts, simply edit the FTP service through the Policy Editor:

1. Click Advanced.
2. Choose Other under the Timeout section.
3. Define the desired value in seconds.

DBEDIT

Check Point has created a new utility to make it easier to work with the database files on the VPN-1/FireWall-1 NG Management Station. The utility (dbedit) allows administrators to make changes to the objects_5_0.C file, such as creating or modifying properties. The utility is designed to replace the error-prone manual editing of the objects_5_0.C file and allow searching of the file based on type and attribute. Additionally, this tool maintains the audit trail for changes to the database, another new feature of VPN-1/FireWall-1 NG.

It is also important to mention that NG handles objects files differently now. In the past, there was an objects.C file on both the Enforcement Module and the management servers. Now, there is an objects.C file on the Enforcement Module and a new file, objects_5_0.C located on the Management Server. Note that a new objects.C file gets created and pushed to the Enforcement Module each time a policy is installed. Editing the objects.C file on the Enforcement Module is no longer desirable because the change will be lost in the next policy installation.

TIP   Every change to the FWDIR/conf/objects_5_0.C file should be done using the dbedit utility.

NOTE   We strongly recommend consulting Check Point technical support before editing the objects_5_0.C file.

To use dbedit:

1. Before editing the objects_5_0.C file:
    *   Close all VPN-1/FireWall-1 NG GUI clients.
    *   Back up the original FWDIR/conf/objects_5_0.C to another folder.
2. Edit the objects_5_0.C file on the VPN-1/FireWall-1 NG Management Server only.
3. From command line, run dbedit. (To learn about the dbedit command options, issue dbedit -h.)
4. Enter a resolvable hostname or IP address when prompted.
5. Enter the username and password of the VPN-1/FireWall-1 NG administrator when prompted.
6. An example command for modifying values in the properties under firewall properties table in the objects_5_0.C file is as follows:

```
modify properties firewall_properties hclient_enable_new_interface false
```

    This command will change the hclient_enable_new_interface (true) property to hclient_enable_new_interface (false).

7. To save the change issue, use the following command:

   ```
   update properties firewall_properties
   ```

8. To exit dbedit, issue the quit command.

9. Install the policy.

CAUTION   Issuing quit to exit will save any change already made. Issuing CTRL+C will kill dbedit without saving any changes.

GUI DBEDIT (Feature Pack 3)

Check Point has introduced a GUI editor for the DBEdit utility in Feature Pack 3. You can download the tool from the Check Point website. The files need to be uncompressed and placed in the same directory as the rest of the FP3 SmartClients: C:\Program Files\ CheckPoint\Smart Clients\NG FP3\PROGRAM. Once installed, you can run the GuiDBedit program by double-clicking its icon in the program directory. A screen shot of the new utility is shown in Figure 21-11.

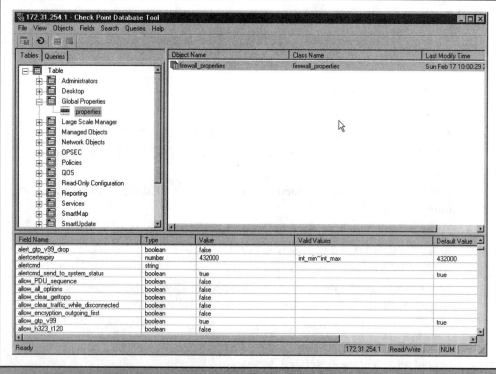

Figure 21-11.   GuiDBedit

MANAGEMENT CONSOLE LOCKOUT

There may be an occasion when the VPN-1/FireWall-1 NG Management Server becomes unavailable due to network problems. Once connectivity has been re-established, you may find that every time you use the Management Console to try connecting the Management Server, an error message appears stating the following:

NG GUI logon error: "connection cannot be established. Another GUI Client is already connected to the Management Server"

Either a pulled out cable or a Policy Editor (or other GUI client/SmartClient) system crash could cause this; it is likely that the TCP layer will not know about a crash until it tries to send the next packet.

In this case, Management Server will not get the disconnect event and will not know a client has disconnected until the client tries to communicate with it.

To avoid waiting forever, the Management Server tries to ping its clients from time to time. The ping interval is 3 minutes by default and can be changed in the registry; follow the steps outlined below.

1. Stop the Management Server by issuing fw kill fwm on the Management Server.

2. Open the Registry:
   - On Unix, use vi $CPDIR/registry/HKLM_registry.data
   - On Windows NT/2000, run regedt32 and go to HKEY_LOCAL_MACHINE\Software\CheckPoint

3. In the FW1\5.0 directory, there is a key called FWMKeepAliveTimeout (it holds the ping interval in milliseconds). Change the value to a shorter interval (for example, a value of 5000 for 5 seconds).

4. Start the Management Server by issuing fwm.

Try to connect to the Management Server again by launching the Management Console. You should be able to connect and start using the Security Policy.

AND FINALLY... IT'S NOT A FIREWALL ISSUE!

I am convinced the above exclamation is made at least once a second around the globe by the firewall administrators of the world. Firewalls can be blamed for just about anything it seems, from a server failing to back up to thousands of duplicate packets being sent from a faulty network switch. Very few of these supposed "firewall issues" turn out to have anything to do with the firewall, but it's surprising just how quickly system administrators and network engineers turn to what seems to be the universal explanation for anything going wrong once a firewall has been placed in between their systems.

A very high percentage of support calls claiming to be firewall problems turn out be something else—mostly routing problems.

CHECKLIST: KEY POINTS IN TROUBLESHOOTING

The following is a checklist for the key points in troubleshooting.

- ☐ List the VPN-1/FireWall-1 NG debugging tools.
- ☐ Explain how the fw ctl pstat command is used.
- ☐ Explain how the fw ctl debug command is used.
- ☐ Explain how the fw tab command is used.
- ☐ Debug the cpd process.
- ☐ Use the Policy Editor in *local mode.
- ☐ Show how the VPN-1/FireWall-1 NG troubleshooting function works.
- ☐ Show how VPN-1/FireWall-1 NG functions overall.
- ☐ Configure the VPN-1/FireWall-1 NG architecture if applicable.
- ☐ Use the resources available from Check Point, your reseller, and the online communities to implement the troubleshooting function in a structured and methodical manner.
- ☐ Learn to recognize when it's not a firewall issue.

CHAPTER 22

Malicious Activity Detection (MAD) and SmartDefense

C heck Point's Malicious Activity Detection (MAD) feature provides a mechanism for detecting malicious or suspicious events and notifying the system administrator. MAD is configurable, allowing administrators the ability to modify the attack detection parameters, turn detection on or off for specific types of attacks, or disable the MAD feature entirely. In Feature Pack 2, this was redefined as SmartDefense. It was further improved in Feature Pack 3 and is now an integral part of VPN-1/FireWall-1 NG.

MALICIOUS ACTIVITY DETECTION (MAD)

MAD is designed to scan the VPN-1/FireWall-1 NG log file and alert the system administrator to any malicious or suspicious events that are occurring. MAD can be configured to meet the specific requirements of an organization.

MAD Attacks

MAD protects networks by alerting administrators to eight different conditions:

- SYN attacks
- Anti-spoofing
- Successive multiple connections
- Port scanning
- Blocked connection port scanning
- Login failures
- Successive alerts
- Land attacks

These attacks will be addressed individually in the "MAD Signatures" section.

MAD Installation

MAD is automatically installed on the Management Module as part of the VPN-1/ FireWall-1 NG installation. MAD is enabled, disabled, and configured by modifying $FWDIR/conf/cpmad_config.conf.

NOTE   When using a DOS editor, look for the DOS-truncated filename: $FWDIR/conf/ cpmad_~1.con.

Global MAD Configuration

Global configuration parameters are those that apply to all MAD attack types.

System Mode

System mode specifies whether VPN-1/FireWall-1 NG should scan for attacks. Setting the system mode to on or off will enable or disable MAD. The default settings for MAD system mode on the cpmad_config.conf file are as follows:

```
#MAD mode
MAD_system_mode = off
```

Memory

If MAD needs more memory than has been allocated, it will exit. Determining how much memory to allocate to MAD will depend on how granular a level of protection is required, balanced against available memory. Memory requirement can be reduced by increasing MAD resolution, but this also increases the probability that some attacks may not be recognized. The MAD memory allocation is defined in kilobytes (KB). The default settings for MAD memory are as follows:

```
#MAD global parameters
MAD_memory = 75000
```

Clean Interval

System administrators can determine how long old events stay in the internal MAD tables. A high, clean interval will reduce CPU usage but will increase memory requirements. The MAD clean interval is set in seconds. The default MAD setting is shown here:

```
# MAD global parameters
MAD_clean_interval = 60
```

Number of Connection Attempts

If the ELA or LEA server terminates, MAD will try to reconnect. Here, an administrator can set the number of times MAD will attempt to reconnect before exiting. Shown here are the default MAD settings:

```
# MAD global parameters
MAD_number_of_connection_attempts = 10
```

Interval Between Connection Attempts

If the ELA or LEA server terminates, MAD will try to reconnect the number of times set as the MAD_number_of_connection_attempts. This parameter will set the interval, in seconds, between those connection attempts. The default setting is shown:

```
# MAD global parameters
MAD_interval_between_connection_attempts = 60
```

Attack Parameters

Each attack type has attack-specific parameters. This allows administrators to customize MAD to a high degree. Customizing is performed in the cpmad_config.conf file.

Mode   In MAD global parameters, administrators can set the mode for MAD to on or off. Each MAD attack signature can be individually set to on or off.

Time Interval   As with the MAD global clean interval setting, each individual MAD attack signature can be set with a Time to Live (TTL) in seconds. When the time has expired, information about the attack is deleted from internal tables.

NOTE   The individual time interval setting supercedes the global time interval setting.

Repetitions   The MAD Repetitions setting works with the Time Interval setting and the MAD global Successive Alerts setting. Repetitions set the number of times an event must occur in the time interval before an action is taken. For example, the successive alerts count the number of alert log entries in the last successive alerts/time interval. If this number is greater than the Successive Alerts Repetitions setting, an action is generated.

Resolution   The resolution MAD parameter specifies the interval in seconds, during which identical log entries are considered to have occurred at the same time. Here is where the administrators balance granularity of protection against memory available. A large resolution value reduces memory usage but decreases the probability that attacks will be recognized. If resolution, for example, is set to 5 seconds, all identical log entries arriving within 5 seconds of the first one are combined into a single log entry. This reduces memory usage but may mask a network attack. It should be noted that the log entries are always individually counted, but they can be combined into a single log entry by this parameter.

Action   MAD scans the log file and generates an alert type, as specified in the Log and Alert tab of the Global Properties setup window, as shown in Figure 22-1.

The Action setting determines what type of alert is generated by MAD. This setting corresponds to the values specified in the Log and Alert tab of the Properties window.

MAD Signatures

MAD detects eight different types of attacks.

SYN Attack

A SYN attack is designed to make a service unavailable by flooding it with connection requests from invalid, spoofed addresses (as discussed in Chapter 16). The backlog queue's buffers fill up with the connection attempts, the server is tied up trying to

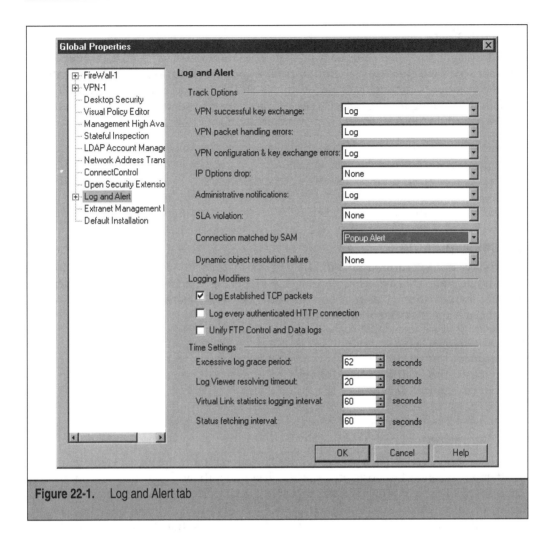

Figure 22-1. Log and Alert tab

acknowledge the connection attempts to invalid addresses, and the service becomes unreachable to legitimate users. The MAD SYN Attack feature is designed to detect this type of attack and to send an alert. Shown here are the default MAD SYN Attack parameter settings:

```
MAD_syn_attack_mode = on
MAD_syn_attack_resolution = 10
MAD_syn_attack_time_interval = 60
MAD_syn_attack_repetitions = 100
MAD_syn_attack_action = alert
```

Anti-spoofing

IP address spoofing is a technique used to gain unauthorized access to computers. The intruder sends messages to a computer from a spoofed IP address, falsely indicating that the message is coming from a trusted host and getting access authorization. The MAD Anti-spoofing feature detects these connections and sends an alert. Shown here are the default MAD Anti-spoofing parameter settings:

```
MAD_anti_spoofing_mode = off
MAD_anti_spoofing_resolution = 300
MAD_anti_spoofing_time_interval = 3600
MAD_anti_spoofing_repetitions = 10
MAD_anti_spoofing_action = alert
```

Successive Alerts

When successive alerts are enabled, MAD generates an action if an excessive number of VPN-1/FireWall-1 NG alerts have been generated. If log activity increases dramatically, it can be an indication of an attack on the network. Shown here are the default MAD Successive Alerts Attack parameter settings:

```
MAD_successive_alerts_mode = on
MAD_successive_alerts_resolution = 60
MAD_successive_alerts_time_interval = 600
MAD_successive_alerts_repetitions = 100
MAD_successive_alerts_action = alert
```

Port Scanning

If port scanning is enabled, MAD generates an action if there are an excessive number of attempts to connect to ports on a specific destination IP address coming from the same source. Port scanning indicates that someone is performing a reconnaissance sweep of your network to identify which ports are open and can be targeted for an attack. This is often a prelude to an attack. Administrators should activate either Port Scanning or Blocked Connection Port Scanning, depending on their port scanning requirements and the memory available to MAD. Shown here are the default MAD Port Scanning Alerts Attack parameter settings:

```
MAD_port_scanning_mode = off
MAD_port_scanning_time_interval = 60
MAD_port_scanning_repetitions = 100
MAD_port_scanning_action = alert
```

Blocked Connection Port Scanning

Blocked connections port scanning is similar to port scanning attacks, but it only watches for dropped or rejected connections. The assumption is that if a connection has been accepted, it is safe and can be ignored. Activating Blocked Connection Port Scanning attribute can be ignored. If a port scanning attack is established, a port connection may be missed. Activate either port scanning or blocked connections port scanning, but *not both*. Which one you activate depends on your port scanning requirements and the memory available to MAD. Shown here are the default MAD Blocked Connection Port Scanning Attack parameters settings:

```
MAD_blocked_connection_port_scanning_mode = on
MAD_blocked_connection_port_scanning_resolution = 5
MAD_blocked_connection_port_scanning_time_interval = 600
MAD_blocked_connection_port_scanning_repetitions = 50
MAD_blocked_connection_port_scanning_action = alert
```

Login Failure

The MAD Login Failure feature detects an excessive number of failed attempts to login to a specific destination IP address from the same-source IP address, indicating a possible attempt to crack a password to gain network access. Note that the Authentication Failure Track, in the Authentication tab of the Properties Setup window, should be set to Pop-up Alert as part of enabling MAD Login Failure detection, as shown in Figure 22-2.

Shown here are the default MAD Login Failure parameter settings:

```
MAD_login_failure_mode = on
MAD_login_failure_resolution = 5
MAD_login_failure_time_interval = 600
MAD_login_failure_repetitions = 30
MAD_login_failure_action = alert
```

Successive Multiple Connections

If an excessive number of connections are opened to a specific destination IP address and port number from the same-source IP address, indicating a possible denial of service attack, the MAD successive multiple connections feature generates an alert. Shown here are the Successive Multiple Connections default MAD parameter settings:

```
MAD_successive_mutiple_connections_mode = off
MAD_successive_mutiple_connections_mode_resolution = 10
MAD_successive_mutiple_connections_mode_time_interval = 60
MAD_successive_mutiple_connections_mode_repetitions = 50
MAD_successive_mutiple_connections_mode_action = alert
```

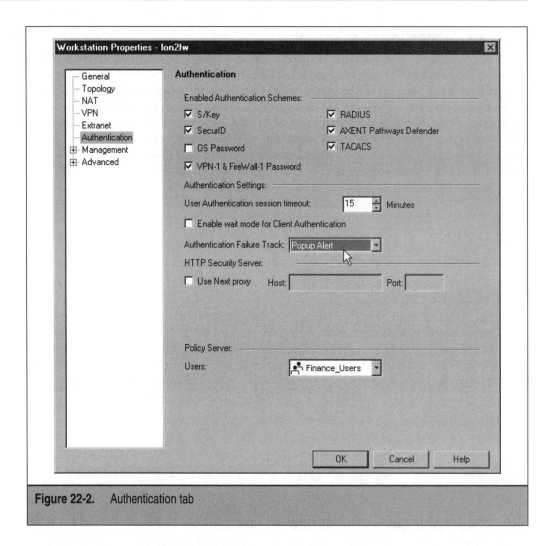

Figure 22-2. Authentication tab

Local Interface Spoofing

Local interface spoofing detects spoofed packets where the IP address has been changed to be an interface of the local VPN-1/FireWall-1 NG Enforcement Module. The default parameters are shown here:

```
MAD_local_interface_spoofing_mode = on
MAD_local_interface_spoofing_resolution = 10
```

```
MAD_local_interface_spoofing_time_interval = 60
MAD_local_interface_spoofing_repetitions = 5
MAD_local_interface_spoofing_action = alert
```

Land Attack

A land attack sends out just one SYN packet, in which the sending device's IP address has been transposed with the IP address of the destination server. When the destination machine tries to acknowledge receipt of the transmission, it ends up using its own IP address, resulting in a loopback condition that will slow or stop the service. The default parameters for the MAD land attack are shown here:

```
MAD_land_attack_mode = on
MAD_land_attack_resolution = 10
MAD_land_attack_time_interval = 60
MAD_land_attack_repetitions = 5
MAD_land_attack_action = alert
```

ENABLING MAD

Fiction Corporation has decided that since e-business is now critical, they require the best security configuration possible for their VPN-1/FireWall-1 NG infrastructure. They would like Check Point's Malicious Activity Detection (MAD) enabled for their perimeter firewalls.

To enable MAD on the Fiction Corporation London Management Module and edit the $FWDIR/cofnf/cpmad_config.conf file and change the following setting:

```
MAD_system_mode = off
```

to the following:

```
MAD_system_mode = on
```

You will now be required to restart VPN-1/FireWall-1 NG to enable MAD. When the Management Module is started, the ELA proxy is started by default. The ELA proxy must be running on the machine running MAD.

To test the functionality of Fiction Corporation's MAD installation, we ran some tests against the London Gateway while System Status was running. The pop-up alert window in Figure 22-3 clearly shows MAD has detected successive multiple connections on the HTTP protocol.

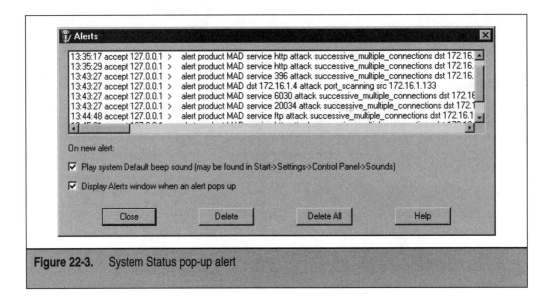

Figure 22-3. System Status pop-up alert

The alerts have also been added to the log. The Log Viewer has been filtered in Figure 22-4 to show the type of log entries that MAD will add.

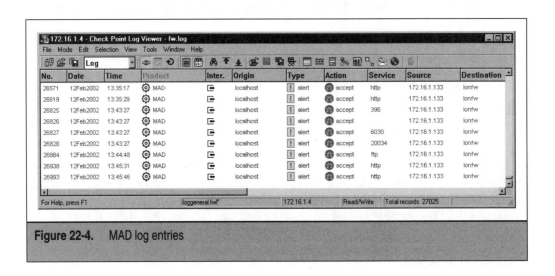

Figure 22-4. MAD log entries

SMARTDEFENSE

Check Point has just announced the release of SmartDefense, which provides centralized control against attacks. This is featured in updates to Feature Pack 2 and is an integral part of Feature Pack 3. SmartDefense is designed to defeat a broad range of attack types, including Denial of Service (DoS), IP attacks, and network probing and web application vulnerabilities. In addition, alerting, tracking, and auditing are all configured centrally, which provides a more complete network defense than MAD. SmartDefense is designed to protect against the following:

- SYN flood
- Land
- IP spoofing
- IP fragmentation
- Illegal and malformed packets
- DNS attacks
- Protocol noncompliance
- DNS attacks
- Application-specific vulnerabilities
- Trojan horses
- Back door and remote administration
- Mobile code (Java, JavaScript, Active-X)
- Hidden file extensions
- Port scanning
- Service scanning
- DOS attacks (Denial of Service Attacks)

SmartDefense is deployed on VPN-1/FireWall-1 NG enforcement points but is defined on the management server.

Configuring SmartDefense

To configure SmartDefense, launch the Smart Client Dashboard and click the SmartDefense button on the toolbar, as shown in Figure 22-5.

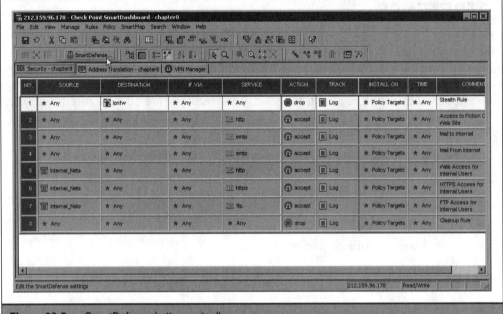

Figure 22-5. SmartDefense button on toolbar

The SmartDefense settings window is launched. There are a number of options that can be configured, as shown in Figure 22-6. Under each category, a detailed description of the attack and the defense is displayed in the window.

SmartDefense is subscription based. Users who have purchased the service can click the Update SmartDefense button to obtain updated defenses and descriptions for new attacks. The Open SmartView Tracker button will open the SmartClient Tracker (formerly known as the Log Viewer) to view only SmartDefense-related events.

Anti Spoofing Configuration

This page is an information page that indicates how anti-spoofing is configured on the gateways. You can change the settings by reconfiguring the individual gateways, as shown in Figure 22-7.

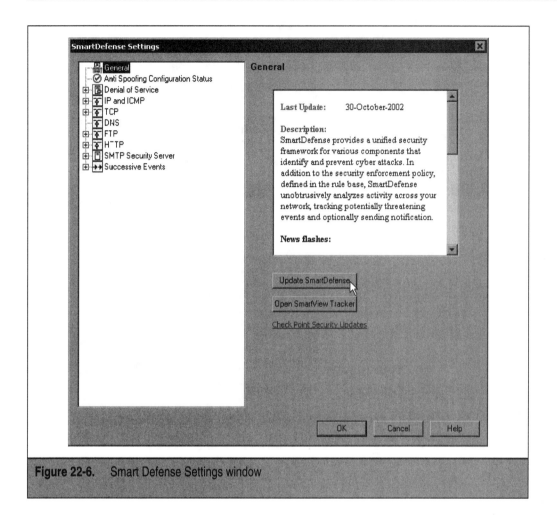

Figure 22-6.   Smart Defense Settings window

Denial of Service

To configure protection against Denial of Service (DoS) attacks, select the checkbox against the options available, as shown in Figure 22-8:

- **TearDrop**   Handles overlapping IP fragments attack
- **Ping of Death**   A malformed Ping packet larger than 64 bytes that causes the targeted host to crash
- **LAND**   A SYN packet in which the source address and port are the same as the destination, i.e., spoofed

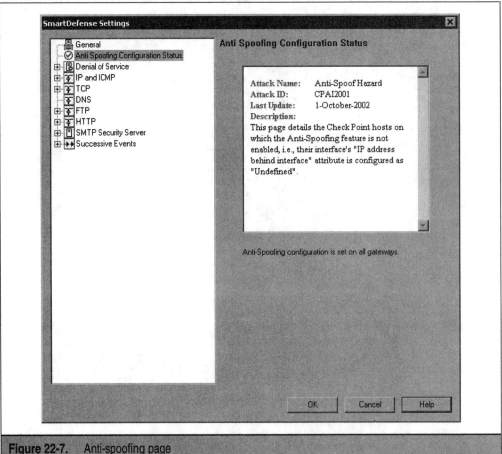

Figure 22-7. Anti-spoofing page

The Advanced button on the page allows the user to define the number of successful events that are required to trigger the specified action.

The settings on the Advanced window are shown in Figure 22-9 and defined as follows:

- **Resolution** The interval (in seconds) over which log entries corresponding to this attack are counted.

- **Time Interval** The interval (in seconds) after which information about an attack will be deleted from the internal tables.

- **Attempts Number** The number of times an event must occur in seconds in order for action to be taken.

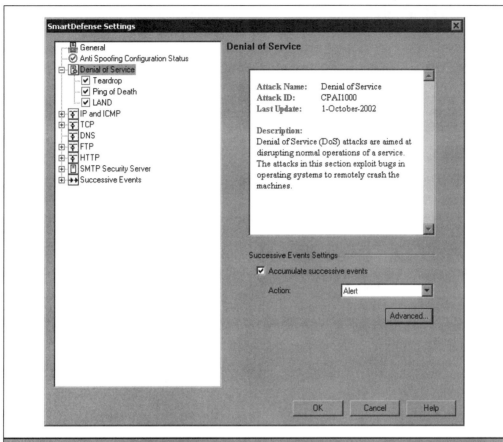

Figure 22-8. Denial of Service settings

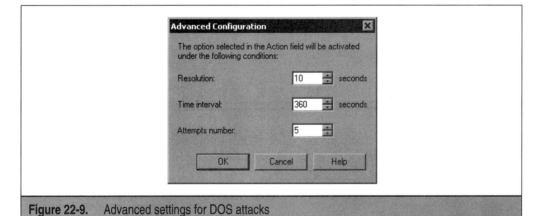

Figure 22-9. Advanced settings for DOS attacks

It is best to run this with the defaults, but if too many alerts are being logged, try increasing the attempts number to ensure a manageable number of alerts are reported.

IP AND ICMP

These settings specify a range of checks on IP and ICMP protocols and are defined as:

- **Fragment Sanity Check**   When an IP packet is too big to be transported on a network topology, it is split into several smaller IP packets and transmitted in fragments. VPN-1/FireWall-1 NG collects all the fragments of a given IP packet before inspecting it to make sure it correctly understands the network traffic.

  This test is mandatory. However, in this page you can configure whether logs will be issued for offending packets.

- **Packet Sanity**   This option performs several Layer 3 and Layer 4 sanity checks. These include verifying packet size, UDP and TCP header lengths, dropping IP options, and verifying the TCP flags.

  This test is mandatory. However, in this page you can configure whether logs will be issued for offending packets.

- **Max Ping Size**   Ping (also known as an ICMP echo request) is a protocol used to check whether a remote machine is up. A request is sent by the client and the server responds with a reply echoing the client's data.

  This option allows you to limit the maximum requested data echo size. This should not be confused with Ping of Death, in which the request is malformed. The Max Ping Size setting allows a configurable setting in bytes for the maximum requested data echo size, as shown in Figure 22-10.

TCP

The TCP section performs a set of TCP tests on packets. To verify that packets are legitimate, the following tests are carried out:

- Protocol type verification
- Protocol header analysis
- Protocol flags analysis and verification

To enable the TCP tests, ensure that the TCP option is checked on the SmartDefense configuration interface.

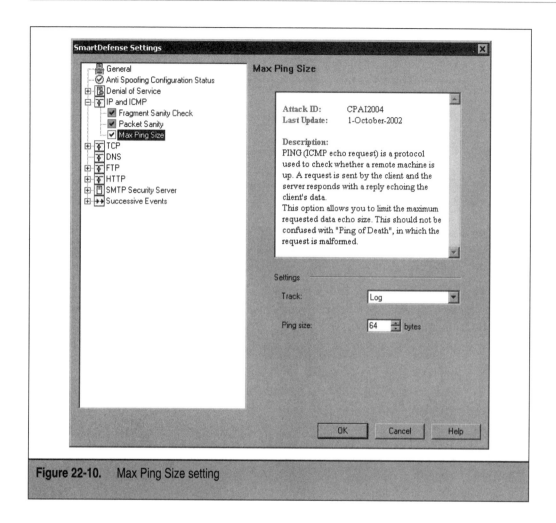

Figure 22-10.   Max Ping Size setting

SYN Attack   The following settings can be made on the SYN Attack screen, as shown in Figure 22-11:

- **Override Modules' SYNDefender Configuration**   Select this option to specify that the settings on this page override the SYNDefender settings specified for individual Modules. SYN attack defense can be specified on a per-module basis or in the SmartDefense SYN Attack page.

- **Activate SYN Attack Protection**   If Override Modules' SYNDefender Configuration is checked, then you can activate protection for all modules. Click Configure to specify the parameters of the protection method in the SYN Attack window.

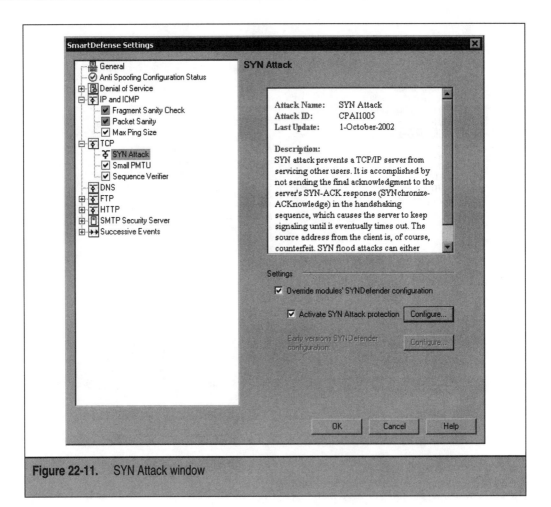

Figure 22-11. SYN Attack window

- **Early Versions SYNDefender Configuration**   Check this option to open the window to configure SYNDefender protection for earlier version modules.
- **SYN Attack window**   The SYN Attack window has a number of configurable settings:
  - **Track**   Select the action to take if an attack is detected.
  - **Track Level**   Select one of the following:
    - **Attacks Only**   The action specified under Track will be taken only when an attack is detected and when it is over.
    - **Individual SYNs**   The action specified under Track will be taken for each SYN packet.

- **Timeout** Specifies how long SmartDefense waits for an acknowledgment before concluding that the connection is a SYN attack.

- **Attack Threshold** If more than the Attack Threshold's unacknowledged SYN packets are detected at any one time, then SmartDefense will conclude that a SYN attack is taking place.

- **Protect External Interface Only** Protect against SYN attacks only on the external interface.

- **SYN Attack window (earlier versions)** This button allows the following to be configured:

  - **None** SYNDefender is not deployed. If you choose this option, your network will not be protected from SYN attacks.

  - **SYN Gateway** Deploy the SYN Gateway method.

  - **Passive SYN Gateway** Deploy the Passive SYN Gateway method.

  - **Timeout** Specifies how long SYNDefender waits for an acknowledgment before concluding that the connection is a SYN attack.

  - **Maximum Sessions** Specifies the maximum number of protected sessions. This parameter is relevant only if Passive SYN Gateway is selected under Method. If SYN Relay is selected, all sessions are protected. This parameter specifies the number of entries in an internal connection table maintained by SYNDefender. If the table is full, SYNDefender will not examine new connections.

  - **Display Warning Messages** If set, SYNDefender will print console messages regarding its status.

Small PMTU A bandwidth attack where the attacker fools the server into sending large amounts of data using small packets causing a bottleneck and degrading performance. The options are as follows:

- **Track** Select the appropriate tracking option.

- **Minimal MTU Size** Define the minimal allowed MTU. Care is required because extreme values can cause problems with legitimate requests being dropped or severe performance degradation.

Sequence Verifier Sequence Verifier is a mechanism matching the current TCP packet's sequence number against a TCP connection state. Packets that match the connection in terms of the TCP session but have incorrect sequence numbers are either dropped or stripped of data.

- **Track** Select the appropriate tracking option.

- **Track On**   Specify the type of out of state packets to be tracked, as follows:
    - **Anomalous**   Track only packets that do not normally appear in legitimate connections.
    - **Every**   Track every out-of-state packet.
    - **Suspicious**   Track only seemingly erroneous packets, unrelated to the connection.

DNS

If this option is selected, all the connections on the DNS port over UDP will be checked to verify they are DNS related. This feature does not support DNS over TCP (TCP Zone Transfer). The only options other than enabling the check is to select the form of tracking required.

FTP

The FTP section offers protection for the FTP protocol.

FTP Bounce   To conform with the FTP protocol, the PORT command has the originating machine specify an arbitrary destination machine and port for the data connection. However, this behavior also means that an attacker can open a connection to a port of the attacker's choosing on a machine that may not be the originating client. Making this connection to an arbitrary machine for unauthorized purposes is the FTP bounce attack. Selecting this option stops an attacker from performing this form of breach.

FTP Security Server   The FTP Security Server has two settings that can be configured via SmartDefense:

- **Configurations Apply to All Connections**   The FTP Security Server is invoked for all connections.
- **Configurations Apply Only to Connections Related to Resources Used in the Rule Base**   The FTP Security Server is invoked when a rule specifies an FTP Resource and/or User Authentication is defined.
- **Allowed FTP Commands**   Check Point recommends that as a minimum the SITE command be blocked, as shown in Figure 22-12. There is a vulnerability in versions of WS-FTP, an FTP Server commonly used on Microsoft systems that allows the attacker to overflow a buffer and execute code on the targeted system.
- **Prevent Known Ports Checking**   Disables known ports checking. This setting should not be enabled unless there is a reason, such as software issues or FTP connectivity issues. Checking this option disables the function.
- **Prevent Port Overflow Checking**   Prevents overflow checking. This setting should also not be enabled unless there is a reason, such as software issues or FTP connectivity issues. Checking this option disables the function.

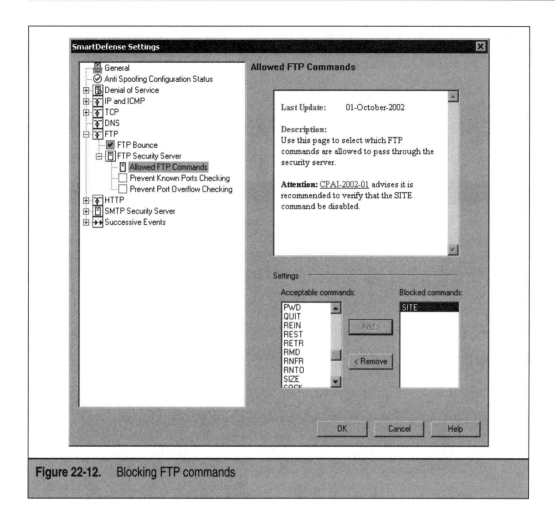

Figure 22-12.   Blocking FTP commands

HTTP

The HTTP page allows the user to configure various HTTP protection options.

General HTTP Worm Catcher   This allows the user to configure various worm signatures. You can import updates from the Check Point website or add patterns manually into the Worm Patterns list. Examples of such worms include Code Red and Nimda.

HTTP Security Server   These pages allow you to select what types of enforcement are applied to HTTP connections passing through the Security Server:

- **Configurations Apply to All Connections**   The HTTP Security Server is invoked for all connections.

- **Configurations Apply Only to Connections Related to Resources Used in the Rule Base**   The HTTP Security Server is invoked when a rule specifies an HTTP Resource and/or User Authentication is defined.

- **HTTP Format Sizes**   Allows you to specify the following, as shown in Figure 22-13:

  - **Maximum URL Length**   Defines the maximum allowed length of URL.

  - **Maximum HTTP Header Length**   Defines the maximum allowed length of the HTTP header.

  - **Maximum Number of HTTP Headers**   Defines the maximum allowed number of HTTP headers.

The next two settings are to prevent malicious content from passing in the HTTP protocol headers undetected by using alternative encoding techniques. Check these options to ensure protection against malicious code hidden in HTTP headers.

- ASCII Only Request Headers
- ASCII Only Response Headers

SMTP Security Server

The SMTP Security Server allows strict enforcement of the SMTP protocol. This can be applied in one of two ways:

- **Configurations Apply to All Connections**   The SMTP Security Server is invoked for all connections.

- **Configurations Apply Only to Connections Related to Resources Used in the Rule Base**   The SMTP Security Server is invoked when a rule specifies an HTTP Resource and/or User Authentication is defined.

SMTP Content   This page allows you to set limitations on variants of the protocols used. Some of these variants are illegal and are meant to fool the content inspection mechanisms into thinking the mail is different from what the client assumes. This allows viruses and other malicious software (malware) to pass through.

- **Maximum No-Effect Commands**   Defines the maximum allowed number of commands sent during the protocol exchange without producing any distinct effect.

- **Maximum Unknown Commands**   Defines the maximum allowed number of unknown commands sent during the protocol exchange.

- **Watch for Bad SMTP Commands**   If selected, enables the SMTP Server to distinguish erroneous SMTP commands.

- **Log When Dropping Connections**   If selected, sends an error notification every time the SMTP Server drops a connection.

- **Add Received Header When Forwarding**   If selected, the SMTP mail headers are to be forwarded to the CVP server for CVP content checking.

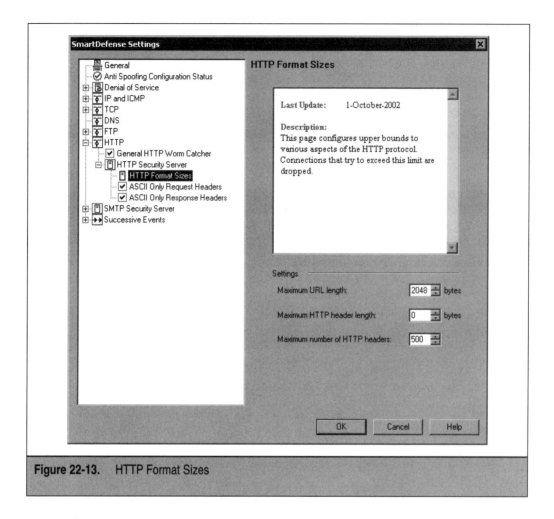

Figure 22-13.   HTTP Format Sizes

Mail and Recipient Content   The settings for this window apply only if an SMTP resource is defined, even if Configurations Apply to All Connections in the SMTP Security Server window is checked. The options listed can be individually selected to be activated:

- **Allow Multiple Content-Type Headers**   If checked, the SMTP Security Server will allow multiple content-type headers.

- **Allow Multiple "Encoding" Headers**   If checked, the SMTP Server will allow multiple "encoding" headers.

- **Allow Nonplain "Encoding" Headers**   If checked, the SMTP Server will allow nonplain "encoding" headers.

- **Allow Unknown Encoding**   If checked, the SMTP Server will allow unknown encoding methods.

- **Force Recipient to Have a Domain Name**   If checked, the SMTP Server will force the recipient to have a domain name.

- **Perform Aggressive MIME Strip** If checked, MIME attachments of all types will be stripped from the message. If unchecked, only the mail headers section and the headers of each MIME part will be scanned. If a relevant header is located, the MIME strip will be performed accordingly.

Successive Events

SmartDefense provides a mechanism for detecting malicious or suspicious events and notifying the system administrator. The mechanism allows you to send alerts when different successive malicious events are detected as listed:

- **Max Memory Allocation Size** Specifies the amount of memory allocated to the detecting mechanism (in kilobytes). If more memory is required, the feature will exit. Memory requirements can be reduced by reducing the number of attacks or decreasing the value of the Reset Accumulated Events property.

- **Reset Accumulated Events Every x Sec** Defines when events will be deleted from SMARTDefense's internal tables. High values reduce CPU usage but increase memory requirements.

- **Logging Attempts Interval** The interval (in seconds) over which log entries corresponding to this attack are counted. A large resolution value reduces memory usage but increases the probability that attacks will not be recognized.

- **Max Logging Attempts** The number of times an event must occur within the logging attempts interval in order for an error notification to be sent.

Successive Events Options Successive Events Options settings are provided under this selection for the following:

- Address Spoofing
- Port Scanning
- Local Interface Scanning
- Successive Alerts

Successive Multiple Connections Page To configure when the tracking option specified under Action will be taken, click Advanced to display the Advanced Configuration window. Configure the following settings: Resolution, Time Interval, and Attempts Number, as discussed earlier for Denial of Service and shown in Figure 22-9.

CHECKLIST: KEY POINTS
IN MALICIOUS ACTIVITY DETECTION (MAD)

The following is a checklist for the key points in Malicious Activity Detection (MAD).

- ☐ Define Malicious Activity Detection (MAD).
- ☐ Show how Malicious Activity Detection (MAD) enhances the capabilities of VPN-1/FireWall-1 NG by adding basic intruder detection capabilities.
- ☐ Identify MAD attacks.
- ☐ Install MAD.
- ☐ Configure global MAD.
- ☐ Show how administrators can be alerted to intrusion activity and take proactive countermeasures.
- ☐ Enable MAD.
- ☐ Identify MAD signatures.
- ☐ Define SmartDefense.
- ☐ Configure SmartDefense.

APPENDIX A

Fiction Corporation's
Initial Proposal

INITIAL PROPOSAL

FICTION CORPORATION

Author	Inti Shah
Date	23 May 2003
Version	1.0
Document Reference	
Number of pages	12

APPROVED BY	*Group IT, Fiction Corporation*	*Fiction Corporation*
Name	Inti Shah	Fred Bloggs
Title	Senior Security Architect	IT Director
Signature		
Date		

Document Control

Amendment History

Date	Version No	
23 May 2003	1.0	Initial Proposal – Secure Internet Connectivity

Distribution List

This document has been issued to the following people as author (A), information (I) and review (R):

Name	Position	A/I/R
Inti Shah	Senior Security Architect, Group IT, Fiction Corporation	A
Fred Bloggs	IT Director, Fiction Corporation	I

Project Documentation

Reference No	Document Title	Author	Version
Reference-V1.07.vsd	Security Reference Design	Group IT, Fiction Corporation	1.07 12/02/02
FOCT-SD-230502.doc	Initial Proposal Fiction Corporation	Group IT, Fiction Corporation	23 May 2003

Contents

Table of Figures

Executive Summary

Fiction Corporation has approached the IT department to provide secure Internet connectivity for their four geographically dispersed locations and provide an enterprise Security Policy that also incorporates their E-business website, which is hosted at a U.K. Internet Service Provider.

Fiction Corporation has stated that they require a robust security infrastructure that connects networks, systems, applications, and users.

The IT Department has developed a detailed solution design that provides a single enterprise Security Policy combined with ease of management. The solution components are as follows:

Perimeter Security	Check Point VPN-1/FireWall-1 NG for perimeter security
Content Security	Check Point CVP integration with OPSEC partner antivirus and URL filtering to protect e-mails at the London Headquarters and enforce Fiction Corporation's acceptable use policy for Internet access
Secure interoffice connectivity	Check Point VPN-1/FireWall-1 NG for secure connectivity between sites
Secure Remote Access	Check Point Policy Server and SecureClient for remote access users and to provide additional security for access to the London Finance network where sensitive data is held
E-business Solution Resilience	Check Point load balancing and high availability to ensure the E-business solution has high performance and resilience as it is mission critical
Security Monitoring	Check Point SmartDefense for monitoring network perimeters for unauthorized access attempts

The solution design document includes a detailed network design and Security Policy Rule Base for all locations.

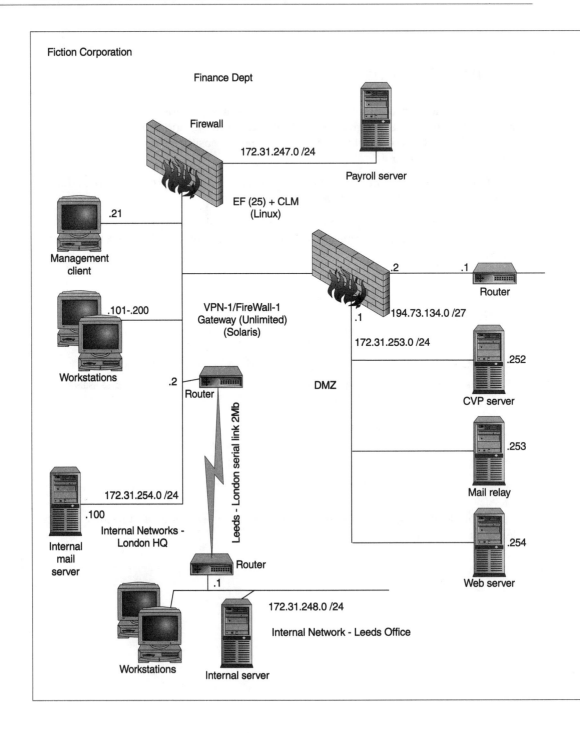

Fiction Corporation

Finance Dept

Firewall

172.31.247.0 /24

Payroll server

.21

Management
client

EF (25) + CLM
(Linux)

.2

.1

Router

.101-.200

VPN-1/FireWall-1
Gateway (Unlimited)
(Solaris)

.1   194.73.134.0 /27

Workstations

172.31.253.0 /24

.2
Router

DMZ

.252

CVP server

Leeds - London serial link 2Mb

.253

172.31.254.0 /24

Mail relay

.100

Internal Networks -
London HQ

Internal
mail
server

Router

.1

172.31.248.0 /24

.254

Web server

Internal Network - Leeds Office

Workstations   Internal server

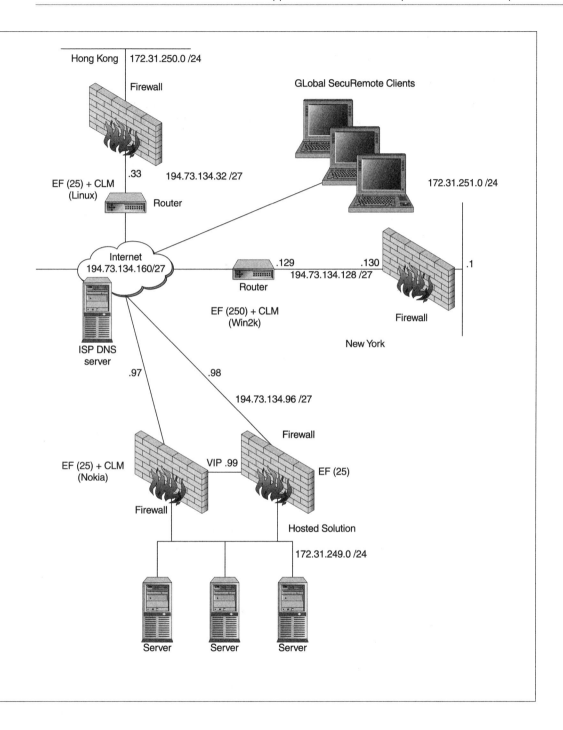

1 Solution Overview

Check Point VPN-1/FireWall-1 NG is recommended for the perimeter firewall solution due to its market-leading technology and capability to provide a single enterprise Security Policy.

1.1 Perimeter security

Group IT, Fiction Corporation has established the following breakdown of user communities:

Site	Users / Hosts	License required	VPN-1
London HQ	2000	Unlimited	YES
Finance Network	15	25	YES
Hong Kong	20	25	YES
New York	10	25	YES
E-business Server Farm	Not Applicable (3 Servers)	25	YES

Hardware and Operating System Selection

Fiction Corporation has chosen different operating systems for their locations because the business has local IT support staff at each site with varying OS support skills. A platform has been selected for each location that is aligned to the preferred operating system in use at that location.

London HQ

The main IT function within Fiction Corporation (Group IT) is located at the London HQ. It has been established that the firewall administrator will be located here. The preferred platform selected for the London Enterprise Gateway is Solaris because Fiction Corporation, Group IT employees have extensive Solaris skills.

Finance Network

Because the Finance Department has extensive expertise in Linux, a Linux gateway has been selected.

Hong Kong

Because the Hong Kong site has extensive expertise in Linux, a Linux gateway has been selected.

New York

Because Microsoft Windows 2000 was already deployed in the New York acquisition, a Windows 2000 gateway was selected.

E-Business Solution

The E-business solution is hosted at Energis Premises in Leeds. Fiction Corporation has chosen to use the Nokia platform for the Enforcement Modules to protect its server farm.

1.2 Management Infrastructure

Group IT recommends that the Solaris Gateway at the London HQ is utilized as the Management Server for enforcement points to enable Fiction Corporation to manage their enterprise Security Policy from a single location.

A single IP address located in the London HQ will be utilized as a management client. Fiction Corporation is planning broadband connections for their firewall administrators so that they can provide out of hours support from their homes. These connections will each have a registered IP address that will be added to the allowed GUI clients list on the London HQ gateway.

Logging of Events

Fiction Corporation has stressed that they require comprehensive logging and audit trails for all Enforcement Modules. Group IT recommends that each Enforcement Module has a Customer Log Module (CLM) license so all logging is carried out on the Enforcement Module and does not get sent to the central Management Module. This will prevent bandwidth saturation on the leased lines that connect each site to the Internet.

Group IT will install scripts that will extract, compress, and transfer log files securely on a nightly basis to the central Management Server.

1.3 Content Security

Fiction Corporation wants to introduce tools to assist in enforcing their acceptable use policy for access to the Internet and at the same time protect the organization against viruses and other malicious code that can be carried in e-mails or attachments or can be downloaded by their employees.

Group IT has selected an OPSEC partner application for antivirus and URL filtering and will make use of the content security functionality within Check Point VPN-1/FireWall-1 NG to deploy this. This will initially be installed only at London HQ, but Fiction Corporation has stated that they plan to extend this to all sites eventually.

The content security application will be installed on a server with a dedicated network connection to ensure maximum performance.

1.4 Secure Interoffice Connectivity

Fiction Corporation wants to connect all their sites together using the Internet. Private dedicated carrier networks are considered too expensive. The main concern in this approach to be addressed is data privacy and security.

Group IT has recommended creating an Intranet VPN which connects all sites together using Triple DES (3DES) encryption. The VPN will utilize pre-shared secret keys for simplicity.

1.5 Secure Remote Access

Fiction Corporation has found that using their existing remote access server is costing them large amounts of money each month. They realize that Internet connectivity using dialup with flat rate costs is much cheaper in the U.K. This will result in significant savings if security concerns can be addressed.

Group IT has recommended the use of SecuRemote for general staff access where security is important but considered low risk, for example, e-mail access.

Group IT has recommended SecureClient with Policy Server for access to the Finance networks where data of a highly sensitive nature is located. The use of SecureClient extends to users within Fiction Corporation's London HQ who also wish to access finance data.

1.6 Security Monitoring

Fiction Corporation has stated that they would like their security infrastructure monitored for availability and logging of suspicious activity.

Group IT will configure SmartDefense in the Management Module. SmartDefense will be used to monitor and prevent intrusion attempts. System Status Viewer will be used to monitor availability and system health of all Enforcement Modules.

1.7 E-Business Solution Resilience

Fiction Corporation has a hosted server farm located at a U.K.-based Internet Service Provider and wishes to provide security against unauthorized access and ensure that they can maximize availability.

Fiction Corporation also wants to introduce resilience for the single web server. Group IT recommends that Fiction Corporation deploy two additional web servers and utilize Check Point Connect Control to offer load balancing. Due to the fact that the site uses custom forms, server persistence will have to be implemented to ensure users sessions always attach to the same web server.

Group IT is recommending that Fiction Corporation utilize Check Point High Availability to provide an Active Standby configuration for the proposed firewalls to ensure that the standby will assume the active role and start processing packets if the primary Enforcement Point fails.

1.8 Group IT Project Methodology

Group IT will follow their methodology for designing and implementing the proposed Internet connectivity solution as follows:

Task	Description
Information gathering	A workshop will be held in which technical information will be gathered and collated and the initial proposal presented.
Initial proposal	An initial proposal document, detailing an outline of the solution components and outline budget, will be prepared.
Requirements definition document	A requirements document will be presented for Fiction Corporation sign off to ensure that both parties have agreed on how to proceed.
Solution design and Security Policy	The solution design will be a blueprint for installation with all IP addresses, static routes and VPN-1/FireWall-1 NG configuration detailed; it will also detail the Security and Acceptable Use Policy for Fiction Corporation. This will require liaison with Fiction Corporation to ensure the solution meets their requirements.
Customer acceptance workshop	A workshop will be offered to discuss and present the solution design to Fiction Corporation and to gain acceptance by Fiction Corporation's employees.
Project/implementation plan	A project plan will be defined with roles and responsibilities agreed upon between the customer and the consultant.

Task	Description
Implementation	Deployment of solution and update of solution design documents will be performed, if required.
Schedule "Go Live" date for Managed Service	Agree upon and complete documents and nominate Fiction Corporation authorized contacts for Managed Service to go live.

This document provides the initial requirements for all of the Fiction Corporation examples used throughout the book. We hope it proves a useful template for your own projects.

APPENDIX B

Upgrading VPN-1/ FireWall-1 NG from Previous Versions

An upgrade can either be done in place using the wrapper installation method to detect and upgrade a previous version, or it can be done manually as described here.

VPN-1/FireWall-1 version 4.0 or higher can be upgraded to NG. If you are using a version prior to version 4.0, you should upgrade to version 4.0 and then perform the upgrade. To upgrade from 4.0 or 4.1, you can alternatively back up your current configuration files and manually merge these in to a new installation. The following files are required:

- **objects.C** This file contains *all* user-defined objects, such as workstations, gateways, and other objects used in the Policy Editor or SmartDashboard.

- **rulebases.fws** This file contains all the Rule Bases that are created.

- **fwauth.NDB** This file contains all user account information for the firewall.

After backing up your configuration files, you can uninstall the previous version and perform a fresh installation of VPN-1/FireWall-1 NG. Next, copy the configuration files to the new directory structure; this will allow you to merge your objects and rules into the new install.

To merge the backed-up files into the new installation, follow these steps. Remember to substitute the full path in place of $FWDIR.

1. Run cpstop.
2. Copy <4.1 objects.C> to $FWDIR\conf\prev_ver_objects.C.
3. Copy <4.1 rulebases.fws> to $FWDIR\conf\rulebases.fws.
4. Copy <4.1 fwauth.NDB> to $FWDIR\conf\fwauth.NDB.
5. Copy <objects.C> from a clean install of NG to $FWDIR\conf\empty_objects.C.
6. Run $FWDIR\bin\fw confmerge $FWDIR\conf\prev_ver_objects.C.
7. Copy $FWDIR\conf\empty_objects.C to $FWDIR\conf\objects.C.
8. Run $FWDIR\bin\fw checkobj.
9. Run $FWDIR\bin\fw cpmi_upgrade.
10. Run cpstart.

You can upgrade to the latest release of NG from a previous version. The following versions can be upgraded:

- VPN-1/FireWall-1 4.0 SP1 and later
- VPN-1/FireWall-1 4.1 SP1 and later
- VPN-1/FireWall-1 NG FP0
- VPN-1/FireWall-1 NG FP1
- VPN-1/FireWall-1 NG FP2

If you are upgrading from a version prior to 4.0, follow these additional steps:

1. Upgrade from that version to version 4.0 SP1.
2. Upgrade from version 4.0 SP1 to NG FPx.

You should upgrade each component in the following order:

1. Upgrade the Management Server and GUI client(s) (when you do this, the version in the Policy Editor is set to NG FPx).
2. Upgrade the VPN-1/FireWall-1 modules.
3. Manually change each module's version in the Policy Editor to NG FPx (in the General page of its Workstation Properties window).

NOKIA UPGRADES

The utilities for installation of packages on the IPSO platform are different from other platforms. You can upgrade from 4.1 SP2 by using the newpkg command if you choose the option to upgrade instead of performing a new install. You should be careful of doing a new installation when upgrading between Feature Packs on the Nokia platform because a new install of an existing version could overwrite configuration information without warning.

The Nokia IPSO operating system can be upgraded manually as outlined using the newimage –I command. Refer to Chapter 7 for further information.

To upgrade, copy the new packages to the /var/admin directory and use the newpkg command to start the installation. You *must* install the SVN Foundation package first, followed by the VPN-1/FireWall-1 NG package. If you have obtained a wrapper version, both components may be included in a single distribution. Choose the option to upgrade from a previous version from the newpkg menu. The currently active installation of VPN-1/FireWall-1 will be offered as the one to upgrade from.

Upgrading VPN-1/FireWall-1 NG FP3 on Nokia

This section outlines the requirements for a successful upgrade to Check Point VPN-1/ FireWall-1 NG FP3. The Nokia platform is easy to upgrade. You can choose which package to upgrade and retain the existing image should you wish to rollback. The steps required to roll back to a previous version of VPN-1/FireWall-1 are also described here.

Upgrade Requirements

Before installing or upgrading Check Point VPN-1/FireWall-1 NG on a Nokia IP Series Appliance, do the following:

1. Make sure you have Check Point VPN-1/FireWall-1 4.1 SP2 or later installed. Upgrading earlier versions on Nokia is not supported.

2. IPSO must be upgraded to the version required for the release of VPN-1/ FireWall-1 you are installing; see the release notes for this information. See Chapter 7 for further information on upgrading the IPSO operating system.

3. If you are installing the separate components, it is essential to install the SVN Foundation (CPShared) package first, then the VPN-1/FireWall-1 NG package, and then any other add-on products.

4. If you attempt to install the same product twice, the installation will fail and result in the removal of the product. If this happens, restart the upgrade installation process again.

Upgrade from Voyager

The following steps list how to upgrade a Check Point installation on the Nokia platform:

1. On the Manage Installed Packages page, turn off FireWall-1 and click Apply.

2. You need to transfer the SVN Foundation known as CPShared and the Check Point FireWall-1 NG packages to the Nokia. To do this, go to the Voyager FTP Install Packages page and download the image from your FTP server. Once you have entered the required information to connect to your FTP server, click Apply, and a list of available packages will be displayed. Click the CPShared package and then click Apply to download it (see Figure B-1).

3. Voyager will then display the package chosen (CPShared) as available for unpacking. Click the CPShared package and click Apply again to unpack it. The unpacked package is shown in Figure B-1.

4. Click the hotlink at the bottom of the Voyager screen as shown in Figure B-1, to install or upgrade CPShared.

5. If you are upgrading from a previous version of NG, you will be presented with a choice of the current versions installed from which to upgrade. If you are not upgrading, the application should appear activated and ready for use in the Manage Installed Packages screen.

6. Repeat steps 2–4 to unpack the VPN-1/FireWall-1 NG package, then, by Upgrade, select the Yes radio button. Under Choose One of the Following Packages to Upgrade From, select the radio button by the version you want to upgrade from, as shown in Figure B-2. Click Apply.

7. Go to the Manage Installed Packages page. The newly upgraded VPN-1/ FireWall-1 NG should be on.

8. Reboot machine.

9. Perform cpconfig.

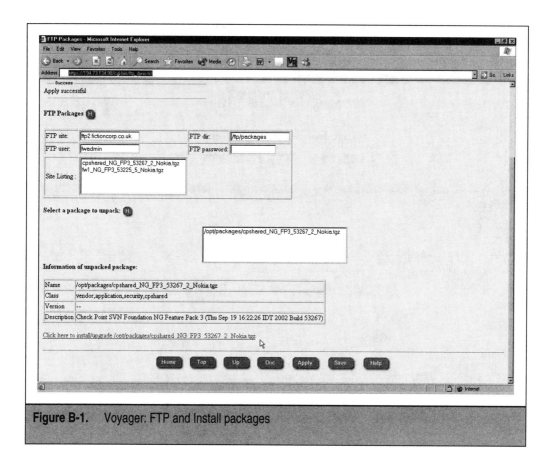

Figure B-1.   Voyager: FTP and Install packages

Upgrade from Command Line

The following steps demonstrate how to upgrade a VPN-1/FireWall-1 installation from the command line:

1. In the Manage Installed Packages page, turn off the VPN-1/FireWall-1 current version.

2. Install CPShared using newpkg command, where x indicates the Feature Pack version and y the build number:

   ```
   newpkg -m LOCAL -n cpshared_NG_FPx_yyyy_y_nokia.tgz
   ```

   If you are upgrading from an NG release, specify the directory to upgrade from with the -o switch:

   ```
   newpkg -m LOCAL -n cpshared_NG_FPx_yyyy_y_nokia.tgz -o $FWDIR
   ```

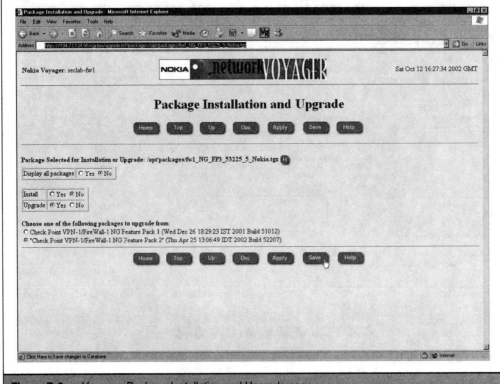

Figure B-2.   Voyager: Package Installation and Upgrade page

3. After CPShared is installed, newpkg continues to list files available in the current directory for installation. If the VPN-1/FireWall-1 NG package is in the same directory as CPShared, it will be listed.

    To upgrade to FireWall-1 NG, use the newpkg command:

```
newpkg -m LOCAL -n fw1_NG_FPx_yyyyy_y_nokia.tgz -o $FWDIR
```

Post-Upgrade

After the initial upgrade process is complete, you will need to complete the installation by following these steps:

1. Install a license. After upgrading from FireWall-1 4.1 to VPN-1/FireWall-1 NG release, a new license for VPN-1/FireWall-1 NG should be installed.

2. Configure SIC. If the Management Server is running in the local machine, cpconfig will ask you to press ENTER to generate an SIC (Secured Internal Communication) key. After an SIC is generated, you'll be asked to save the fingerprint to a file.

3. If it is an upgraded Enforcement Module only, cpconfig asks you to input the secret key used to establish trust, initialize SIC, and communicate with the management server.

4. After cpconfig is completed, you are asked to reboot the machine. Press Y to reboot.

5. Install the new VPN-1/FireWall-1 NG GUI client on your PC. This assumes that the GUI client's IP is in the $FWDIR/conf/gui-clients file; otherwise, you need to run cpconfig to add the GUI clients IP address.

6. Only the local Management Server workstation object automatically changes the VPN-1/FireWall-1 version to NG FP3. If you have Internal Gateway Cluster(s) or other upgraded objects, you need to appropriately modify the new firewall version. These must be changed manually by editing the general properties of the object.

Roll Back to a Previous Version

The following steps list how to roll back to a previous version on the Nokia platform. You can switch back and forth between any of the installed versions as long as you maintain old versions of IPSO on the system if it's required for certain applications.

1. Turn off all the VPN-1/FireWall-1 NG FP3 application packages in Voyager.

2. Apply and save changes to Voyager.

3. Turn on the previous version of the VPN-1/FireWall-1 application package that was running prior to upgrade. Apply and save changes to Voyager.

4. If necessary, switch back to the previous IPSO image from the IPSO Image Management link in Voyager.

UPGRADE VERIFIER UTILITY

Check Point also provides a utility that does pre- and post-upgrade verification checking. Running the utility prior to upgrade highlights potential problems and recommends remedial action, allowing the upgrade to be completed successfully. If an upgrade generates errors while running, the post-upgrade verifier utility analyzes the databases in the $FWDIR/conf directory and will highlight problems identified during the upgrade process and recommend remedial action.

APPENDIX C

Backing Up and Restoring VPN-1/ FireWall-1 NG

As with any critical system, VPN-1/FireWall-1 NG must be backed up in case disaster strikes and the system needs to be restored. VPN-1/FireWall-1 NG is very simple to back up and recover. Certain directories contain the valuable configuration information, and it is these alone that should be backed up regularly. It is unlikely that you would ever need to recover log files or other variable data in the event of a hardware failure; nevertheless, the entire system should be backed up from time to time.

The $FWDIR/conf directory contains the configuration files for VPN-1/FireWall-1 NG and should be backed up frequently. This directory contains the Rule Bases, Objects, and the User database.

The $FWDIR/lib directory should also be backed up frequently. There are several instances where files in this directory, such as the base.def, are modified. If a VPN-1/FireWall-1 NG Feature Pack is installed over these modified files, they will revert to the default installation. This will remove any modifications to these files.

Changes should be kept to a minimum, where possible. This prevents unwanted downtime. A change log should be maintained whenever modifications are made. If a file is deleted or removed, this will assist in a quick recovery of the server.

Do not upgrade VPN-1/FireWall-1 NG with either Feature Packs or full versions without first making a complete backup of the system. This will allow a quick restore. It's rare, but upgrades are not always successful.

On the Windows platform, navigate to the C:\winnt\fw1\5.0 directory. The conf and lib directories are located under the base directory. This directory in a fresh installation of VPN-1/FireWall-1 NG Feature Pack 3 will be c:\winnt\fw1\ng (base directory).

On the Solaris platform, the lib and conf directories can be found under the /var/opt/CPfw1-50 base directory.

The lib and conf directories contain important information required to restore the system if required.

BACKUP AND RESTORE ON NOKIA

The Voyager interface contains a useful method of backing up, retrieving the backup, and restoring it. It's quick and easy to use, and it's a convenient way of backing up before changes are made to the system. Figure C-1 shows the Voyager Backup and Restore Configuration screen. As you can see, the backup options allow a variety of system directories and the critical VPN-1/FireWall-1 NG software to be backed up. In addition, the IPSO settings are always backed up, allowing for a complete system recovery in the event of a failure.

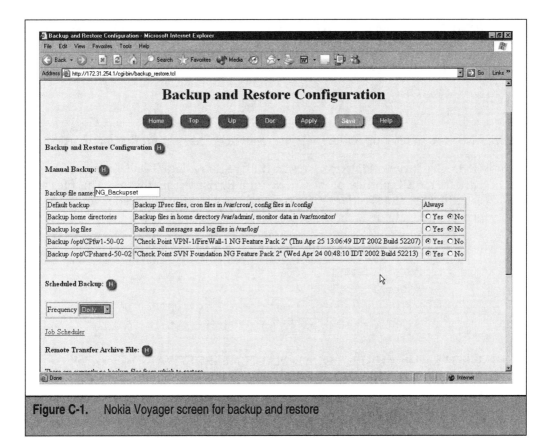

Figure C-1.   Nokia Voyager screen for backup and restore

BACKUP AND RESTORE VPN-1/ FIREWALL-1 NG MANAGEMENT SERVER

The Management Server (also known as SmartCenter Server in Feature Pack 3) is the most critical element to back up because it contains all the configuration information that is pushed down to the Enforcement Module.

Follow this procedure to back up the Management server and copy the following files:

- $FWDIR/conf/Objects_5_0.C

- $FWDIR/conf/rulebases_5_0.fws

- $FWDIR/conf/fwauth.NDB (On Windows systems, this file is only a link to the actual user database file; for example, if the file is fwauth.NDB522, you should rename the real database file—fwauth.NDB522—to fwauth.NDB.)

The Internal Certificate Authority (ICA) and Secure Internal Communication (SIC) files that should be backed up are as follows:

- $FWDIR/conf/InternalCA.*
- $FWDIR/conf/ICA*.*
- $CPDIR/conf/sic_cert.p12

You also need to back up and import the following Check Point Registry portions:

- **UNIX Registry: $CPDIR/registry/HKLM_registry.data**   On Unix systems, back up the SIC portion of the Check Point Registry from this file. This file can be edited using a standard ASCII text editor. Find the SIC section and copy everything under it as shown here:

```
: (SIC
        :ICAState ("[4]3")
        :ICAdn ("o=lonfw..qvihqm")
        :HasCertificate ("[4]1")
        :MySICname ("cn=cp_mgmt,o=lonfw..qvihqm")
        :CertPath ("/opt/CPshrd-53/conf/sic_cert.p12")
    )
```

- **Win32 Registry: HKEY_LOCAL_MACHINE\SOFTWARE\CheckPoint\ SIC**   Use the regedt32 application to export this key so that it can be imported for restoration.

From VPN-1/FireWall-1 NG Feature Pack 2 (FP2), you should also make a copy of all the files from the $FWDIR/conf/crls directory because this will allow you to restore the root certificate and save you from having to issue new module certificates.

Restoring the Management Server

To restore, follow these procedures. Note that restoration will work only if it's performed on the same operating system that was used to create the backup.

1. Install VPN-1/FireWall-1 NG Management Server on replacement or repaired hardware. Ensure the hostname and IP address are the same as previously configured. In addition, make sure that the FQDN (Fully Qualified Domain Name) sent to the CA during cpconfig is identical to the one used previously.
2. Reset SIC using cpconfig on the Enforcement Module.
3. Run cpstop to stop the VPN-1/FireWall-1 NG Management Server.
4. Copy all the files backed up to the $FWDIR/conf $CPDIR/conf directories, maintaining the relative position of the files as backed up.
5. Restore the Registry portions.
6. Use cpstart to start the VPN-1/FireWall-1 NG management server.

APPENDIX D

Using the Check Point Wizard to Create a Security Policy

C heck Point has introduced a number of wizards for completing tasks in VPN-1/ FireWall-1 NG. One of the most useful wizards is the Security Policy Wizard. This will allow a novice user to create a Security Policy and perform address translation on a firewall gateway without having to resort to the complexities of creating objects and assigning these objects to fields in a rule and building up a Rule Base.

In Chapter 8 we walked you through the steps to create a Rule Base. In this appendix, we will again create the Fiction Corporation's London Rule Base, but we will use the Security Policy Wizard to do so.

PREPARING TO USE THE WIZARD

The first step to defining your Security Policy is to ensure that the following information is available:

- IP addressing information
- Object information
- Rule Base required

Once this information has been collected as defined in Chapter 8, proceed to launch the wizard.

USING THE RULE BASE WIZARD

Launch the Management Client by selecting the Policy Editor. When you are presented with the Policy Editor screen, select New from the File menu and you will be presented with the New Policy window, as shown in Figure D-1.

Creating a New Security Policy

In the New Policy window, you are required to do the following:

1. Enter the Policy Name (in Figure E-1, we entered Sample).
2. Select the Policy Type as Security and Address Translation.
3. Click the Wizard button under the Helpers section.
4. Click OK.

The Select Installation Targets window appears. Initially, this is blank, unless you select the option for Specific Modules. If there is more than one gateway object defined, you should select the Specific Modules option; otherwise, leave the defaults and click Next, as shown in Figure D-2.

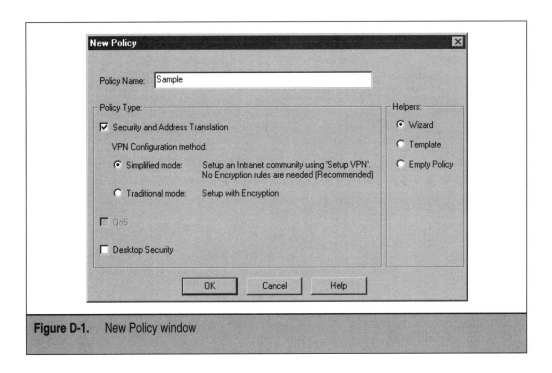

Figure D-1. New Policy window

Click OK to continue. You are now presented with four options for specific wizards. You can select any one of the following:

- **Starter Network** A single internal network with a mail server behind a dual-homed gateway.

- **Publisher Network** A single internal network with public FTP web and mail servers behind a dual-homed gateway.

- **DMZ Network** User-based access to FTP and web servers and a DMZ network; SMTP—POP3 Server in a DMZ network; a protected internal network with user-based policies for selective internet access.

- **Secure Mail** Mail server with SecuRemote Pop3 Access.

NOTE The Secure Mail Wizard will work properly *only* if you are using the VPN version of VPN-1/FireWall-1 NG.

For the Fiction Corporation example, which features three interfaces on the London HQ firewall, select the DMZ Network Wizard, as shown in Figure D-3.

Click OK to continue. This will launch the DMZ Network Wizard.

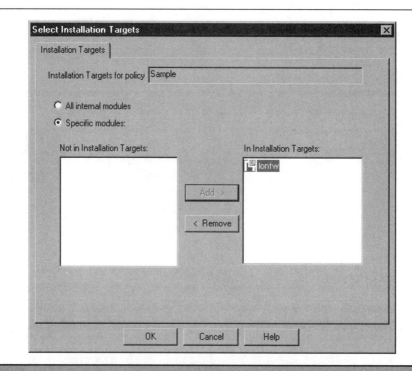

Figure D-2. Select Installation Targets window

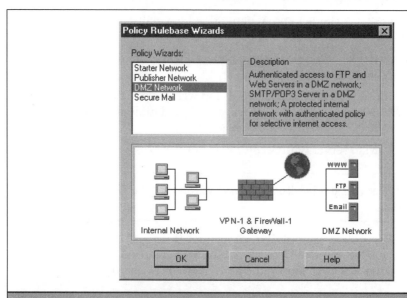

Figure D-3. Policy Rule Base Wizards window

Defining the Gateway

You will now be prompted to select whether the gateway and management server are on the same machine or separate machines. Fiction Corporation gateway has both on the same machine, so select the appropriate button and click Next to continue, as shown in Figure D-4.

In the Gateway Definition screen, select GET to retrieve the firewall interfaces. Click Next to continue creating the Security Policy.

You will be shown a list of interfaces. Click the 194.73.134.2 check box to define this as the external interface, as shown in Figure D-5.

Click Next to continue.

Defining the Local Network

In the Local Network screen, select a name for the internal interface. Enter **Internal_Nets** and click Next, as shown in Figure D-6.

You will now be prompted to add the IP address for the internal network in the Local Network IP Address and Net Mask screen, as shown in Figure D-7.

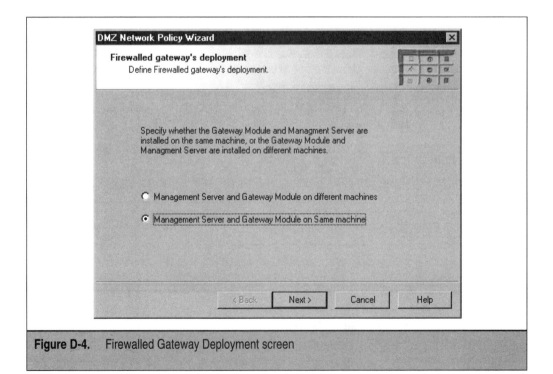

Figure D-4.   Firewalled Gateway Deployment screen

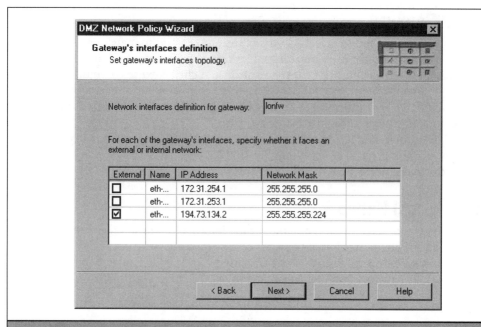

Figure D-5. Gateway's Interfaces Definition screen

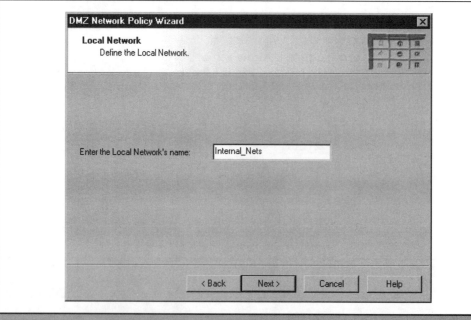

Figure D-6. Local Network screen

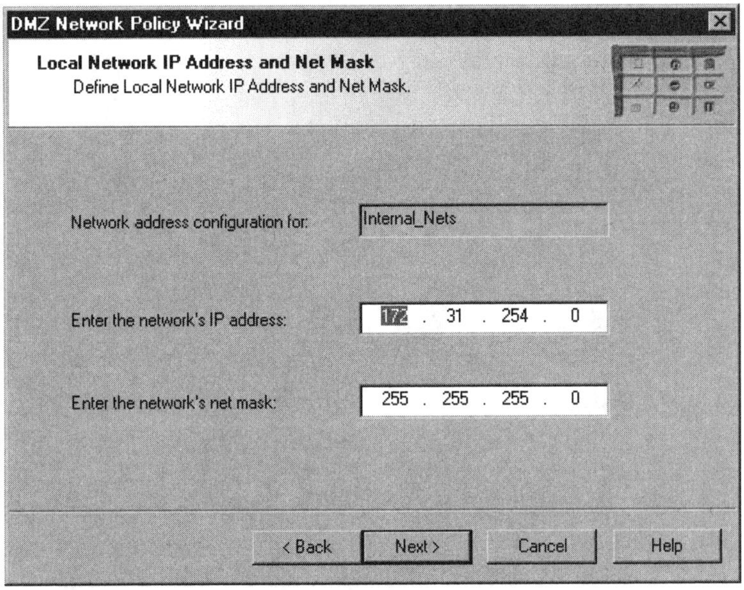

Figure D-7.   Local Network IP Address and Net Mask screen

You will now be prompted to specify if these are valid or invalid IP addresses. Because you are using invalid (RFC1918) compliant IP addresses, select the invalid IP address option so that address translation will be used. Click Next to continue.

In the Local Network Address Translation screen, you will be prompted to enter the hide NAT address for the internal network. This can either be the firewall's external IP address or a specified IP address. Leave the default option of The Gateway's External IP Address, as shown in Figure D-8.

Click Next to continue.

Defining the Outbound Policy

You will now be prompted to specify the type of traffic allowed from the internal network to the Internet. Ensure the option Selected is highlighted and click Next to define which services will be allowed.

You will be prompted to define a collective name for these services. It is recommended that this is left as InternetServices. Click Next to continue. You will now be able to select the Internet services that your internal users will be using.

As you may recall from Chapter 8, Fiction Corporation requires FTP, HTTP and HTTPS. There is no HTTPS option on the Allowed Outgoing Services Group, but you can revisit that once the initial Rule Base has been created.

Select FTP and HTTP, as shown in Figure D-9, and click Next to continue.

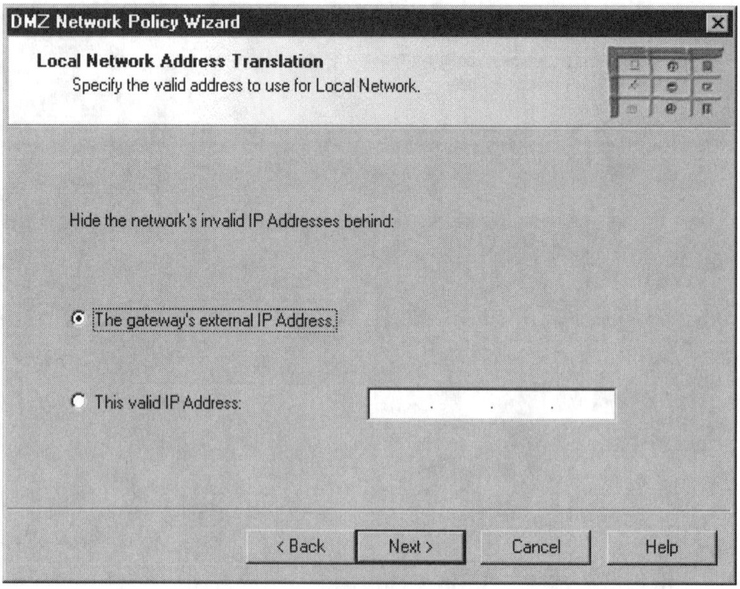

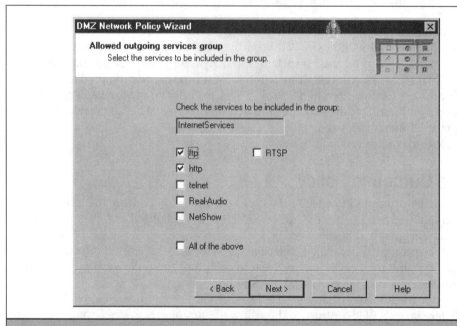

Figure D-8. Local Network Address Translation screen

Figure D-9. Allowed Outgoing Services Group screen

You will now be prompted to name the DMZ. Unless you have a specific name, leave the default. If you want to stick to the convention used in Chapter 8, rename it to Net_172.31.253.0. Click Next to continue.

You will now be prompted to enter the IP address and subnet mask for the DMZ network. Enter the IP address **172.31.253.0** and subnet mask of **255.255.255.0**. Click Next to continue.

You will now be asked if the IP addresses are valid or require network address translation. Select No, as these addresses are invalid.

Configuring a Mail Server

When configuring the mail server, follow these steps:

1. When asked if you want to permit mail traffic, select Yes to configure the mail relay, and click Next.

2. When prompted to give the mail server object a name, select Mail-Relay and click Next to continue.

3. When prompted to enter the mail server IP address, enter **172.31.253.253** and click Next to continue.

4. Enter the valid or registered IP, as shown in Figure D-10.

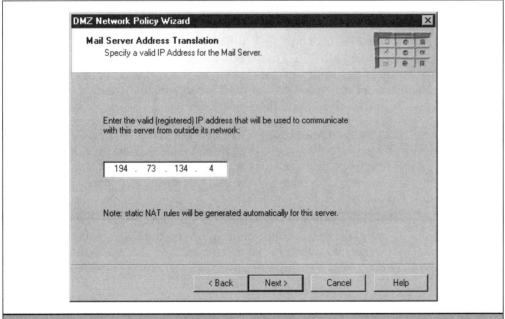

Figure D-10.   The mail server's registered IP

Public Servers Definition

When configuring the public server, follow these steps:

1. When the wizard prompts you to select which public servers need to be configured, make sure that only HTTP is selected, and Click next to continue.

2. Enter the web server's name as Web-Server and click Next.

3. The wizard will then ask for the web server IP address and the valid address for address translation. Enter the following information when prompted:

    ```
    IP Address: 172.31.254.254
    Valid IP address: 194.73.134.3
    ```

4. Click Next to continue.

External Users Access

Decide if you want to restrict access to the public servers to a group of authorized users.

CAUTION   If you select Yes, a user group will be created in the Rule Base. After running the wizard, you must complete the Rule Base by defining authorized users and adding them to the user group.

Select No for Fiction Corporation's Rule Base purposes.

Silent Services

Often your network will see a lot of broadcast traffic that is filling up your logs, especially protocols such as bootp and NBT. You may not want to log this traffic. The wizard creates a rule that drops the traffic but does *not* log it. This traffic is commonly known to firewall administrators as noise or background broadcasts that are not important. Following are some of the services and their properties:

*   **Bootp**   Short for Bootstrap Protocol, an Internet protocol that enables a diskless workstation to discover its own IP address, the IP address of a BOOTP server on the network, and a file to be loaded into memory to boot the machine. This enables the workstation to boot without requiring a hard or floppy disk drive. The protocol is defined by RFC 951.

*   **NBT**   It is best not to allow NBT traffic from the DMZ, inbound to the local network. If this is allowed, a compromised host on the DMZ will be able to connect to internal hosts which are a major security risk. Connections should ideally all be one way, for example, from an internal network to a DMZ network, or from DMZ network to the Internet—not both.

There are obviously exceptions, such as inbound e-mail, where the rule is restricted in some way. Either by making the rule point-to-point (host A to host B only), or service (for example SMTP) specific.

Select Drop and click Next to continue. You have finished using the Rule Base Wizard. Click Finish so the wizard can add the objects and rules to your Security Policy.

Completed Rule Base

You can see the completed Rule Base as defined by the wizard in Figure D-11.

There are a number of things that need amending to finish this Rule Base.

Rule 2 for POP-3 can be deleted because it is not required for Fiction Corporation. This was created because you told the wizard to define a mail server.

The Silent Services rule should really be placed at the top of the Rule Base. This is because VPN-1/FireWall-1 NG examines each rule in order until a match is found. If there is a large number of broadcasts and a large number of rules prior to the Silent Services rule, the firewall will be quite busy processing rules sequentially prior to hitting the Silent Services rule and dropping the broadcasts or other irrelevant services quietly.

You were not able to select HTTPS as a service for the internal users, so double-click the Internet Services object in the Rule Base and add HTTPS to ensure you meet Fiction Corporation's Security Policy requirements.

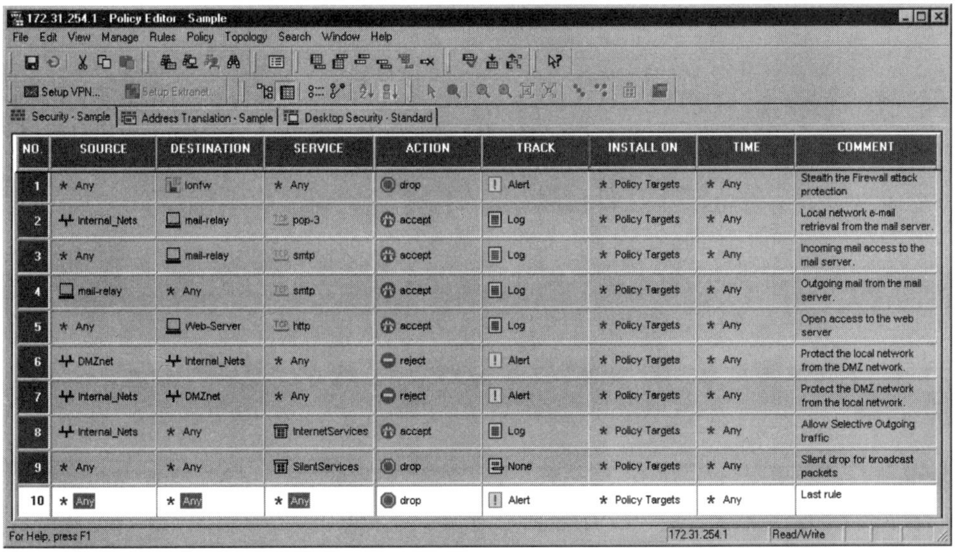

Figure D-11.   Completed Rule Base

Rules 6 and 7 were created to prevent any general communication between the DMZ and the internal network. A general guide is that the DMZ should not initiate any communications to the internal network. If Fiction Corporation users were required to connect to resources in the DMZ, it is perfectly acceptable to have internal users initiate a connection to the DMZ, but not the other way around.

You will need to modify the Rule Base to allow the mail relay to communicate with the internal mail server. This again is a permissible exception to the DMZ golden rule.

We have discussed several ideas about improving this Rule Base, but it should be noted that Rule Base design is dependent on an organization's individual requirements; there is not one right way to design a Rule Base or Security Policy, but there are plenty of wrong ways. We hope that by working through this book and learning about the concepts behind VPN-1/FireWall-1 NG you will be able to design effective Security Policies for your organization or customers.

In this appendix, the VPN-1/FireWall-1 NG Wizard was examined and used to re-create the Chapter 8 Rule Base. There are many different ways to design security policies. An organization should try to define the most effective Security Policy to suit their individual needs.

We have found that the Rule Base wizard is an excellent tool for people new to VPN-1/FireWall-1 NG and also good for rapidly defining a prototype Rule Base.

INDEX

G

 H

N

W

X

INTERNATIONAL CONTACT INFORMATION

AUSTRALIA
McGraw-Hill Book Company Australia Pty. Ltd.
TEL +61-2-9900-1800
FAX +61-2-9878-8881
http://www.mcgraw-hill.com.au
books-it_sydney@mcgraw-hill.com

CANADA
McGraw-Hill Ryerson Ltd.
TEL +905-430-5000
FAX +905-430-5020
http://www.mcgraw-hill.ca

GREECE, MIDDLE EAST, & AFRICA
(Excluding South Africa)
McGraw-Hill Hellas
TEL +30-210-6560-990
TEL +30-210-6560-993
TEL +30-210-6560-994
FAX +30-210-6545-525

MEXICO (Also serving Latin America)
McGraw-Hill Interamericana Editores S.A. de C.V.
TEL +525-117-1583
FAX +525-117-1589
http://www.mcgraw-hill.com.mx
fernando_castellanos@mcgraw-hill.com

SINGAPORE (Serving Asia)
McGraw-Hill Book Company
TEL +65-6863-1580
FAX +65-6862-3354
http://www.mcgraw-hill.com.sg
mghasia@mcgraw-hill.com

SOUTH AFRICA
McGraw-Hill South Africa
TEL +27-11-622-7512
FAX +27-11-622-9045
robyn_swanepoel@mcgraw-hill.com

SPAIN
McGraw-Hill/Interamericana de España, S.A.U.
TEL +34-91-180-3000
FAX +34-91-372-8513
http://www.mcgraw-hill.es
professional@mcgraw-hill.es

UNITED KINGDOM, NORTHERN,
EASTERN, & CENTRAL EUROPE
McGraw-Hill Education Europe
TEL +44-1-628-502500
FAX +44-1-628-770224
http://www.mcgraw-hill.co.uk
computing_europe@mcgraw-hill.com

ALL OTHER INQUIRIES Contact:
McGraw-Hill/Osborne
TEL +1-510-596-6600
FAX +1-510-596-7600
http://www.osborne.com
omg_international@mcgraw-hill.com

Check Out All of Osborne's Hacking Books